JOHN HUME

John Hume

In His Own Words

Seán Farren

EDITOR

FOUR COURTS PRESS

Set in 10.5 pt on 13 pt AGaramond for
FOUR COURTS PRESS
7 Malpas Street, Dublin 8, Ireland
www.fourcourtspress.ie
and in North America for
FOUR COURTS PRESS
c/o IPG, 814 N. Franklin St., Chicago, IL 60610.

First edition, 2018
First paperback edition, 2021

A catalogue record for this title
is available from the British Library.

ISBN 978-1-84682-998-7

Printed in England by
CPI Antony Rowe, Chippenham, Wilts.

To John and Pat Hume

Contents

Abbreviations

BPM	British prime minister
CSCE	Conference on Security and Co-operation in Europe
DUP	Democratic Unionist Party
EC	European Community
EEC	European Economic Community
EMS	European Monetary System
GOC	General Officer Commanding
INLA	Irish National Liberation Army
OECD	Organisation for Economic Co-operation and Development
PIRA	Provisional Irish Republican Army
RUC	Royal Ulster Constabulary
SDLP	Social Democratic and Labour Party
THORP	Thermal Oxide Reprocessing Plant
UDA	Ulster Defence Association
UDR	Ulster Defence Regiment
UKUP	United Kingdom Unionist Party
UUP	Ulster Unionist Party
UVF	Ulster Volunteer Force

Foreword

John Hume is undoubtedly one of the most significant Irish politicians of the last fifty years. He was the product of social upheaval linked to the conflict in and about Northern Ireland and rose to prominence from humble roots when he took a stand against violence – in many ways similar to those who significantly influenced his thinking, such as Martin Luther King Jr and Mahatma Gandhi. This book tracks this trajectory, not in a biographical way, but rather through Hume's own words.

The editor has presented Hume's thinking by collecting his interviews and speeches 'as a testimony to Hume's beliefs and convictions'. He leaves the essence of what these words mean 'for others to judge'. As a result, coming to one's own conclusion on John Hume, the man and the politician, is made much easier. The editor has collected a vast treasure trove of information and curated it chronologically, and it is a gift to researchers, not to mention the next generation, who might not know what Hume stood for. Yet, like any political or social figure, the volume and complexity of his political life, so carefully captured in immense detail here, is also deeply contextual and multifaceted, making any conclusions challenging.

Principally, as you read this collection, Hume comes across as devoted and principled, with a strong belief in hard work and social justice, and a deep commitment to peace and social stability for all the people of Ireland, irrespective of their background. These convictions, as well as his steadfast belief in a united Ireland, continually bump up against a social context of extreme violence, deprivation and political classes wedded to positions that were difficult to shift. This was all taking place within a wider European context of the 1970s and 1980s, where the discourse of political and cultural unity was perhaps in its heyday. As a politician, Hume used this context to develop his own type of politics, which reified economic development and social reconciliation, and pushed for inter-community solidarity and international involvement to cement peace. Aspects of this approach are evident throughout this book, as they are in the essence of the Good Friday Agreement of 1998.

But what specific 'beliefs and convictions' (as the editor puts it) of John Hume come through in this book?

Firstly, Hume is wedded to the idea that dialogue is important and that conflicts can only be resolved through open discussion, even in contexts of strong differences of opinion. Underpinning this is the idea that, certainly in Ireland, there is an interdependency between people that is inescapable. As he noted:

> If we are to live together, the first lesson that we must learn is that we need each other. We will discover how much we need each other, and how we are to live together, only when we sit down and talk about it.

This is integrally linked to the second pillar of his thinking, namely that dialogue was necessary to solve all problems locally because of interdependence, but that globally societies were also interconnected. Hume revered the European Union as an example of how unity and interdependence could be fostered politically and at an international level. He also recognized the importance of the US and its familial and historical connections to Ireland as key to the peace process and stimulating the economic growth necessary to ensure and ultimately sustain peace. Underlying this, while maintaining his own nationalism, was a conviction that nationhood was defined by people and not place or geography.

Thirdly, it is unequivocally clear that Hume opposed the use of violence. There are elements of practicality in his views, that is, that republican violence distracted from the social injustices in the society rather than highlighting them, noting that unionism needs a 'bogeymen' and that 'Irish unity will never be achieved by violence' as it will 'only strengthen unionism'. He also continually highlights the cost of violence to individuals, routinely quoting statistics of death related to the conflict, and pragmatically also noting that 'violence has cost us jobs' and that peace cannot be built on 'the ruins of a shattered economy'. But beyond the pragmatism, Hume shows a deep commitment to what he sees as the more difficult path of non-violence, which he sees as a choice:

> We cannot solve problems of difference by creating divisions. We cannot create peace by using violence. We cannot protect civil rights by attacking human rights. We cannot secure justice by abandoning the rule of law. We cannot achieve freedom by inflicting injustice.

And finally, it is revealing how many times the word 'reconciliation' features in this collection. Hume's view seems to start out instrumentally in relation to reconciliation, that is, that Irish unity is only possible through different traditions coming together, and from his perspective within a united Ireland, saying 'our aim must be not to overcome the Northern Protestant but to seek his help and co-operation'. But as his thinking develops, and perhaps because contact with the other dominant communities intensified over his political career, it is clear that he becomes more committed to the principle of reconciliation at all costs. Finally, Hume sees the 'road of reconciliation' as the only 'real road forward'. Achieving reconciliation at a political level for Hume was embodied within liberal political institutions and a functioning economic system underpinned by a non-violent approach to attempting to achieve one's political aims.

Historians will continue to debate the impact of Hume's philosophy on Irish politics and within the EU, particularly as the context continues to change so rapidly. But if one assesses John Hume's legacy in terms of the themes outlined above, it is clear that, moving forward, at the heart of any process in Northern Ireland are the issues of dialogue; interconnection and managing the process across the borders of Ireland, the UK and the EU; a strong economy; building new shared institutions; and a commitment to non-violence remain central. Hume's approach remains as relevant as ever. However, it is the conundrum of reconciliation that remains elusive.

Hume noted in 1983 that many 'furiously abhor the work of reconciliation', and we know today that, not only in Northern Ireland but globally, some see reconciliation negatively: a sop to the aggressors; a false coming together; selling out one's principles; or some idealistic peacenik concept. But Hume suggests that we have no other choice than to foster reconciliation if we are, for better or worse, forced to share our society with others.

At the same time, at no point in reading this book do you get the impression of Hume as someone who embraced non-violence and reconciliation acontextually or naively. Hume sees reconciliation as needing institutional, political and social support. Reconciliation for Hume is not only people-to-people relationship building. Reconciliation is a profoundly serious political endeavour. As he notes:

> Let that reconciliation start today in this room – between ourselves. Goodwill alone – and I know we have with us today the goodwill of the mass of the people of this island – will not suffice. We must apply all the resources of our collective intelligence, imagination, generosity and determination to this great enterprise and be seen to do it. We must mean business and we must be seen to desperately mean business.

Hume beckons us all to take the more difficult path of mustering our resources to move forward together. Despite the passage of time, his challenge to embrace this type of reconciliation remains profoundly pertinent to politicians linked with the conflict in and about Northern Ireland, as it does to all who claim they want to work toward a more peaceful world.

Professor Brandon Hamber
John Hume and Thomas P. O'Neill Chair in Peace
Ulster University
18 August 2017

Acknowledgments

In the course of compiling this book, I received assistance from family, friends and acquaintances of John Hume, and to them I owe a great debt of gratitude. Foremost among those who assisted me was John Hume's wife, Pat, who supported the project from the outset and who provided copies of many of John's speeches and articles.

Among others who gave significant assistance was Catherine Shannon, professor emerita of Westfield State University, Massachusetts, one of the key organizers of symposia in Boston on the Northern Ireland problem to which John Hume was an important contributor. Professor Shannon kindly provided recordings of sessions from those symposia.

To my SDLP colleague and friend Denis Haughey, thanks are due for assistance throughout the preparation of this book. Thanks are also due to RTÉ and BBC radio archives for permission to use extracts from interviews with John Hume.

My thanks to Kevin Cullen of the *Boston Globe* for copies of articles by and interviews with John published in that newspaper. I am also indebted to Irish and British newspapers that carried interviews, articles and statements from John Hume, from which extracts have been taken.

Gerry Cosgrove and Ann McDonagh, staff at SDLP headquarters, kindly assisted me by locating relevant material in the SDLP's archive.

Librarians and archivists at the Belfast Newspaper Library, the British Library, Derry City Library, the European parliament, the Linen Hall Library, the National Library of Ireland, the library at Parliament Buildings, Belfast, the Public Record Office of Northern Ireland, and at Ulster University, proved extremely helpful in the search for relevant material.

My thanks to Professor Brandon Hamber, John Hume and Thomas P. O'Neill Chair in Peace at Ulster University, for kindly agreeing to write the foreword. Finally, my thanks to Four Courts Press, especially to Martin Fanning and Sam Tranum, for their assistance and advice.

Introduction

John Hume was a hugely influential figure in Irish politics, North and South, as well as in Irish-British politics from the late 1960s until his retirement from public life in 2005. As the Northern Ireland crisis deepened in the early 1970s his influence spread to the US and Europe, and eventually he became one of the most recognizable and widely respected Northern Irish politicians.

Hume first emerged onto the political scene in the early 1960s through his involvement in the credit-union movement, and in campaigns for Northern Ireland's second university to be located in Derry and for improved social housing in the city. From those involvements it was not surprising that Hume became a local leader in the civil rights campaign then underway across the North. The campaign's objectives were electoral reform, an end to the gerrymandering of constituency boundaries, and the replacement of a property-related franchise for local-government elections with 'one person, one vote'. Reform of policing and the establishment of means to guarantee equal employment opportunities were among the other key demands of the movement.

John Hume was one of a new, young generation of public leaders who came to the fore at this time from within Northern Ireland's nationalist community, and he was soon approached to advocate civil rights reform through electoral politics in the Northern Ireland parliament. Successfully elected to the parliament in 1969, Hume quickly became a leading figure in the opposition, and a founder member in 1970 of the Social Democratic and Labour Party (SDLP). He earned a national and international reputation as a politician deeply committed to democratic means of conflict resolution, to non-violence, to partnership government and to reconciliation, principles he steadfastly adhered to throughout the following decades of political instability, and the horrors and tragedies of violent conflict. These principles and Hume's recommendations as to how they could be applied in Northern Ireland provided blueprints for the power-sharing arrangements of 1973–4, the inter-party agreements, the Sunningdale Agreement, the Anglo-Irish Agreement of 1985 and the 1998 Good Friday/Belfast Agreement.

Determined to bring his message wherever he believed influence needed to be exerted to end the violence and allow democratic politics to resolve the conflict, he was prolific in his writings, his speeches, his interviews and his comments. This book, which is not a biography, brings together extracts from many of those utterances to provide a record of – as well as a testimony to – Hume's beliefs and convictions. The extracts are presented along with a narrative written by the editor, to provide context. Assessment and evaluation of Hume's overall contribution to politics and to conflict resolution are for another occasion and are not offered, except in the most general of terms. Essentially, Hume's words are presented for others to judge.

Timeline: significant dates and developments

1937	John Hume is born in Derry, the eldest son of Sam and Annie Hume.
1941–58	John Hume is educated at St Eugene's Primary School, St Columb's College in Derry, and St Patrick's College, Maynooth.
1960	John Hume marries Patricia Hone.
1960	The Derry Credit Union is established, with John Hume as a founder member.
1963	John Hume is elected chair of the University for Derry Committee.
1964	John Hume's seminal article, 'Northern Catholics', is published in *Irish Times*. John is elected president of the Credit Union League of Ireland.
1965	John Hume is elected chair of the Derry Housing Association.
1966	John Hume becomes manager of the Derry-based smoked-salmon business Atlantic Harvest.
1967	The Northern Ireland Civil Rights Association is founded.
1968	An October civil rights march in Derry is baton-charged by the RUC. Hume is elected vice chair of the Derry Citizens' Action Committee.
1969	Hume is elected MP for the Foyle constituency in the Northern Ireland parliament.
1970	The Social Democratic and Labour Party (SDLP) is founded, with Gerry Fitt MP as party leader and John Hume as deputy leader. The Provisional IRA (Provos or PIRA) launch their terrorist campaign.
1971	The SDLP withdraws from the Northern Ireland parliament. Internment without trial is introduced, and the nationalist 'alternative assembly' meets.
1972	British troops fatally shoot civilians on a civil rights march in Derry, on what would become known as Bloody Sunday. The Northern Ireland parliament is prorogued, and William Whitelaw is appointed secretary of state for Northern Ireland.
1973	Hume is elected to the new Northern Ireland assembly. A power-sharing government is agreed with the Unionist Party, led by Brian Faulkner, and the Alliance Party. The Council of Ireland is agreed

with the British and Irish governments and the same three Northern parties – the Sunningdale Agreement.

1974   The power-sharing government takes office in January, with Hume as minister of commerce. The Ulster Workers' Council strike forces the British government to end the power-sharing government in May and to announce a return to direct rule.

1975   A constitutional convention is elected. Hume once again tops the poll in Derry.

1976   The constitutional convention fails to reach agreement. Hume spends the autumn at the Harvard Centre for International Relations.

1977   Leading Irish-American politicians make their first St Patrick's Day statement against violence in Northern Ireland, and US President Jimmy Carter states his support for inter-party agreement. Hume is appointed as a member of European Commissioner Richard Burke's cabinet.

1979   Hume is elected as one of three Northern Ireland members of the European parliament. Hume publishes a key article, 'The Irish question – a British problem', in *Foreign Affairs* magazine. Margaret Thatcher is elected as UK's prime minister, and Charles Haughey is elected as Ireland's taoiseach. Hume becomes leader of the SDLP following resignation of Gerry Fitt.

1980   Secretary of State Atkins convenes inter-party talks, which fail to agree a power-sharing government. Republican prisoners embark on a hunger strike in the Maze prison.

1981   Republican prisoners embark on a further hunger strike; one of them, Bobby Sands, is elected MP for Fermanagh and South Tyrone before he dies.

1982   The SDLP declines to take seats in the new assembly established by Secretary of State James Prior. The party lobbies for a Council for a New Ireland to be convened to agree a common all-Ireland nationalist approach to the Northern crisis.

1983   The New Ireland Forum convenes in Dublin under the auspices of the Irish government. The SDLP, Fianna Fáil, Fine Gael and Irish Labour are represented; Hume leads the SDLP delegation. Hume is elected as MP at Westminster for the Foyle constituency.

1984   The New Ireland Forum reports, but its key proposals are rejected by Prime Minister Margaret Thatcher. Hume is re-elected to the European parliament.

1985   The Anglo-Irish Agreement is signed at Hillsborough by Prime Minister Thatcher and Taoiseach Garret FitzGerald. The agreement affords the Irish government a consultative role in the affairs of Northern Ireland.

1987   The PIRA explode a bomb close to the annual Armistice Day commemoration ceremony in Enniskillen, killing eleven and wounding sixty-five. John Hume and Gerry Adams begin a series of meetings that will eventually include party colleagues; Hume urges an end to the PIRA campaign. Hume is re-elected to Westminster.

1988   The Hume-Adams meetings continue until the autumn. Three PIRA members on a bombing mission are shot dead by undercover British agents in Gibraltar; their funerals in Belfast are attacked by a loyalist gunman.

1989   Hume is re-elected to the European parliament.

1990   Secretary of State Peter Brooke launches a new initiative aimed at convening inter-party talks.

1991   Inter-party and inter-governmental talks are held in Belfast, London and Dublin.

1992   Inter-party talks do not produce agreement, but do produce several important principles for future talks; Hume re-elected to Westminster.

1993   The Hume-Adams talks intensify, focusing on achieving a ceasefire allowing Sinn Féin to join all-party talks.

1994   Hume is again elected to the European parliament. The PIRA declares a ceasefire, and is followed by the main loyalist paramilitary organisations. The Forum for Peace and Reconciliation meets in Dublin, with representation from all parties except the unionist parties.

1995   Preparations for all-party talks get underway. Former US Senator George Mitchell chairs a commission on the decommissioning of paramilitary weapons.

1996   The PIRA breaks its ceasefire, the Dublin forum is suspended, and elections are held to the Northern Ireland Forum for Political Dialogue. Talks involving the parties, except Sinn Féin, commence in June.

1997   In UK elections, Labour returns to government for first time since 1979, and a Fianna Fáil government under Bertie Ahern takes office in Dublin. Political talks in Northern Ireland recommence in June. The PIRA declare a second ceasefire in July, and enter talks in September. Hume is re-elected to Westminster.

1998   The Good Friday Agreement is endorsed in joint referenda, and there are elections to new assembly in Belfast. John Hume and

David Trimble of the Ulster Unionist Party are awarded the Nobel Peace Prize.

1999   Hume is re-elected for the fifth time to the European parliament. Hume receives the Martin Luther King Award.

2001   Hume retires as leader of the SDLP. Hume is re-elected to Westminster.

2002   Hume is awarded the Gandhi Peace Prize.

2004   Hume retires from the European parliament.

2005   Hume retires from Westminster.

2010   John Hume is declared 'Ireland's Greatest' in a public poll conducted by RTÉ.

1937–68

John Hume showed signs of a keen economic, social and political awareness from his earliest years. A highly intelligent and unusually mature youngster, he could hardly have avoided an acute consciousness of the social and economic problems of a deeply deprived city like Derry in the 1940s and 1950s. He was born into a family that moved from one small 'two-up, two-down' terrace house to another during his childhood. The appalling housing shortage in his native city and high unemployment affected the whole community in which John grew up and in which he first learned about Catholic-Protestant relationships. He vividly recalled these circumstances in a radio interview years later:

> My first memories are of living in a single room with my father and mother and five brothers and sisters until I was 5 years old. We lived in that one house because the housing situation in Derry was appalling. From then onwards we lived in a two-bedroomed house [...]
>
> During the war my father worked in the shipyard and when the war ended I was 8 years old and he never worked again. He was unemployed for twenty years and we were all growing up [...] Looking back on it not only was it extreme poverty I wondered how my mother actually succeeded in rearing us [...] and it was only in later life that you realize how extreme the poverty was and realize the sacrifices that in fact were made by parents, my mother in particular [...]
>
> I grew up in Glenbrook Terrace, which at that time was right on the outskirts of the city, on the road out to Donegal, and out the road from us was what they called Springtown Camp, which was a place where the American navy stayed during the war and they built Nissan huts and when they left the housing problem in Derry was so bad that people squatted into it and it became a tin town and it was only in later years when we transformed housing in Derry that we were able to get rid of places like that.
>
> In our street there were three Protestant families and we were extremely friendly. There was no question of any differences between us at all. In fact those families are friends to this very day [...] But there were other streets in the district that would have been totally Protestant and other streets that were totally Catholic and one became very aware of that. I used to notice and I used be amazed when the twelfth of July or the twelfth of August came

around, the marching season, the tension that immediately came into the community [...] and the Protestant community – suddenly some sort of tension went into them. I remember as a child going up through one of the streets and being stuck up against a wall by young Protestant lads. Throughout the rest of the year I played football [with them] and yet at this time I was a papist [...] we were very conscious of that sort of stuff [...][1]

Hume's community was in no doubt as to the reasons for the housing crisis; they knew that the gerrymandered, unionist-controlled corporation in this majority Irish nationalist city used the provision of housing, or non-provision, as a political tool to ensure their own continued hegemony. As a consequence, political and social unrest were endemic in Derry, and gave rise to a deep-rooted bitterness, and resentment of those who controlled the city's government. John's father, Sam, became unemployed when John was 8, and such was the shortage of employment in Derry, and the severe disadvantage of Catholics in accessing it, that he could never find work again. Without her husband's income, John's mother made what few shillings she could doing piecework in the evenings for local shirt factories. Her eldest son, John, as a schoolboy, supplemented the family income by earning a couple of shillings a week from a daily newspaper round. That sense of responsibility for his family was to become a mark of John Hume's character. It developed into an assumption of responsibility for his community, his city and his country – a burden that rested on his shoulders all his life. In John's view, everyone has a solemn responsibility to use every talent that God gave them to achieve the maximum possible benefit for themselves as individuals, for their family, their community, their country and humanity at large. He simply assumed that it was his personal responsibility to solve the social, economic and political problems that beset the society in which he grew up. His son John Jnr would later recall that his memory of his father from childhood was of a man who seemed permanently preoccupied, worried and wrapped up in his own thoughts. That constant preoccupation sometimes made him an uncomfortably taciturn companion. However, it was one of the keys to his magnetic personality. He had a habit of rigorously thinking his way through every situation and every problem that confronted him. When he reached a conclusion, it became an unshakeable conviction. Throughout his life, these settled, unshakeable convictions almost never varied; there is a remarkably steady consistency in his economic, social and political ideas, throughout his life. He communicated these certainties to all those around him in a way that was very reassuring. (Most of us are afflicted with uncertainties and doubts, but not John Hume.) That is what made people look to him for analysis, leadership and a route map for the way forward.

1 Interview with John Quinn, RTÉ radio, 25 June 1992.

Many – perhaps most – of the Hume family's neighbours lived in similarly straitened circumstances, and just as in deprived working-class communities the world over, a powerful sense of community solidarity shaped the social attitudes of Derry's people; neighbours helped each other through the tough times. John's father, Sam Hume, made a singular and highly important contribution to that network of social support. He was known and widely respected for his sharp intelligence, literacy, wisdom, breadth of experience and knowledge of public affairs. John recalled:

> My father had beautiful copper-plate handwriting and he was a highly intelligent man and all the people in the district used to come to my father to write their personal letters for them or to write their letters into the local authorities or the government authorities with their problems. So from a very early age I was very conscious of people coming to the house with their problems, because we didn't have a very big house [...] there were times actually when the people were queued up waiting for my father as he sat at the table writing the letters for them [...] and my father was very committed to helping people to solve their problems because he had a very good knowledge of the whole system as well.[2]

This consciousness of the importance of people helping each other through difficult times was a hugely important factor in shaping the thinking of the young John Hume. The notion that people had to help themselves would lead him into a wide range of activities and projects – the Derry Housing Association, the credit-union movement, the University for Derry Committee, the Derry Development Association, the smoked-salmon business, the civil rights movement, and ultimately the founding of a new political party – all of which had the single aim of helping and improving his own people, his own city and his own country.

Like many other intelligent youngsters from working-class communities, John Hume escaped the limitations of his background, because of the education reforms introduced by the post-war Labour government at Westminster. It enabled him to get a free grammar-school education, and later to go on to university – a pathway previously not open to the children of poor families. Because of the strong religious convictions he inherited from his parents, his schools and his community, that pathway took him to St Patrick's College, Maynooth to study for the priesthood. He took his first degree in history and French, and went on to do a master's degree in history; his thesis was a study of the 'social and economic aspects of the growth of Derry' between 1825 and 1850. However, the restrictions of life as a student cleric gradually became more and more irksome to him; doubts about the solidity of his

2 Ibid.

vocation grew to the point where he concluded that the priesthood was not his destiny. He left Maynooth in 1957 and returned home to Derry. Employment opportunities were scarce, and John drifted into teaching, which was often the only job option available to young, educated Catholics at the time. Unexpectedly, he discovered an aptitude for the profession, especially the teaching of French. His methods brought a high level of success to his students, and were commended by the schools inspectorate. He was an early exponent of the '*écoutez et parlez*' approach, conducting his classes through the medium of French. His success in this kind of teaching brought him to the attention of the French consul in Belfast, who arranged a scholarship for him to spend a month at a French university. Those teaching instincts were to become a hugely important component of his political methodology in later years. When he was criticized for repeating the same ideas time after time, he insisted that he did so because they were correct, and that he would go on doing so until people began to repeat those same ideas to him, as if they were their own original thoughts.

As a young teacher living at home with his father, Hume gradually became immersed in the unofficial social work through which Sam served the local community. His involvement in the life of the community caused him to think more and more about how the people of Derry might address the problems they faced – the lack of housing, the lack of jobs and the endemic poverty and depriva- tion that afflicted such a large proportion of the city's population. His growing reputation as a significant community activist, coupled with his growing fame as a compelling orator in the debates of the city's Columcille Debating Society, propelled him into a leadership role in all matters of concern to the city. The first of these major issues arose out of the programme of 'modernization', introduced by the new prime minister, Captain Terence O'Neill, who succeeded Lord Brookeborough in 1963.

The O'Neill administration's programme of 'modernization' included a proposal for a new university. The natural and obvious choice would have been to locate the new college in Derry. The city already had the nucleus of a university in Magee College, which had a long tradition of higher education, a fine library and a sizeable campus. The city also had a teaching hospital at Altnagelvin. However, there was a deep-seated unease in Derry that the unionist government might regard the establishment of a new university as a useful tool for reinforcing unionist hegemony in Northern Ireland. A pattern had already been set by the decision to develop a new city linking the predominantly unionist towns of Portadown and Lurgan rather than a programmed expansion of the city of Derry, and the concentration of all new development projects in that catchment area within a 30-mile radius of Belfast.

As a consequence of the unease generated by the growing isolation of Derry and the diversion of all developments into unionist areas, leading community figures in the city formed the University for Derry Committee, and John Hume was elected chairman. It attracted support right across the community, including from some of the city's leading unionist politicians. The unionist mayor, Albert Anderson, addressed a meeting called by the committee in the Guildhall in February 1965 and called for a united front to oppose any decision to site the new university in any location other than Derry. This was exactly what John Hume wanted to hear, because he was already thinking of the university campaign as a means of uniting the communities in defence of their city's interests. In an interview for the *Irish Times* with journalist Michael Viney in May 1964, John had said:

> The independence and seriousness of Derry's Protestant, allied to the discipline and resourcefulness of the Catholic, will build the bridge for Derry's future. The symbol of the bridge could be the future full acceptance of the term 'Londonderry' (alongside the ancient name of Derry), for it summed up the two great traditions of the city.[3]

The culmination of the University for Derry campaign was a huge motorcade from Derry to Northern Irleand's parliament at Stormont to argue the city's case for selection as the site of the new university. However, in spite of the support of many of Derry's unionist residents, and perhaps Prime Minister O'Neill's own private inclinations, the inexorable grinding out of the basic unionist agenda could not be stopped. The decision was made to site the new university in the unionist enclave around the small market town of Coleraine. Derry was outraged, as was the general nationalist population of Northern Ireland. The issue became a rallying point for opposition to the sectarian behaviour of the unionist authorities at Stormont. Speaking in Fulham Town Hall in July 1965, at a meeting called by the Campaign for Democracy in Ulster (a body formed by concerned Labour MPs in Westminster, who had begun to listen to and support Gerry Fitt, MP for West Belfast, in his calls for reform in Northern Ireland), Hume said:

> Not a single academic criterion is to be found in the [Lockwood] Report[4] for the choice of Coleraine [...] The plan is therefore to develop the strongly unionist Belfast-Portadown-Coleraine triangle and to cause a migration from west to east Ulster, redistributing and scattering the minority so that the Unionist Party will not only maintain but strengthen its position. The British taxpayer is paying for these schemes. The new university will cost over £200 million. Yet it would appear that the Treasury doles out this size of capital without attempting to scrutinize in any detail the uses to which it will be put.

3 Interview with Michael Viney, *Irish Times*, 9 May 1964.   4 The Lockwood Committee reported in 1965 on future higher education requirements in Northern Ireland.

The tragedy is that this plan comes at a time when the Northern Ireland problem shows more hopeful signs of [an] internal solution than ever before. It is my belief that the problem can only be solved by the people of Northern Ireland themselves, and then only when the mental border that divides our community has been largely eradicated – when bigotry and intolerance have been driven from our shores. There has been a great growth in liberal feeling, but unfortunately, it is my fear that by the time this upsurge in tolerance and right thinking reaches the corridors of power in Northern Ireland, it will be too late for places like Derry, and irreparable damage will have been done. The unionist administration must be taught that they cannot run away from Derry and West Ulster, and that if they seriously want to create a modern community they must treat all citizens with dignity and equality.[5]

Hume went on to appeal to all MPs at Westminster, and to the British public at large, to halt this sinister plan. If they did so they would make a swift and lasting contribution not only to solving the Northern Ireland problem, but, he said presciently, 'also towards a solution that can be applied to the many problems of community division throughout the world'.[6]

John's reference to Derry and West Ulster reflected the belief of many, and not just nationalists, that it was the deliberate strategy of the unionist administration to allow the areas west of the Bann to decline through neglect. Many suspected that the unionist elite hoped that high unemployment rates and severe housing shortages would drive large numbers of nationalists to emigrate to Britain or the United States, and thus preserve the unionist majority in Northern Ireland. In October 1965, a few months after his Fulham address, Hume spoke to the New Ireland Society in Queen's University Belfast, on the motion – 'The west's asleep'.

The people of the north-west reject and resent the suggestion that they are asleep. We feel instead that we are being suffocated. There are those who believe that beyond the Bann, all is wilderness. The charge has been repeatedly made the west is being deliberately neglected. The answer to that charge takes several forms. There are those who say that it is a figment of the imagination of political opponents of the government. There are those who say that the west's asleep, and ask, 'What has the west done for itself?' However, I intend to prove that the neglect of the west is very much a reality. But we must do more than that [...] we must prove that the west has real growth potential and we will begin with the key to the problem, the regional centre

5 Address at a public meeting of the Campaign for Democracy in Ulster, Fulham Town Hall, July 1965; copy in editor's possession. 6 Ibid.

of Derry; for the future prosperity of smaller towns like Strabane depends to a large extent on the development of a large regional centre.

There are over 3,000 unemployed in Derry. An equivalent figure for Belfast would be 30,000. One out of five men in Derry is unemployed. We have 12.5 per cent of all male unemployment in Northern Ireland. Our current figures show 110 boys unemployed while Belfast [with a population five times larger] has only fifty-eight, a statistic which would seem to indicate that school-leavers are being readily absorbed into the working population of Belfast and that future full employment seems assured. Moving out of Derry, on through the north-west to Strabane, we find an unemployment figure of 1,500 out of a population of 7,700. Omagh has 1,000 unemployed in a population of 8,000. Dungannon has a population of 6,500, 1,100 of whom are unemployed. Enniskillen has 1,524 unemployed out of the population of 7,004. These figures take no account of the steady stream of emigration from the west. For instance Derry lost over 6,000 people between 1951 and 1961 [...] the much lower unemployment numbers for the towns in the east, many of them with much larger populations than their western counterparts make an interesting comparison.[7]

Hume went on to criticize the unionist government's economic strategy, as stated in the Matthew and Wilson reports (both of which were commissioned and accepted by the unionist government). This strategy clearly targeted development in eight towns within a 30-mile radius of Belfast, all but one of them overwhelmingly unionist, the exception being Downpatrick. Quoting extensively from United Nations reports, OECD reports and the Stormont government's own statistical research, Hume demonstrated beyond dispute that this strategy ran counter to the prevailing norms of economic development in the rest of the world, but especially in West Germany, which had experienced the most dramatic economic growth of any country in Europe in the 1950s and 1960s. This had been accomplished, he asserted, by a radical programme of decentralization, targeting development in the smaller towns, remote from major urban centres. He dismissed the habitual argument of the unionist authorities, that Derry was too remote, and that communications would be a major problem:

The idea that 70 miles – in 1965 – constitutes remoteness, is clearly nonsense. Professor Wilson himself has said that the transport problems of yesterday are not those of today or tomorrow. It is clear that the expansion envisaged for the north of Ireland will necessitate a second growth centre, and the ideal site

7 Address to the New Ireland Society, Queen's University Belfast, Oct. 1965; copy in editor's possession.

for that is on the Eglinton shore of Lough Foyle [...] It immediately adjoins the Maydown industrial estate and the port is on the other side of the river. This conjures up the enormous possibility – given goodwill – of a massive industrial estate, with a deep-water port and an airport on its doorstep. Such a plan is no more ambitious though it is perhaps more obvious and less difficult than the government's published intentions for the north-east [...] the creation of a new magnet in the north-west would relieve the congestion in Belfast, and create more natural development in Northern Ireland. In its turn the creation of a dynamic growth centre in Derry would bring its share of prosperity to Strabane and dormer towns, and consideration can be given to development plans for these towns in the same fashion as for the small towns in the east. In addition, the availability of labour in the north-west must be an outstanding advantage – 60 per cent of the firms which have come to Northern Ireland since 1953 have come because of available labour. More than half of Derry's unemployed are either skilled or semi-skilled and Derry has the advantage that it is one place in Northern Ireland that could, perhaps, attract back large numbers of skilled workers – former sons – provided that jobs and houses were available.[8]

Unionist opposition at local-government level to the provision of adequate housing in Derry was matched by perceived indifference at regional-government level to the need for job creation in Derry and the west. Therefore, in keeping with the growing determination of many of Derry's leading citizens that Derry must '*farà da sè*' (do it by itself), John and his colleagues began to explore initiatives for job creation. If the government in Belfast was not going to conduct a vigorous development effort in the north-west, then the vacuum would have to be filled by the people themselves. Accordingly, Hume, with his friend Michael Canavan and some other colleagues, set up their own Derry Development Association and drew up a brochure setting out the attractions of Derry as a centre for business development. But in spite of the enormous amount of work they put into their campaign to attract business to Derry, they had little success. Only two companies came to look at the city, and one of those companies – the Goodyear Tyre Company – informed Hume and his colleagues that the department of economic development at Stormont had never mentioned Derry to them, encouraging them instead to explore opportunities in the new urban complex they intended to develop in the Lurgan-Portadown area: the 'new city' of Craigavon. (Eventually Goodyear did set up in Craigavon, but it was never a success, and it closed after fifteen unprofitable years.)

Hume and his colleagues were not discouraged by this lack of success, and

8 Ibid.

decided to set up a business of their own. The River Foyle was one of the best salmon fisheries in Europe, and they began to think about means of exploiting that resource that would create some of the jobs Derry desperately needed. Smoked salmon was becoming a fashionable delicacy in the 1960s and was an ideal development project for Derry, using local resources and not requiring unmanageable start-up costs. With Canavan supplying the premises and the cash, John left his teaching job and went into the business full-time as managing director. It was a huge risk for a young married man to leave a secure teaching job for an uncertain future in a small business. However, it was a measure of the deadly seriousness of his urge to bring about change. Because of the commitment, energy and imagination Hume injected into the project, the company, 'Atlantic Harvest', became a considerable success, and when John went into politics full-time in 1969, the business carried on as a model self-help enterprise.

Hume's personal experience made him very aware of the importance of housing – as well as jobs – to the well-being of families and the general community. He was, moreover, well aware of the work being undertaken by the Dungannon GP Con McCluskey, firstly in the Homeless Citizens' League, and later in the Campaign for Social Justice, to highlight the decisions of the unionist authorities in Dungannon, and many other towns, to deny housing to the Catholic population as far as they could. The same impulses that had led to the creation of the credit-union movement drove many leading citizens in Derry to the conclusion that they would have to build their own houses. An example was set by a prominent community leader, Paddy 'Bogside' Doherty, who, having had his application for a house turned down by the city corporation housing officer, bought a small plot of land and decided to build his own house. This encouraged many others to think that self-help was the only way to solve the housing problem. A driving force in all of this was Father Anthony Mulvey, a Catholic curate who had been involved with Hume, Canavan and Doherty in starting the credit-union movement in Derry. With his encouragement Hume and others formed a housing association and began to raise resources to buy land and build houses. They had some small success, but found that their work was opposed and restricted at every turn by the unionist-controlled corporation, which was determined to prevent housing development in any area which might threaten unionist majorities in unionist-controlled wards. The housing crisis in Derry, and the shameless discrimination in housing provision in many other towns across the North, created a great deal of ill-feeling and gave rise to a swelling mood of discontent, which would eventually erupt onto the streets in the autumn of 1968.

The more John Hume involved himself in self-help enterprises, and in the campaign for economic development west of the Bann, the more it brought him into contact with many other citizens of a similarly practical cast of mind, people who were also thinking about ways that Derry might improve its lot. In the 1960s the credit-union movement had begun to spread from Irish America into the South of Ireland. The idea of a deprived community, pooling its meagre financial resources, in order to create a 'community bank' as a resource for people who had no hope of borrowing from a commercial bank, immediately appealed to John Hume and his friends. Having thought about the matter, and researched the idea thoroughly, the small group of people around Hume decided to go ahead. They pooled their meagre financial resources and established the first credit union in Northern Ireland. The movement mushroomed rapidly in Derry and quickly spread throughout Northern Ireland. During those years, Hume became an evangelist for the credit-union philosophy, travelling the length and breadth of Ireland to spread the word. His magnetic personality, his passionate commitment to the credit-union philosophy of self-help, and his compelling oratory at credit-union meetings, all propelled him to national prominence, and in due course he became president of the Credit Union League of Ireland. At its national convention in the summer of 1968, Hume replied on behalf of the movement to the address of the then taoiseach (prime minister), Mr Jack Lynch. His speech reflected the grounding of his principles in his religious convictions. He was speaking in the context of widespread unrest among young people and workers in many of the cities of the Western world:

> And if we look around the world today [...] we must all be very concerned at what we see. For we see unrest, we see youth revolting in all the capitals of the Western world, we see hunger and poverty, we see violence and peaceful men being shot down in the streets. And all this causes uneasiness and unrest and the world wonders why, and the world asks why. But really, to my mind the answer, and the reason for it all is very simple and the answer is as old as Christianity itself, the answer is simply that man's spiritual and material development have grown and developed apart, so we have nations in the world of great material strength, but they have developed materially at the expense of the spirit. And no less wrong have been the countries of the world that have concentrated too much on the spirit, to the neglect of the material. In short, the material nations of the world today thirst for the spirit, while the poor nations hunger for bread.[9]

He went on to speak of:

> this new Christian approach, this fundamental change in our thinking, this feeling that the Christian must get up off his knees and go out into the

---

9 Address to the annual convention of the League of Credit Unions in Ireland, Cork, 1968; copy in editor's possession.

marketplace, that he must be concerned not just on one day of the week, but he must be concerned with all the problems, with the man who hasn't got a house, the man who hasn't got a job, the man who was hungry. He must be concerned with all these things. This is the new Christianity that is emerging. I think that our movement, starting at the beginning of the 1960s, was an expression in its own small way of the realization of this in Ireland. For surely the credit-union movement is an ideal example of concern for a man's body and his spirit and in my view an example of this basic cry [...] in other words, we should create a nation, and a people that reflect our basic Christian beliefs, a place where people help people, and this is after all the basic idealism of our movement.[10]

In his concluding remarks he related these principles to his developing political thinking:

In short, then, what I am really saying is that today our basic ideals of life and living must invade all that we have to do and say. And in a country like Ireland, it must change our approach to many things. It must change our whole approach to patriotism. It is time [...] that we stopped playing the 'patriot game' in Ireland and started to consider what patriotism is all about. There are many people who talk about, and only very few who think about, what Ireland really is [...] Ireland is people, because people are the basic wealth of the world. Without people we have nothing [...] In the Ireland of today, the true patriotism is that which builds, which sweats, rather than bleeds, and which tries to build up a country which concerns itself with all the problems, social, economic and cultural [...] And through the medium of our ideals of self-help, we believe that we are making a contribution towards this type of society in Ireland today.[11]

Pat Hume would later say that she did not notice John having any particular interest in politics when she married him in 1960. However, his involvement in these various self-help projects, and in the University for Derry campaign, made him very aware of the negative political environment within which he was working. Moreover, he would have been aware of the political ferment in the early 1960s among the growing body of educated Catholics in the North, such as the New Ireland Society at Queen's University in Belfast, and the Belfast-focused National Unity grouping. He would undoubtedly have shared in the general frustration of thinking nationalists with the ineffectual nature of nationalist politics, and the ineptitude of the old Nationalist Party. The first considered state-

10 Ibid. **11** Ibid.

ment of his political views took the form of a two-part article he wrote for the *Irish Times* in May 1964, by way of a reply to an earlier article by the journalist Michael Viney. Viney had spoken of the great political frustration that existed among the Catholic community in Northern Ireland. Hume wrote:

> The crux of the matter for the younger generation is the continued existence, particularly among the Catholic community, of great social problems in housing, unemployment and emigration. It is the struggle for priority in their minds between such problems and the ideal of a united Ireland with which they have been bred, that has produced the frustration [...] It may be that the present generation of younger Catholics in the North are more materialistic than their fathers, but there is little doubt that their thinking is principally geared towards the solution of social and economic problems. This has led to a deep questioning of traditional nationalist attitudes. It must be said at once that the blame for the situation which prevails must be principally laid at the door of the unionist government. But the present nationalist political party must bear a share of it.
>
> Good government depends as much on the opposition as on the party in power. Weak opposition leads to corrupt government. Nationalists in opposition have been in no way constructive. They have – quite rightly – been loud in their demands for rights, but they have remained silent and inactive about their duties. In forty years of opposition, they have not produced one constructive contribution, on either the social or economic plane, to the development of Northern Ireland, which is after all a substantial part of the united Ireland for which they strive. Leadership has been the comfortable leadership of flags and slogans. Easy, no doubt, but irresponsible. There has been no attempt to be positive, to encourage the Catholic community to develop the resources which they have in plenty, to make a positive contribution in terms of community service. Unemployment and emigration, chiefly of Catholics, remains heavy, much of it no doubt due to the skilful placing of industry by the Northern government, but the only constructive suggestion from the nationalist side would appear to be that the removal of discrimination will be the panacea for all our ills. It is this lack of positive contributions and the apparent lack of interest in the general welfare of Northern Ireland that has led many Protestants to believe that the Northern Catholic is politically irresponsible and immature, and therefore unfit to rule.[12]

Hume went on to comment on the fixation in Northern Ireland with religious divisions, and the toxic pressures in each community to conform to traditional tribal imperatives:

12 *Irish Times*, 18 May 1964

This dangerous equation of nationalism and Catholicism has simply contributed to the postponement of the emergence of normal politics in the area, and has made the task of the unionist ascendancy simpler. Worse – it has poisoned the Catholic social climate, to the extent that it has become extremely difficult for a Catholic to express publicly any point of view which does not coincide with the narrow nationalist line. Disagreement with, or criticism of the nationalist approach – or lack of it – inevitably brings down on one's head a torrent of abuse. 'Obsequious', 'crawling', 'Castle Catholic', 'West Briton', are samples of the terms used. The result has been that many Catholics have been unwilling to speak their minds, for fear of recrimination [...] One of the greatest contributions therefore, that the Catholic in Northern Ireland can make to a liberalizing of the political atmosphere, would be the removal of the equation between nationalist and Catholic. Apart from being factual, it ought also to be made fashionable that the Catholic church does not impose upon its members any one form of political belief.

Another positive step towards easing community tensions, and towards removing what bigotry exists among Catholics, would be to recognize that the Protestant tradition in the North is as strong and as legitimate as our own. Such recognition is our first step towards better relations. We must be prepared to accept this, and to realize the fact that if a man wishes Northern Ireland to remain part of the United Kingdom it does not necessarily make him a bigot or a discriminator.[13]

He went on, then, to deal with the constitutional issue, suggesting that the Catholic community should accept the constitutional position of Northern Ireland within the United Kingdom while pointing out that such an acceptance was not inconsistent with the belief that a thirty-two county republic would be best for Ireland. Such a change, he insisted, would remove what was a great stumbling block to the development of normal politics and law. Catholics, he believed, could then throw themselves fully into the solution of Northern Ireland's problems without fear of recrimination. Such an attitude, he insisted, would admit the realistic fact that a united Ireland, if it is to come about, can only come about by the consent of a majority in the North. Hume then turned his attention to the Nationalist Party:

On the party political front, the need for a complete revitalization of the Nationalist Party has long been felt. The 'head without a body' type of party in existence up to the present was bound to lead to political immaturity

13 Ibid.

among Catholics. The necessity for a fully organized democratic party, which can freely attract and draw upon the talents of the nationally minded community, is obvious. It is to be hoped that the new Nationalist Political Forum[14] will create such an organization.

Discrimination, or rather complaints about it, has long formed the main policy of the nationalist political party. One gets the impression sometimes that the deep human problems underlying the statistics are sometimes forgotten, otherwise there would be a more intelligent and sustained criticism and opposition. It must be pointed out that people who discriminate through prejudice believe that they are justified. Catholics can contribute to a lessening of prejudice by playing a full part in public life as some of our religious leaders have been urging. Undoubtedly, in the beginning, they will neither be wanted, nor welcome in many spheres of life in Northern Ireland. But public life means more than service on statutory or other government committees. It means the encouragement and participation in community enterprises [...] designed to develop the resources of the community, and done in conjunction with all those in the community who are willing to co-operate.[15]

Hume then turned his spotlight on the unionist government and unionist leadership in the North. A climate of goodwill had begun to emerge, he suggested, which created an opportunity for a fresh approach, leading to reconciliation. But he went on to warn:

It is well to point out that the considerable heart searching and sincere self-examination going on among Catholics in the North at the moment, does not absolve the Unionist Party from certain obligations if they are sincere about their concern for the future of the North. To date, none of their leaders has shown any response to repeated statements of Catholic willingness to get together. Unionists must realise that if they turn their backs on the present goodwill there can only be a considerable hardening of Catholic opinion [...][16]

Of course, John Hume's warning was not heeded. The decision of the Nationalist Party to accept the role of official opposition at Stormont brought no response. The later decision of the Catholic church leaders to accept a unionist government's nominees to the management of Catholic schools equally failed to produce a conciliatory gesture in response. The work of the Dr Con McCluskey-led Campaign for Social Justice, in documenting the scale and extent of

14 The Nationalist Political Forum was an attempt to bring a variety of nationalist political interests together. It had only limited political success. 15 *Irish Times*, 19 May 1964. 16 Ibid.

discrimination against Catholics in housing and jobs across the North, was blithely ignored. Thus, when the gerrymandered Dungannon rural district council ignored the rightful claims of local Catholic families to be allocated vacant houses in the village of Caledon, prompting the local Stormont Nationalist Party MP Austin Currie to squat in the houses, the pent-up grievances of the nationalist population boiled over and spilled out onto the streets. It also ushered in Hume's direct involvement in politics.

1968–72

The growth of the civil rights movement across Northern Ireland almost inevitably involved community activists like John Hume. The blatant gerrymandering of local-government wards in Derry, the deliberate location of social housing to ensure unionist control of the city's corporation, discrimination in employment practices, and the Northern Ireland government's policies on economic development were among the particular issues that caused him to become involved.

In October 1968 Derry dramatically became a focal point for civil rights protests when police baton-charged a civil rights march and injured several of the marchers. Television images of the attack were beamed around the world, to the great embarrassment of the Northern Ireland government. While not a leading organizer of that march, Hume was elected vice chair of the Derry Citizens' Action Committee, which was established a few days later. The aim was to pursue a civil rights agenda in the city. Later Hume explained why he had become involved:

> I went into civil rights in the early days because I was heavily involved in the voluntary housing movement and the local city council, or corporation as it was called in those days, was the prime example of injustice in the North [...]
> It was the worst case of gerrymandering. To make gerrymandering work they controlled voting rights, housing rights and job rights and therefore there was massive exclusion. What they did in order to control voting was to control housing, and build ghettoes [...] Only Catholics were put into certain areas and in the early '60s the Catholic ward in Derry, the South ward, was filled up and they stopped building [...] because they wouldn't put people into other districts in case it would upset the voting balance. That put enormous pressure on the whole housing front. And as chairman of the housing association we sought to build our own houses and they refused planning permission because we were building in the 'wrong' area. That was one of the major factors that brought me onto the streets in the civil rights movement and of course what is often forgotten is that after, without throwing a stone, we brought it down; three weeks of civil rights protests in Derry without throwing a single stone, Derry Corporation fell. So here was an unjust system that had lasted seventy years and in three weeks, without

1 Interview with John Quinn, RTÉ radio, 25 June 1992.

throwing a stone, it started the whole process of change for the first time in seventy years in the north of Ireland and that process is still continuing. It's that that brought me into politics.[1]

In November 1968 the government announced that the city's corporation would be abolished and an independent, non-elected commission nominated to take over the city's administration. The government also announced that a point system would be used to allocate public housing. This was followed by legislation to allow the appointment of a parliamentary ombudsman to investigate complaints against government departments. A promise that universal suffrage would soon follow was then given by the Unionist Party. By then Hume had decided that while some reform was possible through the pressure of large-scale civil rights demonstrations, more fundamental reform required political pressure as well, and when Prime Minister Terence O'Neill called a snap general election for February 1969 Hume decided to become a candidate. He wanted to use parliamentary influence to ensure that the demands of the civil rights movement would be fully addressed and reform fully implemented. However, Hume's reform agenda widened as he realized that the system of government under the Government of Ireland Act of 1920 was totally inadequate for Northern Ireland's circumstances. Fundamental political reform was essential, though he had not yet determined the actual form it should take. Among his more immediate objectives was the formation of a new, left-of-centre party that would provide the platform for strong opposition at Stormont and for advancing that wider reform he believed necessary.

Hume decided to seek nomination as an independent candidate in Derry's Foyle constituency where the seat had long been held by the widely respected leader of the Nationalist Party, Eddie McAteer. Hume described McAteer as:

> an honourable and highly respected man who had been a natural leader of his generation. However, I felt that our generation was faced with a whole new situation and I sought a mandate in that election to found a party based on social-democratic principles. The fact that I – a young independent – defeated the leader of the Nationalist Party in that election reflected the massive surge of new political interest among the voters and the arrival of a new generation, the first generation who were the products of public education.[2]

It was not an easy decision to contest McAteer's seat:

> I was reluctant to stand against Eddie McAteer but I felt that a more aggressive political attitude and movement was vital. I had the feeling that the

2 John Hume, *Personal views: politics, peace and reconciliation in Ireland* (London, 1996), p. 12.

movement on the streets had attained its immediate objectives, and must be consolidated by political advance. I did not share the fear and forecast of many that my decision would cause a deep division amongst the Catholic people. Any divisions would be temporary, and I believed the people were ready for change [...] I was certain change was in the air and that if I did not enter the field somebody else would.[3]

Hume explained that he stood as an independent because the Nationalist Party had failed to give leadership, had grown content with the status quo and electorally had become happy to hold a small number of seats and not to contest any others:

Is there anyone in this community who doubts that the emergence of the people on the streets was due in part to disenchantment with existing political approaches to the problems of social justice and to the failure of the existing opposition to force the unionist government to abandon their policies which offend against fundamental justice.

Surely now that an election has come the logical conclusion for anyone who has thought about politics is that the methods and approach of opposition politics must change in order that the mistakes of the past be not repeated in the future. That this is a widely held view is clear from the fact that opposition has emerged to the Nationalist Party in almost every seat.

Mr Hume said that people were dissatisfied that the Nationalist Party had not in the past fifty years contested one unionist seat. The same was true again in this election. They appeared to be satisfied with the status quo that had failed – nine safe seats. The present disarray and division in the opposition forces could not possibly be blamed on people who were new to the political scene for they clearly bore no responsibility for it, but it was most definitely due to a failure of past leadership.

The Nationalist Party could not offer the people any more hope of unity today than it had done in the past when it was itself divided. Its youngest and most virile MP, Austin Currie, had received from his supporters what amounted to a mandate to get out of the Nationalist Party and last week's opinion poll showed only 6 per cent of the total electorate supported the Nationalist Party.

The only way out of the present mess is for the people to speak out. And give a clear mandate for a new approach – an approach based on the hard reality that the basic problems of the people – unemployment, housing and emigration – should have priority of attention. Derry is the ideal place to give such a mandate. When Derry spoke on 5 October the results spread through

3 Frank Curran, *Derry: countdown to disaster* (Dublin, 1986), p. 116.

the North like wildfire. Is there anyone who doubts that there will be similar widespread reaction and result from declaring themselves in favour of political change today in the Foyle seat?

The choice facing the electorate is clear – status quo or the hope of a healthy, young and vigorous new movement [...][4]

Principle of consent

Hume intended to break new ground by accepting the principle of consent for any constitutional change in Northern Ireland's status within the UK as a central commitment, and he advanced the proposal to establish a new left-of-centre political party. His election manifesto made these commitments very clear:

> What I stand for fundamentally is a society in Northern Ireland in which Catholic, Protestant and Dissenter can work together to build a new community and base political action on political attitudes rather than use religion as a political weapon. This is a question of issues not personalities, and one which should be fought in open contest without bitterness or rancour. The people must decide.
>
> I will work for the formation of a new political movement based on social democratic principles with open membership and an elected executive to allow the people full involvement in the process of decision-making.
>
> The movement must provide what has seriously been lacking at Stormont, namely a strong and energetic opposition to conservatism, and pursue radical social and economic policies.
>
> The movement must be completely non-sectarian and must root out a fundamental evil in our society, sectarian division.
>
> The movement must be committed to the ideal that the future of Northern Ireland should be decided by its people, and no constitutional changes accepted except by the consent of its people [...][5]

Hume defended his decision to stand for election against critics in the civil rights movement who claimed he was 'letting the movement down' by doing so. His argument underlined the critical need to move into the political arena:

> Some people have suggested that my entry into the political arena will let down the civil rights movement. This is not so. The Derry Citizens' Action Committee was, is and will continue to be a non-political body having among its membership people of different political persuasions. Their polit-

4 *Derry Journal*, 21 Feb. 1969.   5 *Irish Times*, 7 Feb. 1969.

ical differences have not prevented them in the past from pursuing a common aim with strength and unity of purpose. […]

This is not an election about personalities. I am not fighting Mr McAteer, whose political integrity I respect. Rather am I presenting a choice to the people. I am asking them which way do we go. The wind of change is blowing through the north of Ireland. It was created by the people of Derry. I am now asking these same people whether they wish the change to be carried into the political arena. I will do so by presenting them with a choice in the forth-coming election. During the campaign I will explain my policies and my attitudes and ask them to decide.

This is a decision which can only be made by the people as a whole, and not by a few. I am therefore placing the choice clearly before them. I am certain that they will make the right decision.[6]

Making consent a fundamental principle for constitutional change was ground-breaking because, until then, no party of the nationalist tradition, North or South, had ever included this principle in its constitution. To do so would have implied acceptance of partition, and no party that favoured Irish unity had found that possible. So, while upholding the right to democratically express and campaign for Irish unity, Hume strongly argued that unity could only be achieved with the agreement of a majority of the people of Northern Ireland. It could not be achieved by force, as some in the nationalist community argued, notably supporters of Sinn Féin. For Hume, it was not the British government, or the British army that prevented Irish unity being achieved. It was the will of the majority of the people living in Northern Ireland. Therefore, for Hume, force was not only wrong in principle it was also ineffectual, and it completely undermined the very concept of unity. This stance would characterize his whole political career. Another sign of his determination to break with the sterile sectarian politics that had long characterized Northern Irish politics, was his commitment to establish a new political party, one that, as his manifesto declared, would rise above Northern Ireland's ingrained sectarian divisions. In the election, Hume was successful, with 8,920 votes to McAteer's 5,287.

Challenging the status quo

Hume didn't move immediately to establish a new political party. Instead he joined with other representatives from the nationalist community to provide a much more effective opposition than had previously existed, highlighting injustices, probing the government and holding its ministers to account as never before.

6 *Derry Journal*, 11 Feb. 1969.

Hume's maiden speech is an example of his approach, and he soon became one of the opposition's leading and most effective spokespersons:

> The real question that hangs over this house today and indeed over the whole community is: are politics going to remain on the streets or are they going to be fought out in the chamber? With respect, before that question can be answered certain attitudes will have to be clarified. The first is the attitude of people on the opposite benches to the hon. members on this side of the house, because it is without a shadow of doubt the failure of hon. members on the opposite benches to listen to members on this side of the house – who for years have put forward grievances and have not been listened to – that has been one of the causes of people losing faith in parliamentary democracy [...]
>
> Fears and suspicions have been mounting ever since the Matthew Report [on spatial planning] was published in 1961. That report and subsequent government statements showed that in population terms, west of the Bann was going to lose 32,000 people in a two-year period. The 1966 census has already demonstrated that this movement is taking place.
>
> Suspicions were strengthened by the foundation of the new town of Craigavon and by the resignation of its chief planner on grounds that he felt it should have been in Derry. It was further strengthened by the closing of the railways and by the resignation of another Englishman. Both of these people to us seemed to have no axe to grind and one of them pointed out that he was being asked to close the second rail link after the 1970 elections.
>
> Then there was the despicable criminal story of the second university. To me that is where all the present trouble started because that brought the awakening of the public conscience. The prime minister mentioned the new university yesterday and he made reference to the government's wish to maintain university education in Derry and yet in this morning's edition of a Derry newspaper which strongly supports the government the front-page headline refers to the fears in Derry about the future of Magee.
>
> The present minister of education signed an agreement in 1965 that under-graduate education would be maintained in Derry. Already two of the departments which were to be there have moved with the result that the student intake has been seriously reduced. There is a strong feeling among the staff and among the people that rather than being kept alive Magee University College is being slowly strangled and that what we will have in future there in terms of university education is simply adult education. I should like to point out that that would not be accepted by people in Derry of any shade of opinion and I am sure that the hon. and gallant member for Derry City [Commander Anderson, Unionist] will agree with me in that.
>
> Those decisions, plus the reorganization of local government, plus the

movement of functions, for example, of the county council from Derry to Coleraine, including even the count in the recent election, point in one direction and can anyone blame our people in these areas for feeling and fearing that means economic deprivation for the whole area; it means a continuance of unemployment and migration? This is what people feel and all these factors, combined with the basic denial of civil rights, has led to the recent disturbances [...]

I would say that if we are to have a just society it can only be brought about by keeping certain fundamental attitudes and principles in view. It can only be achieved if we believe in the equality of rights of every citizen in our community; it can only be done if we approach the problems with justice in our minds and hearts; it can only be done if we believe in one another and if we are prepared to wipe out the prejudices and fears that are the roots of past hatreds. As I say, that can only be built on the basis of justice and equality [...][7]

Changing attitudes – addressing injustice

Hume frequently stressed the need to change communal attitudes as essential to reconciliation between the communities. He challenged unionist members of parliament to change their attitudes towards his colleagues, inviting them to ensure that parliamentary politics worked for all. He argued that serious grievances, ignored or denied, had left people in majority-nationalist areas west of the Bann without hope. Alongside the university issue, Hume highlighted why the need for reform in the allocation of public housing, a key demand of the civil rights movement, had been so important:

> The allocation system down the years has been that each rural district councillor allocates the houses in his own area. In other words, each petty potentate in each little rural electoral division allocates all the houses in that division and perpetuates himself in power. That is part of the housing policy. Why is housing in the hands of these people at all? Why is it not taken completely out of the hands of all local authorities and placed in the hands of a central housing agency acting through democratically elected local committees? This should put a stop to all the political jobbery which has been a root cause of social injustices which have led to the people taking to the streets in frustration.
>
> Secondly, demands have been made recently for a points system. If there had been a points system in operation in Derry rural district then these allocations could not possibly have been made. I am disturbed to learn that the

7 Northern Ireland House of Commons, *Debates*, 5 Mar. 1969.

points system offered in the five-point package of 'reform' is not to be compulsory. It will have no meaning if it is not to be compulsory. […]

Thirdly, on the question of housing policy again, a good deal of recent unrest has been caused by the fact that people have been forced to live for a considerable time in poor housing conditions and in particular in furnished accommodation at very high rents. There is very little rent control of furnished accommodation […] I admit there are some good landlords who provide good accommodation at reasonable rents but there are many others who do not.

There is an immediate need for legislation to establish some form of rent control or rental tribunal to control furnished accommodation to prevent this happening […][8]

Law and order

Nationalists generally had little or no confidence in the institutions administering law and order, namely the RUC and the courts. This issue became increasingly critical in the spring and summer months of 1969, as civil rights demonstrators, counter-demonstrators and police clashed in towns and villages across Northern Ireland. Such clashes led to accusations of partiality and, at times, of brutality by the police. Deeply concerned about the spreading violence and of the need to somehow develop confidence in the agencies of law and order, Hume believed that fundamental reform was necessary in both. Events in Derry and elsewhere provided examples to illustrate his argument:

I wish at this stage to raise what I regard as a very important matter particularly in the light of the present situation in the community. There is much talk in these tense days as to how the situation can be resolved. One of the major problems that has to be faced is the question of law and order. One of the major difficulties about the solution of our problems is the fact that a large section of our community has absolutely no confidence in the forces of law and order and allegations, which I believe to be justified, have been made about the partiality of the forces of law and order in the community. This being so there are several outstanding matters to which I wish to draw the attention of the house. If the government and the minister are to give the community the assurance that they do not condone partial behaviour on the part of the police force these matters should have been dealt with long before now. The first matter I wish to raise is the question of the police inquiry into

8 Ibid., 3 Apr. 1969.

the events in Bogside in Derry on the night of 4 January [when rioting occurred in the area]. We have still no report on that.

The lingering and smouldering resentment over the events of that evening still persists in Derry and is still responsible for quite a part of the present attitude towards the police. I would have expected that we would have had a report on this some time ago, but we have not.

The second matter, similarly showing that there is some suspicion that things are to some degree being covered up, is the failure to produce, as yet, a report on the incident in Armagh on 30 November involving the *Panorama* team of the BBC and members of the RUC.[9] At that time the then minister promised a quick and thorough investigation and a report and he said he would apologize if he found the complaint of the BBC reporters was well-founded. There are many witnesses and I am quite sure they have made statements, but, as yet, we have no comment from the minister of home affairs on the incident.

The third question is very important in the light of the present situation – the unrefuted information contained in an article by the *Insight* team in the *Sunday Times* last Sunday. It had rather disturbing evidence of apparent collusion between the police and people who were armed to prevent what was a legitimate procession through Burntollet Bridge area.[10] Clear evidence was presented in that article which has not yet been refuted.

That article also stated that a hundred people involved in that 'ambush', as it has been called, were members of the B-Specials force and that thirty have already signed written statements to that effect. There is evidence in that article which has still not been refuted by anyone. Has any effort been made to pursue the evidence contained in that article? In view of the evidence given of police partiality I would ask – and this is directed at the attorney general who, I understand, has been away on government business today and I would expect that he will reply when he has had time to look at the papers in question – that all charges arising out of and since 5 October that are based on police evidence alone should be suspended until there has been a proper and full investigation of police behaviour.

I sat in a courthouse in Derry yesterday and listened to a lot of cases arising out of incidents last weekend. In each individual case the only witness was a single police constable, whose evidence was totally uncorroborated. The result in most of these cases was that pretty hefty and even savage fines – £50 – were imposed, while one person was imprisoned for six months – on the

---

9 RUC officers seized film from a team from the investigative programme.   10 Reference to the ambush of the People's Democracy March from Belfast to Derry at Burntollet Bridge by a loyalist gang.

uncorroborated evidence of a single police constable in each case. In the present situation in the community I would feel that to prosecute people and convict them on such uncorroborated evidence is hardly the sort of justice, or appearance of justice, that this community would expect, particularly in view of what has appeared in a very reputable newspaper through a reputable newspaper team of researchers, namely, that there is considerable evidence of police partiality [...]

I raise these matters now because I am concerned, as are all hon. members on this side of the house, with the situation in the community, one of the root causes being the lack of confidence in the forces of law and order. Members on the opposite side of the house have not ceased to tell us that one man, one vote is no longer enough for us, that it would not satisfy the clamour on the streets. They are quite right, for the simple reason that the people have completely lost confidence, rightly or wrongly, in the impartiality of the forces of law and order [...][11]

Sam Devenny

The most acute local incident to exemplify that concern was the death of one of the first Catholic victims of the period, Sam Devenny, a Derry taxi driver who along with several members of his family was brutally beaten by RUC officers who had invaded his house, allegedly in pursuit of a group of rioters at disturbances in the city. Devenny was seriously injured and died some weeks later in July 1969. Hume starkly outlined the consequences for any support for the RUC, particularly given that the climax of the loyalist marching season was imminent:

Confidence in law and order has broken down [...] because of the fact that some members – I do not say all members – of the force which is responsible for maintaining law and order allow their personal political and religious prejudices to colour their attitude to their duty [...] members of the police force have actually entered people's homes and attacked them by their firesides. They attacked a family in my constituency. They broke the door down with a plank [...] The father [Sam Devenny] was beaten to the ground. He was not involved in the trouble; he was standing at his door. He has twenty-two stitches in his head and serious stomach injuries. His 16-year-old daughter who had just come out of hospital, having an ulcer and appendix operations, was beaten around the back and legs with batons. She is covered with bruises and has had a medical examination [...] The 20-year-old son was beaten on the head, and the 18-year-old daughter was struck repeatedly on the

11 Northern Ireland House of Commons, *Debates*, 29 Apr. 1969.

toe, which had to have medical attention [...] I am not trying to over-dramatize the situation. I am asking this house to understand the reaction of people when this sort of thing happens. Neither am I absolving from blame any stone-throwing vandals who did damage to persons and property in my city on Saturday.[12]

Battle of the Bogside

Sam Devenny's death heightened tensions in Derry, particularly in the city's Bogside area. The annual Apprentice Boys parade, the following month, would pass along the city's walls close to the Bogside, a likely occasion of conflict between marchers and the local community.[13] Calls for the parade to be either banned or re-routed away from the area were ignored. As feared, skirmishes broke out between a crowd that had gathered to protest against the parade, and marchers, and quickly escalated, with residents and Apprentice Boys throwing whatever kinds of missiles they could find at each other. Police sent to intervene came under attack and were soon forced to use tear gas in an effort to disperse rioters. Unsuccessful, the police were eventually withdrawn.

A revolutionary atmosphere then prevailed inside the Bogside as residents realized they had gained a form of control over the area, and a type of local administration was set up, primarily to negotiate with the security forces. Hume was not included and for a time it appeared as if his authority as a public representative could be eroded. He and the Citizens' Action Committee had already experienced severe criticism from extreme left-wing elements in the city, who accused them of being sectarian, and of not being revolutionary. Hume issued a strong rejection of this criticism and a strong defence of the approach adopted by the civil rights movement:

> Since the inception of the civil rights movement I have never made any secret of what I consider the aims of the movement to be – equal rights for all citizens. It is not, and never has been, and it has been repeatedly stated not to be, a movement which seeks to promote either a socialist or conservative society. It seeks only a just society, and the achievement of justice and democracy is surely a necessary first step in the north of Ireland to end forever the equation of religion and politics, before normal politics can take place.
>
> This is the point of view that brought thousands of people on the streets. This is the view that made the civil rights movement a mass movement and

---

12 Ibid., 22 Apr. 1969. 13 The Apprentice Boys are a Protestant association who annually commemorate the 1688–9 siege of Derry by the forces of Catholic King James, the city then being held by a population loyal to Protestant King William.

that has won sympathy and support for it throughout the world. It is a view that can be supported by people holding any political viewpoint and, indeed, that has been the strength of the civil rights movement.

It is, of course, clear that the attainment of civil rights is but a minimum and most people have political goals that go beyond that. But the place to express political views is on a political platform. To seek to use a civil rights platform to express these views is dishonest. To seek to achieve a socialist society by attempting to use the strength of a mass movement is to seek not reform but revolution. These people are now cynically seeking to achieve their aims which are not civil rights by attempting to take over the movement. Any political party could attempt what these people are attempting, but it is to the credit of those parties that have supported the movement from the beginning that they not have tried to preach their own policies from a civil rights platform [...]

I would also point out that the civil rights movement has broken through barriers that have not been broken before. Leaders of different denominations and people of all persuasions have spoken for justice. And can anyone previously remember in the history of Derry when thousands of people of different denominations came together in different churches to pray throughout the night for the peace of a civil rights march? [...]

Finally, I should have thought that it goes without saying that I will continue to press for justice in this society and will remain true to the principles of non-violence that have characterized the civil rights movement from the beginning [...][14]

The situation following the Apprentice Boys parade deteriorated into a virtual siege of the Bogside, and, perhaps not surprisingly, the guns came out. Indeed, over previous months the outlawed loyalist Ulster Volunteer Force had detonated bombs at electricity and water supply stations across Northern Ireland in an attempt to pressurize the government into not conceding civil rights demands. Then, when loyalist gangs, supported by some elements of the police, invaded nationalist areas in Belfast in response to events in Derry, six people were killed. One of the victims was a four-year-old boy who was shot as he lay in his bed.

At an emergency meeting of the Northern Ireland parliament the opposition strongly criticized the government's failure to understand why people in the Bogside resented what they regarded as the Apprentice Boys' arrogant displays of superiority and the partiality manifested by the police in directing their tactics more against the Bogside residents than against the Apprentice Boy and their supporters. Hume's own contribution to the debate was brief:

14 *Derry Journal,* 1 July 1969.

> Probably more than any other member of this house I know what the last few days have meant to people. I had hoped that perhaps crisis could bring out the best in some people in this house but I regret to say that the sterility of this house was never more in evidence than it is today. I do not wish to engage in any verbal battles with anyone, to add to the bitterness that already exists, but after listening to Taylor's speech,[15] which was a jackboot speech in the present crisis, I can only say this in reply: we are quite firm, we shall not be moved. My colleagues and I, Mr Speaker, will say good-bye.[16]

With those words Hume and his colleagues walked out of Stormont. In the meantime, sections of the British army relieved the over-stretched police force in Derry.

By now Hume's worse fears were being realized. In his efforts to make political action relevant to the situation in Derry, Hume persuaded UK Home Secretary James Callaghan to visit the city and briefed him on the need to accelerate reform. Following this visit, UK Prime Minister Harold Wilson and Callaghan met with Northern Ireland Prime Minister Terence O'Neill and his senior ministers. In a joint statement, the first of many Downing Street declarations, the two governments promised rapid progress on the reform programme. They highlighted: the reform of local government, the introduction of a universal suffrage for all elections, measures to ensure equality of employment opportunities, a fair means of allocating social housing and the establishment of the Ombudsman's office. A review of the RUC would be undertaken and the B-Specials would be stood down. In addition, a commission of inquiry into the disturbances would be set up. These commitments, along with the earlier abolition of Derry's corporation and its replacement by a temporary commission, meant that the key demands of the civil rights movement were being conceded. For a while it appeared that Northern Ireland might return to tranquillity. Regrettably, it was not to be.

Civil-rights demands vindicated

When the Cameron Commission[17] on the disturbances in Derry and elsewhere in the North reported in October, Hume was singled out for praise for his leadership and his efforts to prevent or end riots. He hoped that the inquiries and reviews underway, along with the whole reform package, would demonstrate the effective-

---

15 John Taylor, minister of state at the department of home affairs, declared that 11,000 B-Specials constables were to be mobilized to assist the police, a decision deeply resented by Catholics, who viewed the force with great suspicion. The B-Specials were an armed volunteer and part-time police auxiliary, and were exclusively Protestant. **16** Northern Ireland Parliament, *Debates*, 14 Aug. 1969. **17** This commission, chaired by Lord Cameron, investigated the events leading to the violence and civil disturbances in Northern Ireland since October 1968.

ness of the civil rights movement. The main challenge, therefore, was to ensure full implementation of that package. Increasingly, Hume's attention would now focus on constitutional reform and the crisis caused by escalating violence. His immediate plea was for greater understanding and respect between political leaders:

> [T]he government talks about allaying fears. We have heard from many members opposite what their fears of the civil rights movement are. We have heard what they have to say about the civil rights movement. Their attitude was best summed up yesterday when the right hon. member for Enniskillen [Mr West] said that when he saw the hon. member for Dock [Mr Fitt] and Mr McAteer, whom he described as republican leaders, leading the march on 5 October what could he expect the community to think the civil rights movement was? In that moment he summed up the narrow-mindedness that besets the community. He cannot see that a person can support a movement or an idea without involving his political views in it. If hon. members on this side of the house were to set up or give support to an organization for, say, the eradication of disease would hon. members opposite tell us it was being done to subvert the constitution?
>
> The civil rights movement has stated its aims clearly again and again. It has said that it stands for nothing more or less than full justice and equality for all within the constitution of Northern Ireland. That is a position which can be supported by anyone of any political viewpoint. People can support justice in our society; they can support any movement which asks for society to be placed on a firmly just basis without bringing their own political views into it. [...]
>
> For fifty years politics in the north of Ireland have been very easy. In order to be elected all one has had to do is to raise a flag or work up prejudice or suspicion. There has been no necessity to seek election on policies related to the social and economic nature of our community. When a movement tries to wipe out the underlying cancers which divide the people it is met with the same accusations and intransigence. I would point out, as I have done repeatedly in this house in the last six months, that intransigence breeds intransigence and extremism feeds upon extremism. That is exactly what has been happening in the north of Ireland during the past six months [...][18]

Ulster Defence Regiment

Hume's commitment to working peacefully and democratically for constitutional change would soon find expression in a very non-traditional way. When the review

18 Northern Ireland House of Commons, *Debates*, 1 Oct. 1969.

of the RUC reported and, among other reforms, recommended the replacement of the B-Specials with a new part-time army regiment (the Ulster Defence Regiment), Hume made what was for a leader from the nationalist community, a very brave statement. Along with some other nationalist leaders, he called on Catholics to enlist. He believed that joining would show a spirit of commitment to making Northern Ireland a better place for all, and would be an important step towards reconciliation:

> Many Catholics would not like to join the UDR because it is against their tradition, but Catholics must move to make it a neutral force and prevent it being taken over by the B-Specials. Catholics must get involved in all aspects of the North and do away with the prejudice, distrust and sectarian hatred that the Unionist Party needed to continue.[19]

It was an appeal that would soon be withdrawn, as inter-communal violence escalated.

Constitutional reform

At this stage Hume's proposals for constitutional reform were quite modest. He believed that granting full civil rights and equality would allow normal politics to develop, focusing on social and economic matters – in other words, on issues that directly concerned people on a daily basis. Hume, therefore, proposed that the question of Northern Ireland's constitutional position should be dealt with in periodic referenda. The *Derry Journal* reported him as saying that, traditionally, politics was conducted not on the basis of an individual's calibre, nor their policies for dealing with the real economic or social ills of society, but on whether they were for or against the constitution. He hoped that such a proposal would remove the constitutional issue from day-to-day politics:

> It now appears to be agreed on all sides that no change can take place in the existing constitutional position without the consent of the majority of the people in the North, and that any individual or group has the right to campaign for eventual change in the constitution.
>
> In the light of this it would seem to follow logically that the constitutional question should be taken out of politics by having a periodic referendum on it, so that elections could be real elections based on real politics. This would enable parties to contain people with different aspirations for the long-term future of Northern Ireland but who agreed on the basic task of solving the

19 *Irish Times*, 26 Mar. 1970.

present social and economic problems of the state. It should enable people of all shades of opinion to work without prejudice to their own genuinely felt aspirations for the long-term future of the community, to create a really just society in Northern Ireland of which all the people could be proud and in which ancient hatreds and religious divisions would be of the past [...] The civil rights movement in the past year has achieved a lot and the announcement of reforms, if implemented fully, would provide a basis for legislative justice in Northern Ireland. Vigilance was still required to ensure that the reforms, as they went through parliament, were not watered down in any way so that the standard of civil and human rights in their community was as high as it should be in any civilized society [...] However, there is a great danger for the whole community if we feel that legislative justice is all that this community requires to put it right. If the achievements of the civil rights movement are not followed by changes in attitudes then a great opportunity will have been lost and we will gradually slide back into the old divided community [...][20]

In proposals to the Crowther Commission, which was examining models of devolution within the UK as a whole at this time, Hume reflected these same views:

Northern Ireland has been a one-party state since its inception fifty years ago. This is due to the fact that the constitutional link with Britain has been a party political issue and has been the only issue in successive elections. Normal politics have been impossible and anyone holding the perfectly legitimate view that Ireland should be one political entity has been branded and treated as a disloyal citizen. Where one has a permanent minority with no share in power or in decision-making then one has a permanent situation of instability, which is likely to produce periodic outbreaks of unrest as people strive by extra-parliamentary means to find what has been impossible by parliamentary channels – a say in moulding the nature of the society in which they live.

Any review which takes place at the present time should take account of the failures and weaknesses of the existing constitution and should provide a framework, without prejudice to any future changes which may be thought desirable, which will at least ensure full civil and human rights for the Northern Ireland community as a whole. I put forward the following suggestions not as a complete answer to the problem, but as helping considerably towards a solution:

20 *Derry Journal,* 11 Nov. 1969.

(1) It should be stated in any constitution of Northern Ireland that any citizen or group has a constitutional right to advocate constitutional change by peaceful means.

(2) The re-introduction of proportional representation as the electoral system in both Stormont and local-government elections. This will ensure the full representation of minority opinion not only of traditional opposition opinion but also of those who believe in this link with Britain but who cannot accept the sectarian base of the Unionist Party. It will also remove the political advantage of housing segregation, which serves only to perpetuate and strengthen community division.

(3) The introduction of a periodic referendum on the question of Northern Ireland remaining an integral part of the United Kingdom. This would effectively remove the constitutional question from party politics and allow for the development of normal politics.

(4) The enshrinement in the constitution of a bill of rights to ensure full human and civil rights to all citizens irrespective of the government in power.[21]

Hume frequently reiterated his belief that nationalists should opt in, rather than opt out of public affairs in the North. In a speech at Trinity College Dublin (TCD) he began with a plea to those who sought reform to involve themselves in the affairs of Northern Ireland, arguing that it was the most effective means of ensuring that reform would be fully achieved:

Recent events must also produce radical changes in the attitudes of those opposed to the Northern state [...] For it goes without saying that those who have fought for civil rights must also be prepared to accept civil responsibility. Such acceptance will mean involvement in the affairs of the North that has not existed before among those opposed to its existence either because they were deliberately prevented or because, and it must be admitted, they did not choose to be involved. We can no longer opt out.

In short, we must accept the fact whether we like it or not that the Northern state now exists by the will of a majority of its people and that we must involve ourselves at every level of it in order to ensure a better and more prosperous North for all its people and in order to promote the long-term changes that we think desirable.[22]

---

21 Paper dated 3 Mar. 1970, Linen Hall Library, P1072 ND5118.   22 *Derry Journal*, 13 Mar. 1970.

Uniting Ireland

In Hume's opinion, arguing for that involvement did not mean losing sight of the goal of Irish unity. In an article that contains many of his key phrases and messages, he also highlighted to advocates of Irish unity, particularly in the South, the absence of any clear sense as to what unity might mean. He challenged them to replace slogans with a clear vision as to how unity could be achieved and what kind of united Ireland should be envisaged. He castigated those in public life who had only 'discovered' the North because of the civil rights movement, but at the same time he displayed an understanding as to why this had happened. More significantly, he outlined key elements of his own blueprint:

> Since the North hit the international headlines two years ago we have had a surfeit of speeches on the border from Southern politicians who had been silent on the question for years.
>
> They were probably not even aware that the people who lived in places like Belfast and Derry, and who laboured under the injustices of the Northern state regarded some of them as their own leaders – and expected great things from them.
>
> But the lip service to the ideal of a united Ireland did not extend as far as a visit to the North to see how things were in the sacrificed six [counties of Northern Ireland].
>
> All that has changed now, for the people of the North have learned during the past two years that the solution to their problems is largely in their own hands and that interest elsewhere, even in Dublin, is awakened only when they take matters into their own hands.
>
> One result has been the growth in Southern speeches on partition and, thankfully, there is at last emerging a much greater understanding of the problem. From this has come a skeleton of a real strategy for the peaceful solution to what has become known as the Irish question.
>
> I suppose it was inevitable after the bitterness of the happenings of the beginning of the century that the attitude to the North should be largely an emotional reaction, rather than a reasoned position [...]
>
> To look back over the fifty years since the creation of partition is a bit startling. Many leaders have come – and gone – protesting their belief in the ideal of a united country. Most had agreed that it should be brought about peacefully. Yet no party to my knowledge in all those years has produced a detailed blueprint for the peaceful reunification of Ireland.
>
> It seemed to be enough on an election platform to say that partition was an evil and that it must go. The flag would be raised and chests would swell with pride, the blood would get up and one's feelings of being involved in the patriotic game were reinforced.

Meanwhile the border between the people of Ireland grew stronger and its real victims, the homeless and jobless, continued to emigrate.

The failure to produce a policy for peaceful reunification was due in part, I believe, to the lack of moral courage to face up to the emotional unpopularity of some of its consequences. For what is Ireland and what is the border that divides it?

Ireland is not a piece of earth. Ireland is its people. Without its people it is but a jungle. People of varying traditions, outlook and background together form the entity known as Ireland and the unity of Ireland means community of its people.

By the same token the border is not a line on a map. It is a mental border between people, built on fear, prejudice and misunderstanding and strengthened by those who use sectarianism as a political weapon. Its peaceful eradication can only come through the development of understanding, friendship, and the smashing of sectarianism. This is the real task which faces those who genuinely want to solve the Irish problem [...]

Full civil rights in the North are an essential pre-requisite to the eventual and inevitable coming together of both parts of Ireland. Reform is therefore the first step in this direction. Reconciliation in the North – the second step – would then be much easier and, the third, reunification, would be but a matter of time, because the real border, that which divided the people of the North, would be gone [...]

The spilling of sweat together, rather than blood, in the joint effort to build the North and wipe out, as a priority, its serious social and economic ills of unemployment and emigration – problems which in themselves heighten the divisions – will do more for real unity than any amount of flag waving, any amount of emotional speeches.

The completeness of the divide and the size of the problem of reconciliation is seen by the fact that the actions and reactions of the early part of this century in the setting up of the Northern state have resulted in what are virtually two confessional states in Ireland, neither of which is worthy of the best in the Irish people.

What we must now be striving for in the whole of Ireland is a pluralist nation which will be much richer for the full and equal participation of all its traditions. No one group has the right to the ownership of the national conscience or to a surplus of Irishness [...]

In short, in creating the Ireland that we seek to create our aim must be not to overcome the Northern Protestant but to seek his help and co-operation.

We cannot do without him. How else can one create a country where Catholic, Protestant and Dissenter will work together as equals for the betterment of us all? Is there any other peaceful road?[23]

23 *Sunday Press*, 4 Oct. 1970.

By the time of the above article, Hume's election commitment to help establish a new political party had been realized, and a vehicle for the wider dissemination of his views now existed.

SDLP launched

Together with Ivan Cooper and Paddy O'Hanlon, other MPs with a civil rights background, Hume had formed a loose alliance at Stormont. They soon attracted more MPs with a civil rights commitment – Gerry Fitt, Paddy Devlin and Austin Currie – as well as Senator Paddy Wilson. All represented majority-nationalist constituencies. Working closely together as an opposition, their discussions had soon focused on establishing a new political party, the Social Democratic and Labour Party, which was launched in Belfast on 20 August 1970, with Gerry Fitt as leader and John Hume as his deputy. In accordance with his election commitments Hume declared that the party would be non-sectarian, that it would organize in all constituencies and that it would uphold the principle of consent on constitutional change. On being a non-sectarian party, Hume had said:

> I think the document which we have put before the public today, as the statement of principle of this party, speaks for itself – in terms of what this party stands for – and the actions of those present here, in following up this document, and in creating this party in the country when, as Mr Fitt says, we will go into all 52 constituencies [...] The party is committed to these policies and the fact that a man is of one religion or another does not necessarily make him sectarian. And this party is committed not just to being non-sectarian but to opposing sectarianism as one of its principal aims, because sectarianism is at the root of our problems.[24]

Hume and his colleagues hoped to attract cross-community support, as well as members from all traditions:

> From the very beginning the SDLP was happy to include Protestants. In fact of the three of us who fought the first election [1969] two were Catholics and one, Ivan Cooper, was Protestant. To this day, senior members of the SDLP are Protestant, as the important issue for our party is human rights, not religion, and our objective is a continuous respect for the rights and traditions of Catholics and Protestant alike. We are both non-sectarian and anti-sectarian.[25]

24 *Irish Times*, 20 Aug. 1970. **25** Hume, *Personal views*, p. 13.

Violence intensifies

Despite the reforms achieved through the civil rights movement, throughout the rest of 1970 and into the early months of 1971 the security situation in Northern Ireland worsened as paramilitaries from both communities became more active and more lethal. The PIRA, initially proclaiming itself a purely defensive organization, gradually launched an offensive campaign, targeting the security forces and Protestant-owned businesses in an effort to make Northern Ireland ungovernable, and so force the British government to declare its intention to withdraw from Northern Ireland. From the outset, Hume strongly condemned the PIRA's campaign, claiming it was counterproductive and that it would never achieve a united Ireland:

> Violence and men of violence and those who assisted them, either overtly or covertly, have done immense harm to the cause of those opposed to unionism in the North, for among other things they have made it easy for unionists to distract attention from the underlying causes of grievance and by attacking suppression and violence for them to give the impression to the world that all opposition to unionism is violent and suppressive.
>
> When is everyone going to learn that unionism needs bodies like the IRA for survival. It needs bogeymen. Why else when their backs are against the wall do they always draw attention to it. Why else has there been a manufactured IRA scare before practically every Northern election? [...]
>
> The best service indeed that the IRA could give the cause of Irish unity would be to disband, for Irish unity will never be achieved by violence. Violence and the threat of it only strengthen unionism, it only deepens and heightens the sectarian division within the north of Ireland, and it is those divisions which represent the real border in our country [...]
>
> There are, of course, those who will say that nothing was gained in the North except by violence. This is nonsense. The Central Citizens' Defence Committee[26] answered that in one important sentence: 'The struggle for civil rights was assured of success when violence was used against it.'
>
> It was because violence was used against us in the streets by both the police force of the state and by the cudgel-bearing supporters of unionism that we won widespread public sympathy and support. Contrary to what some people argued, it takes far more courage and discipline to remain non-violent and to refuse to retaliate when attacked than to throw stones, bottles, or bombs [...]

26 The Central Citizens' Defence Committee was a Belfast-based organization that co-ordinated several local community-defence groups operating mainly in Catholic areas of the city in the late 1960s and early 1970s.

Violence is today drawing attention away from essential reforms, for press and television no longer carry evidence of the social injustices that afflict Northern society. They carry instead reports of violent actions that are both sickening and senseless [...]

Let us try to understand what the struggle against partition is all about. It is not, as the struggle for independence was, a struggle against a foreign and occupying power. It is a struggle to bring together two sections of the Irish people, and how can anyone with the slightest grain of intelligence imagine that violence by one section against the other can unite them. Reform and reconciliation are the only way [...][27]

The PIRA chose to ignore his appeal.

Nonetheless, Hume continued to argue with increasing urgency the case for constitutional reform. In an address to party members in June 1971, he claimed that a return to the drawing board was needed to reshape the system of government in Northern Ireland. The address marked one of the first occasions on which he proposed the replacement of the form of government established under the 1920 Government of Ireland Act, with one representative of each section of the community – what would later be termed a power-sharing or partnership form of government. He urged the British government to create a new system in which sectarianism would be neutralized, and in which all sections of the Northern Ireland community could participate at every level saying he would:

like to see the British government declare the new system as a principle, and invite all interested groups to submit proposals. Only then can we begin to create a united and prospering community [...] The logic of the British intervention in 1969 has never been faced by Britain herself. The arrival of British troops to maintain law and order, the forcing of reform by the Westminster government on Stormont, and the continuing presence of British watchdogs, is the clearest possible public admission that unionist governments are and were incapable of governing Northern Ireland in peace, justice and stability. Their [Britain's] intervention when allied to the continuing presence of a unionist government [...] [has] created a situation of permanent instability in Northern Ireland, and we have had no less than three prime ministers in two years to prove it [...] The unionist government wants opposition MPs to accept responsibility for ending the violence. But one section [of this community] has been exercising responsibility without authority and I see no similar anxiety among unionist politicians to share authority, decision-making and power in the same way as they want us to share [...] responsibility. Herein lies

27 *Sunday Press*, 22 Nov. 1970.

the root of many of our problems [...] The unionist government fails to condemn violence committed by their own supporters. There was not a word of condemnation about the events in Belfast in August 1969, which were the most horrible that had taken place in such a sick society. To consider their silence in the face of the revelations of the Devenny case, the McCloskey case [...] and the evidence of the B-Specials at the Scarman Tribunal,[28] and of the former attorney general, Mr Peacocke, the Baillie Report about the police in the Bogside and the continuing provocation of the residents of Unity Flats [in Belfast], and no prosecutions to religious hatred, the restraint of the people in the face of all this was remarkable and was to be applauded. Northern Ireland is being asked to believe that the present unionist government will solve its problems. It is a government led by one of the chief architects of Northern Ireland's sick society, and until eighteen months ago one of the staunchest defenders of the injustice-ridden unionist system [Minister for Home Affairs Bill Craig].

With the best will in the world we are in an impossible position, for how can people be expected to believe that the man [Prime Minister Faulkner] and the party that created our problems and who rejected all reasonable and peaceful demands down the years are the man and the party to solve the problem.[29]

Political reform

Later that month, in another debate, Hume strongly criticized the failure to consider such reform and predicted that in its absence the North would continue its slide towards greater instability and inter-communal strife:

Let us admit it, there has been a great moral cowardice on the part of many people who have been elected. There has been a great deal of fence-sitting on fundamental issues on which there should be no sitting on any fence, issues as to whether this community continues along bigoted sectarian lines. That is fundamental: there can be no sitting on the fence on that choice. Similarly, changing this society whether it be done by outright violence or non-violence, is a fundamental choice on which there can be no sitting on the fence. Unfortunately, there are too many people who have sat on the fence and have refused clearly to denounce those who perpetrate violence on the streets, those who attempt to achieve political objectives by violent means, those who have no respect for human life and who seem to think that human lives are

---

28 Francis McCloskey died after being beaten by a baton-wielding police officer during a disturbance in Dungiven, Co. Derry. The Scarman Tribunal reported on violence and civil disturbances in Northern Ireland in 1969.   29 *Irish Times*, 1 June 1971.

expendable as a means of achieving political ends, those who have no compunction in playing politics with the lives of innocent people [...] There is no fence-sitting on this issue, people must get up and say where they stand. Because so many have sat on the fence there unfortunately exists today in the community a great deal of frustration and a great feeling that nothing has changed. When people are frustrated, violence and striking out presents the easy, quick road, but in the long run it is the wrong road. Where civil wars are going on in the world today I am quite certain that the people participating are the ordinary people who, if they had the choice, would regret the steps that led to civil war. We are in a situation today where violence can lead to that situation, and we must make it clear that we oppose it utterly.[30]

This criticism went unheeded and the North continued on the predicted slide. Within a week of that speech the SDLP withdrew from Stormont when the Northern Ireland government refused to order a public inquiry into the fatal shooting by British soldiers of two young men in Derry, who were alleged to have been carrying arms. Hume had justified the party's threat to withdraw by saying:

The importance of a refusal to agree to an inquiry should not be underestimated and will pose some questions which are of far-reaching political consequences. The first question has to do with the role of the British army in Northern Ireland. Has that role changed substantially? We have on record the statement of the Stormont prime minister on 25 May that the British army could shoot on suspicion, a statement later withdrawn because of the strength of our protest. Is shoot on suspicion now the reality?

A second and more important question relates to our role as elected representatives. If, in a situation as serious as we now find ourselves, a demand for an inquiry into events which have outraged our constituents, a demand we feel to be justified, is not granted then what is the justification for our role within the present system? We would point out that throughout the turbulent and difficult period through which our community has gone we have at all times done our utmost to give responsible leadership. We have urged continuing restraint, we have opposed any attempts by our supporters to protest on the streets and we have fought doggedly in parliament to have meaningful reform in order to create the conditions for justice and peace in our society [...]

Our demand for an inquiry is a decisive test of the sincerity and determination of the British government. If it is not granted, as publicly elected representatives, we will accept the logic of our position which is that there is no role that we can usefully play within the present system. If our demand is

30 Northern Ireland House of Commons, *Debates*, 23 June 1971.

not met by Thursday next – exactly a week after the deaths of the two young men – we will withdraw immediately from parliament and will take the necessary steps to set up an alternative assembly of elected representatives to deal with the problems of the people we represent and to become the author-itative voice to negotiate a political solution on their behalf, and we will call on all our parliamentary colleagues to join us.[31]

Once the SDLP had withdrawn from Stormont, it promptly set about making preparations for establishing an 'alternative assembly'.

Internment and the 'alternative assembly'

The situation dramatically worsened in August when the British and Northern Irish governments decided to introduce internment without trial in the hope of blunting the effectiveness of the paramilitaries. Hundreds of nationalists and members of republican movements were arrested and detained, and many were subjected to inhuman interrogation techniques. The widespread violence that followed brought the North to the brink of civil war and severely tested Hume and the SDLP's non-violent approach. In an interview with *Irish Times* journalist Henry Kelly, Hume justified the SDLP's action and spelled out what he believed was required in order to effectively address the crisis that was threatening even wider conflict throughout Northern Ireland:

The Northern Ireland problem is not a security problem, as the British government and Mr Faulkner are trying to show at the minute and I think that events since internment here show that it is not a security problem, that there's not just a small group of agitators in Northern Ireland, that there's a large section of people dissatisfied with the system [...]

We are really in a terrible situation as opposition leaders that our views are not accepted. We think that it's a political solution that is required [...]

Our decision to withdraw [from the Northern Ireland parliament] was an act of political judgment. Many people at the time questioned the wisdom of that judgment. We took it on the basis of the fact that we realized that Westminster policy was drifting and that in fact a decision on repression as the course of action had been taken, and therefore there had come a point when we simply stood against that. We had on many occasions put forward our views to Westminster, but clearly of the two open to them – repression or change of system – they had chosen the road of repression [...]

The system of government cannot continue. That is the reality. We want

31 *Derry Journal*, 13 June 1971.

peace in Northern Ireland, we want justice, we want stability. That can only
come about now by Westminster realizing the realities of the situation. If they
continue to try to bury people in the ground they simply cannot succeed [...]

A removal of the 1920 act as the basis for government here – and I think
we would find a commission running Northern Ireland for a limited period
– is a desirable thing while a permanent solution was worked out [...]

People keep talking about tripartite talks. We are completely opposed to
tripartite talks and the people who make these suggestions are not even
thinking about the problem. There should be either two groups at the talks,
either London and Dublin, or four groups, the unionists and ourselves,
because Brian Faulkner is not a sovereign prime minister, and he doesn't have
a sovereign government. Technically the prime minister of Northern Ireland
is Edward Heath who is prime minister of the UK. Mr Faulkner is the head
of a local administration [...] If Northern Ireland is to be involved in discussions then both sides in Northern Ireland must be involved. [...]

The threat of a Protestant backlash has long hung over Northern Ireland
since 1912 – in fact it created the state. It's that threat that has held Northern
Ireland in the grip of injustice and opposed civil rights and created the
Provisional IRA as a reaction to it. It has opposed every single reform with the
same threat. It has opposed two prime ministers and brought them down. It
is opposing a third now; and it is opposing the British government. And it is
a threat that moderate unionists use when tackling the British government.
They say, 'Unless you preserve us, look what you're going to get.' That threat
has to be faced down before there is any solution to our problem and we'll see
whether the orange card is an ace or a deuce and I believe it will be a deuce.[32]

In the wake of these developments, to publicize its opposition to internment
and its demand for fundamental reform of the government of Northern Ireland,
the SDLP embarked on a campaign of passive resistance. Its campaign consisted
of peaceful demonstrations, large-scale sit-downs, and the establishment of the
'alternative assembly'. The assembly met in the Co. Derry town of Dungiven on
26 October, and in words which were drafted by John Hume, it declared:

The assembly does not recognize the authority of the Stormont parliament.
As Edward Carson said [about unionist opposition to home rule], 'they did
not care two pence whether it was treason or not'. The Northern Ireland state
had been set up by infringing the rule of law which evolved after many years
of work to win agreement between the British and Irish people [...] The
Northern Ireland state and system of government was based on treason and

32 *Irish Times*, 20 Aug. 1971.

had within itself the seeds of its own destruction. Its very impermanence was being shown to the whole world today [...] Government without consensus has led to permanent instability and violence [...] The violent reaction to the failure of government has led to repressive measures such as mandatory sentences and internment [...] The assembly believes that physical violence is wrong. Society is divided – a situation which the present generation has inherited – and violence cannot heal it [...] The real road forward requires patience, which would lead to no bitterness, and it is the road of reconciliation. As W.B. Yeats said of the Protestant people, they are no petty people and they should not demean themselves any longer by being involved with a party based on repression and injustice, but should join the assembly and build a new system, rather than destroy Northern Ireland. We are offering Northern Ireland a new system of government before it is too late and the first step in that direction is to end the present government.[33]

In calling for support for the SDLP's campaign of non-violence Hume directed his arguments especially at young people who were being attracted to violence:

There is no point in throwing stones or petrol bombs or using guns in a confrontation with the British army. Let them use water cannon, gas, rubber bullets or even lead bullets. We shall not be moved. I challenge the youth – it demands far more courage to sit there and let them throw whatever they want to and not to retaliate. The men and women who sat down on Wednesday showed tremendous courage and that should be the basis of our campaign.[34]

To Protestants who might view such protests as directed at them he was careful to say in the course of addressing a large sit-down demonstration against internment:

We are sitting here in thousands and we are determined to end internment and repression and end the system it represents. We have no quarrel with people simply because they are Protestants, and we want to live with them in a situation that will provide peace, justice and stability. We will not raise our hands against them. If there is any suggestion of intimidation in any street against any Protestant it is our duty to protect our Protestant neighbours.[35]

Violence, Hume argued, was no answer to a situation, which was fundamentally one of human relationships and one, therefore, which required a political solution:

33 Ibid., 27 Oct. 1971.   34 Ibid., 22 Aug. 1971.   35 Ibid., 26 Aug. 1971.

If we face aggression with total passive resistance, even in the face of guns, which requires more courage than the use violence, we cannot fail, because the moral conviction of our case will sweep the world [...] there are two views about the Northern question, that it was a territorial division and that it was a human division. The only approach to any realistic solution was to heal the human division.[36]

However, despite Hume's and the SDLP's efforts to promote an exclusively non-violent strategy, and to ensure that the Dungiven assembly would be a workable alternative to Stormont, events on the streets dictated otherwise. The assembly was little more than a very temporary nationalist talking shop. Its value was soon overtaken by the calamity that effectively brought an end to the Northern Ireland parliament, and added momentum to the PIRA campaign – the killing of fourteen people by British soldiers on the streets of Derry on 31 January 1972, a day that has been known ever since as Bloody Sunday.

36 Ibid.

1972–6

Opposition to internment continued to dominate Northern Ireland's politics in the final months of 1971 and the early weeks of 1972. Public sit-downs, marches and demonstrations emphasized to the authorities the bitterness felt within the nationalist community and among its sympathizers at home and abroad. Since it was the Stormont government that had ordered internment, for nationalists the minimum demand was now the abolition of that regime. Protests brought the police and British troops onto the streets, sealing off community-interface areas and, in turn, becoming targets for protestors. On Sunday 24 January 1972, Hume was among civil rights leaders who led a large protest march along the beach at Magilligan, near Derry, to demonstrate outside a British army camp where internees were being held. A week later, at another large protest march in Derry, one in which he did not participate, but which took place near to his Bogside home, British soldiers opened fire and killed fourteen innocent civilians and injured many, many more. Hume likened the killings to the 1960 South African massacre at Sharpeville:

> The British army opened fire indiscriminately on the civilian population attending a peaceful protest in the Bogside today. Their action was nothing short of cold-blooded murder – another Sharpeville and another Bloody Sunday. Their action has left this city numb with shock, horror, revulsion and bitterness. At the time of issuing this statement 12 unarmed civilians have lost their lives,[1] and many more have been wounded. The situation is now grave and critical and I am in touch with political leaders in London and Dublin seeking to have the strongest possible action taken, including the withdrawal of uniformed soldiers from our streets.[2]

In a statement he co-authored with SDLP colleagues, Hume argued the urgency of ending internment and of working for 'a lasting solution', which, notably, they stated would be sought within a thirty-two-county, i.e. all-Ireland context. In essence this meant the involvement of the Irish government in negotiations aimed at achieving that solution, his quadripartite approach. There was now

---

1 Two more would die later.   2 *Irish Times*, 1 Feb. 1972

no prospect that Hume and his SDLP colleagues would return to Stormont. The days of the unionist government were numbered.

> The brutal murder of innocent civilians on the streets of Derry on Sunday has horrified world opinion. Fifteen thousand people demonstrated on Sunday against the repressive policies of Heath and Faulkner and the system of government that has bred them. Stormont has been rejected for many months. There is now no chance of it being accepted. Our first duty is to express our sympathy to the bereaved relatives on the sudden tragedy that has been visited upon them. We have asked the taoiseach to formally declare the occasion of the funerals of these innocent victims to be a day of national mourning, and we appeal to Irish people everywhere to demonstrate through it their sympathy and feelings at the present time. In the immediate situation we call on all those people from cabinet ministers, judges and lawyers downwards – all those who are giving any public service whatsoever to the unionist regime – to withdraw their services immediately and to refuse to participate any further. We regard further participation as condoning the actions that have been taken in the name of Stormont. Urgent political action is necessary to immediately de-escalate the present grave and critical situation if the whole country is not to be plunged into further bloodshed. Such political action should include the removal of internment and the Stormont system that bred it. It should also include the withdrawal of British troops from our streets. We will then engage in talks about a new and more lasting solution and we advise the public that we will be seeking such lasting solution in a 32-county context.[3]

Hume and the SDLP continued their policy of non-co-operation with the authorities by refusing to provide any evidence to the tribunal established to investigate the Bloody Sunday killings, the Widgery Tribunal:

> We will seek an international inquiry. Lord Justice Brigadier Widgery is a man of high integrity, but it is amazing that one who was a lieutenant-colonel in the Royal Artillery and a former brigadier in the Territorial Army should have been selected. No judge who has had long associations with the army should have been given the task of investigating army behaviour, particularly in view of the serious nature of the incident.[4]

3 *Derry Journal*, 2 Feb. 1972.   4 Ibid.

Stormont suspended

Several weeks were to elapse before the British government finally suspended the Northern Ireland parliament, and replaced its government with a secretary of state, William Whitelaw, and a small team of UK ministers. During this period Hume visited the US to brief Irish-American groups on the situation. There, while condemning all violence, he highlighted British army tactics, internment, Bloody Sunday and the use of rubber bullets by the security forces. At a meeting under the auspices of the organization Americans for Ulster Justice, Hume reiterated his call for the disbanding of the Northern Ireland parliament and government, and for negotiations between all parties and the British government. He dismissed the perception that the problem in Northern Ireland was religious saying:

> we respect any religious view and have no wish to dominate any religion […]
> [but] violence is only a symptom of the real problem and the British army's
> attempts to solve the problem by using force only worsens the situation […][5]

Hume returned home just as the suspension of Stormont was being introduced and appealed for an end to violence, especially PIRA violence, to allow political discussions to take place in a peaceful atmosphere. In this appeal Hume couched the causes of the conflict in terms of religious bigotry, and in his belief that the Protestant people of the North had been seriously misled by their politicians. There was, therefore, repeating a point stressed earlier, an obligation on Catholics to assure their Protestant neighbours of their security. He further argued that once bigotry and sectarian attitudes had been eliminated and new, more positive relationships established between Protestants and Catholics, political agreement would inevitably and easily follow. As events would show this was a serious under-estimation of the animosities that lay in the way of agreement:

> Those engaged in the campaign of violence should immediately cease that
> campaign. The British military should cease political arrests and offensive
> actions against the sections of the community they have been antagonistic
> towards.
>
> The people of the Catholic areas of the North are very happy with the
> moves that have been made. We believe that the remainder of the things that
> have to be achieved can, in fact, be achieved by peaceful means and by discus-
> sion because the major obstacle – Stormont itself – is out of the way.
>
> The continuation of a military campaign by the IRA would be a disaster
> because it would be sentencing a lot of people to death, and this would be
> particularly crazy because it would be totally unnecessary now in a situation

5 *Hartford Courant*, 20 Mar. 1972.

where the British government is clearly moving in the other direction and therefore it would be the height of irresponsibility not to accept that and not to attempt to make further progress along the road by negotiations and peaceful means [...] If the IRA continues with their campaign they will be rejected by the people.

In this country we are going to have active co-operation between Protestants and Catholics in order to end this sectarian divide. Those people who have been so misled in the past by political leaders, many of them must feel very isolated and frustrated, and we must recognize that it is our task to assure those people. The worst possible step would be to continue violence because this would play into the hands of extreme unionists like Mr Craig who are arguing that 'these people can never be satisfied and we are in danger and in peril'. I believe a continuation of bombing would be a disaster for the whole community.

The people in the Catholic areas must now stand up and be counted on this issue. Do you, or do you not believe that we have had a major step forward [...] I have no doubt that the people will opt for a complete end to violence and advocate negotiations for a final settlement to the remaining problems.

Those engaged in the campaign of violence should remember that in order to make any society work it needs the consent of a substantial minority [...] That consent we will have to win in the coming months. We will not win it with bombs and bullets.[6]

Arguing that the new situation presented unprecedented opportunities for political progress, Hume continued to press for an end to the paramilitary campaigns, and accused the paramilitaries, especially the PIRA, and unionist politicians of almost willingly conspiring together against the initiatives being planned by Whitelaw to reach new political arrangements:

Mr Faulkner and his colleagues are at it again. They are once again calling for military action against the Bogside and Creggan. They still seek a military solution. They have a cheek for it is precisely those policies pursued by them that have had a major part to play in the disastrous situation to which this community has been reduced.

The truth is the Unionist Party wants to see the Whitelaw mission fail, and therefore has a vested interest in seeing a further escalation of violence so that they can say 'We told you so' and recover their lost power. This is a lesson that needs to be clearly understood by everyone living in the Bogside and Creggan

6 *Irish Times*, 27 Mar. 1972.

areas and we must do all in our power to ensure no such escalation takes place.

We have insisted all along that there is no exclusive solution to our problem. What we have failed to grasp is that it applies to both sides.

While hostilities continue on both sides terrible deeds will be done on both sides and innocent people will suffer on both sides. Each side will react in anger to the actions against them, and it will go on and on until there is total war.

No one wins wars. People lose them.

The first step towards sanity in the present situation is a cessation of hostilities. I believe that the many serious problems that face us can now be resolved peacefully. I believe that internment can be rapidly ended. I believe that the British army can be brought to withdraw from sensitive areas, that political arrests, searches and their attendant evils can be stopped and that an amnesty for political prisoners can be negotiated.

To do so requires a period of peace and calm so that we can grasp these opportunities.

No one believes that the [UK Prime Minister] Heath initiatives are a final solution to our problems. No one has suggested it, but what is believed is that they present an opportunity that must be grasped so that we can end once and for all the sufferings that have scarred the face of this country down the years.

It is the duty of all who claim to serve the people at this stage to listen to the voice of the people and I am certain that the voice of the vast majority in this area at the present time speaks loudly for a cessation of hostilities in order to test the goodwill of Mr Whitelaw.

There are very few certainties in the present situation, but two things are clear. One is that there is nothing to be lost by a voluntary cessation of hostilities. The other is that a continuation of hostilities will lead to further suffering and death on all sides, with no certainty as to the result.

There is a clear and crucial choice facing us, and all who hold positions of leadership at every level of this community should make their choice now and state their position clearly.[7]

Towards a new agreement

The months that followed witnessed rapid movement towards creating the conditions Whitelaw believed would make political negotiations possible. Among the measures taken were attempts, in vain as it transpired, to achieve ceasefires by the

7 *Derry Journal*, 25 Apr. 1972.

paramilitaries, notably the PIRA.[8] There then followed military action to end paramilitary controlled 'no-go' areas in Belfast and Derry, and the first steps in a new political dialogue with the constitutional parties.

While in agreement with the efforts to end paramilitary violence and to regain control of 'no-go' areas, Hume was apprehensive about the effects of the large-scale military action necessary to regain control, coming as it did six months after Bloody Sunday. On the political front, he continued advocating a comprehensive quadripartite approach, and he vigorously defended the position taken by the SDLP, while giving some indications of the elements that could form part of a new agreement. In an *Irish Times* interview:

> Mr Hume spoke in terms of quadripartite talks at which the future of Northern Ireland and of the 'no-go' areas would be discussed. He was sure that the Southern government was preparing for such negotiations and the SDLP would meet the Dublin government in the very near future [...] Mr Hume said that in continuing their campaign of violence the IRA was playing into the hands of right-wing forces who, throughout the truce period, had kept up pressure in order to have the truce broken.[9] These people had not wanted a truce; they had wanted a confrontation between the Catholic population and the British army.
>
> Asked what he saw as possible political developments in the North, he said that the SDLP had insisted on quadripartite talks. They had refused Mr Whitelaw's offer of talks because the terms had been too limited. The party was now engaged in a round of talks with different groups in order to ensure that the final talks would be quadripartite talks. It was essential for the Republic to be involved, if the solution was to be in any way lasting.
>
> He didn't see any solution within the six-county context because the basis of the state was such that no permanent stable structure could be built upon it because sectarianism had been institutionalized by the findings of the boundary commission.[10] The cold logic of the situation was that when Stormont fell, the Government of Ireland Act 1920 also fell. The Government of Ireland Act had been an Irish settlement and anybody who did not see that the new settlement must be in an Irish context was being extremely foolish.
>
> He felt that Dublin must be included in talks. The only objection to that came from unionists, who were objecting on very weak grounds, as Mr

---

8 A PIRA delegation was flown to London for discussions with representatives of the British government in July 1972. The discussions ended when the PIRA continued to demand a British declaration to completely withdraw from Northern Ireland as the only condition for declaring a ceasefire. **9** An uneasy truce between the PIRA and the British army, brokered by John Hume and Paddy Devlin, lasted a few weeks at the end of June and early July 1972. **10** The boundary commission established under the 1921 Anglo-Irish Treaty to determine the actual border between North and South.

Faulkner when he had been prime minister had engaged in tripartite talks with Mr Lynch and Mr Heath. One of Mr Faulkner's proposals was a council of Ireland and if that was part of his solution then it could only be brought about through consultation with Dublin.

Asked for his views about the introduction of a condominium structure of government in Ireland, Mr Hume said that the SDLP had a policy committee which was working to prepare a document for negotiation and had been producing ideas on various topics […] He hoped that the additional troops that had been drafted into Northern Ireland were not going to be used as an invasion force to control the 'no-go' areas of Belfast and Derry, although Mr Whitelaw's statement had made it clear that some action was going to be taken. He continued, 'Let me say this. If such action is taken and there is widespread suffering and even death among the people of the Bogside or Creggan […] I would blame the British army and the British government for taking the action that they did, but I would also blame the Provisional IRA because when people embark on military means of solving problems then they accept the consequences of their policies.

'We have said that war and violence is not the way to solve these problems, we have charted the path which would have lost no human life […] brought no shame on the Irish people […] we stood out for months for the suspension of Stormont, for its replacement by a commission and for quadripartite talks. We first won support from the British Labour Party, then the Heath government itself […] At that stage an end to violence would have meant the total discrediting of the unionist forces; it would have meant the elected representatives of the anti-unionist forces would have been in a very powerful and strong position in which to negotiate a very strong settlement […] that was frustrated by the continuation of the campaign of violence of the IRA.'

Mr Hume went on to say that when the truce had been brought about eventually, it was clear that a path was ripe for a quick end to internment and civil disobedience and that discussions could begin on the problems of the 'no-go' areas as part of a political settlement. All that could have been done peacefully, but the UDA[11] and Faulkner seriously interfered in putting on pressure to have the truce broken during that period and the IRA simply fell into their trap. The Provisional IRA tried to solve these problems militarily and that involved essentially the loss of life and they would have to accept the consequences of that, if by their actions, they forced the British government and army to take action against them in the 'no-go' areas.

He thought it was 'a very definite possibility' that an invasion of the 'no-go' areas by the army would throw the people of those areas into the arms of

11 The Ulster Defence Association was the leading loyalist paramilitary organization at this time.

the Provisionals. Part of the Provisionals' tactics in bombing the centre of Belfast and Derry was to do two things […] to try to provoke a backlash from the unionist side and to try to provoke strong British army action against the 'no-go' areas. 'If these things happen we all know that the emotions of the Catholic population will rise very strongly again. We all know that emotional sympathy will rise in the South, all swinging once again behind the Provisional IRA. If this was the correct interpretation it was a despicable one, because it was using the lives of the people in these areas in order to gain support.'

He agreed that there had been criticism of the SDLP for their decision to take part in talks while internment continued, but he said that this had only come from 'fringe' groups.

The SDLP would be judged on the results of their actions. They had been accused of a 'sell-out' on previous occasions, but they had stood out for the suspension of Stormont, the imposition of a commission and for quadripartite talks. They had been invited to secret talks but had refused. They had been sounded out on their attitude towards a community-type government; to a reformed Stormont itself with a deputy prime minister from the opposition and some cabinet posts as suggested by 'a senior member of the British Conservative Party' but they had held out for the abolition of Stormont, Mr Hume said.[12]

The British army's Operation Motorman, popularly known as the 'invasion' of the Bogside and of other 'no-go' areas that paramilitaries controlled, took place almost as Hume spoke these words. Government control of the areas was quickly and relatively peacefully re-established. Soon afterwards Whitelaw convened an inter-party conference at Darlington in England, but because of internment the SDLP refused to attend. Instead the party published its own proposals in a document entitled 'Towards a new Ireland', the main thrust of which was the claim that a united Ireland would provide the optimal context for peace and harmony on the island. However, since the party accepted that unity could not be achieved in the immediate future, it proposed that Northern Ireland become the joint responsibility of the British and Irish governments and that a cross-community, power-sharing assembly and executive be responsible for devolved matters. Hume outlined the party's approach in a speech in Enniskillen in which he again called for an agreement to be sought in a wider context than that of Northern Ireland itself, and for the unionists to join in creating a new vision for the North, a vision to be ultimately realized in a united Ireland:

12 *Irish Times*, 31 July 1972.

Mr Hume called on the Northern majority, in face of British and international opinion, to reject their past defensiveness and to join with their fellow countrymen to mould the sort of Ireland they wished to see.

'A new vision was needed. It is either that or a return to the instability with the periodic violence, death and destruction which has marred the face of this country in the past and shamed us before the whole world.

'In the weeks leading up to the Darlington conference the whole community has been subjected to a barrage of propaganda from the three unionist parties that attended in what amounted to downright hypocrisy. The projected image of themselves was that they were the only reasonable politicians in Northern Ireland. Yet the very proposals that they were putting forward contained the implicit admission that they did not provide a permanent solution and that they foresaw future political violence.

'The vast majority of people in this community desperately want peace, some are, understandably, so desperate that they would settle for anything without giving any serious thought to future consequences. The aim of truly responsible politicians in the present crisis must be to ensure that the settlement that is arrived at will be a lasting one and that no future generation will have to endure the terrible suffering that the present one has gone through.

'No serious thought [to a settlement] has been given by any of those unionist parties – Unionist, Alliance or Northern Ireland Labour – or if they have, they have not had the courage to face the logic of the Northern Ireland situation, a logic that was all too clear at Darlington.'

Mr Hume said that from much of the discussion at Darlington that it was accepted that normal parliamentary democracy did not work in Northern Ireland, hence the search for new institutional devices. No one asked why, which is surely the most important question of all, the answer to which will lead to a real solution. 'Northern Ireland as a political unit is inherently unstable and it is impossible to find within it a basis for stability which will give a lasting peace that should be the aim of everyone.'

'The solution must be found in a wider context. To say so is not, as our critics have suggested, to dragoon people into a united Ireland against their will. It is to face the cold logic of the situation and to invite all to co-operate in the search for real peace [...]

'Does any serious person in the North, particularly among the oft-quoted majority, seriously think that we can find a permanent solution based on such insecurity. Does anyone seriously want to return to the situation where pledges on the constitutional position are being sought from successive British governments and where elections continue to be fought on this basis?

'I believe no one with intelligence in Northern Ireland wants such a situation and I believe it is time that we all in Northern Ireland, majority and the minority alike, asserted our pride in ourselves and relied on ourselves, rather than on the insecure pledges of a British parliament […]

'Do the majority in Northern Ireland really want a return to the defensive mentality which has characterized their politics to date and which has stultified their positive and powerful qualities, leaving them dependent on a parliament that is not dependable on this issue?'

Mr Hume said that the SDLP's proposals were the only ones as yet put forward by any Northern party that faced up to the real issues. 'We reject the "acceptable to the majority" test to which some prominent Southern voices give so much importance.[13] They do no service to us, for it is a yardstick that has not served the North in the past. Our yardstick will be one that will be just and fair to majority and minority alike and will provide a basis for peace to the whole island.'

'In the short term the SDLP proposals face up to the present realities of life in the North, and give fair and equal expression to the present loyalties of both communities. In the long term our proposals through a national senate with equal representation from North and South do not impose anything on anybody, but invite all, particularly the Northern majority, to reject the defensiveness of the past and to pre-empt the pre-planned and imposed solution and to step forward with their fellow countrymen and mould the sort of Ireland that they want to see.

'As we enter a new Europe in three months time[14] we need a new vision that will end the old quarrels. It is either that or a return to the old instability with the periodic violence, death and destruction which has scarred the face of this country in the past and shamed us before the world.

The SDLP has no apology to make for raising these issues at the present time. They are the real issues facing this community and they require widespread public debate throughout the community before meaningful talks take place. I am confident that anyone who gives our document a serious reading, irrespective of his party, will despite the instant rejection of it by some political figures find it to be pointing a realistic path out of the present sorry mess and one that will coerce no one.[15]

New agreement

British government's recommendations were published in a discussion paper in late October 1972. They enshrined key SDLP requirements, notably that future

---

13 Hume had in mind commentators and politicians like Conor Cruise O'Brien.   14 Ireland formally joined the European Economic Community (EEC) on 1 Jan. 1973.   15 *Irish Times*, 3 Oct. 1972

governments in the North should be cross-community and that new arrangements would have to 'recognize Northern Ireland's position within Ireland as a whole'.[16]

However, with loyalist and PIRA violence continuing at a very high level Hume was deeply concerned that conditions for agreement might not exist. Bearing in mind traditional nationalist antipathy towards the security services and knowing that any agreement would require a change in that attitude, he was particularly concerned about the increasing number of brutal sectarian killings by loyalist paramilitaries and claimed that security authorities were failing to deal with the problem. The party was also very concerned that the referendum proposed by the British government on whether Northern Ireland should remain part of the UK or be united with the Republic, the so-called 'border poll', could be the occasion for an intensification of violence. In meetings with Secretary of State Whitelaw and his security authorities, Hume and his SDLP colleagues strongly expressed these concerns:

> Mr John Hume said last night that during a meeting between the SDLP members of parliament and the British secretary of state, Mr Whitelaw, the SDLP pressed for the removal of internment and pointed out to Mr Whitelaw that it was well known that people connected with the UDA, and UVF who had been engaged in violence were operating in several areas.
>
> Mr Hume said that the SDLP were not insisting that such people be interned but that the normal process of the law should operate against them.
>
> 'I consider it all the more astonishing in the circumstances that Mr Whitelaw continues to employ the internment policy [...] Of course we are not happy with the terms of reference of the Diplock Commission, which is primarily concerned with finding an alternative to internment [...] the SDLP left Mr Whitelaw in no doubt about their opposition to the holding of a referendum in present circumstances. They pointed out the risks to human life that could be involved.
>
> 'We informed him that even in peaceful times protection was required for election agents in many areas. We also objected to the form of question to be put in the referendum. Regarding the SDLP attitudes to participating in the referendum, that will depend on two things – what happens in the British parliament to efforts to get the question form changed, and what attitudes the Irish government adopts.
>
> 'If the Irish government opts for holding a referendum on the same day as the six-county one then the SDLP will go all out to ensure as large a Catholic vote in the North as possible. But if the government in Dublin stands aloof,

16 'The future of Northern Ireland', Belfast, HMSO, 1972.

then the SDLP will have to decide whether to counsel the Catholic voters to participate or to boycott the referendum.'[17]

The SDLP persistently sought assurances from Whitelaw that the security forces would act with impartiality:

> 'We have received consistent assurances from Mr Whitelaw and his security chiefs that the role of the security forces in Northern Ireland is to keep the peace and to act with absolute objectivity against violence from any source. Many of us have questioned whether this is so and have often been regarded as unreasonable for doing so.'
>
> Mr Hume said that the whole range of government action had been against areas where the IRA operates, often causing intense suffering and death to innocent inhabitants of those areas – coercion laws including internment and its attendant evils of brutality and torture, mandatory sentences for riotous behaviour, strong military action, including widespread house searches, shooting of innocent civilians that have brought no redress and Operation Motorman followed by heavy military presence in Catholic areas.
>
> 'It is surely now fair to ask whether similar action has been taken against other sources of violence, particularly those which have emerged since direct rule, or against the organizations from which they spring.'
>
> Mr Hume said it was particularly relevant to ask that question in view of the fact that since Operation Motorman the major source of violence in Northern Ireland had been the sickening sectarian murders that had been taking place nightly and were largely the responsibility of extreme unionist forces. With the best will in the world we can only conclude that there has been a scandalous failure to face up to this problem.[18]

Such criticism of the security forces and of alleged government inaction to deal with loyalist violence would feature very frequently throughout the Troubles.

Unhelpful Southern slogans

From early 1973 the expectation grew that the British government would soon announce terms and conditions for new inter-party talks. In that context, the need for fresh thinking about the North on the part of people in the South continued to be an issue for Hume, particularly in view of the SDLP's emphasis on the need for an all-Ireland dimension to any new agreement. PIRA violence and support for it in the South was a serious challenge. Hume argued that support for the PIRA

17 *Derry Journal,* 3 Nov. 1972.   18 *Irish Times,* 29 Dec. 1972.

was due to traditional attitudes about achieving unity, and to the dangerous messages contained in what he termed 'our mythologies', and called for a national rethink, as this extract from an address to the Wexford Chamber of Commerce highlights:

> For too long we have known what parties are against, we want to know what they are for. It is only when we place before our Protestant countrymen what we really mean, and what we really want, can a basis for a solution be found. Simple condemnation of violence is not enough. It is not enough to simply condemn young people for planting bombs. They do what they have been taught to do. We glorify violence in songs, even in our national anthem. We must get rid of the myth that violence promotes good change in Ireland [...] To keep our people off the immigrant boat is true patriotism – not singing songs of violence.
>
> The real need is to get rid of our mythologies and realize that people are what count. There is real patriotism in building up our country. That is where the real bridge lies between ourselves and our Protestant fellow countrymen.
>
> In this election in the Republic I hope we will not have the old slogans. It means life and death to us in the six counties that these should disappear. Plans and visions of the new Ireland should be placed before the people in this election.[19]
>
> More people had been killed over the past few years in the six counties than in the [Irish] civil war in 1922 [...] the real problems had not been faced and would not until there was a British statesman prepared to stand up to those who wanted to keep the privileged majority in ascendancy. The six-counties strike was blackmail, calculated to force political decisions.[20] On another day [UK Prime Minister] Gladstone said he would not bow to the threat from a privileged group in the north-east but unfortunately Gladstone had been replaced and that threat from the privileged group seemed to be the consistent thing in Irish history which menaced the whole country. There will be no solution until a British statesman stands up to that threat. Waiting and refusing to face up to it has meant nothing more than a running sore of strife and bloodshed.[21]

Later that year, in an address to the Merriman Summer School, Hume again addressed this theme and the responsibilities of Irish governments in promoting new relationships between unionists and nationalists. He strongly advocated Irish

---

19 A general election was soon to take place in the South. It resulted in the first change of government in sixteen years when Fianna Fáil was replaced by a Fine Gael-led coalition.   **20** Reference to a loyalist led strike demanding tougher measures against the PIRA.   **21** *Irish Times*, 8 Feb. 1973.

unity as the optimum solution, and hoped unionists would fully engage in negotiating a new way forward:

> The only people in Ireland who could resolve the issues between Ireland and Britain, with recurring violence and death, were the Northern unionists [...] They should hold their heads high and ask Britain to stand aside while they negotiated a lasting settlement to the problems of Ireland with the rest of the people of Ireland [...]
>
> There were two central themes in Anglo-Irish relations, the internal relations between Catholic and Protestant in Ireland and Anglo-Irish relationships. This was so in 1921 and it was also so today. Partition was a settlement that nobody wanted and it had not worked. The unionists had been given a dominant position and they had maintained it solidly. Their attitude was 'what we have we hold' and 'no surrender'. This siege mentality was based on a deep-seated insecurity and was maintained under the premierships of Craigavon and Brookeborough. It meant total political, social and economic discrimination against Catholics.
>
> The nationalists on the other hand did not believe the state would last. This led to their abstentionism and permanent opposition because they had no hope of achieving change. They became the representatives of the underprivileged in the North. Placed in such a hopeless situation they became inevitably extremely negative in their attitude.
>
> People often ask why there was no development of the labour movement in the North. This could be traced to the fact that the North was founded on a sectarian headcount. This was why it was obvious that Northern Ireland's problem could never be solved in the context of the six-county area. This was a fact that Britain consistently refused to face.
>
> In the South during the period of the long premiership of Mr de Valera and before, very little attention had been paid to the North. No Irish political party had put forward a programme for Irish unity, for instance. There had admittedly been considerable achievements in the Republic. De Valera had taken [Michael] Collins seriously in his statement that the Treaty meant freedom to achieve freedom. He had proceeded to dismantle the [1921] Treaty step by step and he had used the strength of his position to establish the sovereignty of the country.
>
> The explanation of the apathy in the South towards the North could be traced to the tensions which followed the civil war and the fact that the South was engaged in the task of building its own institutions. What was incontrovertible, however, was that the North and South grew apart. Mr de Valera himself had admitted that he had little knowledge of Northern Ireland. This in itself became an encouragement to the unionists to increase their dominance.

A situation then existed in which 23 per cent of the Irish people or 2 per cent of the population of the United Kingdom were dictating relations between Ireland and Britain at a very great price. A great deal of the history of the last 300 years has been related to the whittling away of the power of the Protestant ascendancy. The unionists must realize that their real security could only lie in the community of Ireland.

The present government should not underestimate the strength of its independent sovereign position in the crucial months ahead, nor should it surrender any part of that position to the false liberalism of placating the Northern unionists [...] that same attitude of placation had governed British attitudes towards Ireland for the past three centuries with very tragic results. This was not time for any Irish government to allow its policies to be governed by the same attitudes. Only when the question of the sovereignty of the island of Ireland had been settled could there be any real or meaningful generosity on all sides. The unionists had the key to achieving that situation by asking Britain to stand aside while they agree with their fellow countrymen on the conditions for a new Ireland, independent and sovereign.[22]

It was an invitation that the British government would not accept, even if it was to include Hume's key proposals on governing Northern Ireland, and on its relationship with the South.

Whitelaw's proposals

The opportunity for unionists and nationalists to agree new arrangements was presented when, at the end of March 1973, following consultations with the parties on its earlier recommendations, Secretary of State Whitelaw published the British government's firm proposals.[23] These included an assembly elected on a proportional basis, a cross-community government, and, while firmly cast in the constitutional context of the UK, a formal Irish dimension in the shape of a Council of Ireland. These were broadly in line with Hume's own recommendations, and he warmly and optimistically welcomed the opportunity for comprehensive discussions:

Mr Hume [...] said that the proposed assembly for the first few months and possibly to 30 March 1974 would be a consultative assembly – in other words a conference table. 'As a party we believe that the best solution is one negotiated by the people of Northern Ireland themselves through their representatives and we will of course go to the conference table [...] There is

22 Ibid., 27 Aug. 1973.   23 'Northern Ireland constitutional proposals', Belfast, HMSO, 1973.

no doubt that the best solution is one we agree among ourselves. What encourages me is the spirit of self-determination that is in growing evidence in the last six months.'

Mr Hume urged the cultivation of common ground. 'The conflict is about basic loyalties and if we can resolve that we can find a real opportunity for peace and harmony in Ireland through this conference table and through our existing dialogue with people in the loyalist camp.'[24]

The weeks that followed saw Hume and his party colleagues campaigning for seats in the new assembly that Whitelaw's proposals had promised, elections to which were held in June. Hume topped the poll in the Derry constituency and the SDLP won a total of eighteen seats and was the only party from the nationalist community to win any seats. In the autumn, parties that had accepted the principle of power-sharing – the UUP, SDLP and Alliance – commenced negotiations aimed at agreeing a cross-community executive. In late November, a tentative agreement was reached on the composition of a power-sharing executive. Final agreement would await the outcome of negotiations on the Council of Ireland. Hume welcomed the power-sharing agreement, saying that it:

> involved a partnership rather than power-sharing. For the first time ever in Ireland Protestant, Catholic and Dissenter [...] will be working together to build a new society. All kinds of interpretations will be put by vested interests on what we have agreed and victories will be claimed by many sides. The real victors, if we are to reach agreement [on the Council of Ireland], will be the people of Northern Ireland and, in particular, future generations.[25]

The SDLP would control the ministries of commerce, housing and local government, health and social services while also providing the deputy first minister. The SDLP would also nominate two junior ministers. A few weeks later at the SDLP's annual conference, Hume summed up the challenges and prospects of the agreement, in particular the role of a Council of Ireland, which would be determined at negotiations involving the Irish government:

> The SDLP is committed to implementing a four-year social and economic plan. It is committed to the achieving of full employment and parity of income.
>
> Another part of the plan is devoted to the development of social culture. This is necessary in order to foster better understanding between the communities in the North. The plan is a radical new approach towards resolving the social and economic problems of the North.

24 *Irish Times*, 23 Mar. 1973. 25 Ibid., 23 Nov. 1973.

On power-sharing, we have agreed a representation of seven unionists, six SDLP and two Alliance members. On the voting executive this will be six unionists, four SDLP and one Alliance. The ministries in the control of the SDLP will be those ministries most effective in areas of social and economic change.

On the issue of policing it is a crucial reality that we cannot have a stable society without adequate policing. We are being utterly responsible in insisting that the policing system reflects the community and has the support of the country, otherwise it would bring the executive down round its ears.

On this issue we have got a commitment to setting up a complaints procedure, to local liaison meetings between the police and local councillors but there remains the problem of identification – the need to identify with the new police force.

The forthcoming talks will include the question of the role of the Council of Ireland in law and order. It is at this level that we achieve identification. If we are to accept full responsibility the reason we insist on an acceptable police force is to assure the people of Northern Ireland that the law will be enforced. An acceptable system of law and order is crucial to lasting peace.

All these things will be put on the agenda at this week's talks.

We have come a long way along the road to the creation of a strong Council of Ireland. We have also proposed that the Council of Ireland have a court of human right to implement the European Convention on Human Rights.

We understand that we are asking a lot of the Protestant people of the North. We must applaud the generosity of those who have agreed a consensus. The history of Anglo-Irish relations shows that the problem can only be solved when we have stilled the fears of the Protestant community.[26]

Internment

The SDLP had entered negotiations despite having pledged not to do so while internment lasted. Now the party had to hope that internment would soon be phased out and, as Hume did at the party's conference, had to defend itself by pointing to the gradual reduction in the number of internees and other achievements to which the SDLP had contributed:

I have come to the rostrum to defend the record of the party in opposing internment. Those who formed the SDLP have taken the strongest ever stand against internment and have made it a big issue. They have maintained a

26 Address to 1973 annual conference, copy in editor's possession.

position that many have said was driving them into the wilderness for many months. They have asked for the suspension of Stormont, the setting up of a commission to rule the country, the ending of internment and quadripartite talks. Stormont has been suspended and the commission has been set up and now we have the quadripartite talks and we have a promise of the phasing out of internment. The facts are that in March 1972 there were 545 people behind the wire. The party has consistently and continually pressed for a continuing phase-out and by the summer of 1973, 241 had been released.

The party negotiated a truce and had that truce been maintained internment would have been over long ago. The enemies of the party, violent and non-violent, have done nothing about internment other than make speeches.

Some people recently have met in secret to discredit the SDLP. Execution without trial is worse than internment with trial. If violence ended there would be no justification whatsoever for the continuation of internment.[27]

New dawn

December witnessed the negotiations where the participants – the British and Irish governments, along with the SDLP, the UUP and the Alliance Party – agreed to establish a Council of Ireland to deal with matters of an all-Ireland concern, including a form of oversight on policing. The council would consist of fourteen ministers, seven to be drawn from the North and seven from the South. While the agreement, known as the Sunningdale Agreement,[28] was widely welcomed, it was obvious that a large section of unionist opinion was opposed, and was threatening to frustrate its implementation. However, when the assembly reconvened the following January, Hume, now minister of commerce, felt able to optimistically proclaim hopes for a better future:

> Partnership [...] has replaced conflict as the basis of our political and consti-
> tutional thinking. New institutions of government have been set up based on
> the whole concept of partnership. That is the first step. It is for us now to use
> those institutions and the powers they give us to improve the quality of life of
> our people. We will be judged not by what we say but by what we do [...]
> There is one area where our intentions will be watched with great interest and
> care and where we will be judged by what we do and not by what we say, that
> is, on the whole economic front. Our stated objectives, which are very clear,
> and to which we are fully committed, are to achieve rising standards of living,
> sustained full employment, equality of opportunity and social and economic

27 *Irish Times*, 1 Dec. 1973.   28 So named after the location of the negotiations at the civil-service college in Sunningdale.

justice [...] A great deal [of progress] has already been made, and the opportunities for further advances already exist. Their exploitation to the full for the benefit of Northern Ireland as a whole and for the people can only be achieved through the co-operative effort of all sections of this community. We have it in our grasp to succeed; it is up to every one of us to make the most of it.[29]

Hume continued to express this sense of optimism throughout the early months of 1974. Opening the Northern Ireland office in Brussels, he highlighted signs of economic growth and expansion:

The facts are that since 1969 manufacturing output in our country has risen by over 22 per cent while productivity has risen by over 28 per cent. Moreover in 1972 [...] the 1.5 million people in Northern Ireland exported £91m worth of goods and the total trade of the province was worth £1,854 million, increases of 9 per cent and 7 per cent respectively on 1971.

The fact that this steady economic improvement could only have been possible by the co-operation of a loyal and willing workforce and by a remarkably stable system of industrial relations. I would here pay public tribute to the unions and employers' organizations in Northern Ireland who have succeeded not only in keeping political divisions off the factory floor but have maintained and are maintaining industrial relations which stand comparison with most countries in Europe [...]

I am very happy to announce that there are encouraging signs that these valiant efforts by the working people of Northern Ireland are increasingly being recognized by the investors we seek to attract from overseas. In 1973 my department had its best year ever, with the promotion of close on 10,000 new jobs, an increase of 22 per cent on the previous best and almost 47 per cent better than 1972. Sixty-nine projects were announced as compared with 48 in 1972.

Clearly the word has been getting around in the boardrooms of Britain, America and Europe that Northern Ireland, for all its political problems, has much to offer the industrialist in search of expansion opportunities. It is a process that I welcome, and I am prepared to travel anywhere in the world to encourage it.[30]

29 NI Assembly, *Debates*, 24 Jan. 1974.   **30** Address at opening of Brussels office, *Irish Times*, 7 Feb. 1974.

Darkening clouds

Instead of declining, as Hume and colleagues had hoped, unionist and loyalist opposition to the Sunningdale agreement increased, as did loyalist violence, posing a serious threat to the stability of the new institutions. Hume was particularly concerned that PIRA violence had not abated. Instead, SDLP members were being described as traitors and party meeting places were being attacked.

While Hume hoped that the new political institutions would reduce and eventually help end paramilitary violence, he was also convinced that nationalist confidence in the police was essential if that violence was to be effectively addressed. He, therefore, hoped that arrangements for the oversight of policing that were to be vested in the Council of Ireland would greatly assist in producing that confidence. It was a vain hope, as events were to prevent the council ever meeting, but his optimism that violence would soon end persisted:

> I have never seen in the last five years such a total groundswell against the activities of the Provisional IRA as existed in Catholic areas of the North at the present time. The Provisional IRA's capacity to kill has no relation to their support.
>
> In fairness to the [Sunningdale] agreement, one has to see its implementation before one can understand its real meaning. One of the crucial problems, and we made no bones about it in our election campaign, is policing. It was the area which took up most discussion and we came out with a reasonable agreement on it [...]
>
> Anyone that has been deeply involved in Northern Ireland knew that one of the real problems was the absence of effective policing because in that situation there is no law and order in many areas. If one could create a situation in which the entire community supported the police that would be a major step forward to dealing with what was virtually in some cases an anarchic situation.
>
> The SDLP has always said that its objective was to get full support for a police service in Northern Ireland and towards that end we have come to arrangements in Sunningdale.
>
> With the implementation of these arrangements, which no one need fear, we will be in the strongest possible position to obtain that objective because what in effect these arrangements have been saying and what the new policing arrangements are at Sunningdale, is that we have gone to the heart of the police problem in Northern Ireland, which was the unacceptability of the control of the police force that did exist because they were the arm of one political party.[31]

31 RTÉ 'This Week' interview, *Irish Times*, 7 Apr. 1974.

Despite mounting danger signs over the successful operation of the new institutions, especially the Council of Ireland, Hume remained very optimistic, and on a visit to the US at the end of April, he underlined to Congressional leaders the huge step forward the Sunningdale Agreement had been. He also used the opportunity to criticize those who supported the PIRA:

> The Council [of Ireland] will be a continuing conference table where we can pursue in a legitimate way our aspirations for the development of our unified concept of Ireland which can comprehend and cherish all of the many rich cultural and ethnic traditions we possess.
>
> The Council of Ireland is one of a complex of interlocking series of political structures. Our aim is to build a better society by partnership within Northern Ireland to show that Catholic, Protestant, Planter and Gael can live and work together.
>
> We have achieved the first part of this programme in a power-sharing regional government – the Northern Ireland executive. This itself is a major achievement by any constitutional standards. A minor miracle you may say – if you are a student of Irish history, a major one.
>
> The next stage we are now set upon is to achieve harmony within the island of Ireland and between Ireland and Britain. For this purpose we have negotiated with the Irish and British governments and with our parties in the executive on the formation of the council. I have found an encouraging response from American industrialists to my proposal that they should invest in Northern Ireland [...]
>
> I would ask some of my fellow countrymen in this land when they subscribe to IRA funds whether they would themselves shoot a gun or throw a bomb, for that is what their dollars will do.[32]

Ulster Workers' Council strike

Hume's optimism was soon to be proved misplaced. Less than a month later he was faced with the stark reality that a strike in protest against the new political arrangements, called by a shadowy group known as the Ulster Workers' Council, quickly gathered such support within the unionist community that normal life was slowly grinding to a halt. As the minister responsible for energy, industry and transport, he was soon rendered powerless as groups of hooded loyalists mounted road blocks and prevented deliveries of fuel, goods and services. Critically, loyalist workers in Northern Ireland's power stations were reducing energy to all but essen-

32 Address to congressional leaders, Washington, *Irish Times*, 25 Apr. 1974.

tial services. In the assembly, Hume was forced to admit the extent of the damage being caused to many aspects of commercial and public life:

> The situation on the industrial front is worsening. There is almost complete stoppage in the Belfast area and in provincial areas where the situation was reasonable yesterday it is worsening today. The main reason for this is the lack of electricity. There is clear evidence that many workers are willing to go to work but are either unable to work because of the shortage of electricity or are being prevented from going to work because of intimidation. Our information is that intimidation is on the increase rather than on the decrease. All of this has serious effects on the economy. Industry is losing orders. The damage to the future cannot be calculated. The prospects for new industry have been greatly damaged. Last week we had a successful seminar in Europe to attract new industry but its whole effect is in jeopardy because of the situation. We are talking about jobs for our people. Unless the damage is stopped the spectre of widespread unemployment stares the people in the face. Those are the facts of the situation and the basic effects of the strike.
>
> The body which has initiated this strike calls itself the Ulster Workers' Council. The effects of its strike may well be that we will not have any workers. It says it has called this strike in the name of a political cause. I have always believed that a political cause was supposed to benefit the people in some way [...] All I have to say is that no political cause can benefit from what is happening because what we are facing is not the pursuit of a political objective but anarchy. In those circumstances it behoves every single person with the slightest grain of responsibility to stand up against it.[33]

Within a week the strike had become so widespread that all unionist members of the executive resigned, and SDLP members were dismissed as the British government re-imposed direct rule. After only five months, the brave experiment in power-sharing and partnership had collapsed, and would prove extremely difficult to resurrect. Despite his deep disappointment, Hume clung to the principle of partnership and mutual respect for Ireland's different traditions as the only basis upon which institutions of government could be built, and could survive. In one of his first speeches after the experiment's collapse he strongly defended these principles as fundamental to any solution:

> Any solution to the Northern situation must involve partnership between the two traditions in the North. The drama of the last ten days in Northern Ireland has led many people to believe that a great experiment has failed.

33 Northern Ireland Assembly, *Debates*, 21 May 1974.

Some are glad that it has failed. That great experiment is not dead; certain things will stand the test of time. For the first time in three centuries Protestant, Catholic and Dissenter worked together in a part of this island.

It was purely on the basis of our agreed social and economic policy that members of the executive had come together and they would come together again on the same basis. Their objectives had been clearly stated. They wanted economic and industrial development, and to end unemployment.

They made it clear that where private enterprise could not solve problems, the state would intervene. They sought to increase income levels. They initiated research with the aim of attaining greater worker democracy. They had begun a close examination of the roots of poverty in Northern Ireland. The experiment for the moment has been suspended.

It would be easy for us at this time to obey the call of the bugle in blood that is sounding throughout the land. But if we did this we will go back to the mentality of 'us and them'. It would be easy for us to wrap our flags around us and beat our chests and follow the popular line. Many are preaching that our difficulties call for a much more sane approach than that. It is much more difficult to say we seek not victory for our point of view, but a real solution. Rather than rush in anger to put the boot to the other fellow, we must analyse the problem [...]

There has been three centuries of conflict and now, at the end of the day, there will not be a solution if total victory for one point of view is pursued. This would lead to total civil strife or a three-county North or both.

Sanity demands, when we examine all the options for the people of the North, that we must come to one conclusion: any solution must involve partnership between both our traditions in the North and a partnership between North and South.

Too many people want to become instant patriots and to achieve the great dream of a united Ireland. But there cannot be a united Ireland of value unless it is agreed upon, North and South. Ireland is not just a piece of earth; it is people – Protestant, Catholic and Dissenter – and they cannot be united at the point of a gun.

It is time to cut out the hypocrisy of pretending that the men who use the bomb and the bullet are patriots. They are in fact destroying our country and it is time for people to tell them in a loud voice that they must end their carnage. The united Ireland they seek should be an agreed Ireland.[34]

---

34 Address to annual conference of the ITGWU, 8 June 1974; copy in editor's possession.

Sadly, carnage and mayhem continued and elected politicians seemed unable or unwilling to provide an alternative as they awaited the next initiative from the British government. That initiative took the form of an elected constitutional convention, whose members would again attempt to reach agreement on a form of government, though without the explicit requirement that it be cross-community. The sole condition was that a new executive be acceptable, whatever its format, to both sides of the community. For Hume and the SDLP any accept-able government had to be a power-sharing, partnership one, along with some form of an all-Ireland body. Without those basic elements no proposal would have their support. Following the collapse of the 1974 power-sharing government it was clear, however, that the majority of unionists demanded a return to majority rule and rejected the SDLP's power-sharing and Council of Ireland proposals.

Pressure on policing

As the security situation continued to worsen, the SDLP came under increasing pressure and criticism regarding its position on policing. That position essentially meant that full support for policing from the nationalist community could only be offered in the context of agreed political arrangements. Until then the party would only offer qualified support. Hume frequently answered the party's critics as in the following statement:

> There has been a good deal of politicking recently [...] on the crucial question of policing. It is true that all sections of the population want effective policing. This is especially true of those areas which have been without policing for years, areas that are represented by the SDLP.
>
> There was nothing the SDLP would like to see more than effective policing throughout these areas and the removal of troops from the streets. But this reality must be faced – to put it bluntly if the minority are to be asked to police Northern Ireland, they will want to know first what sort of Northern Ireland they will be policing.
>
> Policing could not be considered in isolation and must be part of the overall settlement. The Sunningdale Agreement contained specific proposals for a solution of the policing problem, designed to create an acceptable system with the full support of the SDLP.
>
> The SDLP had pressed for the ratification of the agreement so that the problem of law and order could be tackled. If the Sunningdale Agreement had been implemented there would have been seen in action the determina-tion of the SDLP and the people they represented to create peace and order.[35]

35 *Irish Times*, 7 Sept. 1974.

Constitutional convention

As elections to the convention approached Hume also made clear the SDLP's key requirements for a successful outcome to its discussions – a power-sharing government and a meaningful Irish dimension:

> To suggest that the Irish dimension could be treated as a form of bargaining counter demeaned the SDLP position, which was a reflection of the basic principle that only by recognizing both traditions in the North could a solution to Northern Ireland's problems be found.
>
> The party did not seek domination but a road of partnership which could overcome the divisions between the two parts of the community and the divisions between both parts of the island.
>
> To abandon the expression of one part, the Irish dimension, would be to throw the situation back to only one dimension. The SDLP challenged both traditions to break from the shackles of the past – they would urge the loyalists to break with the ascendancy and siege mentality and to recognize that their rights and traditions were best protected by their own strength. The loyalists should realize that no constitutional change was possible without their consent. To those who adhered to the Irish dimension the party urged a turning away from a 'spiritual concept of Ireland' which had been used to justify violence and death in an impossible struggle [...]
>
> The SDLP offered a long, hard road of partnership to get rid of mutual fears and to enable people to build together a much better new Ireland and new North, through the co-operation and the sweat of all our people.[36]

On policing he also spelled out the SDLP's approach to how confidence in and support for policing could be achieved:

> The effect of the suggestion advanced by some that the SDLP should declare full support for the security forces would be nil; while those who called for the total disbandment of the RUC and the creation of an entirely new force were being equally unrealistic. The latter course ignored the real core of the problem for it assumed that the policing question was simply a matter of whether one was for or against the RUC. I have no doubt whatsoever because of the widespread war-weariness in the community and the overwhelming desire for normality, it could happen in time that the RUC would return to its pre-1968 level of acceptance. But it would get few recruits from the minority and the Achilles heel would remain to be exploited again by violent

36 Ibid., 30 Jan. 1975.

men. The Achilles heel must be removed. The SDLP is the only party that has kept its eyes firmly on the core of the problem.

Very few people in Northern Ireland will be happy to have continued British-government control of their security.

There is an Irish dimension to law and order in Northern Ireland, particularly in relation to political violence. Loyalists give continued testimony to it every time they call on the South for action, and every time they call for extradition, and every time they accuse the South of providing hiding places for terrorists.

Surely one should look on the problem in a more positive light. In a situation where the institutions of government in Northern Ireland are based on partnership and have full loyalty and consent of both sections of the community, as well as the support and recognition of the South, a totally new situation would obtain.

It would then be possible, as part of the Irish dimension, to have a standing security agreement with the South for dealing with crimes of violence in any part of the island. In such circumstances if any group without a mandate sought to overthrow by violence the agreed institutions in any part of this island, then all the democratic forces North and South could more instantly and in concert be directed against them. There would be no hiding place for anyone. No one, North or South, could escape the law, for both the law and its enforcement agencies would have the democratic consent and support of all sections, North and South.[37]

When elections to the constitutional convention were held, Hume again topped the poll in the Derry constituency,[38] and when it met in June, his opening speech set out in detail the fundamental challenges and issues to be faced:

One of the great weaknesses and causes of failure in this community has been that the ideals which different sections of it have held have been misrepresented by other sections. I am prepared to accept that my colleagues and I may and do misrepresent the ideals and attitudes of those who sit opposite. I am certain that they misrepresent ours, not perhaps through any malice but through sheer misunderstanding. This debate gives us an opportunity to state what our ideals are. The first thing that should be said in a community like Northern Ireland is that ideals are good things when held by a substantial section of the community – ideals which spring from a distinctive culture and

37 Ibid., 20 Jan. 1975. 38 The SDLP increased its overall vote, winning seventeen seats, a loss of two compared with the assembly result.

distinctive tradition [...] This is a much richer place because there is diversity. There are distinctive ways of life and there are differing groups of people in differing countries who have a different approach, yet their very existence is a good thing. The question we have to ask ourselves is, 'Have we learned that lesson?' It often seems to us that the division which exists here is at the root of our problems. Perhaps it is not so much in the division but in our approach to its solution that we make mistakes. There is diversity in Northern Ireland. There is diversity in this chamber [...] The question we must ask ourselves is, 'Should we seek to end that diversity or end the division by conquest or by domination?' In effect that is what both traditions have tried to do for centuries. Each has tried to end the division and the differences with the other by conquest or domination. 'Ourselves alone' has been a powerful attitude in both Irish traditions for a long time. It is the attitude that is dominating the thinking of many people in both sections of our community today.

I believe that both traditions are guilty of this basic exclusivist approach, which feels that one tradition can exist only by getting rid of the other or by dominating the other. The net result of that is to be seen sadly on our respective gable walls and kerbstones. Our culture and our tradition from whatever side we come – this is a terrible commentary on the development of our society over the years – are reduced to scribbling graffiti on gable walls. The very emblems which each side claims to be proud of are painted not only on gable walls but on kerbstones to be walked over. That is a message to all of us of total defeat for the positive development of our traditions. In some senses this has led to the graves of many of our people. It is wrong that two traditions with such rich historical backgrounds should be reduced in the twentieth century to expressing their thoughts on the walls of our streets and on our kerbstones. [...]

In the end the real protection the majority tradition in this part of Ireland has rests in its own numbers, not in defensiveness or siege mentality but in positively coming out, working in co-operation and partnership with the other tradition and building an entirely new society. The same applies to the traditions from which we spring. I have asked you to re-examine the fundamentals of your approach. We have to re-examine the fundamentals of ours. We have been handed down a set of political dogmas that have served us badly. We have been handed down a romantic view of Ireland. We have been given an exclusivist notion of Ireland, a dreamlike thing which bears little or no reality to the life of the people in Ireland.[39]

---

39 Northern Ireland Convention, *Debates*, 19 June 1975.

However, despite his plea for a cross-community, partnership form of government the majority of unionists rejected such proposals, and the convention closed in March 1976 without agreement. SDLP contacts with a number of unionist members of the convention continued for some months, but despite the fact that degrees of agreement were reached on a number of issues, unionists refused to yield in their opposition to power-sharing and in September unilaterally withdrew from the talks. A stalemate had been reached, one that would not be overcome for twenty-two years, and once again, violence was left to dominate the headlines.

Hume's disappointment at the failure to reach agreement found bitter expression in the following extract from a report of an interview in early 1977, in which he was accused of being among the politicians who had failed the people of the North:

> Let's face it people have been saying for months that politicians have failed in the North. That is not so. The only politicians who have failed are those who haven't moved a single inch [...] In this situation all of us have made many efforts to make concessions to try and reach agreement with them. Throughout it all they simply remained intransigent with their 'not an inch' policy and yet it was their handling of the North over a long period in government that led to the situation in which we find ourselves today. So, therefore, I believe there is no future in making concessions to them because there must be a clear change of heart either by themselves through their political representatives or by the people who vote for them before we can reach any political settlement in the North and nothing is to be achieved by any further concessions to them.
>
> I believe that unionists as represented by the UUUC [United Ulster Unionist Council] point to anything that would provide an excuse to prevent reaching an agreement.
>
> We have had long experience of that. Mr West [UUUC leader] has stated categorically that there are no conditions in which he will agree to power-sharing involving those with nationalist aspirations. There are no conditions whatsoever.
>
> In other words if we all became unionists or changed our religion the unionists would then say to us 'but who would share power with turncoats?' That was how intransigent they were and that had to be realized in dealing with them.
>
> We in our view have gone very far to meet them. We are going no further to meet them in the present situation and we must point out clearly now that this nonsense – this attack on politicians that is taking place – must stop because it is only assisting those who are engaged in violence and argue that the people have a choice between politics and war. We must point the finger

clearly and unequivocally at those politicians who are actually hindering any agreement in the North.[40]

Democracy undermined

To Hume and the SDLP, the unionists, by their opposition to power-sharing and their recourse, in May 1974, to intimidation, force and politically motivated strike action, had behaved as in 1912–14 when home rule legislation was defied, and once again had challenged democratic rule in the UK:

> We're not talking about a vast number of people of a state rejecting what a parliament has passed. There are exactly 59 million people in Britain and Ireland. We're talking about a million defying the wishes of 58 million. When you do that as was done in '74 – and '74 did not change the constitutional position of Northern Ireland – it offered a form of government for Northern Ireland that recognized the divisions in that society – that was overthrown by a combination of violence and street action. That meant that the rule of law was overthrown – that's what it meant because in the British system the sovereignty of parliament is the basis of the rule of law. A lesson was learned. Two lessons were learned, one by the unionists which they had learned earlier in this century in 1912 that if they threatened rebellion against the decision of the British parliament they shall overcome. And they did. Another lesson was learned by the minority population in Northern Ireland that when you pursue the democratic process and you overwhelmingly get your point view accepted by 58 million out of the 59 and it is still overturned that there is not much point in pursuing the democratic process, which is the genesis of the violence and the philosophy of violence in Northern Ireland. And those two points of view are at the heart of the deadlock. And it derives from abandoning the rule of law by people who represent themselves as law-and-order people.[41]

The lesson Hume drew from events of 1974–6 was that the British government had to work more closely with the Irish government to create a framework within which the two communities in Northern Ireland could feel less threatened by each other, and more comfortable with the proposition that only by co-operating in a partnership arrangement could peace and reconciliation be achieved. It was a lesson that would take a considerable length of time to be fully grasped.

---

40 *Irish Times*, 31 Jan. 1977.   41 Boston conference, 1984. Recording kindly provided by Professor Catherine Shannon.

1976–81

The three years following the failure of the constitutional convention until Hume's election to the European parliament in 1979, proved an extremely difficult period for the SDLP, especially for its leaders, not least in terms of their personal circumstances. John Hume had been a full-time politician since 1969 but now found himself, along with several of his colleagues, without a paid position – because the assembly had been disbanded and direct rule imposed – but still with a party to lead. Gerry Fitt, an MP at Westminster, remained the only leader with a salary from politics. Nonetheless, the party's group of former convention members were determined to remain in existence, re-designating themselves as the SDLP's 'constituency representatives', while seeking paid employment wherever they could. Meeting regularly, the group vowed to continue providing political leadership to its electorate.

In the absence of any further government initiatives intended to produce cross-party agreement, direct rule from Westminster gradually became entrenched. With that, speculation became rife as to what might ultimately transpire. Two of the most radical possibilities commonly speculated about were a unilateral British withdrawal from Northern Ireland and, secondly, negotiations leading to an independent Northern Ireland. Both gained some support within the SDLP, though Hume was quick to distance himself from each, and was particularly fearful of the consequences of a unilateral British withdrawal.

British withdrawal

In the autumn of 1976 John Hume spent two months at Harvard University, and while there gave an interview to John Dromey of *Harvard Magazine*. This was published at the same time as the debate on withdrawal was taking place within the SDLP and, more generally, in Northern Ireland. Conscious that he was speaking in the one of the most Irish parts of the US, Hume outlined his deep concerns about the likely effects of a British withdrawal:

> I think everyone wants to see British troops off the streets. Nobody wants soldiers on the streets enforcing the law. Our view is that we want to see them withdrawn in the context of a political settlement which allows for institutions of law and order set up with the people's support and with the troops off the streets.

> We [the SDLP] think that British withdrawal without an agreement
> between both sides of the community is very dangerous; it could lead to a
> blood-bath situation in which the Protestants simply seize power in the North
> – so that's a very risky approach. To us the main, permanent element in the
> Irish problem is the relationship between Catholic and Protestant Ireland.
> That will be there whatever happens to the British. The British presence is
> ancillary to that. We would like to see the British presence ended by agree-
> ment between Protestants and Catholics, with a peaceful Ireland left behind.[1]

At the SDLP's annual conference in December 1976 Hume spoke strongly
against a motion calling on the party to demand a British withdrawal. In his intervention in what was a highly charged debate, with several leading members of the
party speaking in favour of the motion, Hume spelled out the key argument
against such a prospect:

> Mr John Hume spoke against the motion not because he opposed the British
> leaving this island [...] he did not believe the British presence constituted the
> kernel of the Irish question. If there was no Protestant population in Ireland
> there would be no trouble and there would have been no need for 1916; if
> there was no Catholic minority in Northern Ireland the present problems
> would never have arisen. It was the relationships of the two communities that
> were vital. The SDLP had offered proposals for long-term reconciliation. 'We
> must tell the loyalists that if you continue "yourselves alone" policy it will
> result in confrontation in which no political party will have a say.'[2]

The motion was defeated.

Later, within the party, Hume set out the choices facing members in a discussion paper, along with the issues that would have to be addressed, if a withdrawal
policy was adopted:

> In the present circumstances the party has basically two courses of action
> open to it:
>
>   a) To maintain and strengthen present policy;
>   b) To change our policy. In the present circumstances such a course would
> seem to indicate that the party move to a British withdrawal situation [...]
>
> Course A – strengthen present policy by taking the following steps:
>
>   1) There should be a strong restatement of the party's present policy and,
> in particular, on the analysis of the problem on which our solution is based.
> Such a statement should underline the achievement of this policy; [...]

---

1 Interview with John Dromey, *Harvard Magazine*, Dec. 1976.   2 *Irish Times*, 6 Dec. 1976.

2) A public campaign by all of the party's representatives to expose loyalist intransigence.

3) A strongly argued case to the British that they adopt a two-pronged approach to the achievement of partnership: (a) that they should use all their resources to convince the community of the value of partnership; and to expose the intransigence of loyalism. If they are prepared to use major resources, particularly in the propaganda field, to break the military will of the Provisional IRA, they should be prepared to do likewise to break the political will of intransigent loyalism; (b) step up their cross-border contacts with the Irish government [...]

4) Initiate major cross-border projects (we should provide a list) and generally raise the whole profile of the Irish dimension.

5) We should openly reject the British contention that the Northern Ireland problem can be solved by the people of Northern Ireland alone and we should strongly restate our position that any solution to be successful must include Dublin and London.

In the event of taking course B the party would have to decide on the following:

a) The steps to be taken to maintain order in the immediate aftermath of either a British declaration or a British withdrawal;

b) The governmental structures that we would propose in the long term as the lasting solution;

c) The means to be used to achieve agreement on such structures by the different representative groups in Ireland.[3]

The defeat of the withdrawal motion, and Hume's stark presentation of what a withdrawal policy implied, effectively ended the party's flirtation with that option.

An independent Northern Ireland

Hume was strongly opposed to the idea of an independent Northern Ireland, and recognizing that it had very little public support, seldom spoke about the option. On one occasion, in answer to a question at a conference in the US, he said:

I think it would be a dangerous option. It would lead to a Lebanese situation very quickly because when you look at Stormont, Stormont was a virtually independent state [...] and it didn't work. It may have worked from a unionist point of view but it didn't work for nationalists. An independent

---

3 SDLP discussion paper, 5 Mar. 1977, copy in editor's possession.

Northern Ireland would be in very grave danger, but I would go close to it in my suggestion for an autonomous Northern Ireland as part of a federal Ireland.[4]

PIRA campaign

In the absence of political movement republican and loyalist terror campaigns dominated public life in the North. Hume remained bitterly critical of the PIRA's campaign, which was then targeting almost anyone it associated in any way with what it termed the 'British war machine'. It was a murderous and futile attempt to make Northern Ireland ungovernable and, thereby, hopefully force a British declaration to withdraw. Targets included not just the security forces but, increasingly, their civilian contractors and suppliers of goods and services, as well as former police and army personnel. Town centres became frequent targets for car bomb and arson attacks. Along with the personal tragedies of death and injury that their campaign was inflicting, Hume denounced its social and economic effects, not least on his native city:

> Never in the long history of Ireland had any organization claiming to represent basic nationalist aspirations reduced itself to the level of the recent Provisional IRA campaign against a section of the Irish people.
>
> The leadership of the Provisional IRA have decided to murder people purely and simply because of the way they work for their living – because they are in business. Is there no one left in the ranks of the Provisional IRA who has even a spark of idealism and who has the courage to stand up to his colleagues and shout 'stop'?
>
> Is there no one who will look back over the past seven years and ask himself: after 1,500 dead and 17,000 injured, after more than 500 bombs, what has been achieved?
>
> It is no excuse to point to the atrocities of others. The Provisional IRA are responsible for their own actions and for the suffering they have brought on their own people. And what has the leadership of the Provisional IRA given in return to the thousands of young people who have idealistically joined their ranks and who now find themselves in graves or in jail?
>
> In our city anyone who looks back over the past seven troubled years will recognize at once that anything that has been achieved has been achieved by purely non-violent and political means.
>
> Derry Corporation has disappeared and been replaced by a democratically

---

4 Boston conference, Mar. 1982. Recording of proceedings kindly provided by Professor Catherine Shannon.

elected council. The last few years have seen a great improvement in Derry's housing situation. On the employment front we have attracted massive new industry. Can anyone doubt that, but for the violence, we would have attracted more?[5]

Hume was particularly scathing in his criticism of elected politicians who supported in any way the PIRA's campaign, especially those in the South. One such was Neil Blaney, who represented the neighbouring Donegal constituency in the Dáil, the lower house of the Republic's parliament:

> The SDLP did not believe in a campaign of violence. They believed in reconciliation between the two communities and had gone to the electorate who had consistently endorsed the party in that policy [...] Mr Blaney [...] spoke from the safety of his Dublin home. He encouraged young people to plant bombs and to go out with guns, go to jail, while his family were not in a position to be retaliated against because of the action of the IRA [...] It [the issue] was a question of relationships between sections of the community and these could not be resolved by violence. It could only make them more bitter. 'Is total victory the only solution? How can you have a solution with total victory [for one side]? What about the million people [unionists] who disagree with Mr Blaney? Do we drive them into the sea?[6]

Cross-border economic concerns

Despite the violence and despite the failure to make any political breakthrough, social and economic progress was never far from Hume's mind, and he availed of any opportunity to press the case for investment and development. Hume believed it essential that democratic politics continue to address day-to-day issues, and was particularly anxious to promote North-South economic links. At a conference that discussed development plans for the north-west (the Derry-Donegal region), Hume proposed the creation of a Lough Foyle Authority to bring together several bodies, on both sides of the border, in order to more effectively manage the lough's economic potential:

> In looking at the development of Lough Foyle [...] here are several key areas that are part of our growth potential – harbours, fisheries, tourist amenities and conservation. At present there are many different authorities on each side of the border with responsibility for all matters pertaining to Lough Foyle.

5 *Irish Times*, 8 Mar. 1977.   6 Ibid., 17 June 1976.

Such an authority could have responsibility for the development of all the harbours and piers in the Lough, as well as for safety of navigation. This would tend to remove the present anomaly whereby the harbours of both Derry and Moville [Co. Derry] are under the ownership of the Derry Port and Harbour Commissioners, and where Donegal have consistently pressed for an independent authority for Moville.

Similarly with the development of the tourist potential, sea fishing, boating, marinas and the extremely valuable fishery potential of the lough and surrounding coast. A related subject to all of these matters is the question of conservation and anti-pollution measures, responsibility for which is also divided between different authorities [...] Many obstacles to co-operation could be overcome if the political will existed on both sides of the border.

Membership of the EEC [...] had lessened the extent of the major problem standing in the way of such progress – the fear of constitutional implications. It is clear that strong and agreed co-operation on social and economic problems can be developed without constitutional implications and can provide clear economic benefits to an intensely deprived region.

The ultimate objective in the development of the north-west should be a strongly integrated region with an overall plan and with a north-west development authority appointed to implement it.[7]

However, with no political agreement there was no forum within which Hume and his colleagues could achieve all this. Interestingly, the proposal anticipated by more than twenty years one of the North-South bodies established following the Good Friday/Belfast Agreement of 1998.

Widening the context

After the convention had shown that a power-sharing arrangement was not feasible in the short term, the SDLP gradually shifted its focus for political progress away from attempting to negotiate with unionists in the first instance, towards several wider contexts. The first focus was Irish-British relationships. Hume quite cogently argued that since it was there that sovereign authority within the two islands lay, it was there the search for a more hopeful approach to addressing Northern Ireland's crisis should begin. Hume contended that it was essential that the Irish and British governments work together to influence the situation by, first, providing the necessary guarantees to both communities, and second, jointly creating the circumstances in which meaningful and, hopefully, successful negotiations could take place. To achieve these objectives, Hume advanced two arguments.

7 Ibid., 9 Apr. 1976.

One of these arguments was aimed at the British guarantee of no change in the North's constitution without majority consent. Hume had made clear since he had entered politics that while he accepted the principle of consent, he regarded the UK government's expression of the guarantee as essentially one-sided. Since unionists were in the majority, the guarantee was effectively saying that the basic unionist position, continued membership of the UK, would remain unchanged even when they rejected and defied British policy on how Northern Ireland should be governed. (Power-sharing and an all-Ireland council had been British government policies since 1973.) In such circumstances, the guarantee was not a neutral position, because it was effectively guaranteeing unionist intransigence:

> It guarantees the position of unionist politicians who, since 1974, have rejected proposals for devolved government in Northern Ireland involving both sections of the community. Is it unreasonable to suggest that this open-ended guarantee has not been a particularly successful basis of policy? Has this produced peace? These are questions that ought to be asked by responsible politicians in Britain and ought to be answered by a responsible government.[8]

Hume's call for the guarantee to be withdrawn was to become one of his central arguments until the guarantee would eventually be modified in the 1985 Anglo-Irish Agreement.

Spelling out Irish unity

To the Irish government and to people of the broad nationalist tradition in Ireland Hume continued to argue the need to move away from the exclusive, romantic 'die-for-Ireland' approach, and towards a more inclusive vision of an agreed Ireland that would cherish all its traditions equally. Working for agreement between unionists and nationalists was the only viable option. That, he argued, could be the only meaningful basis on which to achieve a genuinely united Ireland. He had frequently used opportunities in the South to drive home this message:

> Ireland is not a romantic dream, it is not a flag, it is not just a piece of earth. It is four and a half million people divided into two powerful traditions and its problems can only be solved, if the solution is to be a lasting and permanent one, not on the basis of victory for either, but on the basis of agreement and partnership between both. The real division of Ireland is not a line on a map, but is in the minds and hearts of the people.[9]

8 Boston conference, Mar. 1982. Recording of proceedings kindly provided by Professor Catherine Shannon. 9 *Social Democrat*, Jan. 1976

The US dimension

There was also another dimension to widening the debate – the US. Hume admired the country's political traditions and the constitutional principles upon which politics and all public life were based. He believed these to be worthy of emulation in the Irish context:

> Through a process of development that was never easy or free of problems, Americans have gone very far in giving real practical effect to equality before the law for every citizen and to equality of opportunity for all. America is a country where there is a wider measure of national and political consensus fashioned from rich and broad diversity.
>
> In America there has always been respect for this idea of unity in diversity, and whatever the controversies may be about the value and application today of the old melting-pot concept, there is increasing acceptance of the idea of cultural pluralism. Not without difficulty or devoid of controversy, Americans have achieved religious tolerance and separation of church and state. Written on the smallest coin is the message of greatest value, the cement of American society – *e pluribus unum* – from many one. The tragedy of divided people everywhere, as in Ireland, is that they have pushed difference to the point of division and have not yet learned the lesson that the essence of unity in every democratic society in the world is to accept and respect diversity.[10]

Apart from lessons in creating unity out of diversity, and in developing respect and tolerance for difference, Hume had two more pressing objectives in the US at this time. One was to challenge the support some sections of Irish-American opinion were offering to the PIRA's campaign of violence. The second was to influence leading Irish-American politicians and, through them, the US government to support his approach. Hume's relationship with key Irish-American politicians had begun in 1972 when he received a phone call from Senator Edward Kennedy seeking a briefing on the situation in Northern Ireland. Years later Hume vividly recalled that phone call and the relationships that developed from it:

> I was so astonished at receiving it that I thought somebody was conning me. A voice on the phone said 'This is Ted Kennedy. I'm going to Europe and I would like to meet you to get fully briefed on how you see the situation in Northern Ireland.' I was amazed, but I knew it was him because it was his voice. We met in Bonn, in Germany where he was going. Of course when we met there, we had a very full discussion on the situation in Northern Ireland, and I fully briefed him on the situation as it existed […] There's no doubt

10 Hume, *Personal views*, pp 20–1.

about the enormous assistance that he gave us because following that meeting he kept in regular contact with me.[11]

Following events like Bloody Sunday, support for the PIRA campaign had grown rapidly in some Irish-American centres, notably Boston and New York, with both funds and weapons being sent to the North. The appeal was the age-old one of support for what its proponents claimed was the only way to achieve a united Ireland: a military campaign to force a British withdrawal. It was an appeal that Hume was determined to challenge. He faced this challenge very directly, as in this extract from his speech to the Friendly Sons of St Patrick in Washington in March 1977:

> Both Protestant and nationalist traditions have contributed to the present conflict and confrontation by their exclusivism. Protestant leadership is more negative and stark than it has ever been – 'No surrender', 'not an inch', and 'what we have we hold'. Nationalism is an attitude of mind which says it is patriotic to unite a piece of earth irrespective of what the people on that piece of earth thought. This attitude held that it is not enough to die for it, one must kill for it. It wraps a green flag round us, beats our drums, sings our patriotic songs and lets our chests fill with pride. It defines Irishness in a narrow sectional sense excluding those who do not conform to its narrow mould.
>
> We too can continue with this attitude but we can be certain it will fail, for it has failed before and it will fail again, and we have too many graves to prove it.
>
> The present over-emotional and fanciful make-believe is very different from the original true ideal of Irish republicanism. How sadly has the present vicious parody departed from the doctrine set forth by the organization of the United Irishmen, composed, I would stress, mainly of the Presbyterian Irishmen [...]
>
> Without brotherhood, Irish soil will form only our common grave. But how can we give what the United Irishmen made explicit in the words of 'equal, full and adequate representation'? Given the circumstances of today, given the depth of bitterness and division, that brotherhood can only be promoted by partnership between the two Irish traditions, partnership to govern within Northern Ireland and partnership between both parts of Ireland.
>
> By working together over long and patient years, we can build the under-standing and friendship to replace the prejudice and hatred that now divides

11 Personal communication with the editor.

us. It will be a long and hard road and there are no longer any instant answers.[12]

Hume's focus on leading Irish-American politicians was to yield considerable benefits in terms of political as well as economic support for the case he made. In addition to Senator Kennedy, Hume developed very close relationships with US House Speaker Thomas 'Tip' O'Neill, US Senator Daniel Moynihan and New York Governor Hugh Carey. Collectively, they became known as the 'Four Horsemen'. They issued a statement on St Patrick's Day supporting Hume's approach. This was followed in July by a statement from US President Jimmy Carter promising assistance in the event of a cross-party political agreement.

European context

Hume's third focal point in widening the debate beyond Northern Ireland was the European context. He was a committed believer in the European model of reconciliation through the construction of shared political, economic and social institutions. Northern Ireland had become part of the European Community when the UK joined it in 1973, and by the late 1970s the prospect of a directly elected European parliament offered Northern Ireland an even more direct interest and involvement in the development of these institutions: it was announced that the region would be allocated three seats in that parliament. Furthermore, Hume believed that the whole European project offered opportunities to lift horizons beyond the North's own narrow ground, and for people and communities to co-operate in a context unaffected by local prejudices and local history. Increasingly, Hume stressed this context and the reconciling influences it could have on former bitter enemies. Indeed, since 1977 he had been gaining first-hand experience of the workings of European institutions as a member of Irish Commissioner Richard Burke's cabinet. As with his period at Harvard, Hume used this appointment to acquaint himself not just with the working of European institutions, but also with many of the key personalities involved.

Accepting his nomination as the SDLP's candidate for one of the Northern Ireland seats in the European parliament, Hume claimed:

> We are too small, and divisions in a small community, without a large stage on which to unite, tend to become more bitter and more intractable. Europe offers us that stage, the broader horizon and the issues [...] are ones that will cross the traditional divide in a meaningful way. Europe can be the bridge on which we stand together.[13]

12 *Irish Times*, 18 Mar. 1977.   13 European parliamentary candidate acceptance speech, SDLP, June 1978; copy in editor's possession.

Later, as the elections approached, he stressed the example in reconciliation that
Europe provided:

> 7 June 1979 will be an historic date. The people of the member states of the
> European Community will, for the first time, go together to the polls to elect
> the first directly elected European parliament. It will be an historic act of
> reconciliation among peoples who have been ancient enemies and who twice
> in this century have slaughtered one another with a savagery unparalleled in
> human history. Yet they have been able to agree on a process whereby they
> can grow in harmony and agreement. The lesson should not be lost on the
> people of Northern Ireland.[14]

Hume was also conscious of the value in attracting even wider attention to the
crisis in Northern Ireland. The influential journal *Foreign Affairs* published a
lengthy article of his that contained what many regard as one of Hume's most
cogent analyses of the crisis. Once again, the British guarantee featured strongly in
his argument, as did his condemnation of the PIRA campaign:

> The problem, as I know from years of talking to foreign visitors, is at first
> sight a mass of contradictions. Some of the contradictions are real. London
> for its part, exercises a reluctant sovereignty in Northern Ireland, while
> Dublin maintains a somewhat reluctant claim to that sovereignty. The 'loyal-
> ists' are those proponents of the union with Britain who, while they are
> avowedly the most patriotic of Her Majesty's subjects, put up the most
> stubborn resistance to her government's designs. The Provisional wing of the
> Irish Republican Army believes that Irish unity will be secured by waging war
> against a British establishment which clearly has no fundamental opposition
> to unity, while they ignore (and in their campaign against Britain, further
> incite) those who most adamantly resist the imposition of unity, the one-
> mission Protestant majority. Does this mean things are hopeless? No, but it
> further underlines the necessity, reinforced by horrific events, that all major
> parties to this crisis should rigorously re-examine their own roles, responsibil-
> ities and room for manoeuvre.
>
> The basis of British policy is concealed under layers of good intentions,
> ingenious initiatives, commissions of enquiry, attempted reforms, financial
> aid and a good deal of genial bewilderment. I do not use the word 'concealed'
> maliciously. Many sincere and concerned British politicians and observers
> have the impression that they have tried everything possible to get the Irish to

14 Election leaflet, European election, 1979.

agree together: that is a measure of the extent to which the basic assumption of their policy has become imperceptible to the British themselves [...]

'The British guarantee', as it is called, proved to be a guarantee of permanent exclusive power to one side, the unionists, and a guarantee of permanent exclusion from power to the other, the Catholic minority. Its existence undermined any hope of political negotiation between the two sides in Northern Ireland. It guaranteed the integrity of 'their quarrel'. While this guarantee exists, there is no incentive for unionists to enter into genuine dialogue with those with whom they share the island of Ireland. The suffering and frustration of the people of Northern Ireland overwhelmingly attest to the fact that the guarantee was, to put it very bluntly, a tragic mistake. The price has been paid too long and in too many lives [...]

The unionists of Northern Ireland are justly proud of their heritage and their contributions to the world. As many as eleven American presidents came from their stock. They number field marshals, captains of industry and colonial governors among their great men. They see themselves as pragmatic, hard-headed, sceptical, robust people, and there is much in their history to justify this view. They have shown a corresponding tendency to regard their nationalist Catholic neighbours throughout the island as a more fanciful and less realistic race, and indeed there may be much in the history of the Catholic community to give colour to that view [...]

The unionists are a majority in Northern Ireland. But their political behaviour can only be understood if they are seen, as they feel themselves to be, as a threatened minority on the island of Ireland [...] Theirs are the politics of the besieged. Hence their stubborn refusal to share power with the minority in Northern Ireland, whom they fear as the Trojan horse of the 'real' majority in Ireland, the Catholics. Hence the similarity between their attitudes and those of the whites of southern Africa.

Can this attitude be unfrozen? There are some grounds for believing it can. I have mentioned the Sunningdale experiment, the most promising attempt so far to solve the problem. The main unionist political group at that time, and particularly its leader, the late Mr Brian Faulkner, showed courage and political agility, and the response of most unionists to the experiment was by and large benign. The pusillanimity of the Labour government in London, in failing to resist the predictable destructiveness of the demagogues and paramilitaries on the extremes of unionism, set back the situation almost irremediably; unionist opinion, it must be admitted, shifted further to the right as a result, as evidenced by the growing electoral strength of Ian Paisley. Nevertheless the reality of power-sharing did exist, however tenuously. Unionists, given the right leadership, were seen to be capable of magnanimity. The problem now is to create the conditions where magnanimity can again take hold, this time more securely [...]

If you ask a unionist how real the threat is, he or she will tell you of friends or relatives who have been murdered or injured by the Provisional IRA. What threat could be more real? That, however, is only a vivid and chilling expression of an even greater sense of intimidation. Unionists fear that they would be culturally and racially overwhelmed by the Catholic nationalist majority if they were to join the rest of the island. Would they? This is the challenge to Irish nationalism, to Dublin, to the nationalist minority in Northern Ireland, and to the friends of Irish nationalism around the world.

The campaign of violence of the Provisional IRA has, more than any other recent development, set back and distorted the cause of Irish nationalism in the eyes of unionists, and of British and of world opinion. It is clear that a majority of Catholics in Northern Ireland both favour Irish unity as a solution and reject violence as a means of promoting that solution [...]

The Provisionals have hardened into a ruthless terrorist force which can compensate in terms of experience and technique for what it has lost in political support. It is a long time since commentators invoked Mao and predicted that, as the waters of popular approval dried up, the guerrilla fish would have to abandon the struggle to survive. We can now see that the fish need less water than we had thought. The Provisionals have for years received only insignificant support from the population of either Northern Ireland or the Republic; yet they retain the ability to disrupt and terrorize.

Indeed, their activities have descended to a level of savagery which has numbed the capacity of the public to respond with horror to even their most inhuman atrocities. Life has become cheap – and the entire community to some extent dehumanized. 'Is there a life before death?' asks a piece of anonymous graffiti on a Belfast wall, with some reason. The writer might have asked whether there is any childhood left for the battle-scarred children of the ghettos of that city, and of the rest of Northern Ireland.

Aside from the immorality of its actions, the Provisional IRA campaign has no hope of success. It is, I suppose, conceivable that it might eventually frighten a feeble British government out of Northern Ireland before any process could begin. What would undoubtedly follow would be a serious risk of a bloodbath. This would quickly spread to the South and, after thousands of deaths, would finally resolve itself by the division of the island into two bristling, homogeneous sectarian states, neither stable, both sunk in the obscurantism of their most extreme supporters. No military victory followed by a political settlement is possible in Northern Ireland. That is true not for the Provisionals alone but for the loyalists and the British government as well [...]

In recent years the influence of powerful American leaders of Irish extraction in Washington, notably Senator Edward Kennedy and House Speaker

Thomas P. O'Neill, has brought the issue to the point where the Carter administration has taken a position on Northern Ireland. Their opposition to violence has been crucial. As a result, the support for the PIRA from the United States has been contained and has in fact dropped. That this should have been maintained during the past years of political vacuum in Northern Ireland is an extraordinary achievement. There are many men, women and children in Northern Ireland who are alive today, I am convinced, because of the political courage of these men.

President Carter has committed himself to providing economic aid in the event that a solution acceptable to both sides in Northern Ireland, and to the British and Irish governments, can be found. That was a generous, and unprovocative commitment. It was welcomed by the Irish and British governments as a major incentive to reconciliation, and they were both consulted about it. The Irish question has become a legitimate and serious issue in the Atlantic relationship between London and Washington.[15]

The importance of the US link was to grow substantially over the following decade, leading to President Bill Clinton's significant interventions as the peace process developed, from 1994 onwards.

MEP

The year 1979 was historic in many respects in Northern Ireland, not least for Hume himself. Not only was he elected to the European parliament but, later the same year, he was elected leader of the SDLP following the departure from the party of Gerry Fitt. Margaret Thatcher was elected the UK's first female prime minister and, in the South, Charles Haughey became taoiseach. All three would have critical and interacting roles to play in events affecting Northern Ireland over the next decade.

As a member of the European parliament, Hume now had the opportunity to pursue the wider social, economic and cultural agendas which he had outlined throughout his election campaign, and which he had long championed. During the campaign he strongly criticized his leading opponents from the unionist parties, who wished to remove Northern Ireland from the European Community, arguing that the opportunities it presented were immense:

> To say that Northern Ireland could survive outside is economic nonsense and can only be based on an understanding of world economics thirty years out of date. Also, to demand that the Community solve our problems, and at the

15 *Foreign Affairs*, Winter 1979–80.

same time seek to take Northern Ireland out of the Community as two candidates are proposing only indicates contradictory and confused thinking on the issues.

Northern Ireland needs access to the markets of Europe and outside the Community this would be exceedingly difficult. In such a situation many industries would close and unemployment would increase at least two-fold.

Within the common market there are immense opportunities for our industries to expand and new industries to develop. This is the industrial challenge of the future.

The same is true of our agriculture. Here we have one of the most efficient agricultural industries within the European Community. I shall be pressing for Northern Ireland to be regarded as one of the most important food-producing regions in the community and demanding full advantage of the agricultural market for our produce. [...]

We must recognize that the problems we face in Northern Ireland are problems shared by many regions in Europe and beyond. However, by uniting representatives from such regions an effective voice will emerge to ensure that these problems are tackled as effectively as possible.[16]

Hume lost no time drawing the parliament's attention to the North's socio-economic needs and their links to its political crisis. In a submission to the social affairs and regional committee in November 1979, he called for a special economic development programme for Northern Ireland:

Northern Ireland has at 11.5 per cent one of the highest levels of unemployment in Europe. Forecasts suggest that the level could rise to 16 per cent before the end of the year. Housing is bad, emigration is high. There is a young, growing population. The level of violence is high. Employment has declined in the manufacturing sector, with major sectors such as textiles and shipbuilding under severe threat. Now employment depends on public expenditure on services and subsidies. Membership of the Community has done little to stop the downward spiral of the region.

The establishment of a special economic development programme is called for. This programme, while increasing Community expenditure in the United Kingdom should result in new policies, programmes, measures and structures. The experience gained could be applied to other regions.

The search for peace is linked with winning prosperity. The resolution seeks to provide a common basis on which a broad coalition of members of the parliament can show their practical concern about the situation in

16 *Derry Journal*, 6 June 1979.

Northern Ireland – to establish a programme about which the broad majority of the people of Northern Ireland can agree.

The search for peace and stability is intimately bound up with the achievement of economic progress and decent living conditions, with the provision of jobs and houses. The Community has extensive powers and responsibilities. The relationship between those powers and responsibilities and more strictly 'political' questions is clearly identified by the founders of the Community in the preamble to the Treaty of Paris, when they said they were resolved: 'to substitute for age old rivalries the merging of essential interests, to create by establishing an economic community the basis for a broader and deeper community among people long divided by bloody conflicts and to lay the foundation for institutions which will give direction to a destiny henceforward shared'.[17]

This resolution was adopted, and was followed by an investigation into social and economic circumstances in Northern Ireland, published in the Martin Report, and presented to the parliament in June 1981.

Alongside his determination to obtain support for economic and social initiatives Hume argued that the European parliament should back cultural initiatives, especially those that would support cultural and linguistic minorities across the Community. He was conscious of the situations of such lesser-used languages as Irish, Welsh, Scots Gaelic, Breton, Frisian, Alsatian and Corse, and, along with other MEPs sought greater recognition at European level for those languages and their use in public life. Stressing that the richness of Europe lay in its cultural diversity, in a motion to the parliament in October 1979, he called: 'on the European commission to report by next July on the actions it is carrying out which promote regional languages and cultures and how these can be stepped up so that there can be a genuine policy of support'.[18]

This motion would lead to the preparation of a special report on regional languages and cultures, the Arfe Report, and later to the adoption of a charter of regional languages and cultures and a charter on the rights of ethnic minorities, and to the setting up, in 1982, of the European Bureau for Lesser-Used Languages, located in Dublin.

Membership of the European parliament also provided Hume with opportunities to reach out to new audiences. Speaking at a conference on American-European relationships in Co. Kerry soon after his election, he called on the two governments to act jointly to address a situation that they had a shared interest in having resolved, and he pointed to the support that would be available from US sources were such an initiative to succeed. Effectively, he was outlining

17 14 Nov. 1979, Linen Hall Library, NIPC, P4346.   18 *Irish Times*, 25 Oct. 1979.

the approach that would ultimately be enshrined in the process that would lead to the Good Friday Agreement of 1998:

> The time has come for a positive and decisive initiative. It must be taken by both governments acting together. They should firstly make it clear that there are no longer any unconditional guarantees for any section of the Northern community. There is only a commitment to achieve a situation in which there are guarantees for all.
>
> They should make it clear that there is in fact no solution but only a process that will lead to a solution. They should declare themselves committed to such a process, a process of integration of the different traditions on this island, a process designed to lead to an agreed Ireland with positive roles for all.
>
> They should invite all parties to participate in this process, the process of building a new Ireland. Some will undoubtedly react with an initial refusal but the process should continue without them, leaving the door always open for their participation at any stage.
>
> We ought to be encouraged by the example of unity in diversity in the United States and the European Community where people who a generation ago were slaughtering one another by the million were now represented together in a directly elected parliament.
>
> There can be little doubt that there are those in the US – in the Irish-American community in particular – whose politics on Ireland have been the simple politics of rhetoric. But they are not alone. Here at home we still occasionally and even recently hear the rhetorical sounding of the bugle in the blood.
>
> But more and more the horrors of the past decade have brought ourselves and Irish-Americans face to face with the politics of reality. In recent years the influence of peaceful and responsible Irish-American politicians has brought this issue to a point where the administration has taken a responsible, careful and very generous position on Northern Ireland and for the first time an American president has spoken of the Irish problem.
>
> As a result, support for violence from the US has been contained and has in fact dropped. There are many men, women and children in Northern Ireland who are alive today, I am convinced, because of the political courage and concern of such men as [Edward] Kennedy and [Tip] O'Neill.[19]

---

19 Ibid., 24 Sept. 1979.

Secretary of state's conference

Under Margaret Thatcher's leadership a modest initiative was taken by Secretary of State Humphrey Atkins, who convened inter-party talks in the early months of 1980. While the SDLP had serious reservations about the focus of the talks – they were originally intended to focus exclusively on the issue of devolved government – the party agreed to attend when North-South relations were included on the agenda. However, the UUP declined to participate, and so only Ian Paisley's DUP, the Alliance Party and the SDLP were in attendance. The talks appeared doomed from the outset. However, given the party's commitment to dialogue, Hume used the opportunity to yet again address the question of the British guarantee and, secondly, the SDLP's approach to the RUC. On the latter, the SDLP had remained under pressure to give whole-hearted support to the force, something it firmly believed it could not do in the absence of a political settlement agreed to by both communities.

In the SDLP's submission to the secretary of state's conference Hume spelled out in detail why the UK's constitutional guarantee was viewed as one-sided and unhelpful in the search for a solution. He underlined his view of what he called the traditional loyalist (i.e. unionist) and nationalist positions and why both needed to be re-examined, and in a general manner he indicated the basis for a new agreement:

> The British government's approach to the Northern Ireland problem has been totally consistent since 1920, in that the whole basis of its policy was to under-line and guarantee one identity in a situation where the problem resulted from a clash of identities. It is legitimate for me to ask at this conference whether this has been a successful basis of policy. Has it produced stability? What has it produced? Has it even satisfied those loyalists that it was designed to satisfy? Has it even produced from those loyalists acceptance of the other terms laid down by the British government and parliament for the govern-ment of Northern Ireland? A situation, unique in which the constitutional basis of a community is enshrined only in an act of parliament, is a recipe for instability since, in effect, as long as the constitutional basis for the govern-ment of Northern Ireland is an act of the British parliament, there will always, therefore, be insecurity among the people of Northern Ireland. This has been revealed on countless occasions. Every time a unionist leader meets a British political leader he demands reassurance on the constitutional position, under-lining that he has got no assurance at all. The first step towards moving towards a solution must be a complete re-examination by the British govern-ment itself of its approach to the resolution of the conflict.
>
> As for the loyalist population and the loyalist politicians, the Protestant tradition in Ireland has always sought, and rightly so, to protect its separate

identity. Ireland would be a much poorer place without them. Diversity enriches our country and we should see to it that it is always preserved. What I would ask them to question, however, has been their method of preserving their separate identity because to date they have consistently done so by the exclusive use of power; by holding all power in their own hands; by basically 'an ourselves alone' attitude. This attitude has inherent in it seeds of conflict because by its exclusive nature it is bound, in the end, to lead to conflict. The real security of the loyalist people rests in their own numbers and on their own strength. My appeal to them would be to stand up and negotiate with the rest of the people of Ireland an agreed way in which the people of this island can come together in peace and harmony.

As for the nationalist tradition it, too, has had a fairly consistent approach down the years and in many ways has presented a narrow and sectional vision of Ireland; one which has tended to exclude any understanding of the rights and aspirations of the Protestant population. In its extreme form this tradition has given birth to paramilitary organizations who think it not only right to die but to kill for this tradition. Here again the exclusivist nature of this approach has inherent in it seeds of conflict and it, too, must examine its whole role and what sort of Ireland it was offering. Not a conquest of the North to the South but an agreement on a new Ireland [...]

The alternative role to conflict is partnership. Partnership between the two Irish traditions. It is a necessary means whereby we can reduce prejudice and misunderstandings between us and replace them with trust and confidence. Partnership is not an end in itself. It is an artificial form of government but we have a totally artificial situation which requires, in the short term, artificial means. Partnership is not, as I say, an end in itself. It is a means whereby the people can grow together and replace distrust and hatred with confidence and trust.

Similarly, it is foolish to suggest partnership should be confined to only one part of Ireland. It is also necessary that a similar trust is built between both parts of Ireland. The events of the past twelve months have underlined even more clearly than ever before the fact that the British government alone cannot resolve the crisis in Northern Ireland but that it is a joint responsibility of the British and Irish governments. They should take that joint responsibility now and declare themselves committed to eradicating violence in Ireland forever. They should announce that there are no longer any unconditional guarantees for anyone in this situation, only an objective which would achieve guarantees for everyone and that their objective would be produced by achieving agreed means of living together. The first step in such an agreed means might be a partnership administration in Northern Ireland, agreed among the representatives of Northern Ireland. A further step would then be the creation of machinery, established in friendship, which would examine the differences between the people of Ireland and between Ireland and Britain and create the process which would eliminate, in time, these differences and allow the people to grow in harmony and peace [...] The people of the North must negotiate with the people of the Republic, through their representatives, arrangements whereby the peoples of Ireland can live together in harmony and peace.[20]

Policing

Regarding the highly sensitive issue of policing and the SDLP's position on support for the security forces, Hume presented a very detailed paper to the conference. In it he stressed the effects on law and order resulting from the absence of consensus on the status and governing institutions of Northern Ireland, and why such a consensus was a fundamental requirement to having that situation reversed:

> In Northern Ireland there has always been an absence of political consensus, thereby leaving the state unsupported by a large section of its citizens, who have in turn no identification with those acting on behalf of the state. This vacuum in consensus, support and identity has had disastrous consequences in the field of law and order as can be seen from an examination of that fact.
>
> Because of the situation, extreme powers have to be given to the police and army, allowing them unlimited powers of search and arrest. The exercise of these extreme powers worsens the position and after each incident the degree of rejection increases. There have in eight years in Northern Ireland been some 20,000 arrests and some 300,000 searches [...] These arrests do not account for those held for less than twenty-four hours which are known to be very extensive.
>
> In a normal state an arrested citizen can have immediate access to a solicitor, can only be held for 40 hours without a charge and, generally, if arrested the police are in possession of evidence connecting the citizen with some crime. In Northern Ireland [...] [t]he arrested person may firstly be totally innocent and simply held for the purpose of gathering general information about his or her area. They are not brought to a police station but to an interrogation centre which is equipped with various interrogation devices and staffed with interrogation officers, many of whom have been shown to have committed grave acts of violence against arrested people [...] During the period of internment some 2,000 persons were held for up to four years without having any trial or charge [...] The suffering of those arrested does

<hr />

20 Statement at opening of secretary of state's conference, 8 Jan. 1981, Linen Hall Library, P1045.

not end with detention and deprivation. Many of them have been ill-treated and tortured, as found by the European Court, Amnesty International and the Bennett Inquiry.[21] There have been suicides and attempted suicides by those held. Police surgeons have reacted strongly against what has been done to persons held and have even asked to be removed from their post; 1,521 allegations of ill-treatment or torture have been made over the past four years […] These complaints go back over the ten-year period and have resulted in upwards of £2 million pounds being paid in compensation […]

The lack of community involvement in the enforcement of law and order means that witnesses are not prepared to come forward and testify in court. As a result the police are driven to get confessions as a means of supporting their charges […]

Finally, lack of political consensus leads to an unstable society, a one-sided security force, and a tendency for members of that force to identify with the section of the community that supports them to the extent of even becoming involved in its illegal activities […] The clear lesson is that the whole question of law and order is dependent upon political consensus giving rise to support for the organs of the state and an identity with those enforcing the laws of the state; that consensus in Northern Ireland can only be brought about by a whole-hearted and equal involvement of all the people in governing the area. The bringing about of that involvement is the responsibility of the British government. Until that responsibility is accepted, the terrifying situation in Northern Ireland will continue and worsen, with the vicious circle of lack of consent and identification giving rise to more extreme law-and-order measures, which, in turn, reduce the consent and identification.[22]

Defending his position on the guarantee

The emphasis Hume continued to place on the British guarantee inevitably attracted scrutiny from many quarters. This included an interview with two academics, Seamus Deane and Barre Fitzpatrick, which was published in the journal *The Crane Bag*. Hume was challenged that he was asking too much of the unionists, for whom the guarantee was seen as a protection, without which they would have no option but to fight:

John Hume: But the people who are doing the fighting – the Protestant paramilitaries – are in effect themselves asking for the withdrawal of the guarantee in their proposals for an independent Ulster.

21 The Bennett Inquiry (1978) was into police interrogation procedures in Northern Ireland.
22 SDLP submission to the secretary of state's conference, 30 Jan. 1980; copy in editor's possession.

The question of the guarantee must be put in context. Unionists ran the North for sixty years and it has led to the present situation. I think that is sufficient commentary on unionism.

The British have insisted that any future form of government here would have to be based on partnership. This is really the minimum position for non-unionists in the North. Yet the unionists will not have that either. So on the one hand they want the guarantee but on the other hand they won't accept it when the UK says this is how this part of the UK is to be run.

So to say that withdrawal of the guarantee is asking too much of the unionists – my answer to that is to ask what are the unionists going to give?

I believe that the guarantee has in fact trapped the Unionist Party. They suffer from the siege mentality, and while they have the guarantee they will never engage in any dialogue with the rest of the Irish community. Therefore it acts as a blockade to dialogue interaction.

Seamus Deane: Why do you think that Britain is so insistent on underwriting a unionist position which, as you point out, has sixty years of failure to look back on?

John Hume: Because they have been persuaded by the very arguments which you have just cited; that to do otherwise would cause trouble. I think that they were genuinely afraid of that. I don't think there is any British interest, strategic or otherwise, in remaining in Ireland anymore. Thatcher has said so recently. The only reason they are here is because the unionists want them to stay and they have said that they will not change the status quo without the consent of the people of Northern Ireland.

Now we have started to reply that the consent of the British should be considered as well as that of the unionists, and to ask if there is any price to that British consent. The British have been very honourable in upholding the guarantee – they're now paying up to £1,200 million a year for it, and maintaining up to 20,000 troops; they have bent the law to the point where it is not recognizable as such, and they have been brought before the European Court of Human Rights.

The opponents of the guarantee want the British to withdraw tomorrow morning – I would not agree with that, as it would create a dangerous vacuum. But what the British should say is that there is now no longer any unilateral guarantee for anyone.[23]

Following the secretary of state's conference the British government published a discussion document that suggested Hume's arguments were gaining attention. He acknowledged as much, saying:

23 Seamus Deane, 'Interview with John Hume', *The Crane Bag*, 4:2 (1980).

that institutions of government must have the consent of the minority, along with the rejection of [...] majority rule. I note very clearly that the document states very clearly and firmly that a unique relationship exists between Britain, Northern Ireland and the Republic and that the furtherance of peace and reconciliation can be brought forward in developing such relationships [...] On that basis my party is quite happy to engage in further discussion.[24]

Haughey-Thatcher dialogue

While it would take several more years before significant progress would be made on an inter-party basis, at the close of 1980 Hume was able to reflect that important first steps had been taken, not least because he believed the SDLP approach in the Atkins' talks had prevented the return of unionist majority rule while at the same time witnessing the growing importance of the Irish government's role. Furthermore, as indicated in the discussion document following Secretary of State Atkins' talks, and in meetings between Mrs Thatcher and Taoiseach Charles Haughey, the wider Irish-British context Hume had been emphasizing was being strengthened. Reviewing his first year as party leader, Hume was quietly optimistic that political developments were moving in the right direction:

> In terms of the SDLP our main success has been a negative one, one of prevention. I don't think there's much doubt that at the start of the year the British believed they could restore some form of majority rule and that there would be acquiescence in that. They toyed with the idea of an administration built around Ian Paisley. I believe the SDLP's performance at the Atkins conference and in other private chats, including my own discussions with Margaret Thatcher, put paid to that particular idea.
>
> I said from the start that we were treating the Atkins conference as the first step in a process of discussion, not as an end in itself. I said the process would be an ever-widening one. That's exactly the way it has gone. We got the original terms of reference widened. We got a dual conference going, one where we are able to put forward views on a whole range of matters. Then the process developed further with the involvement of the Irish government. The British government began by saying that it was none of the business of the Irish government, but now two meetings have taken place between the two prime ministers. The key point is that now the two governments are institutionalizing these meetings, something which has never happened before.[25]

24 *Irish Times*, 3 July 1980. 25 Ibid., interview with David McKittrick, 31 Dec. 1980.

In an address to the American Council on Foreign Relations he reiterated his conviction that institutions reflecting Irish-British relationships were needed to strengthen those relationships:

> The British government has again accepted the principle, after having abandoned it for several years, that the government of the Republic must be a joint partner in the search for a solution in Northern Ireland.
>
> The need to give institutional expression to the relationship as part of any process leading to a solution could not only give assurance to the majority that their basic interests were not in any way threatened but also open the way to a statement of the relationships within Ireland itself leading to the lasting peace and stability that is everyone's wish.
>
> No one believes that there is any instant action that would give immediate resolution to the conflict within Ireland. But the summit in Dublin [between Thatcher and Haughey in December 1980] has created a framework within which a progressive process towards a solution could begin – a solution which would at once recognize the unity and diversity of the people of Ireland.[26]

Unfortunately, the crisis caused by two hunger strikes undertaken by paramilitaries in the Maze prison in 1980–1, along with the distraction of the UK government from Irish affairs caused by the 1982 Argentine invasion of the Falklands, intervened before the progress that Hume was hoping for could be developed.

SDLP – 10 years old

The SDLP had marked its tenth birthday in August 1980, and Hume paid tribute to its members, saying that:

> It was an occasion to salute the dedication and self-sacrifice of all those members who have stuck doggedly and determinedly in the often thankless task of working for a peaceful approach to the creation of a just peace in Ireland and to thank all of those who have made a contribution to our party in any way in the past ten years.
>
> Political parties in a normal society survive by being in office or have the prospect of being in office. This has not been so here. To keep a political party in existence in such circumstances, with limited financial resources against the background of the worst violence our country has ever seen, and against the background of splinter groups and individualism, has been no mean achieve-

ment. It is a tribute to the self-sacrifice of many people. It has been a major public service.

The SDLP has survived a turbulent decade as a strong and democratic instrument. It is our hope that in the next decade we shall move into calmer waters and that we will play a major role in fashioning a new society free from fear of violence, injustice and inequality. It is no mean task. Politics is the only way to peace in our divided society. The alternative is conflict.[27]

27 Ibid., 21 Aug. 1980.

1981-4

The hunger strikes mounted by PIRA and INLA prisoners in the Maze prison posed a considerable challenge to the SDLP and, in particular, to John Hume. The strikes were declared in protest against prison regulations on issues such as visiting arrangements, clothing and recreation, and in support of special treatment for what these organizations termed 'political' prisoners. While Hume was able to influence steps towards resolving the first hunger strike, from October to December 1980, he was essentially sidelined from any role in helping to resolve the second, which lasted from March until early October 1981. It was during the second strike that ten prisoners died, the first being Bobby Sands, who had been elected MP in a by-election for the constituency of Fermanagh-South Tyrone in April, a month before he died. The SDLP did not contest that election, nor, despite considerable pressure to do so, did the party contest the by-election to elect Sands' successor. Both decisions resulted in the party being heavily criticized from within its own ranks, as well as from without.

When the first strike was declared, Hume warned about the danger of community conflict inherent in the British government's blunt refusal to concede to the prisoners' demands, especially to wear their own clothing, a right upheld in most Western European democracies. Hume claimed that:

> the gravity of the situation should not be underestimated and warned that unless the issue was resolved satisfactorily there would be an escalation of sectarian tension and street confrontation on a scale that we have not seen for years [...] [and said he] would regard allowing prisoners in Northern jails to wear their own clothes 'as a progressive step' and [...] that the SDLP had lobbied British government ministers to this end.
>
> Referring to the British government's concession last week on civilian clothing, Mr Hume claimed that whether deliberately confusing or not, it had succeeded only in antagonizing one section of the community and causing deep distress in the other, giving rise to a strong heightening of tension.[1]

1 *Irish Times*, 31 Oct. 1980.

After Sands' death Hume warned again of the danger of widespread conflict and, while regretting his death and the pain it had caused his family, he condemned the PIRA and the British government for not preventing that outcome:

> Leadership and discipline are qualities needed in the aftermath of Bobby Sands' death if further violence and suffering are to be avoided.
>
> I regret the death of Bobby Sands particularly because it was so unnecessary and could have been avoided. I have expressed my sympathy with the family who must have undergone insufferable agony throughout the past number of weeks and who, together with the families of the other 2,000-odd victims, are the only ones who understand the full price people are paying for the continuing conflict in Northern Ireland.
>
> I praise the family for the dignity they have shown in the face of what must have been intolerable personal pressure. I have said that the death of Bobby Sands could have been avoided. The British government wanted Bobby Sands to die or to surrender. They could have avoided this outcome with greater flexibility and more sensitivity at various stages of the H-Block dispute.
>
> The Provisional IRA wanted Bobby Sands to have a victory or to die. To have given up his fast without a victory would have meant a humiliating defeat for them, so all the pressures from the organization of which he chose to be a member were to give up his life.
>
> The unionists wanted Mr Sands to die.[2]

Later, when the second hunger strike crisis had reached its peak with the deaths of several more prisoners, Hume continued to urge a resolution through dialogue with the prisoners. As well as criticizing the British government for not engaging in such a dialogue, Hume was highly critical of the approach adopted by prisoners' support groups, and their paramilitary backers. He said:

> the government should talk to the prisoners but [he] had detected no movement. The government's position was that it would not negotiate under duress. Mr Hume said that the SDLP's position was fundamentally different to that of the National H-Block Committee and its constituent paramilitary organizations.
>
> The Provisional IRA and the INLA were engaged in a 'military and violent campaign in which lives of human beings, whether it be the victims of their campaigns, or of their members, are considered by them to be justifiably expendable in pursuit of their political objectives.

2 Ibid., 5 May 1981.

The attitude of the SDLP towards the prison problem was strictly humanitarian.

The problem was no longer merely one of prison conditions because of its effects on the community, North and South. And it was a psychological problem in that the mentality of the prisoners in the Maze is now clearly far removed from the outside world. These young men are starving themselves to death in solidarity with those who have gone before them as much as anything else.

Even the National H-Block Committee and its paramilitary groupings must recognize that organizations which show such scant regard for the basic human right to life have little credibility when mounting a campaign for prisoners' rights and that action by them to end the paramilitary campaign would be a major step in creating the atmosphere to make British government movement on the hunger-strike inevitable.[3]

After the hunger strikes had ended in October 1981, Hume reflected on their effects in his SDLP conference address a month later, saying:

For many ordinary people here, the experience of human life last year became an extended nightmare, coloured by despair for the future and by private and community fear. We who lived through the year know this to be no exaggeration. Thank God, the worst horror that loomed over our lives has now retreated. The damage, the scars, the toll on hope are still glaringly visible. Those brave people deserve our thanks who tried and tried and finally succeeded in turning the tide of misery which had been deliberately unleashed on us at the orders of men of chilling malevolence and which might earlier have been stemmed by a more vigorous and determined government.[4]

European assistance

Despite the ongoing political stalemate and the tragedy of the hunger strikes, Hume continued to campaign for the kind of investment in the North that he had been advocating from the moment of his election to the European parliament. He welcomed the publication in May 1981 of the Martin Report, which addressed the economic and social needs of Northern Ireland. Having highlighted in statistical terms the levels of unemployment and of deprivation experienced in the North, he stated in an address to the parliament:

[W]hat I want to get across to this parliament this evening is the very difficult economic and social background which we as politicians engaged in trying to

3 Ibid., 15 Aug. 1981.   4 Address to the SDLP's annual conference, 1981.

find a political solution to the overall problem of Northern Ireland must work against. It is a social and economic background which is heartbreaking, saps hope and deprives people, especially young people, of their rightful expectation of growing up in a society which will offer them the opportunity of fulfilment. I am personally convinced that the search for peace in Northern Ireland is intimately linked with the winning of better living and working conditions.

Violence has cost us jobs as well as lives, but no one can be asked to build a peaceful political system on the ruins of a shattered economy. It is here in the economic and social sphere that the European institutions have a special role and a special responsibility given to them in the treaties in the inspiring words: 'To create by establishing an economic community, the basis for a broader and deeper community among peoples long divided by bloody conflicts.'

If there is idealism in this Community and if there is a human face, then here is an area which is troubled today and which this Community can step in and help.

The three Northern Ireland members of this parliament – and let us not disguise the fact that we have deep and indeed bitterly divided views on the political situation in Northern Ireland – today make common cause in this parliament. Today we speak with one voice on the issue of economic and social deprivation in Northern Ireland. We appeal to this parliament and to the institutions of this Community for solidarity and for practical help. We appeal to you in the name of the common concerns for the future of all our people in Northern Ireland [...]

A number of detailed suggestions for economic development are made in the report. My two colleagues from Northern Ireland, My Taylor and Mr Paisley, have for their part made a number of extremely valid proposals and suggestions and we together call on the commission to consider these ideas and we intend to develop our thinking and proposals in the month ahead. The approach we are urging to regional policy in relation to Northern Ireland is, in fact, the approach urged by the commission itself and fully supported by this parliament in our advocacy of regional development programmes. We wanted, in other words, to be taken seriously for a change, because for us it is literally and factually a matter of life and death.[5]

Noteworthy in Hume's contribution was his tribute to his two Northern Ireland unionist colleagues, Ian Paisley and John Taylor, and to the manner in which all three had united in advancing the economic and social case – an example

5 European Parliament, *Debates*, 14 June 1981.

of what Hume wanted to see in whatever institutions might be established in Northern Ireland. In his SDLP conference address in November 1981, Hume also reviewed his efforts to secure European investment in social and economic initiatives:

> In spite of its apparent bleakness the year was productive. On the economic front there were two positive and major developments, both resulting from SDLP initiatives. The decision of the European parliament to ask the commission to allocate special assistance to Northern Ireland has resulted in an initial response comprising approximately £16 million for housing in Belfast. This is but a first instalment, and will be built on. The EEC Small Farm Plan worth £80 million, another SDLP policy initiative won by a determined campaign, offers some hope for what has been a devastating year for our small farmers [...]
>
> As a party we have been at the forefront in the fight for economic survival; we must stay there. In the only areas of achievement of progress in our community, we were in the frontline. We have had the successful fight for the introduction of the Agricultural Programme for the Less Favoured Areas, a programme heavily financed from Brussels. In the European parliament we have secured unanimous support – no mean task – for the recognition of the special needs of Northern Ireland, and already in response to that resolution the European commission is bringing forward special programmes. One direct and immediate consequence will be a substantially increased housing programme in Belfast. This is but a first step. Other programmes are under study by a top-level group set up by President Thorn [of the European commission] to investigate how the EEC can best help Northern Ireland and how it can help co-operation in both parts of Ireland.[6]

Acknowledging unionist-Protestant concerns

In the same conference address, Hume argued that when advocating the Irish-British framework and the need for both governments to work jointly in the search for a solution, he was particularly mindful of unionists' concerns. However, he admitted to being 'depressed at the reaction of unionist leaders', because of their negativity towards his plans, despite the fact that he also stressed that the outcome from any negotiations should be acceptable to both parts of the country, and ratified in referenda, North and South:

> The fact is that the Anglo-Irish strategy in its original SDLP conception was designed primarily, not to further SDLP priorities, but to accommodate, to

6 Address to the SDLP's annual conference, 1981.

an extent which some would view as a gratuitous excess, the fears and anxieties expressed by those very unionist politicians of whom I despair. The purpose of the concept was to meet – comprehensively and transparently – all the unionist objections to any dialogue with their neighbours in Ireland. The hysterical leapfrogging of Paisley and Molyneaux, as so often [is the case], prompts one to despair. In this case I hesitate, hoping that the reality – the reality that this policy was basically designed to help them even more so than us – will somehow penetrate some of that granite resistance to reality behind which they collectively cower. I continue to hope […] that one or more of them might discover the wit and the courage to actually say so. Were it not so desperately serious, the prospect of this Gadarene herd racing each other headlong once again over the edge of the real world at the very moment they are handed all the reassurances they had bayed so long for, would be a fine piece of loyalist vaudeville. Alas what we are witnessing on the Northern Ireland stage is another act in a long and repetitive tragedy. It is expressed in slogans of 'no surrender', 'not an inch'. For our part, we abjure any solution in which there would be winners and losers […] So you [unionists] should face reality with us and let us together be grateful that we have an opportunity to do so, before catastrophe overwhelms us all. All we demand is that you and your leaders sit down and negotiate our future with us and the British and Irish governments. For our part we would insist that such talks would have to be ratified in two separate referenda, one in the North, the other in the South […] The principle of consent will be truly respected. I know that many of you do not fully grasp my words. I know that you do not realize that when we say we are proposing an 'agreed Ireland', we mean those words absolutely literally. We mean an 'agreed Ireland' which you would decisively help to shape. I ask you to reflect on our words because they do offer us the prospect of a future together within the limits of what is really possible.[7]

Hume used another opportunity to press this argument when a series of Lenten lectures was organized by an inter-church group, and leading politicians were invited to outline their way forward for Northern Ireland. Hume began by highlighting the difficulty of trying, simultaneously, to reach both sides of the community and to persuade each side to re-examine old attitudes and approaches. He illustrated the difficulty by pointing to the walls being built in Belfast to separate local communities:

It is difficult, sometimes impossible, to bring to each side the dilemma felt by the other. Yet we know that until our leaders and our people manage that

7 Ibid.

breakthrough, we will not make progress in Northern Ireland […] Could we agree that we have all run into a brick wall? I mean this literally not metaphorically. A brick wall is, during these days, being built across Belfast separating the two sides of our community from each other, confirming for ourselves and for the entire world the conviction of the British and our own worst fears that our differences may be insurmountable. Yet the wall is even more significant symbolically than physically. It is no more than a vivid expression – sickening in its bricks-and-mortar finality – of the huge unscaled earthwork that marches all through this community, through every street of Belfast, down every country lane through the churches I am addressing these successive evenings and which looms over the hearts and minds of every single man, woman, boy and girl in Northern Ireland, whether Protestant or Catholic, unionist or nationalist. The fact that a physical wall is being built is no more than a tangible confirmation of what we all have known for years but have not the courage to acknowledge: that we are getting nowhere, that we have indeed run into a brick wall, that we must all sit down and reflect and decide how we can first see over that wall and then unbuild it brick by brick. That wall is a living indictment of everyone in Christian Ireland. It is a living challenge to the failure of past approaches to our problem that has led us to that wall. The particular difficulty about this community, the problem that differentiates it from other communities in crisis, even communities that run into a brick wall, is that we are not all confronted by the wall together; here each side has run into its own side of the wall. It is a challenge to re-examine our past approaches for if they have led us to this, then surely the least we can do is re-examine them.

Take the Protestant tradition. It is an old and honourable tradition in this island. It has produced great people: Swift and Goldsmith will forever exemplify their talent; Grattan and Burke their altruism; and the American War of Independence, the American constitution and as many as eleven American presidents their capacity and their love of liberty. It is moreover that tradition which historically played the first and leading role in propounding libertarian values in Ireland.

Irish Protestants have always sought to maintain their distinctiveness and I admire and commend them for doing so. Yet it seems to me that they have gone astray and put their own heritage at risk. Only look at the results today: unionism has boasted for generations that it is the protection of the Protestant identity and Protestant values, but in the vitriol and sectarian diatribes of the louder voice of contemporary unionism is there the slightest vestige of the fundamental Protestant values of civil and religious liberty? What has gone wrong? […]

The other tradition, my own, has also failed to grasp the fundamental dimensions of our problems. We have failed to define our concept of unity in terms which could be meaningful and truly unthreatening to the other Irish tradition. Because of this fatal omission – the original sin of the nationalist tradition – our inspiration has by default come to mean and to be understood to mean conquest. Unity and unity by agreement should be, if these words have any meaning, synonymous. This must mean the abjuring of conquest and triumphalism. Our failure in this matter – the result of misconception, weakness and illusion – has itself encouraged an extremism which perverts all the higher principles of our tradition. Those who claim the right to kill and the right to die in the name of what they conceive to be Irish unity subvert not only the hope and meaning of unity but the integrity of their own tradition [...]

Northern Ireland today represents unfinished business in the ancient conflict between our two islands. It represents the residual area of failure of the peoples of the two islands to work out their interlocking relationships in a satisfactory way. The problems, resolved elsewhere, have been pushed into this corner of Ireland where, it was hoped, they would be forgotten. The people of Northern Ireland, all of them, have been the victims [...]

I am encouraged by the commitment of the British and Irish governments to construct a framework whose objective is to accommodate a more positive relationship between our two peoples. Within that framework it is my hope that we can build a more positive, stable and lasting relationship among the people of this island. We can have a form of Ireland with a new relationship with Britain that will protect the vital interests of our major traditions. If we have the will to achieve it. Better to build such a framework than a wall in Belfast.[8]

That same month, Hume and Harold McCusker, Ulster Unionist Party MP for Armagh, faced each other on a panel at a conference in Boston. Hume found himself again under considerable pressure because of his belief that, in effect, the British guarantee of no constitutional change without the consent of a majority in Northern Ireland was a barrier to political progress and should be removed. McCusker claimed that if it were ever conceded, the demand would amount to unionists being coerced into a united Ireland. Hume in response stressed that he was not asking that anyone be coerced. Rather he argued that the guarantee had trapped unionists into communal solidarity and had prevented dialogue with nationalists. Tracing the origin of the guarantee Hume argued that the border between North and South had:

8 John Hume, 'The way forward', address in St Anne's Cathedral and Benburb Priory, Mar. 1982. Copy in editor's possession.

created a deliberate majority based on sectarianism and, from the very beginning, I believe that the Protestant population was trapped by that into
sectarian solidarity as a means of maintaining that [majority]. Any politician
who moved out of that solidarity position was immediately regarded as selling
the pass. That is the meaning of 'not an inch'.

And therefore that effectively meant that there was no dialogue with the
minority. Rather it was that the minority was treated as the enemy, and the
history of Northern Ireland shows that successive unionist governments
treated the minority as infiltrators, as the enemy, as people not to be trusted,
as people to be deprived of electoral rights, of housing and of jobs. [...]

Why is it that the only part of the world where it is wrong that we suggest
that people unite is Ireland? And when I talk about unity I'm not talking
about coercion. What I am talking about is sitting down and agreeing how 5
million people in an island that you could put into a corner of Long Island
agree structures to protect what we want to protect. What do the Protestant
people want to protect? Is it their Protestantism or their Britishness, or both?
If it is then we can build structures to protect them. What does the Catholic
population want to protect? Is it their Irishness, their Catholicism, or what?
If it is, then we can build structures to protect them. What we have to agree
is what we have to protect [...]

I am not asking for anyone to be coerced because I don't believe that you
can solve problems by coercing people. What I am saying is that the arrangements we have had up to now have, to put it very mildly, been a failure and
that it's not unreasonable to ask for new structures which will protect what
people want to protect. In asking for new structures I'm asking that they be
worked out by agreement between the different people involved, with Britain
playing a role in bringing about such an agreement. I have suggested what I
would like to see coming out at the end [a form of confederal Ireland] but I
think there might be other suggestions people might like to make and I would
be open to them. All I would like to ask is that [...] each section's basic
identity – what they want to protect – is protected [...]

My point about the guarantee was not a point about sovereignty. Northern
Ireland was deliberately created on a sectarian headcount. You then, having
created a Protestant majority, say to them, 'You can stay linked to us as long
as you have a majority.' I contend that implicit in that is that you are forcing
the Protestant population into sectarian solidarity and you're building sectarianism into the foundations of Northern Ireland and I would submit that
there is sixty years of evidence of elections to prove that every election is a
sectarian headcount. I am further saying that it prevents dialogue. It prevents
any leadership emerging on the unionist side which looks to an accommodation of any description, including the simple sharing of administrative power

in Northern Ireland […] That approach by Britain is a serious obstacle to dialogue […] That is at the heart of the matter.[9]

Two months later the SDLP organized a major conference to mark the bicentenary of what was known in Irish history as 'Grattan's parliament'. Henry Grattan was a member of the Irish parliament in the late eighteenth century when membership was exclusive to men of the established church. He became a champion of legislation to open the parliament to those of other churches, including Roman Catholics. He also favoured the removal of legal restrictions on Catholics and others that had prevented them holding civic offices and from entering, or advancing, in some of the professions. Entitled 'Options for a new Ireland', the conference was addressed by speakers from a variety of traditions. In his address, John Hume again expressed his regard for the Protestant tradition in Ireland:

> The history of Ireland has been for centuries bleak and miserable. By and large those events which our extremists threaten never to allow us to forget do little good in being remembered. Joyce was right to describe Irish history as a nightmare from which he wished to awaken.
>
> Yet the nightmare which continues today, for all the people of Northern Ireland, has occasionally been relieved by an illumination of hope and light sufficient to recharge the batteries of the people with that grinding endurance which has sustained so many generations of the Irish of both traditions.
>
> Such a source of hope was Henry Grattan. In fact, for brilliance, for generosity of mind, for passionate commitment and for sheer love of his country he has few, if any, equals in our annals. He was also perhaps one of the wisest, the most farseeing of all our great men. His convictions – the need for equality of treatment for Catholics, the need to oppose both violence and coercion – were formed in his youth at his uncle's house in Celbridge on the banks of the Liffey. Many years later he wrote, 'Along the banks of that river among the bowers of Swift and Vanessa I grew convinced that I was right. Arguments unanswerable came to my mind and what I then proposed confirmed me in determination to persevere.'
>
> On 17 April 1780, he introduced his declaration of rights in the Irish house of commons and successfully resisted a massive campaign of corruption organized by the administration which sought to suborn him and his followers. His comment on those events is worth recording as an illustration of the consistent nature of direct rule and how well Grattan understood its fundamental weakness. 'We were determined to refuse office and our

9 Recorded at the symposium on Northern Ireland, Boston, John F. Kennedy Library, 19 Mar. 1982.

opinion, and a just one, was that office in Ireland was different from office in England. It was not an office held for Ireland but held for an English government, often in collusion with and frequently hostile to Ireland.' How little things change!

The 17 April 1782 was the greatest and happiest moment of his life. His declaration of rights was triumphantly passed. He ended his speech that day with an invocation of the great names of the Irish Protestant tradition of liberty. 'I found Ireland on her knees. I watched over her with an eternal solicitude. I have traced her progress from injuries to arms and from arms to liberty. Spirit of Swift! Spirit of Molyneux! Your genius has prevailed, Ireland is now a nation and in that character I hail her! And bowing in her presence I say *esto perpetua*!' [...]

The rising of 1798 was an event that filled Grattan with despair. Despite his political convictions he nevertheless saw the oppression which followed as a greater evil and he courageously challenged the administration when in the full flush of its brutality against the rebel Catholics and Protestants. He afterwards wrote of these events that 'the government were so abominable, their measures were so violent that no man could sanction them. There was high treason certainly but these were measures that no high treason, that no crimes could warrant. They did not treat the people like Christians, but like dogs' [...]

We were recently all advised that it is better to urge men to live up to their higher principles than to tell them how far they failed to live up to them. I would like to propose Grattan as a model to which we would all – Dublin, London and the leadership of both traditions in the north of Ireland – aspire. He showed us what could be achieved not alone in terms of actual political success, but perhaps most significantly in terms of political generosity. While Tone and Davis, both Protestants, epitomized the republican ideal – the insistence of breaking the connection with Britain – Grattan might serve as a meeting ground for republicans on the one hand and on the other those who like himself esteemed the British connection but longed for liberty for all the people of Ireland, not just one section of the people.

Grattan was of the Protestant tradition, he expressed its deepest convictions – a commitment to civil and religious liberty, to freedom of conscience, to liberty of the individual. The values were underlined and given powerful and emotive expression at one of the great and generous moments in Irish history and in Irish Protestant history in February 1782 when the Irish Volunteers, most of them Protestant, met in the Presbyterian meeting house in Dungannon to resolve 'That we hold the rights of private judgment in matters of religion to be equally sacred in others as in ourselves. And that as Irishmen, as Christians and as Protestants we rejoice in the relaxation of the penal laws against our Roman Catholic fellow subjects' [...]

We need a new and generous vision to abandon the exclusiveness of 'ourselves alone' in which both traditions have indulged. But first of all we need dialogue. That is what this conference is about. It is not about the immediate production of instant solutions – that is impossible. It is about the making of a major contribution in this community to a real debate and discussion on the forms and structures of government in a new Ireland which can satisfy the needs and aspirations of our different traditions within this island [...] Out of that dialogue would emerge again the sort of visions epitomized by Grattan and his contemporaries.[10]

Prior's assembly

As community tensions eased somewhat following the ending of the hunger strikes, prospects for political progress appeared to strengthen, especially given improved Irish-British relations, evidenced in the establishment of the Anglo-Irish Intergovernmental Council and a number of joint studies being undertaken by the two governments on social, economic and cultural issues of mutual interest.[11] Hume had welcomed this development, and in his Lenten addresses had hoped that local dialogue would follow. However, when the new secretary of state, James Prior, published plans for an assembly, he firmly rejected them. Prior proposed holding elections to an assembly, which initially would only be granted consultative powers. Other powers would not be devolved in the absence of cross-community support, and there was no mention of any provisions for North-South arrangements. With cross-community support highly unlikely to receive unionist endorsement, the SDLP declared it would not join the proposed assembly. In detailing the party's opposition, Hume argued that:

> The basic proposal for devolution of power is that the secretary of state be satisfied that it has 'cross-community' support [...] This can be achieved in two ways – (1) agreement of a 70 per cent majority in the proposed assembly; (2) more than 50 per cent in the assembly provided it has 'cross-community' support. But nowhere in the document is 'cross-community' support defined [...] However, given that an administration is formed the need for 70 per cent agreement would cease and all decisions would be subject to simple majority rule.
>
> What then is the position of a minority minister in such an administration if his policy proposals are defeated by a majority in the assembly? Does the administration fall? [...]

10 John Hume, 'A new Ireland', address to the conference 'Options for a new Ireland', 5 June 1982.
11 Both initiatives resulted from meetings between Margaret Thatcher and Charles Haughey.

It is quite clear that Mr Prior's unworkable power-sharing plans are included only to give a gloss of respectability and 'fair-mindedness' to what is the only concrete proposal in the white paper – an election to a powerless assembly, with powerless committees and well-paid chairmen and vice chairmen.

Such a body would be no more than a dangerous talking shop which could be seriously abused by individual political parties for their own ends [...]

The white paper states: 'the difference in identity and aspiration lies at the heart of the problem of Northern Ireland. It cannot be ignored or wished away.' But the white paper then proceeds to ignore it, for there is not a single concrete proposal in the paper based on what it concedes to be 'the heart of the problem'.[12]

Despite this opposition, Prior pushed ahead with his plans for what became known as 'rolling' devolution, the first step towards which was elections to an assembly, scheduled for October 1982. The SDLP had to decide whether to nominate candidates when the party had decided not participate in the proposed assembly. It eventually did so, but instead of attending the assembly, the party decided that it would seek to persuade the main Southern parties to establish what it termed the 'Council for a New Ireland'. The council, according to the SDLP, would be charged with examining the Northern crisis, and with developing a common set of principles, along with proposals for its resolution. If established, the council would, therefore, address Hume's long-articulated belief that parties in favour of Irish unity should spell out that vision, and what it could mean in constitutional, economic and social terms, before entering fresh negotiations with unionists.

At another Boston conference Hume outlined the context and reasons for both SDLP's decisions:

The basis on which that assembly election was called was a statement by the British government of policy that this assembly would be formed and that power would be devolved to it on the basis of cross-community agreement, meaning agreement between both sections of the community. That is basically the same position as the British government expressed in 1974, and in 1976, and in 1980. We have never been opposed to sharing power. Our problem has been finding people with whom to share it. And in '74 we entered a power-sharing agreement and it was destroyed. In '75 we entered the Northern Ireland convention and accepted the terms laid down by the British government, which were that any proposals had to satisfy the test of cross-community agreement – power-sharing. The unionists rejected it. We went into the conference called by the secretary of state, Humphrey Atkins, in 1980, in which he laid down exactly the same terms. The official unionists [UUP] didn't go to the conference they were so opposed to the concept of power-sharing. I did talk […] to Ian Paisley for six months, at the end of which we reached the same impasse. He said there were no circumstances in which he would share power with the SDLP […] Mr Prior then, for the fourth time in a decade, inspired by Brian Mawhinney,[13] proposes another attempt at power-sharing. Now rightly or wrongly, and before it was launched […] the official unionists said they weren't going to share power with the SDLP under this system. Mr Paisley said the same thing […] I believed them, because I had every reason to believe them, with the experience to prove it. I could not credibly ask my electorate to vote again to go in to negotiate something they knew wasn't possible. There was the whole question of polit-ical credibility involved because the people would have said to me, 'Hey John, who are you going to share power with?' Because we were being told clearly and are still being told very clearly […] that there weren't any circumstances […] Rather than being negative what we did, which I think was a sensible and intelligent thing to do, particularly in the circumstances, we asked the question, 'Why are they saying no to us?' And when you ask that question you go right to the heart of the problem. And the reason why they are saying no […] is because they see power-sharing as a Trojan horse leading them into a united Ireland by a back door.

And when you look at the reason why from 1920 to 1972, when you had one-party rule in Northern Ireland, the ruling unionists discriminated against the Catholics, in housing, in jobs, in voting rights – the reason for that was they saw the growth of that minority taking them into a united Ireland against their will. And when you go back beyond that to 1912, home rule, which was under the crown, was 'Rome rule'. They were then against it.

So my view and my party's view was that if you are serious about solving this problem rather than going into an assembly that everyone knew was going to fail, and destroying our credibility as politicians to the benefit of paramilitaries, that we should address this central question because you cannot discuss any movement in Northern Ireland, any change for the union-ists, any concession that they would give to us, without facing the question of Irish unity, if only because of the negative position of theirs that they fear where that was going to lead.[14]

---

13 A Conservative MP who hailed from Northern Ireland and was a keen proponent of Prior's plans.
14 Recorded at the second 'Symposium on Northern Ireland', Boston, 14–15 Mar. 1984; reproduced by kind permission of Professor Catherine Shannon.

The elections proved particularly difficult for the SDLP since the party was asking its supporters to vote against Secretary of State Prior's proposals and, even more challengingly, to vote for a proposal that had not yet been seriously discussed with Southern parties, let alone with the Irish government, which it expected to convene and fund the new council.

Hume's election message spelled out the essential flaws in Prior's proposals as the SDLP had identified them:

> The importance of this election cannot be underestimated. It [the assembly] is a body without power but which can be given power on certain conditions. The basic condition is that power can be returned to Stormont if there is 70 per cent agreement among its members. What is not appreciated is that even if agreement were reached every decision from then onwards would be by simple majority. The SDLP is taking a firm stand in refusing to fall into such a trap. I am asking you to support us in taking that stand. Unionist leaders have already indicated their intention of using this plan to achieve a 70 per cent vote for the various unionist parties and then on that basis seek a return to majority rule. A solid turnout of voters behind the SDLP is the only way of ensuring that this plan does not succeed. In addition the SDLP will use its mandate, given by you, to continue to represents our constituents in their day-to-day problems. More importantly we will use our mandate to be ready to negotiate on your behalf a meaningful solution. Our problems can only be solved if all the conflicting relationships between the peoples of our two islands are on the table for discussion. Such discussion can only take place in an Anglo-Irish framework. The SDLP will be there to represent you in such discussions. The Prior assembly has nothing to offer except the same political party wrangling that has disfigured our politics. I ask you to stand solidly with us on 20 October in pursuit of these objectives. I ask you also to reject unequivocally those who would advocate or use violence to solve our problems. You can do so by using your vote and your veto on 20 October. Veto the Prior plan. Veto violence […]
>
> Following the election the SDLP will propose to the Irish government the setting up of a Council for a New Ireland made up of members of the Dáil and those mandated in this election. The council should have a limited life and have the specific task of examining the obstacles to the creation of a new Ireland, and producing for the first time ever, on behalf of all elected democratic parties in the country who believe in a new Ireland, an agreed blueprint, so that a debate on real alternatives can begin within the Anglo-Irish framework.[15]

15 John Hume, 'Election message', *Social Democrat*, Oct. 1982.

New Ireland Forum

The SDLP won thirteen seats in the assembly elections, but with a much-reduced vote compared to previous elections. More significantly, the elections witnessed the emergence of Sinn Féin into the electoral process – it won five seats. Following the elections, the SDLP began making its approaches to the Irish government and to Southern parties to convince them of the case for the council. Contact with Sinn Féin was ruled out because of that party's association with the PIRA. At the SDLP's annual conference in January 1983, Hume outlined his expectations for the council:

> In proposing the setting up of a Council for a New Ireland where all consti-tutional politicians committed to a new Ireland would together define what we really wish this new republic to be, the SDLP is doing no more than asking the democratic parties of the republic to join with us in challenging the underlying assumption of British and unionist unwillingness to change and unlocking the key to meaningful dialogue with both.
>
> I am convinced that the difficult process of examining the obstacles will force those parties and ourselves to take many harsh and painful decisions about the definition of Irishness, about the economic implications of unity by consent, about church/state relations, about Anglo-Irish relations, decisions that we would ordinarily prefer to avoid and which public opinion in the South ordinarily does not consider. In proposing this decision-making process, the SDLP is primarily concerned to define and secure the rights of those who, often for good historical reasons, take refuge in the embattled past rather than face today's frightening reality. This means that democrats in the South and in the SDLP must find the humility to acknowledge that we have so far failed to conceive of and to define an Irish identity which adequately accommodates all traditions of this island. Our failure – an intellectual and a moral failure – has unwittingly created one of the principal inspirations of violence. Every day young men kill in the name of 'Ireland'. Their acts of murder reinforce that narrow definition of Ireland which they and so many others have unquestioningly inherited, an 'Ireland' defined in narrow sectional and exclusive terms together with a fanatical hatred of Britain, an 'Ireland' which exists only in the minds of those who speak of it and who kill for it and who die for it, but which bears no relation to the real Ireland, with its rich diversity of traditions and culture. We have for too long stressed this essential unity of Ireland but forgotten about its equally essential diversity. It is this failure to marry both and give them institutional expression that has been the failure of successive generations to solve the Irish problem.
>
> There is no inherited wisdom in this matter. Young and old, we must be ready to question our own inherited assumptions about ourselves painfully,

vigorously, comprehensively and with humility. The word 'new' in our goal of 'a new Ireland' must be given unheard of and unquestionable hard substance. It will surprise, unsettle and shock those in the South as well as the North who believe either that this crisis will simply go away or that it can be solved by benign neglect or that it can be solved by violent conquest. This truly new beginning will have to confront the dilemma set out by Louis MacNeice, a great and fiercely honest Northern poet:

> Why should I want to go back
> To you Ireland, my Ireland?
> The blots on the page are so black
> That they cannot be covered with shamrock
> I hate your grandiose airs
> Your sob-stuff, your laugh and your swagger
> Your assumption that everyone cares
> Who is the king of your castle.
> Castles are out of date
> The tide flows round the children's sandy fancy
> Put up what flag you like, it is too late
> To save your soul with bunting.[16]

The Council for a New Ireland will have to do more than confront these impossibilities: it will be called upon to reconcile and harmonize from them and to forge a new, unheard of, generous definition of Irishness, which will include the sense of British identity. It will be called on to cast this definition in the form of concrete proposals and concrete guarantees for an Ireland very different indeed from that of the North or the South today. It will be called on to back up these proposals and guarantees with concrete proposals for action which will give unquestionable evidence of understanding, goodwill and resolute commitment.[17]

During the weeks that followed this address, Hume and his SDLP colleagues lobbied leaders and members of the South's three main political parties, Fianna Fáil, Fine Gael and Labour, seeking their support for these proposals. Eventually the agreement of all three party leaders was secured, and on 30 May the Forum for a New Ireland, the title eventually chosen, convened its opening session. It was the very first occasion on which the leaders of the main parties of the nationalist tradition, North and South, had gathered to address division in Ireland since the

16 This poem is reproduced with the kind permission of David Higham Associates.   17 Address to the SDLP's annual conference, Jan. 1983.

country had been partitioned in 1921. The opening session in Dublin Castle heard addresses from each of the four leaders. Hume's address echoed many of the same issues outlined at his party conference a few months earlier, with an even stronger emphasis on reconciliation:

> The common goal of which I speak is – and has to be – reconciliation, the reconciliation of seemingly irreconcilable problems on this island. Let that reconciliation start today in this room – between ourselves. Goodwill alone – and I know we have with us today the goodwill of the mass of the people of this island – will not suffice. We must apply all the resources of our collective intelligence, imagination, generosity and determination to this great enterprise and be seen to do it. We must mean business and we must be seen to desperately mean business. I believe that the very fact that we are gathered in this room – that the taoiseach and tánaiste suspend for the purposes of this forum their unique prerogatives to propose and to implement, that the leader of the opposition suspends his natural role of critic of government – I believe that the fact that my three colleagues have been prepared to make these unprecedented political sacrifices in a common effort is a tribute to their seriousness and their generosity and is an encouraging augury of success. The vast majority of the people of the North – those whose hopes are fervently with us today and even those who now doubt our intentions – will not fail to see this occasion for the remarkable and, indeed, unique political event it is.
>
> There is a minority in Northern Ireland and a minority even in this state who furiously abhor the work of reconciliation. Theirs is the way of violence. Their message is hatred. Their medium murder, their achievement division and destruction. This common effort of ours to understand, to build a new Ireland, to reconcile is anathema to them. Why, because they suspect and they fear we might succeed. They can only prevail if our enterprise fails. They can achieve their stated aim of armed political domination in this land only if the forces of despair win out, only if the volcano of cruelty that they remorselessly stoke overwhelms us all. Eighty per cent of the people of Ireland are represented in this historic forum today and their clarion message to the men and women of violence is 'Reconciliation yes, destruction no, democracy yes, your fascism never.'
>
> The world is looking at this forum today but there are two particular audiences to whom we must address ourselves: the unionist people of the North and the British people and government. They must fully understand the seriousness of our commitment and the nature of our effort.
>
> The forum is not a nationalist conspiracy, neither is it a nationalist revival mission. It is nothing less than a major effort – an effort unique in our history

and I believe an effort unexampled in divided societies anywhere in the world – to understand the encounter between our own ethos and the ethos of those who live with us on this island but who refuse to share it with us. This is no academic theoretical experiment but an honest effort to confront the real chilling circumstances of today's Ireland in the full context of the real relationship between Ireland and Britain today. This is the most serious effort that has ever been made by Irish political leaders to face reality and the unionists and the British are entitled – indeed they are invited – to judge our work by that measure, but they are not entitled to ignore it, as it would be seriously against their interest to do so.

The heart of this crisis in Ireland is the conviction, the profound and irreducible conviction of the majority of Protestants in the North that their ethos simply could not survive in an Irish political settlement. This conviction, older than King Billy's throne encrusted and gnarled with generations of embattled struggle, is rejected by the rest of us in Ireland equally convinced by our dark past that we could never impose dominance on others, we who have known better than most the misery and sterility of oppression. The British for their part remain, if not fully convinced by these fears of the unionists, at least not persuaded to the contrary. Hence the paralysis of politics, hence the stagnation and the conflict. There are many other important and complex dimensions to the Irish problem, but there to my mind is its core – the belief by the Protestant tradition in this island that its ethos cannot survive in Irish political structures. This should remain the focal point of our deliberations in this forum and the central target of those who wish to join with us in our important task.

The Protestant ethos I am talking about is not merely theological, although it contains principles such as freedom of conscience which are central to that theological heritage. It contains also and perhaps more importantly a strong expression of political allegiance to Britain which we cannot ignore and which we cannot wish away any more than unionists can wish away our deep commitment to Irish unity. This intractable difficulty we must face squarely in this forum. It will not be easy for us to do so. How do we accommodate in a new definition of Irishness these uncomfortable realities? How would we propose to give to unionists an adequate sense of security – physical, religious, political, economic and cultural – in a new Ireland? Are we, the nationalists of Ireland, prepared to pay the painful political and economic price that this will involve? Do we have any idea of what that price will be? I fear many of us either do not or would prefer not to. The work of this forum will forever deprive us of the excuse of either ignorance or distraction […]

As for unionists, it seems to be in their intelligent interest that we be confronted directly in this forum by their objections to an Irish political arrangement on this island without reservation or apology, in private or in public – as they wish – by members of that tradition. Let me say to unionists: 'We commit ourselves to you and your convictions with deep seriousness in our efforts to understand each other so that we solve this crisis with your agreement and your support.' We seek a solution. We do not seek victory [...][18]

The forum then proceeded to take and debate evidence from interested groups and individuals before producing its report in May 1984.

Maiden Westminster speech

In June 1983, Hume had the opportunity to address the UK parliament and to articulate a similar message, when, as the newly elected MP for Foyle, he made his maiden speech:

I have come here to represent a new constituency in the north-west of Ireland. It contains the ancient and historic city of Derry and the town of Strabane. It is a commentary on the politics of the north of Ireland – or the fact that there is a problem there – that never before has someone with either my religious or my political persuasion stood in this house to represent the city of Derry.

I represent an area which has the unenviable distinction of having the highest unemployment rate of any constituency represented in this house, with 38 per cent in Strabane and 28 per cent in Derry. Those are statistics which interact seriously and severely with the political crisis in the north of Ireland, because that same area has borne more than its share of the brunt of the atrocities that have taken place in the north of Ireland over the past decade. It is the interaction of the economic situation with the political situation that requires a great deal of attention if the problems of that part of the world are to be resolved.

People have wondered about the rise in the political strength of extremism in the north of Ireland. There is no greater example of the reasons for extremism in that area than that we now have a generation of young people who were only 4 years old in 1969 and 1970 and have grown up in a society in which they have always seen security forces and violence on the streets, in which they have been continually searched simply because they are young people, and in which, when they reach the age of 18, they have no hope of any employment because they happen to have come of age during the deepest economic crisis for a long time. Therefore, there are resentments, and there

18 New Ireland Forum, *Proceedings*, 30 May 1983.

are sadistic people who play upon those resentments, [who] point to a British soldier and say, 'Get rid of him and all your problems will be solved.' That simplistic message has an appeal to young people, and people such as myself and members of my party who seek to show that the problems are rather more complex have a difficult task.

If the government were to take seriously the economic crisis in the north of Ireland and make a sensible and determined attack on the problems of youth employment, they would also be making a determined attack on the problems of extremism.

The debate is about defence and foreign affairs. In the [Queen's] Gracious Speech there is reference to the major issue between Britain and Ireland – the problems of Northern Ireland. It also happens to be one of the most serious human issues facing the house. Having come here after surviving over a decade on the streets of Northern Ireland, I have to say with some bitterness that I do not see much evidence that there are many hon. members who think that it is an issue of great human concern.

We have been told repeatedly by ministers, secretaries of state and prime ministers, of whatever party, that Northern Ireland is an integral part of the United Kingdom. We are told by the prime minister that we are as British as Finchley.

I should like hon. members to take any part of the United Kingdom over the past decade and to imagine the following things happening: imagine 2,000 people being killed on the streets in Yorkshire, 20,000 people maimed and injured, and £430 million spent on compensation for bomb damage; two new prisons built and a third under construction; the rule of law drastically distorted, with the introduction of imprisonment without trial; senior politicians and policemen murdered; and innocent civilians murdered by the security forces and by paramilitary forces. Imagine a shoot-to-kill policy for people suspected of crime being introduced from time to time instead of their being arrested. Imagine jury courts being disbanded, plastic bullets used on the streets and innocent children being killed. Imagine paramilitary organizations engaging in violence and the type of interrogation methods that led to the British government being found guilty in the European Court of Human Rights being introduced. Imagine hunger strikers dying in prison in Yorkshire and representatives of the paramilitaries being elected to this house to represent Yorkshire.

If those things had happened on what is commonly called the mainland, can anyone tell me that those events would not have been the major issue in the general election campaign? Can anyone persuade me that any speech made since that election would not have referred to that issue? However, the only hon. members who have referred to it were leaders of two parties in Northern Ireland. Nevertheless, we are told that we are as British as Finchley.

Does any hon. member believe that Northern Ireland is as British as Finchley or any other part of what is called the mainland? Do any hon. members honestly believe that in their hearts? If so, where is the evidence of their concern? The truth is that if every hon. member spoke his heart, he would say that he has psychologically withdrawn from Northern Ireland. The truth is that Britain has psychologically withdrawn from Northern Ireland. Britain and Northern Ireland would be healthier places if that psychological reality were translated into political reality.

The extent of the problem in Northern Ireland today can be summed up by the desperate indictment of a brick wall that has been built between two sections of the community in Belfast to keep them apart and to protect them from each other. That is happening in what is described as a part of the United Kingdom.

That wall is an indictment of anyone who has governed Northern Ireland in the past fourteen years. It is also an indictment of every political party in Northern Ireland. It is an indictment of everyone who has any part to play in the problem. It is an indictment of the unionist tradition, the nationalist tradition and the British who govern from this house. It is an indictment, but it is also a challenge because the only truth that has emerged out of all the suffering of the past decade is that all our policies have led us to that wall in Belfast. The real challenge is to re-examine urgently our traditional approaches to a solution.

Hon. members who represent the loyalist tradition have a lot of thinking to do. Their consistent stance on Northern Ireland has been to protect the integrity of the tradition in an island in which they form a minority. I have no quarrel with that objective. Any country is richer for diversity. I quarrel with the methods of protecting the integrity. Put crudely, that method dictates, 'We must hold all power in our own hands.' That is precisely what has been said. It is a violent attitude. It is an attitude which demands the exclusive exercise of power. The leaders of that tradition have consistently maintained that view, but it invites violence. It is not possible permanently to exclude an entire section of the population from any say in the decision-making process.

The nationalist tradition has also taken a rather simplistic approach. Its argument has often been presented in emotional and romantic terms. Its simplistic definition of Irishness is extremely sectional. It is based substantially on two powerful strands of the Irish tradition – the Gaelic and Catholic – to the exclusion of the Protestant. That narrow definition makes the Protestant tradition feel excluded from that notion of Irishness. In its more extreme form, it is thought right not only to die, but to kill, for that version of Ireland. In those circumstances, we can understand what contribution my tradition has made to the deepening of Irish divisions.

When one considers the streets of Belfast and examines the performance of the organization that represents itself as the ultimate in Irish patriotism – the Provisional IRA – and one considers the bitterness that it has created by its campaign of destruction and killing, one can see how much rethinking and examination we must do if we are to bring about a settlement of the Irish problem and bring forward a definition of Irishness which is inclusive, not exclusive.

The third element is the British government and the house [of commons]. As matters stand, it now has all the power over Northern Ireland. Examination of history reveals one consistent policy. Moreover, it is the only policy that I have heard enunciated here – that Northern Ireland shall remain part of the United Kingdom as long as a majority so wish. On the face of it, that seems to be a democratic statement and guarantee. However, if one looks behind that, one sees that the majority that is being guaranteed was created artificially by a sectarian headcount. When one tells the majority that it can protect itself only by remaining in majority, one invites it to maintain sectarian solidarity as the only means of protection. Therefore, one makes sectarianism the motive force of politics. Northern Ireland has sixty years of elections to demonstrate that that is precisely what has happened.

If we are to break the sectarian mould and the divisions, we must recognize that they cannot continue forever. We cannot deny that 5 million people in a Europe which twice this century has slaughtered its people by the millions could find the wisdom and foresight to say, 'Let us build structures whereby we can grow together at our own speed.' What is wrong with asking for that for our small island of 5 million people? What is wrong with asking to be able to build structures whereby the different traditions can live in peace, harmony and unity in a new relationship with Britain? What is wrong with the government adopting that as a policy objective? That policy was stated by no less a person than Sir Winston Churchill who, on 7 July 1922, in a private letter to Michael Collins, wrote: 'Meanwhile, in the intervals of grappling with revolts and revolution, I think that you should think over in your mind what would be the greatest offer the South could make for Northern co-operation. Of course, from the imperial point of view, there is nothing we should like better than to see the North and the South join hands in an all-Ireland assembly without prejudice to the existing rights of Irishmen.' Such ideas could be vehemently denied in many quarters at the moment, but events in the history of nations sometimes move very quickly. They often move quickly when there is a strong government in power who have the courage to grasp the nettle and face up to reality. Ending divisions in Ireland has evaded statesmen for centuries. Ending the divisions requires strength and leadership. It is not asking a great deal of the government to adopt as policy the statement that Sir Winston Churchill made on 7 July 1922.[19]

European lobbying

With colleagues to deal with the day-to-day business of the forum, Hume continued his lobbying in the European parliament, where he supported the issues he had identified in his election manifesto. The report on promoting lesser-used languages allowed him the opportunity to stress one of those issues – the importance of valuing Europe's rich cultural and linguistic diversity:

> the importance of the issue of minority and lesser-spoken languages in the European Community has been well demonstrated by the reaction in this parliament itself, and by the amount of support from the different groups, and the different nationalities in this directly elected parliament for the protection and the development of minority cultures and languages in the European Community. It is also, of course, an important issue because, in fact, it affects directly some 30 million people in the European Community whose mother tongue is not the dominant tongue in the country in which they live.
>
> It is also important because of the rich diversity of cultures which exist in the European Community and the need to protect and develop such diversity. Since the original resolutions were put in this parliament, some modest progress has been made. We have had a budget heading opened by the commission, which is very welcome, but is only a small beginning. Outside of this parliament, in reaction to the actions taken by the parliament there has also been an important development in that the representatives of the different lesser-spoken languages in the Community have come together to form a European Bureau of Lesser-Spoken Languages. This is a development which those of us who have been promoting this issue in this parliament ought to welcome. And indeed the commission itself should welcome and take note of the setting up, on a voluntary basis, of a European Bureau for Lesser-Spoken Languages. Indeed it is a body which the commission might well use as a sounding board for the development of its policies and projects on lesser-spoken languages. It should consult them, and also consider ways in which it can help that body, both financially and otherwise, to be more effective in its co-ordinating role.
>
> I think it is also in the interests of the commission and the Community in general to recognize that it is from the areas where there are strong and

19 House of Commons, *Debates*, 28 June 1983

powerful minorities who feel threatened that at times has come the most energetic opposition to the whole idea of a European Community, largely because they feel that the creation of this Community threatens further their identity and very existence – and this particularly at a time when they are suffering an immense onslaught from the mass consumer culture [...] If this Community can demonstrate, as is its duty, that the rich diversity of which exists in the European Community, particularly among those people who speak what we describe as the lesser-spoken languages, is going to be not only protected but helped to flourish within the European Community, then we can also harness the enormous energies that those minority groups generate in support of the European ideal, rather than the opposition which, because of justifiable fears, has come from those quarters in the past [...][20]

Violence and economy

The unrelenting campaign of violence, particularly the PIRA campaign, continued to fill Hume with horror. Alongside its human tragedies, he was especially concerned with the effects the campaign continued to have on social and economic investment to support areas of high unemployment:

John Hume mounted a strong attack on the Provisional IRA and Sinn Féin accusing them of supporting a military campaign aimed at destroying jobs and discouraging foreign investment in Northern Ireland. Mr Hume said that the issue of youth unemployment had been seriously exploited by Sinn Féin in an attempt to recruit young people into their campaign.

He listed eleven foreign companies which had left Northern Ireland during the present Tory administration and said that Mrs Thatcher's basic strategy to make existing industry lean and cut off the fat was not designed for an economy like Northern Ireland because she seems to have forgotten that we already were a skeleton here.

The Provos have of course exploited unemployment and have themselves made a major contribution to the unemployment situation in Northern Ireland. Their spokesmen have openly admitted that they support a campaign to destroy the economy, that they support a campaign of killing industrialists to keep out foreign investment.

He said that of the £427 million paid out in compensation since the start of the Troubles in 1968, £338 million was because of industrial and commercial damage caused by paramilitary bombing. Of that £213 million had been incurred in areas like North and West Belfast, Enniskillen, Dungannon, Derry, Newry and Strabane.

20 European Parliament, *Debates*, 10 Feb. 1983.

These, of course, are areas where the Provisionals have been exploiting the resentment against unemployment and among young people in particular. They also happen to be the areas that under the previous unionist regime were singled out for special strangulation […]

Accusing the Provisionals of waging a campaign against their own people in their campaign against economic targets Mr Hume said:

'The SDLP said at the beginning of this campaign that the campaign would expose the contradiction in the so-called military and political approach where on the one hand the objective is to destroy the economy and on the other to show a new image as the champion of the jobless and the unemployed.

'They are trying to show that they have something new to offer. We have pointed out that they have been around much longer than the SDLP and the effects of their campaign are visible and extremely negative. What we are saying to the people of Northern Ireland is that you have a clear choice – build or destroy.'[21]

In a high-profile demonstration of his commitment to counter the economic effects of the violence, Hume agreed in September 1983 to participate in a nine-day investment promotion tour of North America accompanied by Ian Paisley, leader of the Democratic Unionist Party and almost a hate figure among Irish-Americans. Despite being denounced by some Irish-American organizations, Hume made clear the dire need to tackle unemployment in both communities. In response to the criticism he said:

> they were not there to pretend that they had no political differences or that they were trying to hide political differences […] they were agreed on the serious unemployment situation in both sections of the community in the North and were seeking inward investment.[22]

Death penalty

Violence continued to overshadow all other political challenges. Its persistence resulted in a strong demand from conservatives and unionists for the re-introduction of the death penalty for terrorist-related offences. Hume strongly opposed the demand and, in a house of commons debate, argued the case against it:

> This debate is about law and order. There can be few members whose constituents have such a desperate need for law and order as those whom I

21 *Irish Times*, 23 June 1983.   22 *Irish News*, 20 Sept. 1983.

represent. I live in the middle of the Bogside in the city of Derry, an area so ravaged by violence and so disturbed by extremism that outsiders cannot understand how normal life can be possible there. Normal life, as it is understood by most people, is not possible in Derry because there is no law and order, in the usual sense of term. I therefore think that I can understand better than most the yearning for law and order that motivates those who support the motion.

The desire for order is innate in human nature. It is a deep and powerful instinct. It can protect us against chaos and can be the foundation of democracy and freedom. But because those who are lucky enough to have a system of law and order often seem complacent and because those who do not often seem turbulent or cowed into despair, many people forget that no people on earth yearn more for law and order than the deprived, the oppressed and the minorities. If the house does not understand that, it will never understand Ireland, will never understand our awful and terrible history, will never understand that what we all want to stop forever is terrorism in Ireland.

My people want law and order more than any member in this house because they need it more than any member in this house. We must ask ourselves firmly, will the death penalty for terrorism, will hanging Irish terrorists, promote law and order in Northern Ireland or will it destroy law and order in Northern Ireland? That question is central to the debate […]

It is central statistically because far more murders are committed in Northern Ireland than anywhere else in Great Britain. It is central legally because, as has already been said, it would be illogical to introduce the death penalty for Britain alone. It is central politically because the political consequences of hanging Irish terrorists would be so overwhelming as to dominate every other issue in Ireland for the foreseeable future.

Who are the terrorists who would be hanged? An Irish terrorist is a person who for good reasons distrusts British democracy and its application to Ireland and for bad reasons thinks that violence can solve the problems of Ireland. The distrust of British democracy in its application to Ireland is widely shared in Northern Ireland, for good reasons. It is shared by me and I do not have to give lectures on Irish history from 1912 onwards or on the silence of the house between 1920 and 1969 to explain why a substantial section of the people in Northern Ireland have a deep distrust of British democracy. Nor do I have to reiterate my opposition to violence because I do that on my own doorstep every day.

As almost everyone has admitted that the death penalty will not deter terrorists, we must ask ourselves what effect the death penalty would have on society, particularly on a society where terrorists flourish because they move among people who, because of their personal experience, are deeply distrustful of government [...] As terrorists are moving in a society that is deeply distrustful of government and which, in consequence, is deprived of any real sense of security, the effect of the introduction of the death penalty is certain – it would destroy any hope of democracy in Northern Ireland and, in addition, would undermine the reality of democracy in the Republic of Ireland. What is now a disaster in Northern Ireland would, if the death penalty were introduced, become an unmanageable calamity throughout Ireland. There would be many more deaths, both in Britain and in Ireland. If we try to solve a problem by methods that will create even greater problems, is it sensible even to discuss the issue?

When reassessing the British decision to execute the leaders of the 1916 uprising in Dublin, Winston Churchill said that, as a consequence of that action, 'the keys of Ireland passed into the hands of those to whom hatred of England was the dominant and almost the only interest'. Hatred of Britain, the result of grisly experience of generations of Irish life, has, alas, strong roots in Northern Ireland, particularly among young people. It was magnified two years ago by the government's handling of the hunger strike. Never in its wildest dreams could the IRA have expected to recruit the support that was won for it by the British government's tragic mishandling of the hunger strike.

Those who are interested in Northern Ireland will remember the images of that time: the black flags on almost every telegraph pole, the grotesque wall paintings, the nihilistic slogans, the pornography of death, the street violence and the deaths of innocent people.

That hatred, the instability and the macabre display of that time, are as nothing compared with the reaction that would take place in Ireland if Irish men or women were hanged under British law. If the house wants the IRA to win, then hang them.

Reference was made today to the murders which took place in Northern Ireland last night. A UDR convoy was blown up and four UDR soldiers were killed. Does any hon. member not believe that that attack was timed to influence the result of our debate? The leaders of terrorist organizations want to see the introduction of hanging. I live among them and I know their thinking. They would be delighted if hanging were introduced. Let not the house think that the leaders will be hanged. The leaders are not in gaol. It will be the young followers who are sucked into the organizations because of the desperate position in Northern Ireland.

If the house wants the whole of Ireland to be convulsed in a frenzy of hatred, if the house wants once and for all to remove the prospect of a lasting peace, a political solution to the problems of Northern Ireland and the prospect of friendship between our two peoples, nothing would be more certain to bring that about than the hanging of Irish people under British law. This house would then hand over the keys of the whole of Ireland to those who want to come to power by the bomb and the bullet.

Churchill was right when he wrote, in reference to British attitudes in Ireland: 'The grass grows green on the battlefield, but never on the scaffold.' If the house again erects a scaffold in my country, it will turn the whole of Ireland into a savage and bloody battlefield. For the sake of democracy, for the sake of friendship, for the sake of ordinary men, women and children, and for the sake of peace, for God's sake, do not do it.[23]

The motion in favour of re-introducing the death penalty was defeated by a majority of 116.

23 House of Commons, *Debates*, 13 July 1983.

1984-5

As 1984 dawned with no signs of political progress, or of an end to any of the paramilitary campaigns, Orwellian images were frequently invoked to describe these realities. In his address to the SDLP annual conference in January, Hume invoked such images and went on to cast the ongoing crisis in the context of global developments:

> Margaret Thatcher and the SDLP have not agreed on many subjects so far. We find as 1984 begins that we are in disagreement with her on yet another issue, this time a literary one for a change. As she looks out the window of No. 10 Downing Street, Mrs Thatcher finds that George Orwell was wrong about 1984. As you and I look out our doors, be it up the road in West Belfast, among the Sperrins or in the Bogside, we find that he was not wrong about 1984. He was particularly and tragically prophetic when he described the lying slogans that oppressed and confused his hero Winston Smith from every street corner, from every wall and from every system of communication that he encountered: 'War is peace', 'Freedom is slavery', 'Ignorance is strength'.
>
> We know how Winston Smith felt. For be it Mrs Thatcher's own 'Northern Ireland is as British as Finchley' [her own London constituency] or the unionists' 'There is no Irish dimension', or the Provisionals' grotesque 'Murder is democracy', or any of the countless other major distortions of truth that are hailed down on this exhausted community today, for the SDLP the challenge of 1984 is – as George Orwell predicted – to fight the Big Lie and to assert the truth. I believe that in 1984 the truth will prevail.
>
> Mind you although it is now accepted that our crisis here is the most serious in the European Community today, Northern Ireland is not the only crisis which is mired in lies. The very existence of our planet is far more directly threatened by competing lies than by competing rocketry. The arsenals of East and West are primarily swollen, not by the discoveries of science or by exertions of generals, but rather by the lies of those who hold and love power in both camps. The fact that billions of dollars are wasted on these evil machines while billions of people starve or remain sunk in ignorance and ill-health is itself a cruel demonstration of falsehood. Just because we suffer in Ireland does not mean that we do not feel for millions of our brothers and sisters who are the victims of outrage and war and tyranny

elsewhere on earth. On the contrary. As the party of non-violence and justice and of ordinary people, the men and women, young and old, of the SDLP send to the oppressed of South Africa, of Latin America, of Afghanistan and of Iraq and of the whole world a heartfelt message of compassion and encouragement: endure, never give up, we shall overcome.

These words must, of course, be our message to the people of the North. Never were they so badly needed. The political situation is in such tatters that the only way forward now must be to start virtually from scratch; if a team of economists had sought to create under laboratory conditions an example of industrial decline as a warning to the West they could not have succeeded in producing conditions as discouraging as those in which we are forced to bring up our children. Our society, hitherto so strong in traditions and religious values despite our divisions, is in the process of fundamental, almost terminal, disintegration. The individual and communal memories of young people recall only the Troubles, only violence, only tension and hatred. The economic situation offers them little hope. It interacts powerfully on the political scene. Thus for many young people, the hopes and anchors of the future, have become the easy prey of the cult of the Armalite.

These are dark days in the North. Our job is to brace ourselves as never before and offer the people, more clearly than ever before, the only leadership which will create peace and stability now, leadership that is based on non-violence, courage, intelligence and creativity. Not blood but sweat, not tears but brains and endurance. These are the qualities that we stand for now more than ever before. It is up to others also, not just the SDLP, to provide new thinking and new leadership. Even though the SDLP believes that no one is irredeemable, not even Mrs Thatcher, not even Mr Molyneaux, not even Mr Adams – as we look around, the scene is bleak. I said last year that the British had no policy. This year even the British admit they have none. We will not crow over them now. It is a pity that they and the unionists did not see at the time, as we did, what a hopeless charade Mr Prior's assembly would inevitably be. A British politician, Clive Soley, told the New Ireland Forum last week that Britain had no policy in Northern Ireland but crisis management. What management! We may be said to be as British as Finchley but we are treated as though we are far less British than the Falklands. There is at least a British policy for the Falklands, however bewildering, however unaffordable it may seem to most people. There is no British policy for us except the same old set of blinkers for the same old tired unionism nag. Intransigence, by Bigotry out of Guarantee [...][1]

1 Address to the SDLP's annual conference, 1984

Haagerup and New Ireland Forum reports

In the months that followed, Hume welcomed the publication of two reports of which he had been the primary instigator. The first was the European parliament report from the Danish MEP Neils Haagerup, who had been appointed rapporteur for an investigation into political conditions in Northern Ireland. Hume regarded this investigation as a very important acknowledgment of the Northern Ireland crisis by the parliament:

> Mr President, the problem that we address in this debate today is one that is an affront to the ideals on which the European Community was founded. The very fact that this discussion is taking place – the first time ever that a major discussion in an international democratic assembly has taken place on the problems of Northern Ireland – is itself an expression of powerful concern about the continuation of this conflict within the borders of the European Community, an expression of concern and urgency that is summed up in the tragedy itself, not alone in the deaths and injuries of thousands of people and the serious economic crisis which interacts with the political crisis, particularly among young people. These Mr Haagerup has accurately identified, and his proposals, I have no doubt, will meet with unanimous support in this house in the economic sphere.

> However, I suppose for those of us in Northern Ireland, the tragedy and the urgency are really summed up symbolically by the fact that we have come to the stage where it is necessary to build a brick wall to separate Catholics from Protestants on the streets of Belfast; and that this wall is called a 'peace line'. The wall is an indictment of everyone living involved in the Irish problem, because the only message that comes from it is a challenge to all the parties to the conflict to recognize that past attitudes have brought us here and to rethink those attitudes with a view to reaching a lasting peace in Ireland [...]

> The spirit of Irish patriotism in 1984 must have a great deal more to do with spilling sweat than with the spilling of blood. Indeed, Mr President, it ought to have more to do with the real meaning of the Irish national flag. Violence is an affront to the meaning of that flag, which contains the white of peace between the orange and green. It is that version of patriotism that will prevail in the end. That is the very same spirit that motivated the founding fathers of the Community of which this parliament is the representative. Let us remember that the people represented in this chamber, twice in this century alone, slaughtered one another by the million with a savagery that has been unparalleled in human history, yet they had the vision and the strength to rise above the past and to create institutions that allow the people of Europe to grow together at their own speed.

Mr President, is it too much to ask that we can do the same for Ireland, to create institutions which will allow the people of Ireland to grow together at their own speed? The framework in which that can take place has been identified by Mr Haagerup in his report. It is the British-Irish framework. It is the coming together of the two governments to create the dialogue and the process that will bring that about. Let us hope that this debate today will act as a spur to them to get on with the job as a matter of urgency![2]

The second report was that from the New Ireland Forum in May 1984. This report did not reveal the united nationalist voice that Hume had hoped for on the kind of united Ireland its members preferred, or, indeed, even a single agreed analysis of the Northern problem. Fianna Fáil leader Charles Haughey recommended that the report advocate only one solution, namely a unitary state for the whole island, whereas the other parties believed other solutions, such as a federal/confederal state and joint Irish-British authority, should also be included as possibilities. Hume's own preference had been not to include any such precise solutions. Instead, he would have preferred that having acknowledged the legitimacy of the unionist tradition, and having formally committed the parties to an exclusively peaceful resolution, it left open for negotiations the shape and form of a united Ireland. In his address at the close of the forum, Hume ignored the differences that had emerged between the Southern parties and expressed his satisfaction at the level of agreement reached on key principles:

To me personally, the outstanding merit of the report is that it tries to do the most difficult thing of all in the case of the North, which is to tell the truth about that very complex situation. In saying this, I do not pretend that all of our judgments are absolutely correct. I do say that our intentions and our efforts to tell the truth were sincere and rigorous.

In the North where I come from, people have been made dizzy with lies and half-truths, with the malignant Big Lie of those who destroy life while pretending to serve freedom, and the pusillanimous half-truths of those who cannot bring themselves to face the full dimensions of our problems.

This is a courageous, imaginative and generous document and Irish nationalists everywhere can take pride in its achievement. They should do so. The leaders of Irish nationalism have shown the way. We must put our differences behind us and unite in a single, powerful commitment to resolve this problem peacefully.

We must now say to the British government and to British politicians: you may not like everything in this report but you can no longer deny the

2 European Parliament, *Debates*, 29 Mar. 1984.

sincerity and the good faith of our efforts. What we ask you to do is to examine your own situation as we have ours. Irish nationalism has honestly examined its own position and is ready to talk with you. The report provides the basis for such discussion. The people of the North and the people of the two islands cannot afford that you should miss this opportunity.

To the unionists of the North, with whom we share this island piece of earth, Irish nationalism can today repeat de Gaulle's ringing affirmation of reconciliation to the Algerians: '*Je vous ai compris.*' We understand your position. And we accept that before now we may not have fully understood. We ourselves can add, both to the British and to those of the unionist tradition: you too must understand our position. We too have an identity. We too have rights. […] This has been a fundamental episode in the life of this island. It will be seen to have been so by future generations of the Irish and British people who, like those of this generation, will have reason to be forever grateful to the men and women of the New Ireland Forum.[3]

Re-elected MEP

A few weeks later John Hume was re-elected to the European parliament with a significantly increased vote over that he had obtained in 1979. In accepting the SDLP's nomination as a candidate, Hume had reviewed his record over the preceding five years as MEP, claiming that the party could be justly proud that many of the 1979 manifesto commitments had been met. He instanced the Arfe, Haagerup and Martin reports, as well as his campaign to ensure that Northern Ireland's farmers in less-favoured areas would receive special assistance. Looking to the future he identified the wider challenges facing the European community and its role in helping to resolve the conflict in Northern Ireland:

> [W]hen the election is over, and the dust has settled, we face a wide range of problems on the European front. The Community has never been in more serious crisis than it is at this moment. Over the past few years we have seen a progressive breaking down of the consensus which has held the Community together for three decades now. The deepening economic recession of the '70s hangs like a black cloud over the '80s, and has caused a headlong retreat into economic nationalism on the part of major European states, most notably Britain. The continuing deadlock over the restructuring of Community finances, precipitated by Britain, which remains unresolved after the Athens summit, is threatening to strangle the current operation of the Community. There is disagreement over the Common Agricultural Policy and the

3 New Ireland Forum, *Report*, 1984, pp 7–8.

proposals to revise it. And, from an Irish point of view, the Regional Fund and the Social Fund are still too small, and too limited in their scope, to have the sort of impact on our economies, North and South, that is needed to accomplish real progress towards the Community ideal of convergence [...]

In economic terms Europe is now going through the most severe depression since the '30s. There are now more than 12 million people unemployed in Europe. In Northern Ireland we suffer 21 per cent unemployment, and in the most deprived parts of the North the percentage can reach 50 per cent. The nature of the recession we are going through in the 1980s is different from that of previous cyclical depressions. There has been a substantial breakdown of the economic order and that breakdown has caused a panic-stricken retreat into policies of economic nationalism. Each of the major economies has sought to protect its own position by increasing their exports [...] to each other, and by reducing its imports [...] from each other. Thus we have reached an international stalemate with the industrialized countries increasingly preventing each other from attaining a fundamental recovery. The policy of the Thatcher government and other right-wing elements, that expansion of public expenditure will not work anymore, is a serious error. The real truth is that the European countries are so interdependent nowadays that a policy of expansion in one country will only be successful if the other countries follow the same policy simultaneously. We believe strongly that the only way out of this crisis is by the co-ordination of the economic policies of the European states through the European Community. With the assistance of our colleagues in the Parliamentary Socialist Group, we will be working for the adoption of this approach [...]

All of these matters must be seen against the backdrop of the continuing tragedy of Northern Ireland, the continuing violence and the continuing political stalemate. It is, of course, our aim to harness the energies and experience of our European colleagues to help us resolve our political conflict and solve our economic problems. But unless these problems are tackled courageously and with realism here, our European partners will be unable to help. This remains the major task we face. Through the New Ireland Forum we are working to break the deadlock and to generate initiatives and new proposals for the future. The future of our community for some considerable time to come will be determined by the degree of success we achieve.[4]

4 Address to the SDLP's selection convention, 14 Jan. 1984.

Westminster debates the New Ireland Forum's report

In early July, the house of commons debated the New Ireland Forum's report. This provided an important opportunity to advance the case for a formal Irish-British approach to the Northern Ireland problem. During the debate, Hume highlighted, from personal experience, the critical issue of policing and security:

> Reference was made earlier to the recent elections in the North that took place on 14 June. On that day, around the close of polls, I was in my house in Derry when I heard a commotion in the street. I looked out of the window and saw a group of youths in masks filling bottles with petrol. I was not sure whether, in the heat and emotion at the end of election day, the target was my home or a passing military vehicle. Such occurrences are not unusual in front of my house.
>
> There are 650 members in the house. If I ventured to ask them what they would do in such circumstances, 649 of them would tell me that they would pick up the telephone and ring the police. I did not do that. I knew that had I done so I would simply have made a bad situation worse. That is a stark reality of life in areas of Northern Ireland that do not give their allegiance to the union. That situation is described by different people in different ways. I am the only political leader in the north of Ireland who does not go around with a gun in his pocket and who is not driven around by armed policemen. That is because, apart from my objection to the trappings of violence when I am preaching non-violence, any policeman who would drive me to where I live or stand outside my door would be signing his death warrant.
>
> That lack of order in the society that I represent has been described with fancy words. The most recent is 'alienation'. The search for peace and order on the streets, which the people of those areas want more than anything else, will not be achieved by force. It will not be achieved by armed soldiers or police. We have had all that. We have had 20,000 troops on our streets, armed policemen and the toughest emergency legislation in any civilized country in Western Europe. The result has not been order on our streets. The search for order must be based on what order is based on in every civilized democratic society – political consensus.
>
> What I am saying is underlined by the fact that in Northern Ireland today we have a generation of 18-year-olds who have lived through the past fifteen years who know nothing except violence and soldiers on the streets, and who, having built up resentment to that type of society, have nothing but unemployment staring them in the face in our desperate economic situation, making them easy meat for recruitment by paramilitary organizations. That in turn makes a bad situation even worse. That is what makes the problem urgent and that is what gives urgency to the report of the New Ireland Forum.

My colleagues from other parts of Northern Ireland from the other tradition have concerns as well. Their constituents are being murdered because they wear a uniform which people, claiming to be Irish republicans, say makes them legitimate targets. Members of the UDR and RUC are seen as defenders of their tradition. Therefore, their murder is rightly seen as sectarian murder [...]

The purpose of the New Ireland Forum is to begin a reassessment of nationalist attitudes, not, as was so contemptuously suggested by the hon. member for Epping Forest [Sir J. Biggs-Davison], to throw out a lifeline to my party or to any other party. We do not need such a lifeline. The New Ireland Forum is a serious attempt to face up to a serious problem in Ireland. When the representatives – the democratic voice of three quarters of the people of Ireland – speak about a serious problem in that island, the house had better listen. It will be giving another message to Ireland if it rejects the democratic voice of nationalist Ireland and does not give serious attention to what it has to say.

I do not claim that everybody in the nationalist tradition in Ireland is all virtue and that everybody else is to blame. We have only to look at our past approach to recognize the mistakes. We have only to look at the narrowness of Irish nationalism, its definition, its sectionalism, and its exclusionism, tied solely to the Gaelic and Catholic traditions and exclusive of other traditions represented in the house from Northern Ireland, to recognize that that narrowness of itself is divisive. It is pushed to its extremes by those who tell us that the height of Irish patriotism is the right not only to die for it but to kill fellow Irishmen for it as well. It is clear that there is need for a massive rethink in that tradition, and that was what the forum was all about [...]

The unionist tradition is represented strongly in the house. My tradition is under-represented because of the undemocratic voting system that elects people to this house. The unionist tradition in Ireland, as we have heard again today, has always stood for the integrity of Irish Protestantism and for the protection of that tradition within Ireland. That is a noble and laudable objective that deserves the support of everyone in Ireland because any country is richer for its diversity. Any country that does not recognize that the basis of unity is diversity recognizes nothing.

My quarrel with the political leadership of that tradition, is simply that the methods used to protect that integrity have been the wrong methods – that of holding all power in their own hands without surrendering an inch. Again, the mirror image is 'ourselves alone': all power in our hands. That is an inherently violent attitude that can lead only to conflict. There must be a reassessment and a recognition that that tradition is best protected by examining how best to share the island of Ireland with those with whom they share that piece of earth, and what structures, agreements and arrangements can bring real unity based on agreement and acceptance of diversity.

Of course, there are two documents in that tradition that are mentioned on the order paper as 'other documents'. Indeed, the right hon. member for Lagan Valley [Mr Molyneaux] referred to 'The way forward',[5] whose contents are not particularly exciting. However, its tone is new, in the sense that it is completely different from any other document from a unionist party. Some have said that it is a tactical document that is designed to offset the impact of the New Ireland Forum. But I am prepared to recognize it as a genuine document, because I believe that any movement – even only a centimetre – out of the trenches in Northern Ireland should be encouraged. If that [UUP] party's leaders believe what they say when they claim that they want to accommodate the different loyalties in Ireland, I am ready to talk to them.

I am sorry that the hon. member for Antrim North [Revd Ian Paisley] is not in the chamber. But the [DUP] document entitled 'The unionist case' would have been better entitled 'The way backwards' or 'Towards 1690', because it has absolutely nothing to offer. As I expected, we heard about the size of the hon. Gentleman's vote in the recent European elections and about how it must govern the British government's thinking. But we have heard all that before. This problem came in with the playing of the orange card in 1912. The political representatives of unionism threatened that they would resist by violence if the British government did not do as they wished. That overthrew a democratic decision in 1912, and taught unionists the lesson that if they defied and threatened a British government, that government would back down. It also taught others in the nationalist tradition a lesson – that if hon. members win by democratic means in this house, that decision will be overturned anyway. That lesson gave birth to those who believe in violence and force.

Those two attitudes lie at the heart of the Northern Ireland problem and its intractability today, and were both repeated in 1974 in the Ulster Workers' Council strike. Every time a British government moves towards change, they are faced with the same threats from the same sources. The hon. member for Antrim North says that the government does not have the consent of the unionists. Many people talk about consent, but consent cannot be unqualified. We are told that people voted on the basis of opposition to the New Ireland Forum report. The Democratic Unionist Party put an election advertisement in the Northern Ireland press, which was turned down by the *Belfast Telegraph* as being too sectarian. This is how votes were sought: 'Do you know that the pope has appointed Mary as the "Madonna" of the common market

---

5 A discussion document produced by members of the UUP.

and views the EEC as the work of Divine Providence?' That is what the hon. member for Antrim North said. Indeed, the prime minister will be interested in the next few lines of the advertisement, which state: 'Do you know [...] that Mr John Gummer, the chairman of the Conservative Party, has stated that the common market will help to take the Protestants back into the church of Rome?' [...] Furthermore, the right hon. member for Strangford [Mr Taylor] was said to be a member of the British Conservative group in the European parliament and so associated with 'Gummer's pro-Vatican stance'. The hon. member for Antrim North said that people should vote for him instead of the right hon. gentleman for that reason. That is the sort of thing that people voted for.

If consent is refused because of prejudice, we cannot allow prejudice to determine political change. I could cite further examples of such prejudice. For example, Lisburn council is run by the Democratic Unionist Party. It does not have many powers, but one of them is to collect the dustbins. However, it refuses to collect them on the Poleglass housing estate because it will not collect Catholic bins. The council will not give its consent to that. Under public-health legislation, the minister has to force the council to collect them. If that council will not collect Catholic bins, who can ask me to sit in an assembly with such people when its purpose is to achieve power-sharing? Does the secretary of state think that I have lost my marbles, or that my electorate would think anything of me if I did that?

If consent is refused, reasonable reasons must be given, and they must not be based on prejudice. The veto handed over in the British guarantee to unionism has been extended to a veto against all change, and has thus paralysed political development in the north of Ireland. There has been some complaint today that the forum's report is too harsh on previous British attempts to solve the Irish problem. That may or may not be so, but it is true that all previous attempts have failed. That is the harsh reality. Consequently, the British government, no less than the rest of us, must start making some reassessment.

The position of successive British governments has not changed since 1920, because they have only one position and that is the guarantee to Ulster unionism that there will be no change in the constitutional position of Northern Ireland without the majority's consent. There is no other policy. The policies on power-sharing and security have not been implemented because of the unionist veto, thus making a bad situation worse.

Because that guarantee was given to a population that was created on the basis of a sectarian head count – that is how Northern Ireland was created – solidified sectarianism in Northern Ireland has encouraged the majority who want to protect their rights to maintain sectarian solidarity. Consequently, sectarianism has remained the motive force of politics in the north of Ireland, and every election proves that. Until that is changed, there will be no movement.

Any security policy or system of order must be based on political consensus. The absence of that political consensus in the north of Ireland is the Achilles' heel that has been exploited by every terrorist. Those who live there know that. There will be wholehearted community backing for the forces of law and order only if that community gives its loyalty to the institutions of the state. One must create the political situation to allow that.

Today, the secretary of state said that the three options in the Forum Report were not on, because they did not have the consent of the unionist population. What is the British government's view? Let us hear what they think of those proposals. Let us not hide behind the unionists. I am sick and tired of people representing Irish unity as something that should not even be talked about. […]

That brings me to the New Ireland Forum itself, about which much has been written and said. A major consensus within Ireland, within a democratic nationalist Ireland, should be heeded. Any rejection of it should be carefully considered, because of the massive advantage given to other people. We are not talking about an extremist document. The document says clearly and honestly that the narrow ground on which we have concentrated for a solution up to now – the narrow ground of Northern Ireland – does not deal with the whole problem. Relationships between the communities in Northern Ireland are only part of the problem. The relationships within Ireland and between Ireland and Britain are the problem. Northern Ireland illustrates the failure to solve that problem. No attention was paid to that problem by the house from 1920 to 1969.

Only within a British-Irish framework can the solution be found. The most important aspect of the report is not the three options, but the views of Irish nationalists about the ways in which realities must be faced if there is to be a solution. We also say that we are willing to examine other ways of accommodating those realities and requirements. If we are praised by the government for being willing to look at all options, it ill-behoves the government to start ruling out options themselves.

I invite the house to read chapter 5 of the report carefully. It contains a list of realities which must be faced if we are to solve the problem. Hon. members should say with which realities they disagree. If they agree with the realities, surely they must agree that the only major proposal in the forum report is to get the governments together to create the framework and atmosphere in which the realities can be discussed to bring about an end to the Irish problem.

All options and all points of view must be considered. Nothing should be ruled out and nothing should be ruled in. There should be no preconditions to allow people to stay away. That should be the beginning of the real dialogue if we are to find solutions to our problems.

I end where I began, in my own city. This house of commons was elected on 9 June last year. Those with an interest in such matters know that 9 June is the feast of Columba, the founder of Derry. In his early days, he was regarded as a rather turbulent priest who caused conflict between the clans in the north-east of Ireland. He thought that stubbornness and pride were the causes of conflict. He went into exile in Iona, where he became a substantial influence in determining the culture and civilization of most of Scotland. When he was there, he crowned a Scottish chieftain on the Stone of Destiny, which subsequently became the Stone of Scone and which now lies in Westminster Abbey. It was taken back to Ireland once because of the trouble between the clans. He called a convention because he believed that negotiation and discussion without preconditions were a better way to solve the problems than going to war. There was a difference of opinion between the Dalriada, a clan from the area represented by the hon. member for Antrim North – the people of the Antrim coast and the people of south-east Scotland – and the people of the clans in the area covered by my constituency. The problem was to whom should the Dalriada pay tribute – the Irish high-king or the king of Argyll. The solution was simple. Columba said, 'Let them pay tribute to both.' In that way he solved the complex identity problem and preserved the unity of the Irish clans. Since then, he has been known in Irish history as a dove of peace. There should be a dove of peace in government today.[6]

Despite Hume's strenuous efforts, the British government did not quickly accept the case for a formal Irish-British framework. Instead, the situation seemed likely to move in the opposite direction when, after a meeting with Taoiseach Garret FitzGerald in London in November, Margaret Thatcher categorically ruled out the three options highlighted in the forum's report – a united Ireland, a federal/confederal Ireland and joint authority. Her statement, characterized by her explicit ruling 'out' of each option, seemed likely to put a brake on the process, at least in the short term. Later, when asked what his reaction was to Thatcher's dismissal of the three options, Hume said:

Just because the BPM [British prime minister] said 'out, out, out', that did not mean that I was going to walk away. Political development would never

6 House of Commons, *Debates*, 2 July 1984.

take place anywhere if you took 'no' for an answer to a political demand. There was deep and justifiable anger in Ireland following the PM's triple negative. I believe that that anger (and the strength of it) had an effect on Britain and on the ruling party in particular. It was noticeable that comments from that direction became a lot more conciliatory thereafter. My own reply in a nutshell, was, 'OK, you've rejected the three main options that were put forward. What about the fourth one? We are open to any suggestion that anybody else has to bring forward.' It was that kind of response – from others, as well as myself – that led to the 'Anglo-Irish' talks between the governments at Westminster and Dublin and to subsequent developments.[7]

In the meantime, the violence continued, unabated. The PIRA's bomb attack on the Conservative Party conference in Brighton in September was one of the most dramatic and brutal examples of its capacity to sustain its campaign. The one positive note came from some within the unionist parties who were offering the prospect of dialogue. Hume's address at the SDLP's annual conference reflected on all these issues. He began by referencing the comments about Orwell in the previous year's speech:

> A year ago as we were looking ahead I quoted the perverse slogan of Orwell's novel *Nineteen Eighty-Four*: 'War is peace'. Orwell was right about 1984; 1984 saw nuclear arms entering space. Even Orwell could hardly have written the script as globally the superpowers insisted that the road to peace lay in accumulating more and more nuclear arms and locally the Brighton bomb was extolled as a 'bomb for democracy'. Famine racked much of Africa, stirring to unequalled generosity our own collective famine memory and instincts. The mounting number of cruise missiles and Soviet SS-20s coincided with rocketing youth unemployment, with Northern Ireland, as usual, beating all sides and all records.
>
> The beginning of wisdom is to see that all of these problems are inter-linked. I think that we in the party know and feel this more strongly than almost anyone else. We may not all have the expertise, but we *know* what is wrong in Africa, what is wrong in Cyprus, what is wrong in the Middle East and, yes, what is wrong as the United States and the Soviet Union face each other across their Himalayas of nuclear gunpowder. We *know* that the will to peace and the will to justice are not strong and not urgent enough. That will, if we were strong enough, could transform the global economy by transferring the resources wasted on nuclear weapons to the developing world, thereby creating the growth in world markets that would enable the Western

7 Address at Milltown Institute of Theology, *Guilty parties* (Dublin, 1985).

economies to tackle their unemployment problems in the rising tide. If that will had been strong enough in London, Northern Ireland would not be dangerously divided today [...]

Nineteen eighty-four saw two major advances for our party. The first was the successful conclusion of the New Ireland Forum. The second was the party's smashing victory in the European elections, which pundits had forecast as a difficult race for the SDLP. Well they – and we – maintained our consistent record [...]

Nineteen eighty-four ended with requests for talks from unionist leaders. We in this party take those requests very seriously indeed and we have made our position clear. We are committed to the democratic political process. And so we are committed to dialogue. We will enter dialogue with any democratic party and our approach will be based squarely on the problem as we see it and on proposals that we see as adequate [...] and necessary, in other words, on the Forum Report in all its aspects. No party in Northern Ireland has set out its position, its analysis or its proposals more clearly or in more detail than the SDLP [...]

In saying that, we take requests for talks very seriously, but we are obliged to have in mind that talks which fail would damage the political process. The experience of the SDLP with our opponents over the past ten years' experience – which, were it not for the death and destruction in Northern Ireland in those years, could only be described as bad political farce – entitles and obliges us to insist on that question.

Much of that experience is recent. We witnessed the sectarian triumphalism after Chequers.[8] Even in recent days we have seen the mask drop again in various ways. We have heard the ugly sectarianism of Mr Taylor, one of the most senior figures in the official unionist party. One after another over the years, unionist-dominated councils have been found wanting: Lisburn, Craigavon, Armagh, Cookstown. Because some unionists couldn't stomach the fact that Derry, my own native city, is no longer their gerrymandered fief, their political leaders at Westminster this past week have sought to establish two councils rather than one; this was the culmination of a declared campaign to smash power-sharing in Derry, which unionists know has always been and remains on offer from the SDLP.

Are these the attitudes of people who want a new beginning? We are told, however, that these are people who want to make a new beginning. If so, they will not find the SDLP wanting. The SDLP will engage in dialogue on the basis that I have stated. Accordingly I will be making informal approaches to

8 Unionists had greeted Mrs Thatcher's dismissal at a Chequers press conference of the forum's proposals with considerable glee.

the other party leaders to clarify the questions I am raising with a view to creating reasonable ground for fruitful dialogue and to emphasize again that we seek accommodation for our differences not conquest. Those who fail to recognize and accept the diversity of their country or their community will never unite it.

I now address those who claim to speak and to wage war for me, for you and for the rest of the Irish people, the provisional republican movement. I would like in particular to address myself to their supporters and to ask one simple question: Can any human being – you or I – evade responsibility for the consequences of the methods that we use to solve our political problems? Surely the answer must always be No. What responsibility does the Provisional Movement accept for the consequences of the methods they use? A Sikh shot Mrs Gandhi. Who suffered? Within twenty-four hours there were thousands of dead Sikhs. Does Mrs Gandhi's killer bear any responsibility for those deaths which were the direct consequence of his action? Who are the dead in the North? The majority of civilians killed are from the Catholic community. So are the majority of young people in jail. The same is proportionately speaking on the dole queues. It is the Derrys, the Strabanes, the Newrys that have been blasted as 'economic targets'; it is principally the jobs of their people that have been bombed to extinction as though those communities didn't have enough unemployment inflicted on them from other sources already [...][9]

Referring to the New Ireland Forum, Hume argued that it contained the seeds of a solution:

If we were to distil the essence of the approach of the Forum Report [...] it would be [in] paragraph 4.15 of the report. I quote:

the solution to both the historic problem and the crisis of Northern Ireland and the continuing problem of relations between Ireland and Britain necessarily requires new structures that will accommodate together two sets of legitimate rights:
  – the rights of nationalists to effective political, symbolic and administrative expression of their identity; and
  – the rights of unionists to effective political, symbolic and administrative expression of their identity.
  So long as the legitimate rights of unionists and nationalists are not accommodated together in new political structures acceptable to both, that

9 Address to the SDLP's annual conference, Jan. 1985.

situation will continue to give rise to conflict and instability. The starting point of genuine reconciliation and dialogue is mutual recognition and acceptance of the legitimate rights of both. The forum is convinced that dialogue which fully respects both traditions can overcome the fears and divisions of the past and create an atmosphere in which peace and stability can be achieved.[10]

The forum's recognition of unionist rights marked the first time Ireland's main political parties with roots in the nationalist tradition had given unionists such explicit recognition. It was this recognition that would later become a bedrock principle of the 1985 Anglo-Irish Agreement and, more than a decade later, of the Good Friday/Belfast Agreement in 1998. The hope now was that the two governments would work more closely together to create a framework for the inclusive dialogue that Hume believed essential if a worthwhile comprehensive agreement was to be reached. The fact that the unionist parties were seeking talks gave some hope of progress.

However, in an initiative that was greeted with a mixture of surprise, welcome and condemnation, Hume participated in a radio discussion with Sinn Féin leader Gerry Adams, during which Adams invited him to address his party's *árd-chomhairle* (executive). Hume indicated that he would prefer to talk to the PIRA's army council, justifying his suggestion by saying:

> As I understand it, Sinn Féin is subject in all matters to the army council [...] If I am to talk to the Provisional Movement I want to talk to the people who are making the decisions in order to ask them to cease their campaign of violence.[11]

Hume later expanded on the reason why he had asked to meet the PIRA leadership:

> Well, we are used to taking risks in our part of the world. The matter arose when I was taking part in a discussion on BBC radio with the leader of Sinn Féin. It was he who extended the invitation. I thought to myself, 'Well, he expects me to say no, and he will then, rightly, attack me for saying no, because I am going to talk to Ian Paisley, who had a record of dealing with violent organizations in one way or another.' That is why I agreed to meet the leaders of the provisional republican movement. I hoped it would give me the chance to talk to the people who take the real decisions in that movement, to the men who literally call the shots. I wanted to talk to them about their

10 Ibid.   11 *Irish News*, 2 Feb. 1985

campaign of violence, and especially about my belief that it is destroying the country, North and South.

My agreeing to meet the Provos was heavily criticized by the British and Irish governments and by unionists in the North. But it was very popular 'on the ground', among people where I live. I cannot see that there is anything to be lost by dialogue because, in essence, if I were to refuse to talk to anybody in the North who is either engaged in violence or who has been engaged in violence, or who has used violent organizations, or has talked to violent organizations, I'd be talking to myself.[12]

The meeting was arranged, but then aborted when the PIRA representatives insisted that it be filmed. Hume's attempt to directly engage with the latter in order to persuade the paramilitaries to end their campaign had failed. Furthermore, given the hostile unionist reaction, Hume's initiative also ended any prospect that unionist parties would meet the SDLP, at least in the immediate future. Consequently, hopes for progress now rested on negotiations between the two governments which were aimed at strengthening their co-operation in addressing the Northern crisis. Hume kept pressing his case for an Irish-British framework. Speaking to the annual congress of the Confederation of European Socialist Parties, he said:

there are flickering signs that just over a decade after joining the EEC, Ireland and Britain may be able to find a way out of the 'dark tunnel' in which their relations had been trapped since the seventeenth century. The solution to our problems lies in finding democratic institutions and structures with the necessary economic backing, in which consensus and acceptance of difference can be accommodated as they are in the societies in which you all live. The European Community, with its history of conflict far deeper than ours, and its experience of conflict resolution, is an inspiration to us and a flame of hope [...] If we are so fortunate to find that we can work out a political framework for the accommodation of our differences in Northern Ireland are we unreasonable if we ask our European colleagues for solidarity, if by insisting that they contribute to the underpinning and preservation of such a framework by offering to assist with a major and essential programme of economic reconstruction?[13]

On a more philosophical note, at the Merriman Summer School in August, Hume discussed parliamentary democracy, and the lessons to be drawn from the

12 Address at Milltown Institute of Theology, *Guilty parties* (Dublin, 1985).   13 *Irish Times*, 11 Apr. 1985.

Irish experience, particularly the North's experience since partition. It was a wide-ranging speech, which analyzed why previous attempts to establish parliamentary bodies in the North had failed, the principles upon which any future attempts should be based, as well as a strong condemnation of violence. It is also clear from this address that Hume was anticipating much of what, in principle at least, would appear a few months later in the Anglo-Irish Agreement:

> I want to talk about what are the foundations of parliamentary democracy and can they be laid in the northern part of this country, bearing in mind the context of the wider relationships, North and South, which exist in Ireland and the very nature of the creation of the North and the South.
>
> I find in the different parliaments I have wandered around, one thing that strikes me most of all, coming from the North, is how many parliamentarians take it for granted, never even consider the nature and the foundation stones of parliamentary democracy. We in the North don't have them all and there-fore have to think about them all the time. If the litmus test of the parliamentary system was the number and variety of parliaments, then we could in the North claim to be the most parliamentary place on earth. If parliaments solved problems, our problems would have been solved ten times over.
>
> From its very inception the North had two parliaments. It had a parlia-ment at Westminster taking control over matters concerning the crown, defence, foreign affairs, treason, titles as well as naturalization, trademarks and coinage. These were matters which were excepted from local jurisdiction and local power. Then, as well, we had the parliament at Stormont with the powers conferred on it by the Government of Ireland Act 1920 – the general power to make laws for the peace, order and good government of Northern Ireland [...]
>
> This major power which was conferred on Stormont at this time reflects a couple of major ironies. The first was the fact that the unionists didn't wish for any such parliament, and they only received it because of the achieve-ments of Irish nationalists. I often think that when we lay blame on other people for things in politics which we don't like, that we might sometimes think that maybe the things we don't like might have something to do with the consequences of our own methods. I am talking about partition when I say that. It is often said that partition is the direct result of British attitudes and British attitudes only. I think it's time that we considered the proposition that perhaps the methods that we Irish use might have something to do with the creation of partition. Because if we look about at the state of different parts of the world today, if we look at Cyprus, the Lebanon etc., we see that in every society where violence was used as a means of healing a divide, the

net result was the drawing of a line between the two sides of the divide. And indeed if we look at the North today, it is staring us in the face. If the violence continues, one possibility is very clear – another line will be drawn. And then we will obviously also blame someone else for that, and we don't think that perhaps it was a consequence of the methods that we used ourselves, and didn't think this through [...]

The second irony was of course that once it was set up, it enabled the unionists to mark out and preserve their wholly dominant position in the north of Ireland, to strengthen their sense of their own independence, a sense that led them to actual outbreaks of violence in 1974.

The Stormont parliament fell in 1972, and, as I say, it wasn't the only parliament that served in the North. It was succeeded in 1973 by the assembly, one which was shorn, in particular, of the security powers of Stormont. This was hardly on the statute books before it was prorogued as a result of the loyalist challenge to Sunningdale and the collapse of British will. Since then we have had different forms of assembly in the north. We have had Merlyn Rees' constitutional convention in 1975. We have had Humphrey Atkins' constitutional conference in 1980. And we have had James Prior's rolling devolution assembly of 1982, which still staggers on, on one leg. There has been a stream of British discussion papers with enough suggestions for forms of government and variations of them to provide constitutions for hundreds of states.

That underlines the fact that parliaments of themselves and varieties of them are not the litmus test of a parliamentary democracy. The first defining characteristic of a democracy is, as it always has been, consensus. There cannot be a fixed and unchanging majority and minority about matters of importance in any democratic society. Parliamentary democracy works on the assumption that its citizens agree on certain basic things: that they agree on who they are, and how they wish to be governed. This is the rock upon which a parliament is built, and no form of parliamentary democracy or parliamentary assembly, however intricate its balloting procedures, can be built, or can work without that rock of consensus. It is a search for that rock, that consensus and that consent that is the search for peace and stability in the north of Ireland. That is not to say that all members of a society must share the same culture or the same aspirations. In fact something which appears a contradiction is when you look across the world at all the countries that are united countries, and you ask yourself the question: why are they united? The answer appears to be a contradiction. Every country is united because it accepts diversities. That is a lesson which we in this country have yet to learn. The acceptance of diversity is the essence of unity. And unless we learn that we will never, ever, ever, unite this country. And the acceptance of diversity means the acceptance of things that perhaps we do not like. It means the accommodation of difference, and the acceptance of differences that are perhaps very different from our own traditions, backgrounds and cultures. For if we look at any society where any one tradition tries to dominate another it can only end up in division [...]

That leads me to the second defining characteristic of parliamentary democracy, which is non-violence. I do not mean the mere avoidance of violence, I mean the positive assertion of political activity as an alternative to war, not just as a means to a particular end, but as a value in itself, a recognition of a higher form of social organization it is not easy to reach and maintain, and must be worked at, and sweated for. This is essentially a rational approach to politics. But man is also moral, and morality also requires the conduct of political activity by peaceful means. It is extraordinary that violent societies are often churchgoing societies, where individuals attach great importance to the role of religion in their lives. This is another factor for the discussion of parliamentary democracy in Ireland – the role of the churches.

It is a major influence and it is certainly true of Northern Ireland today. It is a place where religion has a very deep influence on people's lives, and they have no difficulty in accommodating the ten commandments in their personal lives while they commit or advocate acts of violence and injustice in their political lives. There can be a complete disjunction between the two: the words of churchmen condemning murder and strife fall on the heedless heads of the men of violence and the men who perpetrate injustice [...] why is it that communities that belong to the same Christian tradition, a tradition that upholds humility and peace, why is it that they produce such bitter, endless strife? This is a question which should be examined and answered by churchmen [...]

Continuing on the second criterion of non-violence. It is often claimed of course by those who are violent that non-violence and parliamentary methods have achieved nothing. They, correctly of course, see that non-violence and parliamentary methods are one and the same. They often say that this has achieved nothing in the north of Ireland. I think that those of us who have been engaged on these methods – parliamentary and non-violent – have perhaps been a little remiss in spelling out what actually has been achieved. When I think of why I went onto the streets of the North in the non-violent civil rights movement [...] what we were looking for was simple things like one man one vote; like the fair distribution of housing, more housing [...] [like] jobs, a fair distribution of them. These are the three basic areas. That was only fifteen years ago and that was a not a long time. What has happened in the meantime? We have one man one vote [...] It [Derry] was the worst-housed city in 1967, when I sat in an office in Castle Street, as chairman of the Housing Association, a self-help body, and felt frustrated at the lack of any political attempt at house building, interviewing people night after night and seeing the desperate housing situation face-to-face. Today we have one of the best-housed cities in these islands, achieved by non-violence and by asking [...] that housing should be taken out of the hands of politicians, and given to an independent technocratic body, the housing executive, which has been done [...]

Violence [...] invites defeat, and it destroys that which is worth having. Edmund Burke once spoke of this when he was rebuking the British government for its failure to conciliate America. He said, 'A further objection to force is that the thing you fought for is not the thing that you recover. But what you recover is depreciated, sunk, wasted and consumed in the contest.' If you lived where I lived you would know that those words are true: 'sunk, depreciated, wasted and consumed'. The violence of the past ten years has done a lot of that apart from the fact that it has killed 2,500 people and that it has maimed 20,000 people. 'Nothing less will content me', said Burke, 'than whole America'. Nothing less will content us, than Ireland whole [...]

Those who state that Irish unity is the only answer, British withdrawal is the only solution – they never tell us how they are going to do it. They measure every suggested solution against that ultimate objective, and describe it as a sell-out if it is not that ultimate objective. They seek all or nothing. They always end up with nothing. It is like the man who goes into negotiations, comes out with 60 per cent and is told that he has sold out because he did not get the other 40 per cent.

The third group, and I would like to include my own party in this, is the group that looks at the problem and says, 'Here is how we propose to go about it.' And our approach has been what we used to call in the '70 the 3Rs – reform, reconciliation, reunification. First of all we have to recognize the fact that all the principles that applied in 1920 do not apply today, because since 1920, two separate entities have grown up in Ireland, with all the consequences of that, which were dealt with in great detail in the Forum Report [...]

The North is there. Our view is that the first step towards a solution is to seek equality for all citizens there – that must be the basic thrust in the civil rights movement. And based on that equality to then move on to reconciliation, because reconciliation can only be based on equality [...] And reconciliation and the breaking down of barriers between sections of the community that are equals of its very essence creates unity and that will be the road, that will be the chart, and therefore any proposal that is made by anybody for progress, for development, our yardstick would not be the ultimate, our yardstick would be: will it help us along that road? [...] the framework in which we must see the solution is the framework of the problem, the British-Irish framework. That is the framework [...] in which a breakthrough took place in 1980, in the historic meeting between Mrs Thatcher and Mr Haughey, in which the Anglo-Irish process was first set up, the framework within which the solution is being sought today. That is the framework [...] in which the talks are taking place today between the present government and the British government on the basis of the Forum Report [...][14]

In the months that followed, speculation mounted as to what the outcome to ongoing Irish-British negotiations would be. Hume was very conscious that support from the US and from Europe for whatever might be agreed would be crucial. In an address in September to a conference on Ireland and European-US relationships Hume stressed the historic background to these relationships:

throughout the seventeenth and eighteenth centuries the Irish people looked to the continental [European] powers as political allies. During the nineteenth and early twentieth centuries they looked to the Irish-American community. When both parts of the island acceded to membership of the European Community in 1973 this was not an unprecedented involvement with the Continent; people had sense of renewing a connection from which they had had been distracted by a century of turbulence and sometimes horrific events.

The situation today is intriguing: the earlier links with the Continent have been renewed but now rest on the solid foundation of the treaties of the European Community. The links with America were founded on the connections of blood, friendships and heritage between 4.5 million people on this island and upwards of 16 million people in the United States; the relationship has deepened and matured as the Republic has developed politically and economically and as the Irish in America have prospered and built on their extraordinary political achievements of the past hundred years.

These two global relationships have played major roles in the fortunes of Ireland in recent years. From America came tourists and much of the industrial development which created the impressive economic development of the Republic in recent years. From Europe have come the economic benefits of membership of the Community which have transformed life, particularly in the Republic, and also a sense of political dignity and statehood, again in the

14 Address to the Merriman Summer School, 23 Aug. 1985; copy in editor's possession.

Republic, which prior to membership, had been stifled by a claustrophobic bilateral relationship with the neighbouring island.[15]

A few weeks later, in an address to the National Democratic Foundation in the US, he stressed the example America had provided in the struggle for civil and human rights, and its support for a peaceful, non-violent approach towards resolving the problems of Northern Ireland:

> Yours is a state where there is consensus fashioned from rich relationships and broad difference. From many you have one. We however do not yet know such consensus. We have not yet devised structures which accommodate difference and ensure stability.
>
> We know that the emergence of that consensus in the United States was not easy. That it is only in more recent times that minorities really feel they have approached that equality that is theirs by right. Your party leaders played a noble role in that achievement. It was not simple. There were times of panic and times of indifference. There were times of hope and times of despair. There was social progress and there was social pain. But you saw it through, and you will see it through again.
>
> For ourselves we know the scale of our task, but we are not daunted by it. We have been tested by discrimination, bigotry and state violence, but we have not been tempted by revenge. We have been hurt, misrepresented, and handicapped by the violence of others but we have kept faith with our own non-violence. We have been troubled in a political vacuum but we have held true to our political values.
>
> Our challenge is not easy, but the choice is. There is no other way. We cannot solve problems of difference by creating divisions. We cannot create peace by using violence. We cannot protect civil rights by attacking human rights. We cannot secure justice by abandoning the rule of law. We cannot achieve freedom by inflicting injustice.
>
> We have no illusions that a solution lies somewhere over the rainbow. We know the path is long and stony. We do not seek to mislead people by promises of instant solutions. We do not hide from our responsibility by hiding behind unrealistic and uncompromising demands. We seek to help people not to use them. We seek to allay fears not play to them. We seek to ease tensions not exacerbate them. We try only to solve problems, not exploit them.
>
> We want to thank you for the assistance that many in your party have given us. Standing by us has not been easy for you. You too have had to pay

---

15 Address at Waterville, Co. Kerry, 23 Sept. 1985; copy in editor's possession.

the price of abuse, misrepresentation or even rejection. Clearly the only reward that you seek is a new Ireland. We owe it to you as well as to ourselves and our children, that we should fashion that new Ireland [...]

I wish to pay tribute to the achievements on human rights of the Carter-Mondale administration. But I want to assure you that our own problems will not distract us from doing what we can in the fight for human rights in the modern world. Know that when we seek to find those who have disappeared, when you seek to allow families to bury their executed dead, when you seek to free the dissident, when you seek to secure justice for those crushed under cruel apartheid, we are at one with you. Together we are at one with the feeble, the deprived and the true.[16]

In the context of rising expectations as to what the Irish-British negotiations would produce, Hume was also anxious to contrast the possibilities from patient, political engagement with the dangers and threats of a violent approach. He again forcibly argued the dangers of outright civil war inherent in the mounting demands from the PIRA for a British withdrawal:

The most likely response would be that the vacuum left by the British army would be filled by people with arms. Seizing territory as a bargaining counter is par for the course. If you need examples just look at Cyprus and the Lebanon. I am not interested in getting the British army out of Ireland if this leaves behind an even more divided society. Nationalists in Northern Ireland are faced with two difficulties, one is the British presence, the other is their relationship with the unionists. Resolving the first difficulty must be done in a way that does not exacerbate the other [...]

There is no precedent to justify the militant republican attitude that if they drove 'the British' out then 'the Irish' would sit around a table and come to an agreement. One quarter of the people of Ireland regard themselves as British. This is no tiny percentage such as [Europeans] in Rhodesia or Algeria but a substantial number that is concentrated in one geographical corner of Ireland.

If you face that fact, if you actually care about the future of the people of this island then you must approach the problem in a more prudent fashion to ensure that the end result gives you a peaceful and stable island.[17]

Hume continued his attack on the PIRA and its campaign of violence, which he condemned with particular vitriol:

16 Address to the National Democratic Foundation, *Congressional Record*, 10 Oct. 1985.   17 Address at Milltown Institute of Theology, *Guilty parties* (Dublin, 1985).

Then there is the [...] alternative to the SDLP, the Provos under their banner of 'principled leadership'. They bomb factories and shout about unemployment, they shoot a teacher in a classroom, kill school-bus drivers, kill on campuses and then lecture us on education. They kill, maim and injure and they carry out attacks in hospital precincts and then tell us about protecting the health service. They rob post offices, leaving people without benefit payments and then they preach to us about defending the poor. They talk about housing. When we deliver £65 million of European aid for housing, Danny Morrison [of Sinn Féin] says it is a bribe to wean people in Belfast away from republicanism. In short, houses for Catholics are bad for republicanism. We have heard that before, was that not the unionist position from 1921 to 1998? Houses for Catholics are bad for unionism? On Friday evening their housing spokesman complains about a £6 million cut in the budget of the housing executive in Northern Ireland as a whole. On the same Friday evening their military wing blows £2 million of public money in a single street. They criticize the British government on Kinsale gas,[18] and they blow up the electricity interconnector [between North and South]. They rightly condemn the execution of a young black poet in South Africa but they execute a young unemployed man in a back lane in the Brandywell [in Derry], or they execute a trussed up young couple in the back streets of West Belfast. They condemn British brutality yet use it themselves. Are kangaroo courts any improvement on Diplock courts? Are punishment beatings and shootings the answer to community crime? So much for principled leadership [...]

Then, there is the reaction to the continuing Anglo-Irish talks. The SDLP are 'collaborators', 'helping to legitimize the British presence', 'sell-outs' etc. etc. Have we not heard all that before? Was that not how we were described in the '70s because we fought elections? When they told people not to register for their vote and to burn their vote? Now they fight elections and we hear nothing about legitimizing the British presence. Instead they go into a court to a judge appointed by the British crown to defend their democratic rights but they will not send their leader, appointed, not by the British crown but by the people of West Belfast, to the British parliament to defend their rights. If, of course, there are some gains or advances from the Anglo-Irish process, it will be their achievement, they say. They will claim any successes but blame others for their failures. They remind us of the cock that crowed and claimed to have turned on the sun but accepted no responsibility for the rain.[19]

---

18 Plans to supply the North with natural gas from the Republic's Kinsale field were under discussion at the time.   **19** Address to the SDLP Annual Conference, 9 Nov. 1985.

Within a week of the conference the Anglo-Irish Agreement was signed at Hillsborough, an event that precipitated considerable political turmoil within the unionist community, but which received a general welcome by nationalists. For John Hume and the SDLP the agreement marked a watershed in terms of the Irish government's role in the affairs of Northern Ireland. The two governments undertook to consult and in so far as possible to reach agreement before taking significant decisions affecting the North. The framework within which Hume believed a solution could be reached had at last been put in place. There were also commitments to police and judicial reform, and to enhancing cross-border economic and security co-operation. Politically, the British government also made clear that if the people of Northern Ireland ever wished to unite with the Republic, it would facilitate such an eventuality. Hume welcomed the agreement and, in particular, the new Intergovernmental Conference that would oversee its implementation. In a speech to the house of commons, he stated:

> I was glad to see a full house at the beginning of the debate. That is the first achievement of the Anglo-Irish Conference. It shows that the serious human problem facing the peoples of these islands has at last been given the priority that it deserves. It has been put at the centre of the stage [...]
>
> This is the first time that we have had a real framework within which to address the problem. The problem is not just about relationships within Northern Ireland. One need only listen to the speeches of Northern Ireland members to know that it is about relationships in Ireland and between Ireland and Britain. Those interlocking relationships should be addressed within the framework of the problem. The framework of the problem can only be the framework of the solution, and that is the British-Irish framework. There is no road towards a solution to this problem that does not contain risks. The road that has been chosen by both governments is the road of maximum consensus and is, therefore, the road of minimum risk. We should welcome that [...]
>
> The divisions in Ireland go back well beyond partition. Centuries ago the leaders of Irish republicanism said that they wanted to unite Ireland by replacing the name of 'Catholic/Protestant/Dissenter' with the common name of 'Irishman'. That was in 1795. Thirty years before partition Parnell said that Ireland could never be united or have its freedom until the fears of the Protestant minority in Ireland could be conciliated. This is a deep problem. It will not be solved in a week or in a fortnight. The agreement says that if Ireland is ever to be united it will be united only if those who want it to be united can persuade those who do not want it to be united. Sovereignty has nothing to do with maps but everything to do with people.
>
> The people of Ireland are divided on sovereignty. They will be united only

by a process of reconciliation in which both traditions in Ireland can take part and agree. If that happens, it will lead to the only unity that matters – a unity that accepts that the essence of unity is the acceptance of diversity [...]

For the first time [this agreement] sets up a framework that addresses the problem of the interlocking relationships between the people of both Irelands. It is the approach of maximum consensus. It is the way of minimum risk. For the first time – this is a positive element in the agreement – it respects the equal validity of both traditions. That is what the right hon. and hon. members of the Unionist Party are complaining about. It is not a concession to me or to the people whom I represent. It is an absolute right to the legitimate expression of our identity and of the people I represent. Nobody can take that from us. The recognition of the equal validity of both traditions removes for the first time every excuse for the use of violence by anybody in Ireland to achieve his objective. A framework for genuine reconciliation is provided. Both sections of our community can take part in it.

Several hon. members have said that the SDLP has a double veto on devolution. I have already said several times to them in public, but let me say it again so that they may hear it, that I believe in the partnership between the different sections of the community in Northern Ireland. That is the best way to reconcile our differences. By working together to build our community we shall diminish the prejudices that divide us. The agreement means that I am prepared to sit down now and determine how we shall administer the affairs of Northern Ireland in a manner that is acceptable to both traditions.

The second question that appears to excite people about my party's attitude relates to the security forces and to policing in Northern Ireland. Our position – this is not a policy but a statement of fact that applies to every democratic society – is that law and order are based upon political consensus. Where political consensus is absent there is an Achilles heel. Violent men in Northern Ireland take advantage of that Achilles heel. For the first time the Intergovernmental Conference will address that question. It has committed itself to addressing that question. It has also committed itself to addressing the relationship between the community and the security forces. I want to give every encouragement to the conference to do so at the earliest possible opportunity. If it does so, it will have our fullest co-operation. I want the people whom I represent to play the fullest possible part, as do any citizens in a democratic society, in the process of peace and order. While we await the outcome we shall continue to give our full and unqualified support to the police force in impartially seeking out anybody who commits a crime in Northern Ireland.

What is the alternative to the process of reconciliation and the breaking down of barriers? Why should anybody be afraid of the process of reconciliation? Anybody who is afraid has no confidence in himself or herself. It means that they cannot engage in a process of reconciliation. If they cannot retain mutual respect for their own position as well as for that of somebody else, they have no self-confidence. Therefore, they should not be representatives of the people of Northern Ireland. The only alternative is the old one of hopelessness, tit-for-tat, revenge – the old doctrine of an eye for an eye which has left everybody blind in Northern Ireland.[20]

In the European parliament a few weeks later Hume again welcomed the agreement in similar terms, drawing parallels between the new Intergovernmental Conference, its proposed inter-parliamentary body and its secretariat, with European Community institutions:

This house will no doubt note that the institutions set out in this agreement are rather similar to the institutions of the Community that we represent in this chamber. The Anglo-Irish Conference is the equivalent to the council of ministers, the proposed inter-parliamentary tier is the equivalent of this house and the secretariat is the equivalent of the commission. Those similar institutions have enabled the peoples of Western Europe represented in this house [...] to end conflict and war on the continent of Europe and to grow together at their own speed. This being the case, is it an exaggerated hope to express in this chamber today that the same institutions set out in the Anglo-Irish Agreement can provide a similar opportunity to the people of Ireland to grow together at their own speed and to end conflict, hatred and violence in that island.[21]

Notwithstanding the commitments to respect the democratic wishes of the electorate on any change to Northern Ireland's constitutional status, unionist opposition to the role of the Irish government in the North's affairs was such that any prospect of inter-party talks was immediately frustrated, and delayed until that opposition had run its course. In the meantime, the SDLP's deputy leader, Séamus Mallon, won a seat in the constituency of Newry-Armagh when fifteen unionist MPs resigned and forced by-elections in their constituencies as an expression of their opposition to the agreement. Given these developments, Hume and his colleagues focused their attention on ensuring that the agreement's commitments on equality, police reform and equity were upheld. They felt that at last developments were creating a more level playing field between themselves and unionists.

---

20 House of Commons, *Debates*, 26 Nov. 1985.   21 European Parliament, *Debates*, 12 Dec. 1985.

1985–6

Given the scale and intensity of unionist opposition to the Anglo-Irish Agreement, the following eighteen months of 1985–6 witnessed hardly any attempts to initiate cross-party discussion, let alone negotiations. In this context Hume and the SDLP could only emphasize that they remained available for talks. While continuing to make the case that the agreement offered the framework essential for addressing the constitutional and political problems affecting not just relationships within the North, but relationships between Ireland and Britain, Hume also addressed several more specific high-profile issues of the time, some of an all-Ireland nature, others more global. These included church-state relationships, the case for a divorce referendum in the Republic, apartheid in South Africa, the pressing social and economic needs of sub-Saharan Africa, regional development within the European Community, nuclear energy and the plight of those he believed had been falsely convicted and imprisoned for planting PIRA bombs in Britain.

Church-state relationships

On church-state relationships Hume argued for complete separation:

> If we are talking purely and constitutionally, the only democracy in Western Europe, at the moment, where there is not complete separation between church and state is the United Kingdom. It is the only country where the head of church is head of state, and where there are seats, as of right, in the national parliament for bishops of a particular church.
>
> I do not believe that it benefits any country or people when the attitudes of a particular church are legislated into the law of that country. If you go down that road, you come to extreme examples, such as Iran and Iraq, where the private morality of an individual church becomes the total legislation of the country. That sort of identity is not necessary. I believe if you are a Catholic, you do not need acts of parliament to make you a better Catholic. The day you need an act of parliament to make you a better Catholic, your lack of faith in your own faith becomes self-evident.
>
> There needs to be a wide-ranging debate on church and state, so that people know exactly where they stand. It should be made clear, for example, that the church must preach the ideal. Nobody should ask the church to

weaken her teaching on any issue. That is the basic role of the church: to preach the ideal. The role of the state is quite different. The state has to deal with the real. Real things happen with legal consequences.[1]

Divorce in the Republic

A critical example of an issue that affected church-state relationships in the South was the Republic's constitutional prohibition on divorce. The government of the day argued in favour of the prohibition's removal, and a referendum to remove the prohibition was called. Hume argued that divorce legislation was required to address the situation of marriage breakdown, and not, as some suggested, as a gesture to please unionists in the North:

> Answering questions at a meeting of the Association of European Journalists, Mr Hume accepted the view of the Roman Catholic church that politicians must look at the social consequences of divorce legislation, because divorce did create serious social consequences.
>
> 'If there is going to be a referendum on divorce in the Republic – and that decision must be taken by the Republic's political parties – people must know precisely what kind of divorce law they are voting on.'
>
> Asked if the Republic should introduce divorce to please the unionists Mr Hume replied 'the South should not be changed to please the North, but should introduce change on its own merits'. It was his view that there was a need for a law in the Republic to deal with the legal consequences arising from marriage breakdown.
>
> There were also legal consequences for those who obtained a decree of marriage nullity from the Catholic church but discovered that there was no civil law to deal with their situation.
>
> Mr Hume said that if the political parties in the Republic agreed to the holding of a referendum to remove the constitutional ban on divorce, it would be futile to ask for a 'yes' or a 'no' answer. 'You will get all kinds of extreme debating positions on this, highlighting the Californian divorce law and other situations. So I am saying before you have a referendum let the people know exactly what you are talking about. Let them know the specific law that would be proposed.'[2]

In the event, the referendum seeking support to remove the prohibition on divorce which took place the following June was lost. Hume's reaction to the result

---

1 Address to the Milltown Institute of Theology, *Guilty parties* (Dublin, 1985).   2 *Irish Times*, 7 Dec. 1985.

was brief: 'I cannot say that I am delighted by the result.'[3] The prohibition was eventually removed following a later referendum in 1995.

Africa

Hume spoke out against apartheid in South Africa on several occasions. Receiving the human rights award of the American Federation of Teachers, he described apartheid as 'the greatest single crime against humanity in the world today'.[4] Earlier, in a house of commons debate in June 1986, he had highlighted the desperate nature of the situation in which the black population in South Africa found itself, and the limited choices they had to address their plight:

> All hon. members seem to agree – that is, if they mean what they say – that apartheid is an evil and inhumane system that should go. There seems to be general agreement about the remarks of the EPG [European Parliamentary Group] that the South African situation threatens the worst bloodshed to be seen since the Second World War. Consequently, I wish merely to ask what hon. members would do if they were black South Africans faced by that situation. What would they do in a situation where the normal democratic rights and processes do not exist? They do not have a vote or access to any of the normal democratic institutions to deal with the assault on their fundamental human dignity, nor do they have the right of peaceful protest. They are banned when they try it; they are shot and gassed.
>
> In such circumstances is it not remarkable that there has not been a great deal more violence? Martin Luther King said of South African blacks twenty years ago that they had withstood abuse and persecution with a dignity and calmness of spirit seldom paralleled in human history. How much more is that tribute due to the South African blacks today? The right hon. member for Brighton, Pavilion [Mr Amery] listed many areas in which there had been massive violence and admitted that there had been a great deal less in South Africa. The question that Conservative members have to ask themselves is, what would they do as blacks with no access to any peaceful method of redressing injustices?
>
> What are the blacks doing? Those who see that violence brings its own evils are asking us for something moderate. They are asking Britain to do less than it did when its territorial rights were threatened in a small dispute in the South Atlantic affecting only 1,800 people. Then the British government asked for international sanctions, which they backed up with great physical force. The blacks in South Africa are not asking for that. They are asking

3 Ibid., 28 June 1986.   4 Ibid., 9 July 1986.

simply for international sanctions to help them create circumstances in which dialogue can begin between black and white about the creation of a non-racial democracy in South Africa. That is all they are asking.

In Tokyo some weeks ago the leaders of the most powerful industrial nations met, rightly, to discuss the threat of international terrorism and to take action to deal with it. I say 'rightly' because it is a serious problem, but it is in no way as serious as the problem which, in the eyes of eminent world statesmen appointed by the leaders of the Commonwealth, threatens violence and bloodshed on the scale of the Second World War. Mr Shultz, the American secretary of state, walked out of that Tokyo meeting and said, 'Gaddafi, pal, you have had it; you are isolated.' What is wrong with the same leaders meeting again to discuss the serious situation in South Africa and with Mr Shultz, or anyone else, saying, 'Botha, pal, you have had it; you are isolated'?[5] What is wrong with taking the necessary steps to ensure that he is isolated?[6]

At the SDLP conference 'Africa – the challenge of change', Hume gave a keynote speech in which he stressed the responsibility to have concern for the human condition in general, not just in one's own situation, saying:

We have decided to focus our conference on Africa. We have done so because in that 'vast and complex continent', as Martin Luther King described it, there are many interlocking issues which are crystallized in underdevelopment, mass poverty and injustice. We have done so because we are conscious of the fact that many of us, understandably, think broadly in terms of a Third World, with little sense of peoples' identities or culture, whatever about our concern for their living conditions.

It is perhaps appropriate that the SDLP should look at the condition of Africa and the relationship of our part of the world to it. Our party was founded out of the civil rights movement. The movement took much of its inspiration from the civil rights movement in America under Martin Luther King. It is not widely enough recognized however that much of Martin Luther King's own inspiration had come from Africa and the words of its leaders and authors, and particularly at a time when Africa was apparently achieving its political independence.

Many of Africa's hopes have unfortunately been cruelly frustrated. Our speakers today will give us some account of this and the various factors underlying those problems. Among those factors is the historic underdevelopment

5 P.W. Botha was president of South Africa at this time.   6 House of Commons, *Debates,* 17 June 1986.

and abuse of Africa under colonialism, continuing economic colonialism and exploitation, poor aid programmes and inadequate and sometimes inappropriate development programmes. In our conference we will want to look at those factors which we can help to change [...]

I have no doubt that people here have a commitment to world justice. That has been shown in the response to various fund-raising initiatives for famine relief or development. It has been shown by the thousands of letters which people here sent to political representatives and the hundreds of petitions from all sorts of groups, schools and communities. I do not believe that this has been appreciated or reflected by the media [...]

The issue which most occupies concerns at present is the situation in South Africa. We will discuss the nature of apartheid and its effects on people's lives. I think that people here often underestimate the reality of apartheid, perceiving it to be just a thoroughgoing scheme of political discrimination. For individuals, communities and entire peoples, it is that and more, amounting to a fully comprehensive denial of human rights and dignity in all areas of life. It is a crime against humanity and we must make every effort in solidarity with the struggle of people in South Africa to bring apartheid down. That includes comprehensive and total sanctions.

But as this conference will bear out there is more suffering in Africa than under apartheid and that poses uncomfortable issues for people in the Western world. We must face the fact that at a global level power relationships and economic circumstances betray many of the hallmarks of apartheid. Power and wealth is concentrated in the hands of a minority. In a situation of plenty the majority of people suffer underdevelopment, lack education and health facilities, face malnutrition and work for a less-than-meagre living while producing wealth or resources for others [...]

I have told American audiences, 'We in Ireland can, I believe, have a special role on these issues, given our history [...] Ireland knew famine in the last century, it is for that reason that our country has been so moved by the present famine of Africa. We know that our famines were not simply natural disasters. History shows that the Irish people were starved or forced to leave their native land because of unjust distribution of land, poverty and extortion which forced the production of cash crops for the wealthy abroad instead of food for the hungry at home, trade structures which knew no morality and unequal power relationships between countries. These are the same injustices and absurdities which crucify Africa today.'[7]

7 Address to the SDLP conference, 'Africa – the challenge of change', 25 Oct. 1986.

Regional development in the European Community

Hume was a fervent advocate of regional development within the European Community. He believed that properly planned regional development would arrest the growth of the Continent's major conurbations. Such development would lead to more even growth outside conurbations, thereby offering an effective antidote to the social decay, crime, violence and drug-taking so characteristic of large cities. In an address to a conference at University College Galway in September 1986, he argued for a more effective and financially strengthened European Community regional policy:

> Present policies have failed to generate the sort of economic growth and development which would bring living standards in the peripheral regions up to the Community average. 'Convergence' is the word that is used among eurocrats – and it hasn't happened. [...]
>
> In short, existing Community instruments have so far proved inadequate to the task of stimulating development of the regions in any real sense. There have been signs of a Community willingness, on occasions, to take more dramatic initiatives. The regional aids given to Ireland and Italy after the launching of the EMS [European Monetary System], and the introduction of the Integrated Mediterranean Programme, have been signs that the Community can take greater formal powers in this area. But as the commission itself has stated, 'unless regional policy can be developed [...] the process of integration within the Community will come to a halt'.
>
> What sort of regional policy will stimulate the development of the depressed regions, and promote convergence? I have long believed that a policy which aims to create a 'Europe of the Regions' is the only policy that makes sense socially, economically, culturally and politically.
>
> One of the most worrying aspects of economic development patterns in recent times has been the concentration of growth in huge urban areas. The massive overpopulation of the major European and American conurbations, with the consequent strain on all of the public services, has generated enormous social problems. The drift into the cities, and the erosion of traditional communities, has often been accompanied by a breakdown of order and an upsurge of antisocial behaviour. There is a strong and growing body of thought which insists that this growth pattern must be halted and reversed if the social decay, crime, violence and drug-taking is to be contained. There are, therefore, powerful social reasons for a dynamic regional policy to preserve and expand traditional communities in the weaker regions. Such communities hold people together in a relatively harmonious equilibrium, through a network of family and community constraints and pressures which generate considerate behaviour [...]

There are powerful cultural reasons for a regional policy which preserves and expands traditional communities. It is in such communities that the full richness of our cultural heritage, in all of its regional diversity, is preserved. The decay of such communities, the erosion of their languages and regional dialects, and the disappearance of their particular cultures would leave us all a lot poorer. It was for this reason that I proposed in 1980 a programme of measures to preserve regional languages and dialects [...]

Above all, there are powerful economic reasons for a dynamic regional policy. Some years ago the Brandt Commission produced a report which fundamentally argued that the development of the Third World was not just a moral imperative but an economic necessity.[8] Even in terms of crude self-interest, the developed countries can only gain in the longer term by the substantial transfer of resources to the poorer nations. The generation of prosperity and higher living standards in the Third World could in turn revive world markets, expand world trade and revive the flagging economies of Europe [...]

If these principles are applicable on the world scale they are equally applicable on the European and national scale. 'Convergence', therefore, is not a welfare policy; it is probably the only policy for economic growth which offers some hope of an economic revival [...]

Can we in Ireland take advantage of this renewed commitment to integrated programmes on the part of the commission? Quite simply, we can and we must. I have been working within the parliament to bring into existence an integrated programme for the rural areas in the North. Yet even within so small an area there are distinct regions with their own particular local needs and problems – my own north-west for instance, the city of Derry and its natural hinterland, Donegal, Tyrone and County Derry. Similarly there are distinct regions within the Republic, with their own local character and particular needs and problems. Connacht needs a different type of development programme from the city of Dublin [...]

I would suggest there is a need for change at national level. Up to now development policies at the national level have favoured concentration and centralization. If development is to be decentralized then power needs to be decentralized. Strong decentralized participating communities can best identify local needs, and discern local opportunities, and they can bring a motivation into play which remote centralized bureaucracies do not have. This does not necessarily involve a rivalry between the periphery and the centre, but rather a dynamic tension which can stimulate both in a partner-

---

8 Willy Brandt was a former chancellor of West Germany, who headed a commission that examined economic trends in the developing world, and published its report in 1981.

ship for progress. Such a partnership could, as John Healy has said, 'harness the dynamic of the regions', in a new growth of national prosperity.[9] If this is to be done, then regional administrative structures must be developed which can undertake the work.[10]

Nuclear energy

At the SDLP's 1986 annual conference, in Newcastle, Co. Down, Hume addressed concerns about nuclear power, which had grown considerably following the explosion at the Chernobyl plant in the Ukraine. Immediate concerns existed because of the Sellafield nuclear plant in Britain, close to the Cumbrian coast on the Irish Sea:

> We live in a small world. Chernobyl and its aftermath confirmed that forever. It also highlighted the awesome risks of nuclear power, risks of which we are all too well aware, particularly here on the Co. Down coast, where a range of nuclear installations face us across the Irish Sea. Most of them have safety records that give grounds for deep concern, whether it be accidental discharges into the sea or the atmosphere, ageing structures or easy-going management.
>
> Our source of particular concern is Sellafield. Over three hundred accidents have taken place there since the 1950s. Earlier this year a series of errors and accidents followed misleading attempts at reassurance. It is irresponsible to add to it a THORP plant, which will process waste with much higher levels of radioactivity. The risk of a single accident in a century with all its awful consequences for humanity removes all justification for the use of nuclear power. No generation, for its own comfort and economy, has the right to put future generations at risk. [...]
>
> The SDLP held a special conference earlier this year to examine the threats posed by Sellafield. It was a clear indication of our concern to be as informed, thorough and responsible as possible in our approach to this major and fundamental issue. With these credentials we will continue to press for a shutdown of the Sellafield plant and, through our membership of the Confederation of Socialist Parties and our international contacts, we will continue to press the case for non-nuclear energy policies.[11]

---

9 John Healy was a well-known Irish political and social commentator. **10** Address to the conference 'The future of regional development', University College Galway, 26 Sept. 1986; copy in editor's possession. **11** Address to the SDLP's annual conference, 22 Nov. 1986.

Imprisoned unjustly

To the litany of PIRA atrocities were added the injustices being suffered by those falsely imprisoned for bombings in Britain in the 1970s that had taken many lives – in Birmingham, Guildford and Woolwich. Hume, along with the other SDLP MPs, Séamus Mallon, Eddie McGrady and Joe Hendron, campaigned for their release. Hume spoke movingly about these injustices in the course of a European parliament debate:

> Fifteen years ago this week, twenty-one people were having a drink in pubs in Birmingham and were blown to bits. Let it be clear that it is the totally unanimous view of this house that the greatest injustice that can be committed is murder, because there is no redress for that injustice. People can come out of jails; people cannot come out of graves. Let that point be very clear.
>
> What was also understandable was the wave of anger and emotion that swept Britain after the atrocities of Birmingham and Guildford. What is not, however, acceptable is that the anger and emotion should distort the basic principles of justice. That has already been accepted in the case of the Guildford Four.
>
> Might I say that as an Irish person I was very proud of the demeanour of Mr Conlon and Mr Hill on their release?
>
> A lot of people in Ireland have much to learn from those two people, particularly from the dignity and lack of bitterness they showed and the generosity they showed in thanking those British people who led the campaign on their behalf – leaders of church and state and ordinary people. Those same leaders of church and state are asking the same questions about Birmingham. They are supported today by representatives of all twelve member states. I would hope that both of those arguments together, those of distinguished British people and the representatives of the twelve member states will be taken seriously by the British authorities and that they will respond positively to them. It is also a great injustice to the twenty-one Birmingham people who cannot come out of their graves that the wrong people are spending their lives in jail for that horrible crime.[12]

The Guildford Four were released in 1989, the Maguire Seven in 1990 and the Birmingham Six in 1991. The real culprits were never caught.

---

12 European Parliament, *Debates*, 23 Nov. 1989.

1986–8

With unionists maintaining their unwillingness to enter talks as long the Anglo-Irish Agreement was in force, Hume was anxious to ensure that its benefits were clearly understood, and that its implementation would be as complete and as rapid as possible. He firmly believed that the agreement marked a major watershed in dealing with the conflict, that it would help resolve many outstanding nationalist grievances and, critically, that it would provide the most effective political framework for resolving the conflict. In an article in the journal *Studies* he strongly argued this latter point:

> What I find remarkable is that the Anglo-Irish Agreement bears no resemblance to the descriptions by its critics. One wonders if they have either read it or understood it or whether party prejudices have run so deep as to blind their judgment. The framework for the process [...] ought to be the Anglo-Irish framework. Firstly, because it is the framework of the problem. The relationships that are in conflict are not confined to the North; they are within Ireland and between Ireland and Britain. The framework of the problem, the British-Irish framework, should be the framework of the solution. Secondly, it is the framework of maximum consensus, since it is based on the consensus of the 59 million people of both islands, rather than the consent of 1.5 million of them. Thirdly, and because of that, it is the road of minimum risk. Every road towards an answer is fraught with risk. The road of minimum risk is the road based on the democratic consensus of the people of both islands.
>
> The framework that has been created is the Anglo-Irish Conference, which is in effect a permanent council of ministers from Britain and Ireland meeting on a regular basis, serviced by a permanent secretariat, to deal with a wide range of problems affecting the people of Northern Ireland. It is a decision-making process which is much fairer than any previous such process and which is the ideal framework, firstly, for tackling immediate grievances within the North and ensuring equality of citizenship, and secondly, for dealing with the wider relationships which have a direct bearing on the problems of the North. It is, in short, an opportunity to use the democratic process to the full in order to pursue the healing process [...] It is not a solution to the Irish problem, which is the false assumption on which many of its opponents criti-

cize it. It is a framework of opportunity whereby we can move together towards a solution. It is permanent, and future governments, using the framework, can make their contribution to the healing and building process. More importantly, when taken in conjunction with the declarations embodied in the agreement, it removes completely the slightest justification for the use of violence in Ireland to achieve political objectives.

There are two declarations, only one of which has received detailed public attention. There shall be no change in the status of Northern Ireland without the consent of a majority of its people. That is a statement of fact. Does anyone believe that the people of Ireland can be united by force, or coercion? Does anyone believe that they can be united without agreement? Is not the evidence of divided people elsewhere that attempts to unite them by force have led only to partition and re-partition?

The second declaration is that if a majority in the North wish for Irish unity then the British government will facilitate and legislate for it. This is a clear statement by the British government that it has no interest of its own, either strategic or otherwise, in remaining in Ireland. It is a declaration that Irish unity is a matter for Irish people, for those who want it to persuade those who don't. It is a clear challenge to all who really believe in the common name of 'Irishman' to do what has never been done, to enter a sustained period of persuasion, of breaking down of barriers. To seek to do so by bullets is an approach not alone of cowardice but one that reveals an almost total lack of self-confidence.

The process involved is not one that any Northern Protestant need fear if he or she enters the process with self-confidence. They must be part of the process, part of the building. What emerges must have their hallmark too and must respect and cater for the diversity of the Irish people. In the second half of the twentieth century, what is the alternative?

The harsh truth is that we will be sharing the same piece of earth for a long time to come. We can live together or we can live apart. Living apart has not been very pleasant and has brought out the worst in us all; living together and growing together will be painful and difficult. There will be many hiccups, many setbacks but the goal is worth achieving and it will take time. Is there any other way?[1]

Hume was also anxious to demonstrate to the men and women of violence that democratic politics worked and could achieve worthwhile and very practical results. In an address to his own Bogside branch of the SDLP he posed and answered the question 'What has been achieved?' as follows:

1 *Studies*, winter 1986, 204–9.

The two governments, as a result of an international agreement, are sitting together at a permanent conference table dealing with the problems of Northern Ireland. That is the very far-reaching step the significance of which has been underestimated by all the critics except the unionists. If the public were to read tomorrow morning that a permanent Anglo-Argentinian Conference had been set up to deal with the problem of the Falkland Islands, would the world, as it did in our case, not applaud a significant development?

That permanent intergovernmental framework is the means whereby the steady process of building a solution to our deep-seated problem can take place if those who are party to the problem have the will to take the opportunities presented. It is also the best way because it proceeds with the consensus of the 59 million people of both islands rather than with the veto of 1 per cent of them. In addition the framework will survive existing governments so that future governments can continue the building process [...]

The unionist political leadership recognizes that they have lost their unconditional veto, a veto which in our view goes to the heart of the problem and the removal of which is an essential first step on the road to a solution. Not only did that veto not serve the people of Northern Ireland well, it did an extreme disservice to the unionist people themselves in setting them apart from their neighbours and from those with whom they share this piece of earth, thus ensuring permanent instability. In addition the muscle of that veto was the ability of the unionist leadership to blackmail and threaten any British government that tried to tamper with that veto. The success of that blackmail confirmed leadership in uncompromising hands and convinced some in the nationalist community that only violence worked. That vicious circle has paralysed political development and has damaged all sections of our community. In cutting through that vicious circle the present British government is doing a service to our whole community and is creating the circumstances where dialogue without domination can take place. In that stand both they and the Irish government deserve the solidarity of all right-thinking people on both islands because it is crucial to the eventual resolution of this conflict. When that dialogue takes place is a matter for the unionist leadership. We are ready when they are and they should remember that as long as they refuse, then all decisions will be taken within the new process which basically is direct rule with an Irish government input, and from the viewpoint of SDLP supporters that is better than anything we have had to date [...]

In the meantime, and in the short term, the Anglo-Irish Conference has been dealing with the internal grievances within Northern Ireland that it promised to address in the communiqué accompanying the agreement one year ago [...]

Quite a lot of progress, contrary to the perception being promoted by opponents of the agreement, has been made. Ending a serious hunger strike earlier this year was one of the first acts of the Conference. Progress has been made on a number of other issues which although not major have been a source of irritation throughout years of unionist rule and [on which] pressure for change was consistently resisted, e.g. street names in Irish, registration of 'I' voters,[2] and reform of flags-and-emblems legislation. On a more meaningful note, the decision to demolish both the Divis and the Rosville flats has been taken. Major proposals for police-complaints procedures similar to those obtaining elsewhere have been tabled by the British government for discussion and the SDLP has put forward its own proposals. Movement is clearly underway. Again, a major discussion paper detailing the full extent of religious discrimination, with new proposals including sanctions against guilty employers for dealing with it has been tabled by the government. Again, the SDLP has joined in the discussion by submitting our own proposals, and new legislation is underway. The same commitment has been expressed in relation to human rights. The Irish government has submitted a far-reaching proposal for a bill of rights and the British government has responded with proposals for a declaration of rights. Again clear movement is underway. On the economic front a substantial international fund has been set up to help areas of high unemployment and the Newry-Dundalk area has benefited from improved road proposals.

There has been some disappointment about a lack of movement in the crucial area of the administration of justice, and in particular the Diplock courts. The British government has rejected the Irish government proposals for a three-judge court, but since the agreement recognizes that there is a problem in this area the British government has a responsibility to now bring forward its own proposals and to come to agreement with the Irish government. In the same area it is clear that progress has been made in bringing the supergrass system to an end and proposals for legislation to amend the Emergency Provisions Act in relation to arrest, bail and length of remand are on the table for the present session of the house of commons. Not bad for one year I would argue, particularly when compared to the total lack of movement on many of these issues over many years. In short, politics and the political process set up by the agreement are actively working and the result is a much fairer decision-making process for the population at large.[3]

2 'I' voters were excluded from voting in local-government elections in Northern Ireland. The 'I' indicated imperial elections only, i.e. Westminster.   3 Address to the Bogside branch of the SDLP, 13 Nov. 1986.

Fair employment

Among the more pressing issues which Hume and the SDLP wanted to see addressed was that of equality and fairness in the workplace. Reports from the Fair Employment Agency continued to reveal a significant under-representation of Catholics in workplaces across the North, not least in the public services. The essentially exhortatory approach to addressing the issue contained in the 1976 Fair Employment Act was clearly not working and pressure was mounting for stronger legislation. Adding to local pressure for legislative reform was a campaign in the United States that was directed at US companies with subsidiaries in Northern Ireland. This campaign aimed to oblige such companies to adhere to what were called the MacBride principles, a set of principles on employment practices in Northern Ireland named after Seán MacBride, former Irish politician.[4] John Hume, who had frequently used his visits to the US to promote economic investment, was very critical, not so much of the principles themselves, but of the aggressive manner in which he viewed the campaign being conducted. For his criticism he became a target for some sections of Irish-American opinion and was forced to defend his approach:

> John Hume, the leader of Northern Ireland's moderate and predominantly Catholic Social Democratic and Labour Party, says that those Americans pushing for the MacBride principles to ensure equal opportunity for Roman Catholics in Northern Ireland 'just don't know the damage they are doing'.
>
> 'The American campaign against the MacBride principles is allegedly being waged on behalf of people I represent,' Hume said in an interview last week. 'I regard the people behind it as serious and sincere, but they're not helping us – they're doing us damage' [...]
>
> 'There's nothing wrong with the principles as principles,' Hume said, 'but their main effect is disinvestment in Northern Ireland. We need jobs and not principles if we're to tackle our problems of discrimination and unemployment.' [...]
>
> Though praising the commitment of those Americans pushing the MacBride principles, Hume said they miss the point. 'Even if all jobs were provided fairly in Northern Ireland, which they're not, we'd still have 25 per cent unemployment.' [...]
>
> The threat of MacBride, Hume said, can cause a US company considering investment in the European Community to take up proposals from other countries – Ireland, Belgium, Italy or wherever – which offer aid and tax incentives similar to those provided by the British in Northern Ireland.

4 Seán MacBride was a former IRA leader and, later, Ireland's minister for external affairs and an international human-rights activist.

Discrimination against Catholics in Ulster had to be attacked on the ground, not in America, Hume said, noting that the British 'have already published a green paper suggesting sanctions against unfair employers' [...]

While critical of some activists, Hume praised the vast 'mass of Irish-Americans, who are against violence from whatever its source and who do not support the IRA' [...]

'The IRA and its political wing, Sinn Féin, have been hurt by the accord, the infighting inside the Irish National Liberation Army and the party's poor showing in the recent Irish elections. Their claim has always been that they're waging war on behalf of the Irish people,' Hume said. 'Well, they're waging war on behalf of 0.93 per cent of the Irish people,' which was Sinn Féin's percentage of the vote in the elections.[5]

Later, in an *Irish Times* article, Hume again defended his opposition to the MacBride principles campaign and, in particular, to what he described as Sinn Féin's cynical support for the principles while at the same time supporting PIRA attacks on shops, factories and other business premises that effectively destroyed employment opportunities. The twin-track evil of discrimination, as practised by the unionist governments, required a twin-track remedy, he argued:

> If you look at discrimination in Northern Ireland as practised by the unionists when they were in power, it was very thorough and very exhaustive. But it was a twin-track policy that they adopted. East of the Bann there was plenty of employment and Catholics were discriminated against and this was particularly true of public employment which was under the control of the government and the unionist local authorities.
>
> Places like Derry, Newry, Strabane, Enniskillen and West Belfast were starved of investment and jobs. If you look at the allocation of industry under the unionist government of the 1950s and 1960s it is quite clear that there is a pattern of locating industry in a discriminatory fashion.
>
> Therefore if you are to defeat and cure what has happened in the past in terms of discrimination, you need fair employment law with teeth and an agency with teeth to implement it and you need inward investment into areas of high unemployment.
>
> There is only one way you can defeat the past discrimination against places like Derry, Strabane, Newry and West Belfast and that is by the affirmative-action programme of putting in new jobs. We can't have fair employment in Strabane without employment, and anything that blocks that employment coming in hinders our strategy of achieving fair employment.

5 *Boston Globe*, 8 Mar. 1987.

My advice to our friends in the United States was and is if you really want to help us then encourage investment in areas of high unemployment in Northern Ireland. That is a positive thing to do. The effect of the MacBride principles campaign, whether people like to admit it or not, is to stop investment coming, and that is bad for us [...]

During the 1970s, the IRA assassinated the head of the Grundig Company in Northern Ireland and the head of the Dupont Company, the reason being they wanted to drive jobs away.

That is still their policy. And we had the amazing contradiction a few weeks ago of Gerry Adams calling for investment in jobs in West Belfast and a week later the IRA blowing up factories in the same area. What does that tell you about their attitude towards fair employment?

It is utterly cynical and they are the only party that supports this campaign in the United States because they see, as I see, that it stops jobs coming in here and by stopping jobs coming in, they create a lot of discontent among young people and use that discontent as recruitment and fermenting unrest.[6]

Speaking at the SDLP's 1987 annual conference, Hume outlined the party's position regarding fair employment, and argued the consistency of its two-pronged approach to the issue, while also highlighting his continued reservations about the MacBride principles. There was, he said:

the need for strong fair-employment legislation and the need for substantial new investment and job creation in areas of high unemployment. The fair employment legislation must be strong and clear. It must involve sanctions against offending employers, including withdrawal of government grants, and laws which make discrimination illegal. But everyone must recognize, as we have consistently done, that fair employment legislation alone will not itself solve the serious imbalance of employment opportunity between the different sections of our community that is now accepted by everyone including government. We could never have solved the serious housing problems of Northern Ireland if we had insisted only on a fair points scheme for the allocation of housing. The desperate housing problems of many areas of Northern Ireland could never have been dealt with unless, in addition to the points system we also had thousands of additional houses built and the finance available to construct them. Similarly with employment. The best fair employment laws in the world will not of themselves provide one extra job in Strabane, in Newry, in Derry, in West Belfast or in any other areas of high unemployment. There is also need for a substantial and preferential drive by government to encourage investment in those areas.

6 *Irish Times*, 24 Sept. 1987.

The SDLP was the first party, and for a long time the only party to produce far-reaching proposals for a charter of rights in the employment field. Sinn Féin produced their document only a few weeks ago now that they realize the importance of the issue. I will not dwell on the contradictions of an organization whose political wing produces documents on fair employment while their military wing blows up the employment which they wish to be fair. The SDLP proposals have been placed before the British government and placed through the machinery of the Anglo-Irish Conference. The response from the British government has been a consultative document, which for the first time from a government source sets out the full scale of the discrimination problem to be faced. Other documents from government appointed bodies, like the Standing Advisory Commission on Human Rights and the Fair Employment Agency, have been equally forthcoming in both statistics and proposals. The extent of the process of discrimination and of the serious imbalance in opportunity for Catholics is now clear to everyone and accepted by government. I take it that this unprecedented frankness in describing the extent of discrimination in job opportunities against the Catholic population represents a determination by government to deal with it.

In facing up to the problem we must be frank, because we can only make a positive contribution to its resolution if we identify the problem accurately. The unemployment problem, and therefore the employment opportunities for Catholics, is not all to be laid at the door of the government. We should not forget that as far back as 1974, only six years after the beginning of the civil rights movement, this party had for a short period ministerial responsibility for industrial development. By May of 1974 unemployment, at 5.8 per cent, was at its lowest ever. Fourteen hundred jobs which had been signed up, and a factory allocated in Newry, never came because of the kidnap and murder by the Provisional IRA of the general manager of the company in question. Six hundred manufacturing jobs for Strabane were never announced because the UWC strike made the proprietors turn on their heels. Thirty-nine thousand jobs were lost directly in manufacturing industry between 1970 and 1980 because of the Provo bombing campaign against economic targets; £11 million worth of damage to both economies, North and South, resulted from the same campaign. It does not take a genius to recognize that if those jobs and that money were in the economy today the employment opportunities for Catholics would be much greater since we would clearly have a great deal more employment to distribute fairly [...]

The MacBride principles campaign in the United States is also a factor in the whole discussion on fair employment [...] We have no quarrel with the principles. Indeed our own proposals to government are much stronger.

Our concern is based on the fact that certain aspects of the campaign may
tend to discourage investment and we would much prefer if our friends in the
US encouraged industrialists to come to areas of high unemployment. I have
already had discussions in the United States with many of the leaders of the
Irish-American labour coalition, which has been to the forefront of this
campaign. Let me make clear that neither I nor anyone else in this party has
any doubt about the integrity of the intentions of that coalition in relation to
fair employment in Northern Ireland, an integrity that was clearly demonstrated to me by their willingness to seek ways for some of the substantial
pension funds that their unions control to be invested in areas of high
unemployment in order to counter any suggestion of disinvestment. The
same cannot be said of certain other individuals and organizations like Sinn
Féin and their American allies with whom the American-Irish coalition has
no connection whatsoever.[7]

Administration of justice

Hume was also anxious to draw attention to other significant achievements that
had resulted from the Anglo-Irish Agreement in order to demonstrate the efficacy
of a political approach to addressing nationalist grievances, as opposed to the
violent approach adopted by the PIRA and supported by Sinn Féin.
Notwithstanding the failure to reform the Diplock courts, the notable achievements included several long-standing demands affecting the administration of
justice and policing:

In the run-up to this year's general election we listed the areas in which
progress has been made, considerable progress on those issues in eighteen
months compared with the total lack of it for the many preceding years [...]
there has been the marked improvement in banning, re-routing and policing
of potentially provocative parades; supergrass trials are at an end; in bail applications the onus is no longer on the defence to show that bail is safe but is
now on the prosecution to show that it should not be granted; periods on
remand are being shortened by the availability of more judges, allowing
scheduled cases to be heard outside Belfast, and there is now a provision to
enable the secretary of state to set statutory time limits for the period between
first remand and trial; there are now statutory guidelines on admissibility of
confession evidence which render confessions obtained by the use or threat of
violence inadmissible and allow confessions to be excluded in the interests of
justice; suspects are now entitled under law to have a person outside informed

7 Address to the SDLP's annual conference, Nov. 1987.

of their arrest and whereabouts and have automatic access to a solicitor after 48 hours […][8]

Economic development

Hume's efforts to attract investment did not stop at trying to persuade overseas companies to invest in Northern Ireland. He constantly used his American contacts to also promote opportunities to develop trade links that would benefit local enterprises, particularly small and medium-sized companies. Secondly, he used his membership of the European parliament to influence rural and agricultural policies that would benefit communities and farmers, especially those in poorer or less-favoured areas.

With regards to promoting trade links, he became directly involved in the Boston Ireland Ventures initiative, which aimed at creating trade links between Boston, Derry and Donegal. The initiative resulted from contacts with Irish-American Mayor Ray Flynn of Boston who was anxious to direct investment towards border regions in particular. The initiative enabled companies from Derry and Donegal to participate in a number of trade fairs in Boston while investors from Boston supported the development of a shopping complex in Derry.

Rural development

By the mid-1980s the European Community was engaged in extensive discussions on removing internal barriers to free trade so as to achieve a single internal market. Hume was anxious that, in achieving a single market, less-favoured – i.e. economically disadvantaged areas like those in Northern Ireland – would not be further disadvantaged. He outlined his concerns:

> The final ratification of the Single European Act and the consequent drive to complete the internal market should concentrate our minds on the fundamental purposes of the Community. To date the lofty rhetoric on social and economic cohesion has not been matched by action to achieve the convergence of living standards which was one of the major principles and purposes of the founding fathers. In fact the gap between the richer and poorer regions of the Community has widened.
>
> The danger in the completion of the internal market is that it will accelerate the widening of that gap that it will lead to greatly increased specialization of production and an uneven distribution of gains from trade. If these dangers are to be avoided then we need a new approach both at commission and council level, and within the member states themselves.

8 Address to the SDLP's annual conference, Nov. 1987.

On the one hand the European Regional Fund must be greatly increased – at least doubled, as recommended by the president of the commission, and there must be greater concentration of resources of the fund in the most deprived areas of the Community. In a report I presented to the European parliament last month, I argued that the Republic should be permitted to receive a higher rate of Community contribution towards defraying the cost of regional projects and programmes, following the precedent of the 70 per cent authorized for Portugal. The same considerations, obviously, must apply to Northern Ireland.

In conjunction with this and with a more regionalized approach to development, governments, North and South, must proceed rapidly to submit proposals to the commission and the other member states to provide new sources of employment in rural communities. We should also be seeking selective exemption from the restrictions on agricultural production, as the Republic is doing, on the basis that the range of alternative enterprises available to our farmers is very much smaller than in other member states with different climates and soils. The Maher Report on my proposal for an integrated rural development programme for the rural areas of the North[9] has laid the basis for such a strategy. I call upon the government to take steps now to seek such a programme for our rural areas from the European commission. They are pushing an open door if they do.[10]

Enniskillen massacre

The one dominant issue on which no progress was being achieved was the violence that marked daily life in Northern Ireland. On the day the SDLP concluded its 1987 annual conference, 8 November, the IRA committed one of its most horrific attacks, the bombing of the war memorial in Enniskillen on Armistice Sunday, which killed eleven and injured more than sixty of those gathered for the annual commemoration ceremonies. Hume issued one of his strongest condemnations of the PIRA:

> I join other hon. members in expressing abhorrence at the appalling atrocity yesterday, which was an act of sheer savagery. The choice of the occasion yesterday, when people were commemorating the dead of two world wars, who came from every section of every community of both islands, was cold and calculated and designed to stir and hit the deepest emotions of the unionist and British people. It was the deepest act of provocation against the

9 T.J. Maher was an Irish member of the European parliament who prepared a report on rural development.   10 Address to the SDLP's annual conference, Nov. 1987.

unionist people that has taken place in my lifetime. I sincerely hope that no one will fall into the trap that has been laid by retaliating, because the doctrine of an eye for an eye leaves everybody blind.

This house can do no more today than endorse the prime minister's statement yesterday that there should be no hiding place anywhere in these islands for those who committed the atrocity. We should also endorse the Irish prime minister's statement that every step would be taken by his government, together with the British government, to ensure that those who committed the atrocity are brought to justice.

There is a lesson to be learnt by the representatives of Northern Ireland. It is clear to me, as it must be clear to anyone, that it is the past attitudes in Northern Ireland that have brought us to where we are today. Unless we are prepared to re-examine those attitudes, we will stay the way that we are. If we are to live together, the first lesson that we must learn is that we need each other. We will discover how much we need each other, and how we are to live together, only when we sit down and talk about it.[11]

Hume-Adams

In the wake of the Enniskillen tragedy Hume responded positively to approaches made on behalf of Gerry Adams that they should meet, notwithstanding the criticism he knew would be directed at him for doing so. The meeting, held in late 1988, led to several further exchanges between the two party leaders and also meetings attended by leading members of their respective parties. Documents were exchanged outlining each party's position on ways to end the conflict and to making comprehensive negotiations possible. The SDLP's document took the form of the following letter from Hume to Adams, which set out the party's approach and outlined its essential critique of the PIRA's campaign, which Sinn Féin continued to support:

Dear Gerry,

Following our recent discussion, I promised to put to you in writing a summary of the views that I put to you on that occasion with a view to their consideration by your organization and with a view to developing more in-depth discussions at future meetings. You promised to do likewise.

The views I put to you on that occasion were broadly in two parts, firstly my comments on the analysis and methods of the Provisional Movement and secondly, arguments and proposals for a peaceful political alternative. I now

11 House of Commons, *Debates,* 9 Nov. 1987.

repeat those points in writing. Of necessity they are brief but I hope they could be developed in much greater depth and detail in any forthcoming discussions.

The basic method used by the provisional republican movement is of course the IRA campaign.

The price of that campaign is already clear to everyone, not least to the members of that organization themselves. And to their families. Lives have been lost, people have been maimed, young lives have been wasted in prisons, untold damage has been done to the economy of this island as a whole, destroying hopes for the future of many of our young people and forcing them to leave and therefore diminish Ireland. The statistics are well known and do not need repetition.

The people who have suffered most and the areas that have suffered most are the very people and areas that are represented by either the SDLP or Sinn Féin. The other constant irritation to people are the numerous complaints about harassment by security forces – house searches, heavy military presence on the streets – providing constant strain and tensions in the daily lives of people who have enough problems, given the economic circumstances in which most of them are living. The justification given by the authorities in Northern Ireland is that all these activities by the security forces are a reaction to the IRA campaign and are consequences of that campaign. A great deal of relief could therefore be brought to ordinary people by ending the campaign and removing the stated justification for security-force activity.

It is not an answer to suggest that the British presence is the primary source of our problems, and therefore the cause of all the violence. It is not enough to suggest, as Provisional spokesmen frequently do, that the cause of all the violence is the British presence in Ireland. All of us take our own decisions and use our own methods for dealing with that presence. We must also take responsibility for those methods for dealing with that presence. We must also take responsibility for those methods and for their consequences, particularly when such consequences can be foreseen. The IRA must take responsibility for their methods, as they do, but also for the foreseeable consequences of those methods, which have brought so much suffering to Irish people.

It is also clear that there is little chance of those methods succeeding in the foreseeable future in achieving the stated political objectives of the IRA. Does anyone in Ireland, even among supporters of IRA, believe that the present British government will accede to the demands of the IRA made by force? Does that not mean that the whole country and the members of the IRA and families of the IRA face at least another decade of what we have just been through, with all the suffering and without any guarantees of achieving their objectives at the end of it?

Is it not time for the IRA and the members of the provisional republican movement to seriously reconsider the methods that they have chosen to achieve their objectives, or are they in danger of moving to a situation – or are they already in it – where the methods have become more sacred than the cause?

Even if the stated objectives of the IRA were to be achieved in the manner which they have been set out, we in the SDLP would argue that that would not bring peace to Ireland but would lead to much greater chaos and to permanent division and conflict among our people. That is a serious charge but it is a view that is shared by the vast majority of the Irish people, who do not endorse the use of force to solve political problems in Ireland or to achieve national objectives. It therefore deserves serious attention and consideration by members of the provisional republican movement, if they are open to genuine dialogue as to the way forward. It is a view that is also shared by a wide spectrum of British political opinion who wish to see permanent peace in Ireland and who are sympathetic to the Irish cause.

The objectives of the provisional republican movement are a British withdrawal from Ireland or a declaration of intent to do so within a given period. In our view there is no difference in practice between these two objectives because once a declaration of intent is made then the effect is no different from an actual departure. The political vacuum is immediately created and as all experience of such situations show the vacuum will be filled immediately by force as each section of the community moves to secure its position. This route is the route of maximum risk and is a risk which we believe no one has the right to take unless they do so with the full authority of the Irish people.

What is the risk? In such a vacuum the likelihood is that the British army would become inactive. In the knowledge that their government has decided to withdraw all responsibility, does anyone think that soldiers would be prepared to risk their lives? Each section of the community would seize its own territory and we would have a Cyprus/Lebanon-style formula for permanent division and bloodshed. What would the 12,000 armed members of the RUC do? What would the 8,000 armed members of the UDR do? Is it not likely and natural in the emotionally charged atmosphere that would obtain and in the absence of any acknowledged authority that they would simply identify with the community from which most of them come and become its military defenders? And what would happen to the Catholic community in such circumstances, particularly in those areas where they are most vulnerable?

Is the risk involved in such a military policy not an awesome one and likely to ensure that the peace and unity of Ireland will never come? And would the contemplation of such risks and such consequences not justify a complete reappraisal of their methods and their strategy by the provisional republican movement? Or have they reached the stage where their certitude about both their methods and strategy amounts to the fact that their methods and strategy have actually become more sacred than their cause (their cause being a united, independent and peaceful Ireland), and to discuss them or to contemplate changing them is unthinkable? Such an approach is a purely military approach, and as has already been admitted on all sides, there can be no military solution.

There is a political alternative and in our view the political road is the only one that will ensure that there is lasting peace in Ireland. For the SDLP, Ireland is first and foremost its people; the territory is secondary since without people the territory isn't much different from any other piece of earth. The tragedy is that the people of Ireland are deeply divided, and have been deeply divided for centuries on some fundamental matters. But it is the people of Ireland who have the right to self-determination. It is the Irish people who have the unalienable right to sovereignty. Unfortunately the Irish people are divided on how to exercise the right to self-determination. The Irish people are divided on how to exercise the right to sovereignty. It is the search for agreement among the Irish people on how to exercise these rights that is the real search for peace and stability in Ireland. It is a search that has never been seriously undertaken by the nationalist/republican tradition in Ireland and it is the real challenge facing us today if we have any belief in the future of the Irish people as a whole. Does the provisional republican movement accept that the search for agreement among the people who live on the island of Ireland (which means in practice agreement between what has become known as the people of the unionist and nationalist traditions) on how to exercise self-determination is a search that cannot be conducted by force? And does anyone believe that if such agreement were reached that any British government could refuse to endorse it?

Indeed the present British government has made clear in an internationally binding agreement that if such agreement on the exercise of self-determination took the form of Irish unity that they would in fact endorse it. Is that not the clearest possible challenge to the nationalist/republican tradition in Ireland to begin the task of building a new Ireland with our unionist fellow citizens, an immensely difficult task given our past but one on which substantial and steady progress can be made in the absence of military and violent activity?

Is that not the challenge that has also been put two centuries ago by Wolfe Tone and never really taken up in his oft quoted but misinterpreted diary statement of his objectives and methods:

To subvert the tyranny of our execrable government, to break the connection with England, the never-failing source of our political evils, and to assert the independence of my country – these are my objects. To unite the whole people of Ireland, to abolish the memory of our past dissensions and to substitute the common name of Irishman in place of the denomination of Protestant, Catholic and Dissenter – these were my means.

It is surely clear from that that Tone was stating with great clarity that his means or method of breaking the link with Britain was to unite the people of Ireland first.

And does that challenge not also remove all justification for the use of violence because does not the British declaration on endorsing and accepting agreement among the people of Ireland on Irish unity not make clear that Britain is now saying that she has no interest of her own in being here and that her only interest is to see agreement among the people who share the island of Ireland.

We in the SDLP would therefore like to pose some questions to the provisional republican movement, with a view to creating the conditions in which all military and violent activity will come to an end:

1. Do you accept the right of the Irish people to self-determination?
2. Do you accept that the Irish people are at present deeply divided on the question of how to exercise self-determination?
3. Do you accept that, in practice, agreement on exercising that right means agreement of both the unionist and nationalist traditions?
4. If you accept 1, 2 and 3, would you then agree that the best way forward would be to attempt to create a conference table, convened by an Irish government, at which all parties in the North with an electoral mandate would attend? The purpose of such a conference would be to try to reach agreement on the exercise of self-determination in Ireland and on how the people of our diverse traditions can live together in peace, harmony and agreement. It would be understood that if this conference were to happen that the IRA would have ceased its campaign. It would also be understood in advance that if such a conference were to reach agreement, it would be endorsed by the British government.
5. In the event of the representatives of the unionist people refusing to participate in such a conference would you join with us and with other nationalist participants in preparing a peaceful and comprehensive approach to achieving agreement on self-determination in Ireland? Would we in fact and in practice take up the challenge laid down by Tone?

6. I think that you might agree that if we were to proceed successfully down such a road that the atmosphere throughout Ireland would be transformed and that the international goodwill would be overwhelming to such an extent that many things which seem either difficult or even impossible now would become attainable.

Naturally the points that I am making in this letter are of necessity brief and I am looking forward together with my colleagues and yours to going into them in depth in a spirit of genuine dialogue. May I also add that in spite of all the pessimism that is around and indeed my own realistic sense of the obstacles that lie in the way, I sincerely hope that we will be successful in attaining an objective of bringing an end to all military and violent activity in the northern part of Ireland.

Yours sincerely,
John Hume[12]

While several meetings between members of the two parties and, separately, between Hume and Adams on their own, took place over the following months there were no immediate positive results. The Sinn Féin leadership refused to accept the need for an end to the PIRA campaign in advance of wider talks taking place, and the SDLP declined to join with Sinn Féin in any political initiatives, such as the campaign for stronger fair employment legislation, as long as it supported the PIRA's military activities. Hume's most detailed comment on these talks and Sinn Féin's failure to respond positively to his argument against the use of politically motivated violence was contained in his address to the SDLP's annual conference in November 1988. In his comments he again sharply criticized the provisional republican movement for its campaign of violence, and its refusal to acknowledge the devastation it was causing.

I had talks with them [Sinn Féin] recently. The talks were designed to explore whether they [the PIRA] were willing to lay down arms and join the rest of the people of this island in the lengthy and difficult search for peace based on real self-determination. I put some questions to them about the price of their means and method, about the consequences of victory for their viewpoint, about peaceful alternatives which already exist. They replied with sheaves of paper reiterating well-worn declarations about nationhood and the rights of the Irish people to self-determination while ignoring the single most self-evident fact that strikes every human being in the world as they look in on

12 Letter to Gerry Adams, Mar. 1988, SDLP archives.

Ireland – the Irish people are divided on that very question, the question of how to exercise self-determination. Agreement on its exercise will never be brought about by force and violence but only by dialogue and all the signs are that such dialogue will be neither easy nor brief.

For people who proclaim their Irishness and their pride in Ireland so loudly and so forcefully they are remarkably lacking in either the self-confidence or moral guts to sit round and talk with their fellow Irishmen and persuade them that their vision of Ireland is a better one. Their decision in particular to use guns and bombs to 'persuade' their Protestant fellow Irishmen is not only an extreme example of lack of faith in their own beliefs or in the credibility of them, it is an attitude of extreme moral cowardice and a deeply partitionist attitude. For its real effect is to deepen the essential divisions among the Irish people.

And it isn't just the unionist people who are their victims. Leaders of Sinn Féin have been saying recently that the nationalist nightmare has not ended. They are dead right because they and their military wing are the major part of that nightmare. There is not a single injustice in Northern Ireland today that justifies the taking of a single human life. What is more the vast majority of the major injustices suffered not only by the nationalist community but by the whole community are the direct consequence of the IRA campaign. If I were to lead a civil rights campaign in Northern Ireland today the major target of that campaign would be the IRA. It is they who carry out the greatest infringements of human and civil rights, whether it is their murders, their executions without trial, their kneecappings and punishment shootings, their bombings of jobs and people. The most fundamental right is the right to life. Who in Northern Ireland takes the most human lives in a situation where there is not one single injustice that justifies the taking of human life?

Let the record speak: up till last Saturday 2,705 people have died in the twenty-year period of the current Troubles; 31 per cent of these were members of the security forces; 14 per cent were members of paramilitary organizations; 55 per cent were ordinary civilians, men and women from both sections of our community, 69 per cent of whom were from the Catholic community and 31 per cent from the Protestant community. And who killed those people?

The statistics are devastating: 44 per cent were killed by the Provisional IRA and 18 per cent by their fellow travelling 'republican' paramilitaries; 27 per cent were killed by loyalists; 10 per cent were killed by the British army; 2 per cent were killed by the RUC; and 0.28 per cent by the UDR. In short, people describing themselves as Irish republicans have killed six times as many human beings as the British army, thirty times as many as the RUC and 250 times as many as the UDR.

And wait! One of their claims is that they are the defenders of the Catholic community. Of the 1,194 members of the Catholic community who died, 46 per cent were killed by loyalist paramilitaries, 37 per cent by people describing themselves as republicans and 17 per cent by the security forces. [...]

In the past twenty years republicans have killed more than twice as many Catholics as the security forces and in the last ten years have killed more than the loyalists! Some defenders! [...]

My challenge to any of those people in Ireland, North and South, today who regard themselves as republicans is to accept the straightforward offer made to them in our talks. Lay down your arms once and for all. Join the rest of the people of Ireland in the search for ways and means of breaking down the barriers with our Protestant fellow citizens, in persuading them to join us in building a new Ireland that reflects our diversity and respects all our traditions, and in persuading the British government to commit all its resources to the same end. If they were to do so, then the atmosphere in this whole island and in the North, in particular, would be transformed and the nightmare of all our people would be truly at an end.[13]

Anglo-Irish Agreement three years on

The third anniversary of signing of the Anglo-Irish Agreement provided Hume with the occasion to again outline the opportunities it had presented for a comprehensive dialogue, as well as what it had achieved. Both were very important in light of his attempts to persuade the PIRA to end its campaign of violence. His argument was that the hard grind of democratic politics did yield positive results. In an article published in the *Derry Journal*, Hume emphasized that, with the agreement:

> a final settlement of the Irish problem has not been reached. We do believe that an opportunity has been created by the agreement in the setting up of a permanent Anglo-Irish institution to make progress towards our goals of peace and reconciliation. It is an opportunity that can be developed if it is taken up with goodwill on all sides.
>
> In short the new Anglo-Irish institution that was set up was a vast improvement on what had been the previous decision-making process – Stormont and direct rule – but it was not and is not a solution to all our problems. It is a method of dealing with them whereby both governments commit themselves to working as closely as possible, using all their resources, to deal with the problems that we face. They have not and will not always agree but they are committed to reaching maximum agreement in their

13 Address to the SDLP annual conference, 1988.

approach to the problems that we face. Is there a better peaceful way of tackling our deep-seated problems?

Critics of the Anglo-Irish Agreement have criticized it for not being what it was never intended to be: an instant solution to our problems. It is a framework and if its critics on all sides were to join in using the institutions and in taking the opportunities created by it to resolve the conflicting relationships here that only we can resolve, then progress towards peace and reconciliation would be very swift indeed. And what alternatives have the critics offered? On the one hand the unionists have offered nothing. They have given not the slightest public indication to anyone that they have moved one inch from their 'ourselves alone' approach to holding power. On the other hand the Provisionals continue to offer death and destruction with its attendant bitterness that is now disillusioning even some of their most fervent supporters. Is there anyone who doubts that if the Provos were to lay down their arms and all political parties with an elected mandate were to enter into dialogue with the objective of resolving relationships within the North, within Ireland and between Ireland and Britain, that the atmosphere would be transformed and the goodwill generated enormous? Those who refuse to enter such a process are admitting they do not want a solution, they want victory for their own view which they wish to impose on everyone else. In other words they have become a major part of the problem [...]

However, we are all aware that if all our grievances were removed tomorrow they would recur in another form if the underlying disease or problem is not dealt with. It is at this level that I think the most interesting progress has been made [...]

The unionists, of course, fully realize the significance of the Anglo-Irish Agreement and fully accept that it meant a loss of their veto and a major shift in the British position. It also, therefore, as a consequence, challenges some of the fundamentals of physical-force republicanism because it removes their stated reasons for what they call 'the armed struggle'. Put succinctly the British government has made clear that in the essential quarrel that divides us here, union or unity, they will accept the wishes of a majority in Northern Ireland. That means, as I have said so often, that Irish unity is a matter of those who want it persuading some of those who don't. That position may not be everything that a republican would like them to say but it is a significant enough shift to remove all justification for the use of 'armed struggle'. It is now also clear to the nationalist community in the North that most of their grievances today are a direct consequence of the IRA campaign and would disappear if that campaign ended. Harassment of young people by security forces, house searching, troops on the streets, prisons full of young people, deaths particularly of innocent people [...] Then there is the high unemployment, with its lack of hope for our young. In 1974 when I was minister for commerce there were 220,000 employed in manufacturing industry. Today, there are 90,000! Both the size of today's unemployment and our failure to attract new jobs and investment have a great deal to do with the continuing violence and indeed were part of the IRA strategy when they were assassinating industrialists.

If the IRA campaign were to end tomorrow, the troops would be off our streets within weeks, with all the consequences of that. We could begin the process of emptying our prisons particularly all those young people sucked into violence in the intense sectarianism of the 1970s [...] More importantly for the long term, we could begin to heal the divisions among the people and combine to tackle the problems of breaking down the barriers in a process of real reconciliation, harnessing the enormous goodwill and energy that would be released by the ending of all military activity and violence. This too is the challenge that the Anglo-Irish Agreement has put up to the nationalist people but has been obscured by the attention given to the unionist reaction. It is up to all democratic politicians who support this agreement to clarify that challenge to the people at every opportunity and to promote the maximum debate.[14]

14 *Derry Journal*, 15 Nov. 1988.

1988-91

While unionist opposition to the Anglo-Irish Agreement, and, in particular, to the role it conferred on the Irish government in the affairs of Northern Ireland, remained strong, signs slowly emerged that some unionists were beginning to move away from the demand that the agreement be removed completely before talks would be possible. Instead they were demanding that it be suspended for the duration of any talks. So, while he was convinced that the agreement effectively modified the British guarantee and had created a more level playing field, Hume sought to re-assure unionists that the agreement protected their constitutional, human and civil rights through the explicit commitment of both governments to the principle of consent for constitutional change. The agreement should not, therefore, be seen as a threat to the basic unionist need for constitutional protection. Critically, he argued that the agreement provided a solid framework within which to negotiate a way forward between the two communities in the North, and between North and South:

> The American theologian Reinhold Niebuhr once composed a prayer which if my memory serves me, ran something like this: 'Lord give me the serenity to accept the things I cannot change, the courage to change the things I can, and the wisdom to know the difference.'
>
> It is a prayer much invoked by politicians, from John F. Kennedy onwards, and it is easy to see why. The struggle to reconcile what is desirable with what is possible lies at the heart of every political process and the true sense of where that point of reconciliation lies is the greatest gift, or 'wisdom', that any political leader could pray for. A prayer in these terms could serve very appropriately as the opening invocation to the search for political understanding on this island.
>
> There are things we cannot change in the situation we are now called on to grapple with. We cannot alter the history of Ireland which has left such a bitter legacy of division to those of us who live in this island today. We cannot simply wish away the reality that there are two traditions in this island which perceive the meaning of being Irish in quite different and, in part, opposing ways.
>
> We cannot deny that each tradition has a radically different perception of the conditions necessary to serve its liberty and well-being and to give

political expression to its identity. Nor can we change the political and geographical facts of life that events in Northern Ireland are so close to Dublin and London that the pattern of these events must be of concern to them, not as a matter of choice, but of political necessity.

Indeed, to put it another way, settling the totality of relationships is what settling the problem is about and the best possible framework for that process is the framework which encompasses all those relationships.

Our starting point in Northern Ireland has been defined for us by realities such as these. To recognize these realities is a precondition for effective action and not a recipe for fatalism. There are many things that we can and must change and the process will indeed require courage. We cannot change the facts of history but we can change the impact these facts have on us.

We have inherited deposits of anger and frustration in each tradition, secure in its own sense of justification at the failure of the other to conform to the role which has been prescribed for it. That has translated into the 'no surrender' or 'ourselves alone' symmetrical denials from the heart of each tradition of the reality or relevance of the other. It has been these addictive simplicities that have been the staples of unionism for so long.

It is the achievement of the Anglo-Irish Agreement that it has challenged these simplicities, even if the response of the unionist leadership, characteristically, has not yet gone beyond the stage of presenting it to their followers as simply an act of treachery against unionism.

The agreement is a powerful symbolic expression of the political truth that peace and stability in Northern Ireland cannot simply be attained by denying the reality of the validity of the nationalist community, any more than it can be attained by denying the reality of unionism.

The agreement does not solve the Northern Ireland problem, but it points in the direction where a just solution may be found. That lies, in the words of the agreement itself, in a recognition by both governments of the 'need for continuing efforts to reconcile and to acknowledge the rights of the two major traditions that exist in Ireland', and recognition and respect by them for the 'identities of the two communities in Northern Ireland and the right of each to pursue its aspirations by peaceful and constitutional means'. The agreement is not, therefore, a point of arrival or an end but a point of departure for those continuing efforts it speaks of. It is not, as we have frequently said, the solution but the best possible peaceful framework within which progress towards a solution can be found. It establishes between the two governments the mechanism of the conference and secretariat to work out the practical corollaries of that recognition of the equal validity of the two traditions.

The mechanism is firstly a safeguard against the development of any new discriminatory policy in the running of Northern Ireland. It provides a point of scrutiny which is involved with the administration as of right and is entitled to be heard within that administration without losing the right to speak out whenever the defence of the basic principles of the agreement should call for it.

Secondly, the conference and secretariat mechanism is involved in the more complex task of dismantling the legacy of past discrimination. No one would suggest here that the rate of progress is as rapid as could be wished. There are forces of inertia or resistance to be overcome even in an area as clear-cut as fair employment.

The continuing campaign of IRA violence provides an all-too-convenient arsenal of counter-arguments to those opposed to major change on sensitive issues such as the behaviour of certain members of the security forces, the reform of the courts or changes in the prison system [...]

There is, however, a further dimension of the agreement which we should not lose sight of. It is the constant theme of unionist propaganda against the agreement that is now an obstacle to dialogue between the two communities in Northern Ireland. If unionist enthusiasm for dialogue had been seriously in evidence prior to the agreement, or if we could be certain even now that an eagerness for dialogue existed for its own sake, not as a tactic, that position might command deeper sympathy. Nevertheless it is worth looking at in its own terms.

Fruitful dialogue between the communities in Northern Ireland, vital as it is, is not the elementary and simple first step which outsiders sometimes believe. To have any meaning it presupposes some readiness to change, and it was because the entire unionist programme amounted to a denial of change that such dialogue never prospered.

It is only fair to recognize, however, that each community would have brought its own baggage of fears to such talks. For the nationalist community there was the fear of a final seal on a British imperialist or colonialist purpose which might deny the right to work for an Ireland governed in peace and harmony by all of the people of Ireland without that outside involvement which is at once the symbol and effect of our present division.

For the unionist community there was the spectre that a process of dialogue would bring about the realization of their worst nightmare and prove that fatal first step on a slippery slope that would incorporate them against their will in a political system they found alien.

The Anglo-Irish Agreement provides reassurance to both sides on these crucial points. The agreement does not banish the aspiration to Irish unity from the agenda. On the contrary it represents a formal acceptance by the British government that the nationalist identity and aspiration is of equal validity with the unionist. It pledges practical support for Irish unity if a majority of people of Northern Ireland give their consent to that measure.

Equally importantly, from the point of view of unionist fears, both govern-ments affirm that any change in the status of Northern Ireland would only come about with the consent of a majority of the people of Northern Ireland and recognize that the present wish of a majority of the people of Northern Ireland is for no change in that status. By declaring that they will accept the wishes of the people of Northern Ireland, whether those wishes are for union or unity, the British government have declared themselves neutral in the basic quarrel between us; that is a significant advance.

The determination of both governments to work together under the agree-ment to ensure that those who adopt violence for political ends do not succeed is not just an important practical demonstration of their commit-ments to safeguards for the rights of the unionist people but also for the future peace and stability of the whole island.

The agreement, therefore, is not about denying political realities on either side, or denying fears and aspirations, which, whether we regard as well founded or not, we must accept as real. It is about integrating all these realities into a process aimed at overcoming the formidable obstacles in the way of peace and stability on this island […][1]

Nearly four months later, on 13 January 1989, in a wide-ranging interview with *Irish Times* correspondent Frank Millar, Hume commented in depth on the signif-icance of the Anglo-Irish Agreement – the reasons why it was necessary, some of its positive achievements and his hopes for political progress:

The reason was to create, first of all, a framework within which a solution could be pursued and in that sense the framework of the solution has to be the framework of the problem. For the very first time we have a framework which is addressing all the relationships which go to the heart of this problem. One of the reasons why we disagree so often with the unionists in our treat-ment of the problem is that we disagree about what the problem is. I will state clearly that the problem is the failure to resolve these relationships, a number of them, the central relationship being that of the unionists and the rest of the island, and then the relations between Ireland and Britain, and within the North. So that essentially is what the Anglo-Irish Agreement is about, it's about treating the disease. Now while the disease remains to be cured, which is the politics of it, the symptoms keep recurring. One of the symptoms being the administration of justice, the relationship between the Catholic commu-nity and the security forces. I think that most people would accept that since the Anglo-Irish Agreement was signed there has been, for example, a distinct

1 *Irish Times*, 3 Oct. 1988.

improvement in one area which gave grave offence to the Catholic community and that was the handling of parades, and Orange parades in particular. Because we could never see the reason why such provocative parades – by provocative parades I mean triumphalist marching through Catholic areas – were allowed. I have no objection whatsoever to the Orange tradition being celebrated in Ireland, it's part of our tradition. But it should be done in a manner that is neither triumphalist nor provocative. It should be done in a genuinely celebratory manner. I believe in that area there certainly has been an improvement. On the question of the administration of justice, I think there are many people who would argue that you are more likely to get a fair trial now in Northern Ireland than you would get in Britain if you are an Irish person being tried for an offence concerned with violence. They would argue that one of the reasons for that is the existence of juries in Britain for such trials, because of their emotional nature. We would accept the reason why, in Northern Ireland, it was necessary to remove juries, because of intimidation and so forth, which is self-evident. But that being so, we would have argued that the responsibility, therefore, should not be left on the shoulder of one person, and that is why we would argue for three-judge courts rather than one-judge courts.[2]

In answer to questions from Millar about attitudes towards the security forces, especially questions about the attitude of those who supported the PIRA, and who claimed that the agreement had not effected any change on the ground, Hume argued that:

it's in the interests of people like Sinn Féin and their supporters to keep on saying we don't see any change. In fact, there is an identity of interests between the IRA and the unionist opponents of the agreement. I mean every time the IRA commits an atrocity the unionists use it as a reason for saying that the Anglo-Irish Agreement has failed. In other words, they are, if you like to use an old phrase, living off the backs of the IRA.[3]

Asked by Millar about unionist allegations that Hume and the SDLP in general had been living off the backs of the PIRA, and that without the PIRA there would never have been the Anglo-Irish Agreement, Hume replied:

The IRA are against the Anglo-Irish Agreement, although I hear them sometimes saying that they are responsible for the advances. Those sorts of contradictions I don't have much time for. Basically the IRA existed in the

2 Ibid., 13 Jan. 1989.   3 Ibid.

1920s, the 1930s, 1940s and the 1950s. They had campaigned in all those periods and they failed miserably, and the only time any change started to emerge in Northern Ireland was in the non-violence of the civil rights movement, which challenged and asked a very simple question of the unionists; can you give us justice? And can you survive with the answer 'yes'? It was a completely new approach. We started the process of change in Northern Ireland, which is working and the IRA came in on the back of that. They have prolonged the process and they have made a solution much more difficult to find. Now it suits the unionists, of course, to make those sorts of charges, but in fact the real allies in Northern Ireland have always been the unionists and the IRA [...] they are natural allies, and they are natural allies in trying to bring to bring down the Anglo-Irish Agreement, because any peaceful person must accept that in a society where you have a conflict of identity, the best possible way of dealing with that problem is for the governments that represent the identities to work as closely as possible together to resolve it.[4]

Faced with the claim that since unionist leaders believed that Hume would only settle for a united Ireland in any negotiations, there was, in reality, no point in negotiating with him, he replied:

What I am concerned about isn't concepts. I am concerned about the fact that Ireland has for too long concerned itself with territorial attitudes rather than the fact that there are people who live on an island and that the people who live on the island are divided [...] There are societies in the world where the differences are far deeper than ours, but yet they live together in perfect peace and harmony because they know how to accommodate their differences. All I am saying is that unity for me means – it means agreement on how we share the island. That is what unity actually means. Unity without agreement isn't unity at all, it's conquest and you are back to that. And what I am saying is that it is time for the representatives of the different traditions in this island to sit down together and decide how they are going to share this island, how they are going to protect their traditions in a manner that is satisfactory to both sides. Now that could be a hell of a long search, but that is the real search and that is the search we have got to be engaged in. It's easy to indulge in name calling, to say: 'Well I don't trust you.' The unionists don't trust me – fair enough, maybe I don't trust them. I don't have to trust them, and they don't have to trust me. What I have to do is trust myself and what they have to do is trust themselves to represent their own people, anywhere, with anybody else and come to a settlement that protects their own people. And I

4 Ibid.

have to do precisely the same thing, whether I trust Paisley or not is irrelevant.[5]

Asked if his definition of 'self-determination for the Irish people is the agreement of all the people on this island on some basis on which to share the territory', Hume answered:

Oh, absolutely. My definition of self-determination is self-evident: it is that the people of the island as a whole should sit down – first of all. There's a lot of people saying the Irish people have a right to self-determination. Nobody disputes that, but what they seem to ignore is that the Irish people, if one defines the Irish people as the people who live on the island of Ireland, are divided on how to exercise that right. That division goes very deep. That division goes back beyond partition. It goes back a very long way. Therefore, if we are going to exercise self-determination then the people of the island as a whole have got to agree, have got to reach agreement. But when they do reach agreement on how they are going to share the island, then I believe you have the basis of real unity because you have got agreement and the essence of unity is agreement. [...] [Y]ou see one of the problems is that throughout this century the people of the island as a whole, either North or South, have never been given an opportunity to speak on how they are to be governed, apart from elections, which is choosing their government. They have never been allowed to speak on the system of government for the island as a whole or on relationships within the island as a whole. And, therefore, what would be the outcome of discussions between representatives of both parts of the island, I couldn't forecast. I wouldn't attempt to forecast because if I am quite genuine in saying that I want the different representatives to come to the table and discuss the shape of the future island, then I just leave them free to put on the table whatever they wished to put on that table. To prejudge the outcome would be wholly wrong and politically foolish.

Given the implications any agreement might have for the Republic's constitution, in particular articles 2 and 3 of the 1937 constitution which claimed jurisdiction over Northern Ireland, Hume accepted that it would have to be changed significantly, or even replaced:

The one thing that is absolutely certain is there's no chance whatsoever of any government in the Irish Republic changing the constitution or proposing a change in the constitution to the people of the Republic of Ireland in advance

5 Ibid.

of any settlement. That would be regarded as not being politically very wise either. But what has been accepted always by all parties in the Republic is that any new settlement which involves the unionists and themselves would mean their willingness to look at the possibility of an entirely new constitution. Most political leaders in the Republic have said time out of number that in the event of a settlement between themselves and the unionists they would not object at all to considering a new constitution. I think that is self-evident.[6]

European Community elections

In the absence of any immediate prospect of inter-party talks, Hume's attention moved to the upcoming European elections, for which he was again selected as the SDLP's candidate. In his election manifesto Hume again stressed the SDLP's strong commitment to the European project, and to the goal of European unity. John Hume's worldview is also evident in his expression of concern for the developing world and for the environment, issues which other politicians in Northern Ireland seldom, if ever, addressed:

> Alone among the major parties [in Northern Ireland] in this election, the SDLP is strongly committed to the European ideal and to the concept of a united Europe. We believe that it is only through unity in Europe that we can build greater peace, prosperity and freedom for our peoples. No country can confront alone the major economic challenges of the 1990s. The European framework offers us, in Northern Ireland, a means of escaping from the suffocating policies of Thatcherism and, by joining with our European partners, in the promotion of economic development, the extension of social justice and human rights, and the achievement of equality of opportunity.
>
> The European Community, with selective and co-operative growth, can become the most dynamic area within the world economy in the next decade. The achievement of a single market will, in itself, bring huge economic benefits. The Cecchini Report estimates that at least £7,500 million will be saved by doing away with unnecessary paperwork and delays involved in getting goods past border controls.[7] There will be further cost savings for industry in the economies of scale which the single market will bring and in the greater efficiency which the liberalization of services and capital will entail. Cecchini estimates that up to 7 per cent could be added to the European Community GDP, that prices would fall by up to 6 per cent and that up to 5 million new jobs could be created. This kind of economic growth

6 Ibid.   7 The Cecchini Report examined the costs and benefits of the European single market.

would enable the EEC to make a decisive contribution to the creation of a new international economic order which would facilitate greater growth in the developing countries, and a solution to the Third World debt problem [...]

As well as a clean and beautiful natural environment, a proper social environment is vital to the construction of a 'people's Europe'. Every citizen of Europe, and of the world, is entitled to a full education, a job with a fair wage, a decent home to live in, a comprehensive system of social security and health insurance, and freedom to live without fear. The creation of employment continues to be our greatest priority, and that is why our central proposal is a co-ordinated policy of expansion of the European economy. However, as well as creating jobs we must guarantee equality of rights, and opportunities for all citizens, and especially those who have experienced disadvantages in the past, such as young people; women; racial, linguistic or religious minorities; the disabled [...]

The reduction of antagonisms and armaments in Europe, and the world, is an absolute priority for member parties of the Socialist Group. The European Community is the nucleus of the peaceful and free union of the democratic states of Western Europe. As such it can play a key role in creating rapprochement between East and West, and must pursue that role by more positive and active diplomatic means. Our purpose must be to bring about nuclear disarmament, to revitalize the process of negotiation on the reduction of conventional weapons and forces, and thus to make the world a safe place to live in.

The people of the world are entitled to live in freedom from fear. They are entitled to live in freedom from hunger, disease and poverty. Simple justice dictates that we cannot continue to tolerate the social, economic and cultural exploitation of the Third World. We in the Socialist Group will continue to demand that the EC give a consistent and meaningful level of development aid as a basic feature of its common external policy [...]

The European Community must be a pillar of human rights in the world. The European parliament has been and will continue to be an important forum within which constraints can be exerted on the member states to observe proper standards of human rights within their own jurisdictions.[8]

Hume retained his seat, with over 25 per cent of first-preference votes.

---

8 'Manifesto for the European parliament elections', SDLP, 1989.

Dialogue with the PIRA and the unionists

While still awaiting a unionist commitment to enter talks, Hume used the twentieth anniversary of the arrival of British troops on the streets of Northern Ireland to reflect on the consequences, immediate and longer-term of that event, placing it in an historical context that emphasized the need to address Anglo-Irish relationships in their wider European context. Hume's emphasis on this context was crucially important because his reflection was part of the indirect, but very public argument he was conducting with the PIRA leadership at this time, hoping to persuade them to reassess their whole terrorist campaign. In retrospect, the article summarizes the central messages that Hume and his SDLP colleagues would bring to the negotiations that would take place over the next few years and which would lead to the Good Friday Agreement in 1998:

> The arrival of British troops on the streets of Northern Ireland was the beginning of the end of the Stormont parliament and indeed the end in practice of the 1920 Government of Ireland Act. The arrival of the troops signalled the end of the 'non-interventionist' stance by successive British governments since 1920. Apart from their financial subvention they had consistently refused to intervene even in the face of the incontrovertible evidence of serious and blatant discrimination.
>
> The first unionist ever to give voice to the real significance of 14 August was Desmond Boal,[9] one of the few unionists who did apply his mind to the future. A fortnight after the arrival of the troops he raised in Stormont an incident involving British soldiers in Mamma's chip shop on the Shankill Road [Belfast].
>
> Mr Boal made a number of points, but concluded: 'In my respectful submission there can only be said to be an encroachment to some extent on the powers given to the Northern Ireland government by the 1920 act. Perhaps these powers have been voluntarily relinquished by the Northern Ireland government. I see the attorney general shakes his head. He is entitled to his opinion. I am entitled to mine. I take the view, and I am not deterred one iota from stating it by the negative shaking of the attorney general's head, that there has been some eating away, some erosion of the powers given to the Northern Ireland government by the 1920 act by our voluntarily giving over of the control of the streets of our country to the GOC [general officer commanding], who is not under our command. I do not put it any further and I do not wish to debate it but I simply state that that is my opinion. Not for the first time will that opinion later be shown to be right.'

9 British troops arrived on 14 Aug. 1969 to patrol the streets in Northern Ireland.

He was right. Governments do not govern unless they have complete control of security and once the British army came onto the streets of Northern Ireland it was only a matter of time before the British government resolved the contradiction and took direct control, thus taking the first serious step in the process necessary to finally settle the problem of Ireland – the removal of absolute power from the unionists and the ending of the one-party state.

At the same time another event took place which had a fundamental effect on the events of the ensuing twenty years. A loyalist mob, led by a Stormont MP and including police and B-Specials, burned 500 Catholic homes in Bombay Street [in Belfast] and killed nine people. The traumatic effect of that pogrom gave birth to the Provisional IRA and gave them credibility as a 'defensive' organization. It also ensured that many of the young people of that generation, particularly those in West Belfast who had experienced the horror of that pogrom, became committed to the Provisional IRA, not with any deeply worked-out philosophy, but as a powerful emotional reaction to what had happened to their own people on their own streets.

It was a short step for the leadership of the Provisional IRA to move from defence to attack and to launch their mistaken and costly campaign [...]

That campaign has brought an inevitable reaction from the British army, fundamentally changing the role it came to exercise on 14 August and bringing it into conflict with the Catholic community on many occasions, the worst being Bloody Sunday. There can be no doubt that British soldiers were warmly welcomed on the streets of Derry and Belfast in 1969 by the Catholic population, who saw outright civil conflict staring them in the face, with the RUC and B-Specials on one side.

It is worth asking what would have happened had the troops not arrived and the 11,000 B-Specials been deployed, who would have defended the Catholic population? The Irish army? They would no doubt have been able to get to Derry and to Newry but what would have happened to the rest of Northern Ireland? The most likely outcome would have been an immediate Lebanon-style situation from which we would never have recovered.

The Provisional IRA campaign to force a British withdrawal from Ireland by physical force is based on a seriously flawed analysis of the nature of the Irish problem in the second half of the twentieth century. It also seems to regard physical force as a principle rather than as a means, given their refusal to consider the consequences of the campaign for their own people. Their method has become more sacred than their cause. They regard the British presence in the north of Ireland as *the* problem.

They seem to think that the British interest in Ireland is the same as it was in the seventeenth, eighteenth, nineteenth and early twentieth centuries and has not changed. They completely ignore and underestimate the nature and the depth of the division between the Irish people who live on the island of Ireland. They struggle for the right of the Irish people to self-determination but ignore that the Irish people are divided as to how that right should be exercised and have contempt for the right of the same Irish people to determine the method to achieve agreement on the exercise of self-determination.

They ignore the changes in the world around us, which has become a much smaller place and which has changed the nature of British interests in Ireland and its relationship with Ireland and with other European countries, relationships which in these past centuries went to the heart of the Irish problem.

The British interest in Ireland has changed in this the last quarter of the twentieth century. Britain's interest in Ireland and in preventing self-government related directly to Ireland's historic links and friendships over the centuries with the other peoples of Europe, particularly Spain and France, and in the danger of Ireland being the back door to England's traditional enemies.

The rebellion of O'Neill and O'Donnell and their Spanish and Roman links led to the plantation of Ulster, with all its consequences. The rebellion of Eoghan Ruadh led to the Cromwellian plantation; 1798 and Ireland's links with France led directly to the Act of Union. In response to all that the Irish people became obsessed with the British and our European vision narrowed considerably.

Now Britain has joined with France, Spain and Ireland as well as other European countries in accepting the necessity of interdependence, in the smaller world of the late twentieth century. Ireland poses no threat to England and indeed the Irish are now in a position where we can once again renew and develop our European links and vision, and indeed, because of those links, and because of common interests and problems with many parts of Europe and because of the respect for the Irish in Europe we can become part of the European majority in the new emerging Europe, if we are prepared to apply our minds and our efforts to it [...]

The rich cultural and regional diversity of Europe is something to which we have a major contribution to make in maintaining, shaping and developing. Indeed, it is interesting to note that those who fear the new Europe most are English nationalists like Mrs Thatcher. They rightly sense that it is the death knell of concepts of nation states and sovereignty which led the imperialism and dominations of past centuries.

We are living through the development of a new phase in European history. In the past the city state moved to the nation state. Now, in today's much smaller world we are shaping and moving into entities which reflect that world. And a Ballymena man will be no less a Ballymena man because he can get to Brussels today as quickly as he could get to Belfast a century ago.

All this has implications for our ancient quarrel and opens up new opportunities for its resolution. We should note that this is one issue on which the whole of the Irish people did express their self-determination when majorities in both parts of the island voted to join the EC [...]

The British government makes it quite clear that Irish unity and independence is a matter for those Irish people who want it to persuade those who don't, and if they do, Britain will take the necessary steps to recognize and bring about the new reality.

Even if Britain has interests in Ireland today it is quite clear from this declaration that in the event of agreement being reached by the divided people of Ireland, those interests would be set aside.

We are now at the heart of the problem, which is the fundamental differences between the people who share this island. This has been the aspect of the problem that has received very little attention over the years by those who describe themselves as republicans. The truth is of course that we have not had very many republicans in Ireland. We have had plenty of extreme nationalists [...]

The central relationship that goes to the heart of our failure to achieve stability in Ireland is the unionist distrust of the rest of the island. It is this distrust that led them to exclude Catholics from any say in the old Stormont and eventually brought it down. It is that distrust that brought their opposition to and downfall of the power-sharing executive. Until that distrust is removed, until that relationship is resolved to the mutual satisfaction of both sides, nothing will be stable.

It should also be clear that any proposal for resolving the relationship may be put on the table and none excluded, and that it is for the unionist people to define their own identity and ethos as they see it and not as the rest of us see it. It would be the major task of the [inter-party] conference to accommodate the differences as presented there.

Furthermore, to demonstrate that we are serious about our commitment to partnership and agreement in building our new relationship, it should be made clear in advance that any agreement reached would have to be endorsed by referenda, both North and South, requiring a majority in both. The joint referenda proposal is central to the whole process since it reassures the unionists, and from a nationalist/republican point of view, it would be the first time that the Irish people as a whole would have been asked to endorse how we live together and share this island.[10]

10 *Irish Times*, 14 Aug. 1989.

Two weeks later, at the Merriman Summer School, Hume returned to a very early theme of his when he challenged Northern nationalists to adopt a more positive approach to participation in the public life of their society now that the Anglo-Irish Agreement had resulted in considerable progress in addressing grievances, especially those related to employment practices and security-force behaviour. He also continued to argue that the agreement had not harmed unionism and that unionist leaders should seize the opportunity to engage in comprehensive talks:

> Northern nationalists need to recognize that despite the legitimacy of past grievances 'the world does not forever owe us a living and that given equality of treatment we should not only be quite capable but anxious to stand on our own two feet and use our talents in playing a positive and constructive role in society'.

> Mr Hume said he believed the European dimension fundamentally altered the questions of sovereignty that have dogged us for so long, and warned that in the challenges that lay ahead it would no longer be enough to nurse alienation […]

> 'The whole of Ireland has suffered and is suffering from the cancer that is our failure to accommodate our differences. If we in Ireland cannot meet on the narrow ground that is Ulster let us meet on the broader ground of Europe.'

> Economically, both parts of Ireland had much to gain from concerted action and had common problems which working together could help to solve.

> 'I believe that when we compare ourselves to the rest of Europe our differences will be less apparent and that we will discover that we have much in common, that we have similar values and have an identity of interests on many issues.

> 'I look forward to the day, for example, when all Irish people can enjoy Orange marches as part of a shared past and don't see them as displays of menacing supremacy.'

> Mr Hume again stressed the need 'to sit down and talk about how best we are to resolve our differences'. He had no hidden agenda […] and certainly no wish to do violence to anybody's allegiances or destroy anyone's way of life.

> Though he accepted and took no joy in the reality of unionist shock and anger, mistrust and fear, in reaction to the Anglo-Irish Agreement […] it surely had been clear for some years that neither Britain nor Ireland were prepared to play old, worn-out roles of confrontation.

> 'This has been one of the most culpable failures of the unionist leadership, that they were so imprisoned in their history that they could not recognize

what was happening, preferring to see treachery and plots where none existed. I have many times asked that leadership to name a single unionist in Northern Ireland who has been damaged by the Anglo-Irish Agreement. There is none to be found. Instead they use every IRA atrocity as evidence of the failure of the agreement – an ironic identity of interest.'[11]

In November 1989 the secretary of state, Peter Brooke, indicated that an end to the PIRA campaign would open the door to Sinn Féin's participation in inter-party talks. At the SDLP's annual conference the same month Hume added to the mounting pressure on Sinn Féin by again highlighting the number of ordinary people killed by the PIRA. In doing so, Hume strongly defended the SDLP against those who, because of the party's stand on policing, claimed it was 'soft on terrorism':

> The security field – issues of justice, order and violence – continues to be the most difficult area. The party has always recognized that in the absence of consensus on how we are governed the symptoms of that disease will appear in different forms. The last few months have been no exception. The SDLP approach has always been very consistent. We are resolute in our adherence to the impartial and proper application of the rule of law. While others have sought to bend, breach and brutalize the rule of law in the name of protecting society and democracy we have stood firm in our commitment for sound lawful frameworks, due process and civil liberty as the very oxygen of democracy. As we have challenged abuses of democracy, miscarriages of justice or untoward security-force behaviour, we have been continually pilloried and misrepresented as being soft on terrorism. The truth is that our detractors are soft on justice and the proper rule of law, and, at times, descend to the level of the terrorist.
>
> We refuse to countenance any abuse of, or attack on innocent people as 'regrettable but acceptable and tolerable mistakes'. We recognize that the biggest and most basic mistake is to invite such terrible risks to ordinary citizens by dismissing the proper rule of law or democratic standards. In recent times, we have had stark examples of what I am talking about.
>
> Let us not forget those in our midst who are now the dispensers of the greatest injustice of all – the taking of human life [...] Up to the end of October 2,770 had died in Northern Ireland arising directly from what have become known as the 'Troubles'. Not one of those people will come out of their graves. The injustice of murder can never be corrected.[12]

11 Ibid., 26 Aug. 1989.   12 Address to the SDLP's annual conference, 6 Nov. 1989.

Dictators and oppressors

In a 1990 New Year's address aimed at the PIRA, Hume used some of his strongest language in criticizing the movement when he described it as acting as 'dictators' and 'oppressors'. He called on ordinary people to make clear to those supporting violence:

> that there is no cause in Ireland, North or South, that justifies the taking of human life. People should make clear that the greatest perpetrators of injustice in the north of Ireland today are those organizations which take human life; that there is no injustice worse than murder; and those who use such seriously unjust methods to bring about change become themselves dictators and oppressors.
>
> The SDLP leader asserted that any organization which had the support of less than 5 per cent of the Irish people and which insisted on forcing its will on the people by force could justifiably be described as oppressors and dictators.
>
> The self-determination of the Irish people about the methods of achieving their political objectives had been clearly expressed in elections North and South and those who refused to accept it could justifiably be described as enemies of the people of Ireland [...]
>
> Let us hope that in 1990 there will be those in their ranks, hopefully in their leadership, who will have the moral courage to recognize in public what they all know in private – that their methods are leading nowhere, only to increased suffering for the people of the North. Are the Provos the only people in Europe today who need guns to achieve their objectives, apart of course from dictators?[13]

The above remarks contain a clear indication that Hume was aware of a debate going on within the leadership of the PIRA about their campaign and that at least some had realized that after twenty years it was achieving nothing in terms of its political objectives. At the same time some progress was being made towards creating the conditions in which inter-party discussions and, possibly, meaningful negotiations could take place, involving the SDLP and the unionist parties. Hume made clear that he was prepared 'to meet anyone, any time about anything'. In June, it appeared that talks would soon commence, and Hume welcomed the development:

> I join the secretary of state in saying that everyone in Ireland and in Britain wants his initiative to succeed. Contrary to the impression given by others

13 *Irish News,* 1 Jan. 1990.

who have spoken in the debate, the goodwill of the Irish government in the matter is totally unquestionable.

I should place on record my own appreciation for the immense efforts that the secretary of state has put into a difficult task, the sensitivity that he has shown to different points of view and to the integrity and dedication with which he has pursued the objective of bringing us all round the table. We all acknowledge that he has made considerable progress, and I look forward to the talks. I also pay tribute to the right hon. member for Lagan Valley [Mr Molyneaux], the hon. member for Antrim, North [Revd Ian Paisley] and the leader of the Alliance Party, who is in the Strangers' Gallery, for the integrity and goodwill with which they have approached the talks. We must develop that spirit in the full knowledge that we face a difficult task because there are deep differences and divisions. The talks will be a serious beginning in dealing with the problems.

We are helped by the wider atmosphere in which we work today. The unionists are celebrating the three-hundredth anniversary of the battle of the Boyne. Some feared that the celebration might turn out to be divisive, but we should remember who was there in 1690. In addition to the Irish, the Danes, the Dutch, the Germans and the French fought on both sides.

Since 1690, all those countries have settled the differences between them, but Ireland has not. They have settled many deeper differences and have moved on to a wider European scene. There are lessons for us in that, as the origins of our problems are European. From a nationalist republican point of view, the English presence in Ireland was due to Ireland being considered the back door for her European enemies. The plantation of Ulster was England's response to O'Neill's and O'Donnell's links with Spain. The Act of Union was England's response to the French invasion of Ireland in 1798 [...]

Can anyone seriously say today that Britain has an economic interest in Ireland, when the British taxpayer is paying £1.5 billion a year to keep our economy going? Does anyone believe that Britain has a strategic interest in Ireland in a nuclear world, and that a military presence is necessary for strategic reasons? Does anyone believe that, when everyone knows that if the violence stopped the troops would be off the streets in a matter of weeks?

We have the legacy of our past, but the meaning of sovereignty and independence has changed. Today we have shared sovereignty and interdependence. The issues about which we quarrelled in the past are gone, but our legacy is a deeply divided people. What does the IRA say about that? It says that we are being prevented by force from exercising the right to self-determination. Is that true? The people who live in Ireland are deeply divided about precisely how to exercise their right to self-determination. Agreement on how to exercise that right cannot be achieved by force or physical violence, but only through dialogue and peaceful means [...]

Let us leave aside the past and agree to build institutions in Ireland that respect our differences, but we must do that in agreement, as agreement is at the heart of the matter. There is no way in which we can solve our problems by one section of our people countering another. It is no longer about pushing difference to the point of division; it is about accommodation and respect for difference. Having set up in agreement those institutions which respect our differences, we can then work the common ground, which all hon. members representing Northern Ireland would agree is substantial. Our economic interests in particular will increase as we move into the single market. By spilling our sweat rather than our blood, we can break down the differences between us and grow together at our own speed. That is the strategy that I believe we should follow.

After a terrible twenty years, there is a spirit abroad that demands political leadership and talks between the governments involved as soon as possible. I wish the secretary of state well, and I am confident that it will not be too long until the remaining loose ends are tied up, so that we can begin the difficult, but I hope successful, process of bringing lasting peace to our people.[14]

Unfortunately, it would be almost another twelve months before inter-party talks would commence. In the meantime, as the PIRA continued its campaign, Hume's frustration at the violence and the lack of political progress were evident in his address a few months later to the Merriman Summer School:

On 1 January this year I addressed them [the PIRA] directly in a New Year's statement. I pointed out that as they entered 1990 they might reflect on the facts of their twenty year old campaign. They might reflect in particular that their so-called 'mistakes', their Enniskillens, were not in fact exceptions, they were direct consequences of the very nature of their campaign, and because of that, irrespective of other arguments, render their campaign totally unjustifiable. I pointed out that up till 1 January 1990, 55 per cent of all people who had died in the so-called 'Troubles' in the North were innocent civilians – people killed in so-called 'accidents' or in tit-for-tat revenge killings by loyalist paramilitaries. It is clear, therefore, I argued, that if their campaign continues in 1990 that at least one of every two people who die will be totally innocent civilians, because this is the pattern that derives from the very nature of their campaign and there would not be justification in 1990 in statements of regret or apology because they knew in advance that that is specifically what was

14 House of Commons, *Debates*, 5 July 1990.

going to happen [...] Is there a single injustice in Northern Ireland today that justifies the taking of a single life.

My view of course is that these thoughts must strike the leaders of this campaign, but they immediately cast them aside because it would appear that they are lacking in one essentially quality – moral courage. The leadership required, given the nature of the IRA, to admit that they should abandon what they call 'armed struggle', would require enormous moral courage and real leadership, which appears to be non-existent. If there are any in their ranks who have that moral courage and they need republican precedents for their actions, they should remember a man called Pearse who once issued a statement calling on his followers to lay down their arms lest they bring too much suffering on their own people. Are there any such people in today's Provisional IRA? If there are and they have the moral courage to change to totally peaceful methods, then no single act in this century would do more to build new relationships or to transform the atmosphere on this island and to begin the process of breaking down the barriers between our people which are the real problems on this island today and which are the real legacy of our past and which are in fact intensified by the IRA campaign [...]

If both parts of Ireland can enter into new relationships with Greeks, Italians, French, Germans etc., it is surely long past time when they should be forging new relationships with one another. If bitter enemies like France and Germany can build new relationships can we not do the same? And can we not learn from the experience of Europe? [...]

[S]urely we can apply exactly the same lessons and methods to our problem, to grow together [...]. How? Let the British and Irish governments together follow the example of the European Community. Let them make a joint declaration that the divisions among the people of Ireland and the prejudices that are at their root are the regrettable consequences of our history and are not in the best interests of the people of Ireland or of the European Community; that the two governments have decided to leave the past aside; that they have decided to build institutions in Ireland, North and South, which will respect differences but which will allow the people in both parts of Ireland to work their common ground together and through doing so over generations, spilling our sweat and not our blood, to grow together, like the Europeans, at our own speed. That common ground, largely economic, is already considerable and will become even more considerable as we approach 1993 [the introduction of the European single market]. Indeed, with the removal of commercial borders and the creation of the channel tunnel that common ground and economic interest will intensify as we become offshore islands of the united Europe.[15]

15 Address to Merriman Summer School, Aug. 1990; copy in editor's possession.

Twentieth anniversary

At the SDLP's annual conference, when the party celebrated the twentieth anniversary of its foundation, Hume began his address by recalling its founding principle of non-violence, and what had been achieved through it. Again he contrasted the SDLP and the civil rights movement's approach with that of the PIRA, whose leaders he accused of perpetuating a campaign that was both immoral and impractical in terms of achieving its goals. Hume also expressed his frustration at the lack of urgency in convening inter-party talks and blamed unionists for putting barriers in the way by adding precondition to precondition:

> It is once again a pleasure and an honour for me to address you as party leader. It is a particular honour for me to do so on a weekend in which, twenty-two years ago this very day, 25,000 people stood on Derry's bridge in one of the most moving and outstanding examples of non-violence that this island has ever seen.
>
> Our message was simple – give us justice. We pointed out that any society built on injustice could not survive that question. Within three weeks, without a stone being thrown, Derry Corporation, the symbol of the worst injustices, which had survived fifty years including an IRA campaign in every decade, had fallen and the transformation of this city had begun. Three years later the reverberations created by that movement brought an end to the Stormont regime itself. It did not survive the question. The basic and unanswerable demand of the civil rights movement was equality of treatment for all citizens in the North and once that was achieved we had every confidence that all other problems, particularly the deep divisions among our people, could be solved by normal democratic and political means.
>
> The party was born out of the civil rights movement and was fundamentally based on the same philosophy that we have steadfastly pushed ever since. It is best summed up in the words of one of the great men of the twentieth century that I have quoted often – Martin Luther King – words that are quite prophetic when applied to the violence on our streets today:
>
> 'Violence as a way of achieving justice is both impractical and immoral. It is impractical because it is a descending spiral ending in destruction for all. The old law of an eye for an eye leaves everybody blind. It is immoral because it seeks to humiliate the opponent rather than win his understanding; it seeks to annihilate rather than convert. Violence is immoral because it thrives on hatred rather than love. It destroys community and makes brotherhood impossible. It leaves society in monologue rather than dialogue. Violence ends by defeating itself. It creates bitterness in the survivors and brutality in the destroyers.'

The tragedy for this society and this country was that there were people at that time who, in spite of the new energy, new vision and new hope generated by the civil rights movement, believed that change was worthless and unpatriotic unless it was steeped in blood. Their basic view of Ireland is as a piece of territory. Its people are expendable [...]

The IRA analysis of the Northern Ireland problem is as irrelevant to current realities as Ceauşescu's demented ideas were to the welfare of the Romanian people. The IRA are the true heirs of the old imperialism. Their tools are death and destruction, their aim is conquest through fear and terror, their mindset in sectarian divisiveness. The 'mistakes' that they admit are the murders of innocents. Their doctrine is an eye for an eye and they are blind. By their own standards let them be judged.

They proclaim the proclamation of 1916 as their bible and basic guide. Have they ever read it? Let me quote it: 'We place the cause of the Irish people under the protection of the Most High God, whose blessing we invoke upon our arms and we pray that no one who serves that cause will dishonour it by cowardice, inhumanity or rapine.' Was the blessing of the Most High God on the bomb that made a human time bomb out of Patsy Gillespie?[16] Was there no cowardice in making people carriers of death to others? Was there no humanity in the killing of Louis Robinson[17] or any of the other recent victims?[18]

Hume firmly believed that recent British government declarations on the future of Northern Ireland had made it clear that it would not place any barriers in the way of Irish unity should that be the wish of the majority of its people. To resolve the immediate crisis Hume once again called on both governments to convene a conference at which all parties would be invited to argue for their own proposals. He accused the unionists of not responding to previous calls for talks, saying:

I have to confess that I find their approach difficult to understand. They said they could not talk to us while the Anglo-Irish Agreement remained in existence. [UUP leader] Jim Molyneaux recently described it as 'a miserable narrow-minded contradiction'. Yet he will only talk to us through the secretary of state of the government that negotiated the agreement and registered it with the United Nations.

In addition, it has emerged that they will only talk to the South as part of a delegation led by the same government. And yet this party will not stand

16 Gillespie was forced to drive a van in which a bomb had been placed to a British military checkpoint outside of Derry. He and five soldiers were killed when the bomb exploded. 17 An RUC detective abducted and murdered by the PIRA. 18 Address to 1990 SDLP annual conference.

beside the same secretary at a ceremony in Belfast to remember the dead of two world wars. In trying to understand this contradiction my only logical conclusion is that like the Provos, the unionists do not have the confidence to stand on their own feet and represent their own people without additional assistance.

In reality it was the repeated failure of unionist politics to discard outmoded ideas of domination which led the two governments, working in the closest co-operation, to agree a structure designed to guarantee the rights of both traditions on this island. The agreement was therefore an admittedly circumscribed effort to remove the concrete causes of much of the 'sectarian and political confrontation' Mr Molyneaux refers to.

Both governments accept that the agreement is not written in stone. It can be built upon and transcended. The current political initiative is designed to see if the willingness exists on all sides to make political progress. Yet, I must once again ask, where is the willingness on the unionist part?

Despite all the evasions and subtle double-talk the reality regarding the talks process is clear. The unionist parties laid down three preconditions for their participation. Both governments after due consideration and clarification agreed to respond to these as a basis for commencing comprehensive negotiations.

No sooner was this stage reached than the unionist parties stipulated a new precondition, 'substantial progress' had to be achieved in one area of the talks before discussion could begin in other areas. It then transpired, as I have said, that there was a further precondition: the unionist parties declined to participate in North-South talks in their own right; instead, they wanted to be members of a delegation led by the secretary of state.[19]

The Olof Palme memorial lecture

In the same month, Hume delivered the Olof Palme memorial lecture in honour of the assassinated former social-democratic prime minister of Sweden who had won an international reputation for his approach to conflict situations. Hume addressed the Northern Ireland crisis in a European context, and also argued that it would be in Ireland's interest to become involved in closer international co-operation, particular with post-communist Central and Eastern European states, especially under the auspices of the Conference on Security and Co-operation in Europe. Citing the example of post-Soviet Europe, he drew attention to Palme's approach to resolving conflict, saying that:

19 Address to the SDLP's annual conference, Nov. 1990.

Olof Palme always strove to analyse and tackle problems on a holistic rather than a reductionist basis. He assessed and addressed problems within their wider context and saw that developing new relationships and structures among nations was not an idle and remote game of statecraft but is crucial to providing positive prospects which will touch the lives of ordinary people [...]

Change in Europe is continuing apace at two levels. One is the growing integration of the European Community based on the realization that the democratic nation state is no longer a sufficient political entity to allow people to have adequate control over the economic and technological forces which affect people's opportunities and circumstances. The task is to ensure that those arrangements and institutions which develop shared policies and programmes are democratically based. The issue is the need to optimize the real sovereignty of the peoples of Europe rather than ossifying our democratic development around limited notions of national sovereignty which only give space to multi-national vested interest. [...]

The transforming scene in Eastern and Central Europe has opened the prospect of the 'common European home'. That has been powerfully symbolized by the Paris Charter, signed less than two weeks ago at the meeting of the CSCE [Conference on Security and Co-operation in Europe] [...]

We should not forget that when Brezhnev first proposed what is the CSCE the reaction of most people ranged from apathy to cynicism. Above all leaders in the West, Olof Palme saw the attractions even then of pursuing this then obscure facility in international relations. He could see a scenario where such a framework would be accepted as an essential and effective way in which the whole breadth of Europe could enjoy security with each other rather than defence against each other. His whole approach to the arms race and the intensification of military alliances was to cut through the rhetoric of prejudice and suspicion. He proffered the devastating simplicity that we can only obtain security with others rather than against others [...]

In a recent far-reaching speech, the British secretary of state in Northern Ireland has stated in pretty bald terms that Britain has no selfish strategic or economic interest in Ireland. His assertion is that Britain is not out to manipulate or maintain its presence or partition in Ireland by way of fulfilling British interests. He underlined that Britain is not opposed to political unity in Ireland and went further in saying that if a majority of people in Northern Ireland express a wish for a united Ireland then Britain would make the necessary political provision to facilitate that [...]

We should also bear in mind that the European single market and the whole 1992 process will have an important impact on the border as we know it in Ireland. This should neither be exaggerated nor underestimated.

This process will allow the border to ebb substantially from economic life in Ireland. It should also provide a context which will require and should inspire policy programmes and administrative instruments which will be cross-border and all-Ireland in scope [...]

This in itself cannot remove political division. But it will allow the real essence of that division to be addressed rather than being distorted and deepened by economic, social and administrative divergences and rivalries [...]

Having presented the potential for new relationships within Ireland and between Ireland and Britain against the background of a changed and changing Europe, I should perhaps indicate something of the role which Ireland might play in that context.

Like Palme's Sweden, Ireland remained neutral from military alliances, whatever about its democratic or ideological affinities. Current developments serve more to vindicate that position than invalidate it. They do however call for a realignment of that neutrality to update it to present realities and potential achievements.

In this I propose not that Ireland join NATO, whose relevance is more questionable now than previously. Instead I am suggesting that Ireland can play a particular role in promoting and enhancing the possibilities offered by the CSCE scenario. I believe that it can identify a common cause not just with other neutral Western states but also with countries of Central and Eastern Europe who want to escape from the two military conglomerates. In doing so Ireland can play a role that would complement the efforts of those in NATO member states who want to work to achieve real and complete pan-European security, offering true peace rather than maintaining European defensive modes, albeit with less tension.

I think that is the challenge that Palme's vision offers to Ireland and as I say it complements the challenge it offers to responsible peace-building in Britain.[20]

While Hume was convinced that the Anglo-Irish Agreement had provided the parameters within which comprehensive negotiations could take place, unionists objected to any talks taking place while the mechanisms established under the agreement continued to operate. Suspension, they argued, had to mean the complete suspension of all aspects of the agreement. Hume, along with both governments, argued that while the agreement could be replaced, they would not accept its complete suspension. Winning support for any compromise proved tortuous. Nonetheless, progress was made and the year ended with some hope that talks would take place in 1991.

---

20 Olof Palme memorial lecture, Nov. 1990; copy in editor's possession.

1991–3

Discussions on the conditions under which inter-party talks could take place continued throughout the early months of 1991, with sufficient agreement being eventually reached to allow talks to commence in June. Along with the SDLP, the parties to those talks were Alliance, the DUP and the UUP. The agreed format for the talks was that they would consist of three strands, each strand a reflection of Hume's analysis of the key relationships and issues to be addressed: political and constitutional relationships within Northern Ireland; political and constitutional relationships between the North and the South; and political relationships between Ireland and the UK. It was accepted that the UK government would chair Strand 1, that an independent chair would preside over Strand 2 and that the two governments would jointly address Strand 3 issues. Initially, to meet unionist concerns, a time gap of twelve weeks between meetings of the Anglo-Irish Conference was declared, within which talks would take place. In a speech at Westminster, Hume welcomed the announcement that talks would occur, saying:

> May I join other hon. members in welcoming the secretary of state's statement, which is long overdue. Like others, I express my appreciation of the integrity, dedication and honesty with which he has approached these talks during the past fifteen months. Although there have been many obstacles and hiccups along the way, I should also like to pay tribute to the Irish government and to the leaders of the two unionist parties. Although there are many difficulties, it is fair to say that all parties approached the talks positively and constructively. I hope that the same spirit is brought to bear on the many obstacles that lie ahead.
>
> I am particularly pleased that all the relationships that are at the heart of the problem are now on the table for discussion, because otherwise we will not solve anything. It is important to note that no agreement can be reached unless agreement is reached on all the conflicting relationships that lie at the heart of the problem. The challenge that faces us is historic and I hope that the spirit that has governed the approach to the talks will continue into the talks themselves.[1]

1 House of Commons, *Debates*, 26 Mar. 1991.

At the opening session of the talks Hume presented the SDLP's analysis of the issues to be addressed. He began by outlining how the SDLP believed the talks should proceed:

> In our view – and we have said so many times in public – it is essential that before we seek solutions to the Northern Ireland problem we ensure that we understand what the nature of that problem is and, just as importantly, that to the greatest extent possible, we understand each other's perception of what it is. The analysis should be followed by the setting out of the requirements or criteria which, based on the analysis, should be necessary in any realistic attempt to resolve the problem. Only then should we – or indeed can we – move to a discussion of the institutions and structures which could be devised to give expression to those requirements.[2]

Hume went on to outline the party's analysis of the nature of the problem:

> The Northern Ireland conflict is the last negative legacy of the ancient quarrel between the peoples of Ireland and Britain. It is clear that the ultimate resolution of that conflict can only come about within the context and framework of the wider Anglo-Irish process [...]
>
> It is equally a lesson of the past seventy years that once a relationship of mutual respect has been established, the Irish and British peoples have shown themselves capable of working together to heal old wounds and hurts. There is every reason to believe, therefore, that if in this current process we can succeed in establishing a new basis of mutual trust between the two traditions on the island, then the healing process on this island also would be both rapid and irreversible.[3]

Given that one of the key aims of both unionist parties in entering the talks was the removal of the Anglo-Irish Agreement, Hume emphasized its significance for the nationalist community:

> From the inception of Northern Ireland until the signing of the Anglo-Irish Agreement in 1985, the nationalist identity was denied political expression and validity, and nationalists were excluded from effective participation in the institutions of government. The particular significance of the Anglo-Irish Agreement was the acknowledgment – first signposted at Sunningdale – by the British government of the legitimacy and validity of the Irish identity of Northern nationalists, and that any way forward in Northern Ireland had to

2 'The SDLP analysis of the nature of the problem', May 1991; copy in editor's possession.   3 Ibid.

incorporate a formal 'Irish dimension'. For the nationalist community that dimension must be a fundamental element of whatever new arrangements might emerge from the current process.[4]

Hume balanced this key requirement with a clear recognition that unionists had a parallel demand:

> From a unionist perspective, therefore, whatever may emerge from the current process will have to be such as to guarantee their sense of identity and to assuage their fears in terms of the perceived threats posed by Irish nationalism to their ethos and way of life.[5]

He then enumerated several key requirements and issues that would have to be addressed if a successful outcome to the negotiations was to be achieved:

> 1) The political process alone can lay the foundation for political progress. The people of Northern Ireland are deeply divided. The only consequence of violence is a more deeply divided people. We, by contrast, believe that the political process is the only means through which the commitment to peace and justice that exists in both communities can be channelled to create the conditions for an agreed future, which protects the identities and promotes the interests of both communities and traditions. [...]

> 2) The problem must be addressed and resolved within the context of the three central relationships. As we made clear earlier in this paper, the unionist and nationalist traditions define themselves in terms of aspirations and loyalties which transcend the confines of Northern Ireland. There is, therefore, widespread acceptance – including among unionist politicians – that the Northern Ireland conflict must be addressed and can only be resolved in the context of the totality of Anglo-Irish relationships – within Northern Ireland, within the island of Ireland and between Ireland and Britain [...]

> 3) The two traditions must aim to reach agreement on how best to share the island of Ireland. In the discussions the SDLP held with Sinn Féin in 1988, we stated 'it seems to us to reveal a deep misunderstanding of the Ulster Protestant tradition to suggest that it is largely the British influence and not their own reasons that make [unionists] wish to live apart from the rest of the people of Ireland'. We also stated 'the harsh reality is that whether or not [unionists] have an academic right to a veto on Irish unity, they have as

4 Ibid. 5 Ibid.

a matter of fact based on numbers, geography and history and they have in the same way as Greek or Turkish Cypriots have a factual veto on the exercise of self-determination on the island of Cyprus [...]

4) The Anglo-Irish Agreement represents an irreversible breakthrough in understanding and tackling the underlying causes of Anglo-Irish conflict [...] The abiding reality, recognized by the Anglo-Irish Agreement, is the right of the Irish government to involvement in the affairs of Northern Ireland. This right is explicitly embodied in the agreement and has been lodged formally with the United Nations on behalf of both Britain and Ireland [...]

5) Changes in Europe and beyond have profound implications for Ireland [...] New factors and new understandings are constantly entering into the political calculus for tackling the problems within Northern Ireland and within the wider relationships of the two islands of Ireland and Britain. In this regard, changes in the relationship between the two countries which have been occurring in the context of the European Community are of particular significance. The EC is undergoing a vibrant debate as to the form and substance of political authority which, whatever the eventual outcome, will profoundly affect the nature of life in these islands and in the Community at large in the twenty-first century. We are all aware of the discussion regarding the degree to which the evolving Community will require the pooling of sovereignty by the member states so as to meet the common tasks. Clearly these developments have the most profound implications for our relationships on this island.[6]

To these constitutional and political issues Hume added the need to reform the judiciary and policing, and to provide mechanisms to protect human rights. Finally, the SDLP submission highlighted the human, social and economic costs of violence and political instability, which had affected the whole of the North, and which would require the combined efforts of all to address.

Regrettably, due to time constraints, but essentially as a result of unionist unwillingness to allow the talks to proceed following a meeting of the Anglo-Irish Conference in July, they were suspended. No substantive progress had been made.

In his annual conference speech, which was much more international in its reflections than many previous speeches, Hume had little apart from the following to say about those talks, which, when resumed, he still believed had the potential to produce a comprehensive agreement that would:

6 Ibid.

transcend in importance any previous agreement (including the Anglo-Irish Agreement) ever made because it would for the first time give all sections of our people the security that they want and allow them to work together and to ultimately break down our outdated barrier.

Our approach to the Brooke talks was based, as everyone knows, on that overall strategy that at the end of the day is designed to involve the settlement of all relationships, because such an agreement, emerging from such talks, would be aimed at giving security to all. It would remove the objections to such talks that are based on the existence of other agreements, whether of 1920 or 1985. That is why we have called, and call on Mr Brooke again to convene such talks without delay. I would hope that the unionist leaders would respond in the same spirit. I believe that all our people and people everywhere would applaud.[7]

While talks would reconvene in March 1992, only one brief meeting took place before a British general election forced their adjournment.

Single European market

In the meantime, the imminence of the European Community's summit on the single market and possible monetary union became key focal points of John Hume's attention. His 1991 conference speech devoted considerable attention to the European agenda, and his remarks underlined his passionate commitment to an ever closer union between the peoples of the Community, as well as his belief in the Community's very positive benefits for the people of Ireland:

> As we approach the Maastricht Summit, our voice will be heard as well. In advance of that summit there will be a two-day meeting in Brussels of the leaders of all the social-democratic, labour and socialist parties in Europe to discuss our attitude to the agenda of the summit and to make a major declaration on our positions and the challenges posed by economic and monetary union and political union to all of the people of the EC including ourselves [...]
>
> The conference at Maastricht is devoted to updating the EC treaties on political union and on economic and monetary union, in short to intensify the process of European unity begun as far back as 1956 when the first six members came together. It seems to me that some of those voices raised against the evolution of political and economic union, particularly in the British Conservative Party, want to ignore reality and to forget what the

7 Address to the SDLP's annual conference, 1991.

European Union is all about. Do they think of what sort of Europe the EC has replaced? Have they ever cast their mind back to the history of Europe in this century alone? Have they forgotten the slaughter of millions of people that the Europe of the past represents – two world wars in this century alone, with all their devastation, allied to the conflicts of every generation in previous centuries? If all of the people of that horrific past had been offered a European Union, would they not have been prepared to pay a price for it? [...]

But a price doesn't even have to be paid. Economic necessity underlines and underpins the idealistic reality of a united Europe. The facts are, and some people refuse to face them, that the nation state has outlived its usefulness and its day has come and gone. No nation state can live apart in today's world, politically, economically or environmentally. The world is a smaller place. We are interdependent. Could any one of the twelve member states live apart from the rest, with economic and political barriers separating them? Could they survive economically?

None of this rules out the fact that the Maastricht Summit faces major challenges, both political and economic. Everyone accepts the concept of a single market. Is it possible to have a genuine single market without a single currency? The creation of a single currency will of itself substantially reduce costs to intra-Community trade. Everyone accepts that the single market will substantially increase economic growth. Paperwork and delays at borders alone at the moment cost an extra £7 billion per year. The removal of borders will reduce that cost, reduce prices to the consumer by around 6 per cent and create an estimated 5 million new jobs. The real challenge is to ensure that these jobs are not centralized in the richer regions of Europe but are shared also with the poorer regions. Hence, economic and social cohesion is a major issue of Maastricht [...]

We [the Socialist parties] are also committed to the Social Chapter to provide equality of treatment and basic social rights to workers right across the new Europe. Our proposed Social Chapter demands that these rights must include:

- fair wages and hours of work;
- the right to work and to paid holidays, sick pay and redundancy pay;
- the right to information, consultation and participation for company workers, particularly in multi-national firms;
- the highest standards of health and safety protection;
- full childcare provision, maternity and paternity leave;
- vocational training and retraining for older workers;
- equal treatment and equal opportunities for women and men;

- the right of the elderly to minimum income to protect them against poverty.[8]

Later, Hume attempted to reach out to the unionist community, where most of Northern Ireland's eurosceptics were to be found, by publishing an article on European unity in the Belfast *News Letter*, the daily paper, which, in general, supported the unionist position. In it he emphasized the importance, past and present, of Ireland's links with Europe:

> [T]he Irish problem is European in its origins. In centuries prior to the Act of Union the Irish had very strong links with the rest of Europe and very many common interests. It was precisely the fear of those links that led to the colonization of Ireland and to what has become known as the British presence.
>
> The battle of the Boyne was a major battle in a European war in which Dutch, Danes, Germans, French and English all fought. It was the links with Spain and O'Neill and O'Donnell that led to the plantation of Ulster. It was the French invasion of Ireland in 1798 that led to the Act of Union. There is no doubt historically that the British presence in Ireland was a presence to defend her own interests, both military and economic, and to prevent Ireland being used as a back door by her European enemies.
>
> All that has now changed. Both Britain and Ireland have now built and are continuing to develop new links with those same European countries. The world is now a smaller place. Sovereignty and independence, the issues at the heart of war in Europe and the issues at the heart of the British-Irish quarrel, have changed their meaning
>
> The basic needs of all countries have led to shared sovereignty and interdependence as we move inevitably towards the United States of Europe, and as we in Ireland rid ourselves of this obsession with Britain and rebuild our links with the rest of Europe [...]
>
> In Northern Ireland we can continue to close our eyes to the changing world around us and we will continue to be left behind.[9]

Hume also addressed himself to a Southern audience that was preparing for a referendum to determine whether the Maastricht Treaty, which had been signed in February, should be endorsed. To people in the South, he argued:

> It is interesting to look at the voices that are strongly opposing the European Union and Maastricht. I noted in the British parliament that they were all

---

8 Ibid. **9** *News Letter*, 6 Mar. 1992.

voices of nineteenth-century British nationalism. The opponents on the Continent are similar, the Front National in France and the emerging neo-Nazi forces in Germany and elsewhere. History will not be too kind to nineteenth-century nationalism. It created not only two world wars but imperialism as well, and humanity has paid and is paying a terrible price [...]

There is no shortage of such a mentality in Ireland and a referendum on a complex issue gives it the opportunity to emerge. Referenda are at their most democratic when they are on clear single issues. When they are about complex issues, the public and democracy are best served by paying attention to all the forces in a democratic society who are responsible to them and whose job it is to consider the matters in question in detail – government, opposition, trade unions, and the industrial, business and farming communities. In Ireland they have all urged 'Yes' to European union and they are right. What they are saying is that Maastricht is not totally perfect but it is a steady and positive step in the revolutionary process of a united Europe. One would have thought that every human being would want to move not only towards a united Europe but towards a united world! [...]

The institutions [of the EC] that were set up were institutions that respected difference and diversity but allowed the peoples of Europe to work their common ground together – to spill their sweat not their blood and to grow together at their own speed into a new Europe, the essence of whose unity is based on acceptance of diversity. The evolution continues.[10]

The referendum in the South endorsed the Maastricht Treaty, with 69 per cent of the votes cast in favour.

Brooke talks

The announcement that the talks would reconvene in Belfast occasioned a lengthy debate at Westminster. In his contribution Hume began by referring to the deaths of thousands of people and by pointing to the so-called 'peace' walls in Belfast, and the indictment that both the deaths and the wall implied on all sides for the failure to resolve the crisis, but he warmly welcomed the talks:

One of the worst things that has happened – it is one of the greatest indictments of us all, and I include everyone who is involved in the problem – is that in Belfast, which is the most churchgoing city in Western Europe – that includes those on both sides of the religious divide – it has been necessary to build not one wall but thirteen to protect one section of a Christian people

10 *Irish Times*, 8 June 1992.

from another and to separate them from one another. That is where I want to begin […]

As I have said, I welcome the talks. I welcome the fact that, for the first time during the existence of the problem, all aspects of it will be on the table for discussion, with all the relationships that are involved. We shall be talking about our relationships within Northern Ireland and relationships between North and South and Britain and Ireland.

I recognize that, in agreeing with Strand 2, the unionist political leadership is saying that it is willing to take seriously the argument that is advanced by some of us that that is a central factor in dealing with a solution to the problem. I do not underestimate the fact that that shows political leadership. The unionist leadership is willing to discuss North-South relationships with the Dublin government. That is, in a sense, in keeping with its tradition. Craigavon, Northern Ireland's first prime minister, talked regularly to the people in Dublin in attempts to reach agreements with them. In 1938, shortly after the 1937 constitution was passed, one of Craigavon's great quotes was: 'We cannot forever live apart. In today's world, no group of people can live apart.'

It is obvious that the relationship between unionist people and the rest of the island is central to the problem we face. I say that because, in 1912, when the house voted democratically for home rule for Ireland, the unionist people felt that they could not live with it. That reflected their relationship with the rest of the island. When the Stormont parliament was set up, the unionist government excluded the nationalist population, by and large, from any say in how the place was run. They did so for the same reason: fear of links with the rest of the island. They opposed the Sunningdale Agreement for the same reason: they feared assimilation with the rest of the island. That is why they have opposed the Anglo-Irish Agreement. I may be reading the unionists incorrectly, but that is my perception of unionism. I would welcome being told where I am wrong when we get round the table. I hope and believe that our dialogue will be deadly serious.

Until that relationship is sorted out, nothing will work. When I say 'sorted out', I mean to the satisfaction of unionist people as well as to the satisfaction of the rest of the people of the island. That is why we propose that, before there are talks with the Dublin government on how we shall live together on the island, an agreement should be reached that any agreement should be endorsed on the one day by means of a referendum within each part of the island.

That reassures the unionist people that when we say 'agreement' we mean it. That undermines the extremists who use guns, because, for the first time ever, the people of Ireland as a whole will have spoken. That will be the basis for lasting peace […]

If we analyse areas of conflict in other parts of the world – not only in Northern Ireland but in the Middle East and South Africa, for example – we find that mentality. In effect, it is we, ourselves, alone. That approach obviously excludes others. In the end, such a mentality is bound to lead to conflict.

There is another way. Again, it is simple and straightforward. Our experience of history – and the unionist people's experience – should teach unionists that their real strength and, at the end of the day, their only strength, lies in their own numbers and their own people. They must stand on their own feet, and negotiate their own relationships and agreements with those with whom they share a piece of earth.

I believe that the unionist mentality – the belief that they can trust only themselves – reflects their fear that the rest of the island wishes to subsume them, or indeed to wipe them out: that feeling is, of course, reinforced by the IRA campaign. Let me quote what should be a unionist slogan, from John Hewitt, the well-known Northern Irish poet, which expresses the deep anxiety felt by the unionist people. He said: 'This is our country also, nowhere else; and we shall not be outcast on the world.' I agree with that. I think that the objective of my side of the community should be to reassure the unionist people that, whatever approach is adopted to a solution of the problems, we have not the slightest interest in making them outcasts [...]

Let us build institutions in the north of Ireland which respect our differences, but which allow us to work our common ground, which is considerable. Let us, too, build institutions by agreement between both parts of our island – institutions which allow us to work our common ground and, by doing so, to break down the barriers of prejudice and distrust, the fruits of which – results, rather; I should not call them fruits – have been such tragedy in the past.

I have no doubt that, if we reach such agreements and vote for them, as I suggested earlier, by working together over the years, we shall erode our prejudices and grow together at our own speed, in two or three generations, into a new Ireland built on respect for diversity – an Ireland built by its people working together.

I do not think that it will be easy for us to reach such agreements in the current talks, but in the meantime, while we are doing so, let us get working on the common ground anyway, in order to break down the barriers of distrust between us. The common ground is obvious. We are one of the areas with the highest unemployment in the whole of the new European Community. Why do we not work together to tackle that, and, in doing so, turn our disadvantages into advantages?

All over the world, there are people who tell us that they are proud of their

Irish heritage. The Irish, both of the North and of the South, are the biggest wandering people in the world – we are a bigger wandering people than the Jews. The most recent census in the United States showed that 42 million people declared themselves to be Irish. The same is true in Australia and Canada – and many of those people have made it in business, politics or whatever.

Why do we not use that card, as some of us have already done, making contacts with people in senior positions in the United States, and asking them to use their influence? We say, 'Okay, so you want to help Ireland. A pint of Guinness on St Patrick's Day is all very well, but how about some real help, such as considering some investment?'

As we play the green card in such places as Boston, I believe that our unionist friends could play the orange card in places such as Toronto. The hon. member for Antrim, North [Revd Ian Paisley] could use the links which his political and religious tradition has with the southern states of America. Let us get together and harness those energies in a positive rather than a negative sense, to bring development to our people. We are not asking people for charity, because we have something to offer. We are offering them a foothold in the biggest single market in the world, and we speak the same language.

While we are talking, and trying to build confidence and trust in our people, let us work the common ground together. Let us spill our sweat and not our blood. Let us at last give hope to our people. All of us who know the problem know that we will not solve it in a week or in a fortnight, but if the people see us engaged in strategies that lead in the right direction, they will stand behind us.[11]

The talks continued over the following months but then ended inconclusively in early November. Reflecting on the engagement between the parties, Hume struck a surprisingly positive note in his address to the SDLP's annual conference, claiming that while there had been no agreement, a considerable degree of common understanding had been reached on parties' positions. His hope was that an early return to talks would build on that understanding. Significantly, given what would soon emerge regarding his renewed contacts with Sinn Féin leader Gerry Adams, Hume also pointed to some slight changes in what Sinn Féin was saying about the need for any agreement to win support across the divided people of Ireland:

Before the talks began, we were under no illusions about the major difficulties that lay in the way of reaching agreement. We have always recognized that a few

11 House of Commons, *Debates*, 5 Mar. 1992.

years is a very short time in the history of a people, particularly a deeply divided people, and if a solid basis of agreement was to be reached that it would probably take considerable time. That has turned out to be the case. However, we ought to recognize as well that considerable progress has been made. For the first time ever all aspects of our problem were under discussion. It has been agreed that any agenda for a lasting solution must resolve not only relationships within the North, but between North and South and between Britain and Ireland. In short our problem is not, as it has been wrongly described for so long, 'the Northern Ireland problem'. It is in fact a British-Irish problem and indeed it was the failure of Britain and Ireland to sort out their relationships satisfactorily that led to the creation of Northern Ireland. In essence the failure was pushed into a corner called Northern Ireland and was left to fester for almost fifty years until it finally burst. It is now back at the heart of the British-Irish agenda and cannot move back from there. That in its own way is substantial progress. Secondly, even ten years ago no one would have forecast that the British and Irish governments, the SDLP and the two unionist parties would sit round the same table and in spite of our differences engage in serious and constructive dialogue. That too is substantial progress and in its own way is evidence of the seriousness of the unionists in seeking a solution even though our differences also remain substantial. Where further progress may have been made, and time will tell, will be in whether we have developed deeper perceptions of one another's difficulties, problems and necessities.

Our approach to these talks has been clear and unequivocal and we would hope to continue the process, which has begun, of developing a deeper and less prejudiced view of one another by making as many contacts as we can with the unionist community, particularly at community level, in order to put to them directly our approach to a settlement.

From the beginning we avoided the traditional approach to talks of putting our detailed proposals on the table on day one. Such an approach, as experience has shown, not only will not produce a settlement, it will not even begin to develop the trust and understanding that are essential pre-requisites to reaching agreement. Instead we insisted that everyone should put their analysis of the problem on the table and begin the process of identifying the common themes and political realities that would have to be faced up to in any solution. That approach has led to a great deal of constructive dialogue and I think to a better understanding of our differences.

Our approach has been based fundamentally throughout on the basis that our task was not to seek victory, nor to wipe out our differences, but to build a society which respected our differences, which created institutions which respect our differences and which allow us to combine our energies in tackling our common problems [...]

The one organization that could make the greatest contribution to creating the atmosphere in which all this could happen is the provisional republican movement. Their attitude, as expressed by their methods, is that difference is a threat and therefore should be destroyed. In the process they not only do not remove difference they intensify it to the point of division. Does it never occur to them that difference is not a matter of choice it is a mere accident of birth and upbringing? Had those who killed human beings in the name of the IRA been born and reared on the Shankill Road or in Birmingham, do they not realize that they might have been the young policeman or the young soldier that they killed? How can you unite with people by killing them? What sort of world would we live in if everyone treated difference as a threat? The normal answer from the Provos to such criticism is 'What about ...', not seeming to realize that even if their what-aboutery was correct all it means is that they are taking their standards from those about whom they are complaining. Let me remind them again of what Martin Luther King said: 'If you use the methods of the oppressor you will end up worse than the oppressor.' The IRA have killed six times more human beings than the British army, the RUC and the UDR put together.

In recent times the political leaders of the provisional republican movement have indicated that they accept that any solution to the problem of Ireland must involve the agreement of the divided people of this country. Let us hope that they will follow that welcome approach to its logical conclusion and use all their influence to persuade the IRA to lay down their arms so that our entire community can get down to the essential task, the healing process of breaking down the barriers of distrust and prejudice that stand in the way of such agreement [...][12]

Economic challenge

Ever conscious of the need to maintain a focus on economic development, Hume strongly attacked the British government's strategy for development in Northern Ireland:

> We cannot accept the dogma outlined by the government in its so-called strategy paper for Northern Ireland, 'Competing in the 1990s', which relies on the free-play of the market. This approach was judged last Tuesday not to be good enough for the United States. If it does not work there, and if the United States needs an active partnership between government and the market how much more essential is it for government to have an active role in a weak, peripheral region? The real world, not the world of dogma, requires

12 Address to the SDLP annual conference, Nov. 1992.

government to have responsibility, to provide assistance and to use resources to exploit opportunities.

Once we see ourselves as something different from a region of the United Kingdom, new possibilities emerge. In fact, regional performance has always been – and is now increasingly – influenced by the international economic system. For example, new technology or the reorganization by companies of their production and supply chains, for reasons that have nothing to do with the national economy, may radically change a region's prospects, as the people of Magherafelt discovered last year when a multi-national branch closed down. We have to learn to link directly into the international economy in the context of the world's supply, production and distribution networks, otherwise the world will pass us by.

In particular we must make a massive effort to train and educate all our people. By European standards the British educational system stands out because of the high percentage of young people leaving the education and training system with inadequate or no skills. Here in Northern Ireland we obtain very good 'A' level and university degree results, but are even less successful than the British system in providing basic skills and training to the overall population. This neglect, apart from its cost in the waste of human talent, is suicidal in terms of economic development. For we know that two out of three jobs will be affected by the new information technology, and that the new technology is making an impact – not, as predicted, by eliminating jobs but rather by creating a huge need for training and retraining.[13]

Poverty on the European agenda

At a conference on poverty in Europe in Derry in December 1992, Hume argued that poverty and its consequences amounted to:

> one of the most fundamental problems in Northern Ireland and the rest of the European Community. But it has not received the attention it deserves from government or from European institutions as a whole. Indeed all the available data shows that far from improving, poverty has increased in recent years. Despite the theories of Reaganomics and Thatcherism that the free market would ensure a trickle down of wealth throughout society, the result has been an ascending cascade towards the top. Wealth has been concentrated while poverty has been spread more widely [...] Throughout the European Community, millions of citizens experience living standards well below a reasonable level [...] Poverty is a scourge but it can be overcome. Provided the

13 Address to the SDLP annual conference, Nov. 1992.

political will and vision is there, it can be conquered. There is no mystery about the causes of poverty, the problem is the lack of determination to address these causes. Chief among these causes is unemployment. Not only are millions deprived of employment, the massive financial costs of unemployment drain resources which could otherwise be used to deal with other causes of poverty [...]

For those in employment, low pay is a major burden. Despite efforts to implement equal pay legislation women are the prime victims of low-wage economics. Then there are those who are so excluded from the labour market that they are not even counted as unemployed, or whose prospects of employment for lack of skills or experience would be remote even in a period of boom.

If we are serious about dealing with poverty, a fundamental reappraisal of economic and social policies pursued throughout the Community is required. While many initiatives can be taken within the context of Northern Ireland, there is a clear need for a European anti-poverty strategy.

Poverty is clearly a social as well as an economic problem. The social dimension of the Community must be enhanced urgently. The concept of a social Europe has always been present in Community legislation and practice, but unfortunately it has always occupied a secondary status. Social initiatives have traditionally been by-products of economic policies, not positive innovations in their own right.

There has been much controversy over the Treaty of Maastricht. No one would claim it is perfect but it received the [support of the] overwhelming majority of the Community's elected representatives in the European parliament. An important consideration for those of us who supported it was the creation of new Community competences in the social arena, and the introduction of qualified majority voting in certain areas. Eleven out of twelve member states accepted the Social Chapter. The isolation of the British government should, I hope, provoke a serious campaign for opting back in to the European mainstream.

A social Europe is a political and economic necessity. Without it the strains of economic integration and modernization will cast the future of the Community into doubt. There is also a danger that the development of economic and monetary union will be used as an excuse to cut social expenditure. That would be very short-sighted, and we must resist any such antisocial policies.[14]

---

14 Address to the conference 'Poverty on the European agenda', Derry, Dec. 1992. Copy in editor's possession.

New North, new Ireland, new Europe

Hume again displayed his international outlook in an address to a congress of the European socialist parties some weeks later. He drew inspiration for resolving Northern Ireland's conflict from the huge changes, achieved non-violently, in Central and Eastern Europe and their implications for a new world order:

> We have seen the powerful cast down and those who had been outcasts chosen to lead free peoples. To an Irishman, who, in his lifetime, has led people in the streets in mass non-violent protest against the denial of basic civil rights, who with my party steadfastly upholds the democratic process in a society where the taking of human life is seen by some as the only means of change and by others as the means of upholding the status quo, where the doctrine of an eye for an eye leaves blindness in its wake, such scenes cannot fail to be deeply moving. The silent dignity of masses of people gathering in non-violence will bring about more change and will expose in minutes more repression than years of gunfire and bloodshed. Those who use the methods of the oppressor tend to end up worse than the oppressor. I bring with me today a symbol of past divisions and present realities. I have it here. Yes it is a piece of a wall, but it is not from the wall on which the people of Berlin danced and which they helped tear down. It is a piece of the 'Belfast Wall' taken from one of the many walls that have been built to separate divided communities throughout the city. While barriers between peoples are crumbling across a Continent, even as we speak another such wall is being built in Belfast and has been given by some the grotesque name of a 'peace line', as if the bleak desolation created in parts of that city after twenty years of violence could be described as peace.
>
> This lump of concrete reminds us that while walls may separate people, the real barriers cannot be seen because they exist in the hearts and minds of the people themselves and are built of hate and violence and fear. They are barriers that can only be overcome when we overcome our fears and have the courage to trust one another and learn to accept and respect our differences. They are also a challenge, for in reality they were built by past attitudes and the challenge is, if those walls and what they represent are to fall, to re-examine those past attitudes, all of them. [...]
>
> Recent events in Eastern Europe also show that new ideas can sweep away obstacles which seemed immovable, and just as the darkest hour comes before the dawn, new beginnings can emerge just when we face despair. But I do not despair. As someone who has devoted my life to politics and the democratic process, I say with complete and utter conviction that there is no political problem that cannot be solved by men and women who choose to put aside

former animosities and work together to find solutions, and who are prepared to act in a spirit of goodwill and trust. I say too that the time has come for us to tear down the walls which separate us and find a new liberty in freedom from hate and freedom from fear [...]

Let there be no doubt that there is deep concern and fear in the developing countries that our pre-occupation with the single market and with Eastern Europe will yet again put their problems on the back burner. Let us reassure them. If we accept, as we do, that one of the travesties of the arms race and Cold War was that it maintained such dreadful injustice and misery, then we must make a new global co-operation and meaningful North/South dialogue one of the prizes to be won from the changing East/West relationship. We seek a new European order, yes, but within a new world order.[15]

Hume sensed the new spirit of hope sweeping across Central Europe in the wake of the collapse of communism, and the great attraction, in the countries concerned, of becoming part of the European Union. His hope was that Northern Ireland's crisis would be positively affected by a similar period of hope and reconciliation.

15 Address to the Congress of European Socialist Parties, Berlin, 1993; copy in editor's possession.

1993–4

The revelation, in April 1993, that John Hume and Gerry Adams had renewed direct contacts precipitated what can be described as probably the most controversial period of Hume's political career. Since the 1988 talks between the SDLP and Sinn Féin, Hume had maintained a kind of public dialogue with the leadership of the PIRA, continually posing questions about the morality, legitimacy and efficacy of its campaign, particularly in light of that movement's stated objective of forcing from Britain a declaration of its intent to withdraw from Northern Ireland. Occasionally the two men debated publicly, as in a BBC radio interview in March 1992, during that year's general election campaign. Adams argued his party's right to be present at any negotiations based simply on its electoral mandate and irrespective of anything else, including its links with the PIRA. Hume agreed that while Sinn Féin had a mandate from its electorate, that mandate could not justify a place at the negotiating table as long as Sinn Féin maintained its support for the PIRA. Hence his efforts to persuade the republican movement, through his talks with Adams, to abandon its campaign of violence:

> Mr Hume said he did not think that the IRA had wider support than Sinn Féin. 'I am also quite certain,' he added, 'that in all previous elections Sinn Féin have made it clear that a vote for Sinn Féin was a vote for unequivocal support for what they termed the armed struggle.'
>
> 'It was not their opponents who invented the phrase "a ballot paper in one hand and an Armalite in the other".[1] However, there is nobody who would be more delighted to see an end to the violence than myself and the vast majority of the people of Northern Ireland. Anything that has anything to contribute to that end I would be happy to look at. Violence is the biggest problem facing our people. Peace in our streets is the biggest issue because there is not a single injustice in Northern Ireland today that justifies the taking of a human life [...]
>
> 'What I would like to see is a complete cessation of the IRA campaign and that Sinn Féin can take their place like any other political party around the table [...] My understanding is that the provisional republican movement is a movement which has got a military wing called the IRA and a political wing called Sinn Féin. That is how I understand it and how the public understand it.

1 The phrase was first used by Sinn Féin publicity officer Danny Morrison when he talked about Sin

'If that is true', said Mr Hume, 'then obviously Sinn Féin can have an enormous influence in bringing the IRA campaign of violence to an end. Because, as Gerry Adams appears to be agreeing, violence has no contribution of any description to solving this problem.'[2]

Knowing that Sinn Féin had to meet this condition, Hume renewed his meetings with Adams. Following their meeting in 1993, the two leaders issued a joint statement that set out very succinctly the purpose and focus of their meetings:

> A meeting between us held on Saturday, 10 April, in our capacities as leaders of the SDLP and Sinn Féin has given rise to media coverage, some of which was ill-informed or purely speculative.
>
> We are not acting as intermediaries. As leaders of our respective parties we accept that the most pressing issue facing the people of Ireland and Britain today is the question of lasting peace and how it can best be achieved.
>
> Everyone has a solemn duty to change the political climate away from conflict and towards a process of national reconciliation which will see the peaceful accommodation of the differences between the people of Britain and Ireland and the Irish people themselves.
>
> In striving for that end we accept that an internal settlement is not a solution because it obviously does not deal with all the relationships at the heart of the problem.
>
> We accept that the Irish people as a whole have a right to national self-determination. This is a view shared by a majority of the people of this island though not by all its people.
>
> The exercise of self-determination is a matter for agreement between the people of Ireland. It is the search for that agreement and the means of achieving it on which we will be concentrating.
>
> We are mindful that not all the people of Ireland share that view or agree on how to give meaningful expression to it. Indeed, we do not disguise the different views held by our own parties.
>
> As leaders of our respective parties we have told each other that we see the task of reaching agreement on a peaceful and democratic accord for all on this island as our primary challenge.
>
> We both recognize that such a new agreement is only achievable and viable if it can earn and enjoy the allegiance of the different traditions on this island, by accommodating diversity and providing for national reconciliation.

Féin taking power.   **2** Report of a Radio 4 debate, *Irish News*, 21 Mar. 1992.

We are reporting our discussion of these matters back to our respective parties. They have fully endorsed the continuation of this process of dialogue.

We will be picking up on where the talks between our parties ended in 1988 and reviewing the current political situation.

As at that time, we engaged in a political dialogue aimed at investigating the possibility of developing an overall political strategy to establish justice and peace in Ireland.[3]

In light of British statements, particularly by Peter Brooke, secretary of state for Northern Ireland, that it no longer had any 'selfish political or strategic interests in remaining in Ireland', Hume had prepared the following draft, which was to undergo several revisions over the following two years before emerging, in the hands of the two governments, as the Downing Street Declaration in December 1993. Its contents reflected the significance Hume placed on the European context, as well as his thoughts on self-determination and his emphasis on having the agreement of the people of Northern Ireland for any settlement to be durable:

(Proposed) Joint declaration by both British and Irish prime ministers

1. Leaving the past aside and regretting the pain and suffering caused by past failures to settle the relationships of the peoples of both islands satisfactorily.
2. Recognizing that the implementation of the single market and the coming into being of the European Union with the effective removal of all borders fundamentally changes the nature of British/Irish relationships. Further recognizing that future developments leave both parts of Ireland as the only part of the new Europe with no land links with the other regions, will intensify the common ground between both parts of Ireland and intensify the need for maximum co-operation to achieve maximum benefit from the European Union.
3. Regret, however, that there remains a serious legacy of past relationships – a deeply divided people on the island of Ireland. This is a major concern of both governments and both deeply regret that these are the last remaining such divisions in the new European order.
4. Both governments recognize that these divisions can only end with the agreement of the people, North and South, in Ireland.
5. Both governments therefore commit themselves to using the maximum resources to create the atmosphere in which such agreement is made easier. Both governments find it unacceptable that these are the last remaining

3 Joint statement from John Hume and Gerry Adams, 13 Apr. 1993.

divisions in a Europe that has already ended many more deep and bitter quarrels. They will, therefore, promote intensive co-operation at all levels to strengthen the process of agreement.

6. The British government reiterate yet again that they no longer have any selfish political or strategic interest in remaining in Ireland. Their sole interest is to see peace and agreement among the people who inhabit the island and will devote all their available resources to that end.

7. For its part the Irish government recognizes that the traditional objective of Irish nationalism – the exercise of self-determination by the people of Ireland as a whole – cannot be achieved without the agreement of the people of Northern Ireland. It would, therefore, commit itself to working for institutions of government, North and South, which would respect the diversity of the people of Ireland [...], but allow them to work their substantial common ground together in order to build the necessary trust for an agreed future. In order to pursue that strategy it would set up a permanent Irish Convention in order to plan and implement the steps and policies required to break down the barriers which divide the people of Ireland which prevent the exercise of agreed self-determination. If the British government refuse the joint declaration, the Irish government would proceed to set up the convention with the additional objective of planning and implementing the policies required to persuade the British government to adopt our strategy and objectives. Membership of the convention would consist of elected representatives of all parties in Ireland who share the objective of a united, self-determined Ireland.[4]

Not surprisingly, Hume was again widely criticized for having re-engaged with Adams while the PIRA continued its campaign. But having already embarked on talks with unionists in 1991–2, he felt it was impossible to ignore the opportunity to return to his dialogue with the republican movement in order to persuade its leaders to end the violence, and so enable Sinn Féin engage in the political process. Unionist criticism was loudest, but critical voices also came from sections of Southern opinion, political and media.

Anxious to defend these talks, Hume availed of the opportunity provided by an invitation to deliver a lecture on the theme of 'Christianity and Politics' at St Thomas' Church of Ireland church in Belfast, to outline his case to a Protestant and, presumably, mainly unionist audience. He also wanted to allay some of the fears that his contacts with Adams had created. In particular, he emphasized that any agreement would have to be put to a referendum in both parts of the country:

4 Eamonn Mallie & David McKittrick, *The fight for peace: the secret story behind the Irish peace process* (London, 1996), pp 118–19.

In order to underline our commitment to agreement, the SDLP have proposed, and it has been endorsed by the Irish government, that any agreement reached should be endorsed in a joint referendum held on the same day in the North and in the South, requiring a yes from each.

This proposal is to reassure the unionist people that we mean what we say when we talk of agreement. From a unionist perspective such an agreement would not just be validated by a majority of people in the North but would have the approval and allegiance of nationalist Ireland – North and South.

From a nationalist point of view it would be the first time ever the people of Ireland as a whole would have endorsed the institutions of government North and South. This is the true basis of lasting peace and order because for the first time ever institutions of government would have the total loyalty of the people; it would be a meaningful expression of self-determination in a real situation.[5]

Answering his Southern critics directly, Hume was particularly caustic in his criticism of Conor Cruise O'Brien, the former Labour politician and academic, who had been to the fore among Southern critics of the Hume-Adams talks. O'Brien had accused him of leading a very sectarian party, to which Hume responded:

In recent times there has been quite an amount of ill-informed, to put it charitably, misrepresentation of the views of myself and my party in relation to the most serious problem facing this country.

It is quite clear that these commentators have paid no attention of any description to what we in the SDLP say or do in the North or else, which is more likely, they are just deeply prejudiced and, in the long tradition of prejudice, quote statements either selectively or out of context to justify their prejudices.

The most recent statement by Conor Cruise O'Brien is a powerful example of both irresponsibility and deep prejudice. He said in Belfast that I had turned the SDLP into a 'deeply sectarian party'. If I were seeking advice on how to be sectarian, then the first person I would consult would be Conor Cruise O'Brien. Dr Ian Paisley seems to think that he is a very worthy source given that he had no difficulty in reprinting, in full, an article by O'Brien in his *Protestant Telegraph* as justification for the views of his own party. And just recently a loyalist paramilitary organization in justification of their attacks on what they describe as pan-nationalism quoted Mr O'Brien.

O'Brien didn't seem to notice that two leading Belfast SDLP councillors whose homes that organization tried to burn down recently, came from the

5 Address in St Thomas' church, Belfast, 9 May 1993; copy in editor's possession.

Protestant and Catholic communities. Neither does he bother to note that of the four senior officers of the SDLP, two come from the Catholic community and two from the Protestant community [...]

The most recent selectivity of quotations relates to the words 'the Irish people have the right to self-determination'. That is not just the language of Sinn Féin and the IRA [as O'Brien had alleged], but the language of the League of Nations and the United Nations. Because such views are central to the serious problem of the North, in keeping with my responsibility, I addressed that very question on numerous occasions in both speeches and articles, and it is evident that these commentators didn't even read them, or chose to ignore them.

I have repeated that it is people that have rights, and not territory, and that they tragically are deeply divided as to how that right is to be exercised, and that agreement can never be reached by any form of force or coercion [...][6]

Despite his critics, Hume's discussions with Adams continued and, in what was an attempt to force both governments to respond to the opportunity for peace they believed existed, they issued another joint statement in September:

Our discussions, aimed at the creation of a peace process which would involve all parties, have made considerable progress. We agreed to forward a report on the position reached to date to Dublin for consideration. We recognize that the broad principles involved will be for wider consideration between the two governments. Accordingly, we have suspended detailed discussions for the time being in order to facilitate this.

We are convinced from our discussions that a process can be designed to lead to agreement among the divided people of this island, which will provide a solid basis for peace. Such a process would obviously also be designed to ensure that any new agreement that might emerge respects the diversity of our different traditions and earns their allegiance and agreement.[7]

A month later in the house of commons, Hume vigorously defended his talks with Gerry Adams against very strong criticisms from unionist and conservative MPs:

As we look to the future, we face a number of choices. The first choice is the status quo. A number of people are comfortable with that because the Troubles do not affect them; the Troubles affect people in the poorer areas –

6 *Irish Independent*, 12 May 1993.   7 Second joint statement from John Hume and Gerry Adams, 25 Sept. 1993.

that is where the violence is and where the troops are on the streets. It is not a solution. The second choice is a scorched-earth policy, turning Northern Ireland into an internment camp. That is not a solution. The third is a minimalist agreement between the unionists and ourselves, with the extremism and violence continuing. That is not a solution. The fourth choice is to face reality. One recent positive development is the fact that both governments, and all parties from Northern Ireland in this house, have agreed that if we are to solve the problem rather than merely discussing who wields the power in Northern Ireland, we must deal with all the relationships which go to the heart of the problem and sit around the table to do so. I believe that if we sit around the table in an atmosphere of peace the dialogue will have a much greater chance of succeeding.

Unfortunately, there are in our society a substantial number of people who vote for political organizations which support violence and what they call 'armed struggle'. If one happens to be a public representative in that society, does one not have the responsibility to do everything in one's power to try to bring that violence to an end, in particular, by talking to people?

I make no apologies for entering into dialogue with Mr Adams for the objective of bringing a total cessation to all violence. That is the objective and we can achieve it by talking, despite the risks involved and the irresponsible accusations hurled at us, and at myself in particular, by people from other political parties, and the fact that people's lives are put at risk by such irresponsible criticism [...]

A lot of people have been hurling quotations in respect of what I am supposed to have said with Mr Adams. As an example of what I am talking about, let me ask the house what it disagrees with in the following language, which is the language that we have expressed together: 'The exercise of "self-determination" is a matter for agreement between the people of Ireland. It is the search for that agreement and the means of achieving it on which we will be concentrating [...] We both recognize that such a new agreement is only achievable and viable if it can earn and enjoy the allegiance of the different traditions on this island, by accommodating diversity and providing for [...] reconciliation.'

Our second statement says: 'We are convinced from our discussions that a process can be designed to lead to agreement among the divided people of this island, which will provide a solid basis for peace. Such a process would obviously also be designed to ensure that any new agreement that might emerge respects the diversity of our different traditions and earns their allegiance and agreement.' Can anyone in the house claim that an agreement among the divided people of Ireland which respects their diversity and earns the allegiance and agreement of all the traditions is not an objective for which all hon. members should be working and to which the government should be totally committed?

At the end of the day, I have said publicly that the dialogue in which I am engaged has been the most hopeful sign of lasting peace that I have seen in twenty years. I do not make statements like that lightly. I believe that the dialogue in which I have been engaged is a dialogue of real hope [...] At the end of the day, as our statement made clear, this process must involve both governments, and all parties. Its objective is an agreement that has the allegiance and agreement of all traditions [...] I should like to see the two governments meeting next week. I am standing here and telling the government that I believe that we have a real process of lasting peace and a total cessation of violence on the basis that I have just stated. I am saying to them, 'Hurry up and deal with it.' The government must hurry up and deal with it because the process and the opportunity exist [...] I do not underestimate the risks that I have taken in entering into the dialogue, but if, by talking to someone, I can make a contribution to saving human life and creating the circumstances in which we shall never, as we are doing today, stand condemning the murders of yesterday, if by dialogue as elected politicians, who surely were elected to talk – what is wrong with talking, particularly if it can bring about lasting peace? I say directly to the government that I believe that there is a real basis for lasting peace and the total cessation of violence. I hope that they will examine it in detail and respond positively.[8]

Ireland West investment conference

While he awaited a response, Hume addressed wider concerns at a conference that discussed the economic and social conditions west of the Shannon and west of the Bann. On many indices these regions showed significant disparities when compared with the east of the country. While decrying the disparities, Hume's approach was not to indulge in 'begrudgery' at the expense of the east, but rather to seize opportunities to create new centres of development in the west:

> The material conditions for a new partition are emerging. But just as I would argue that the North-South divide has been destructive for both parts of Ireland, a new socio-economic partition between east and west would be equally damaging to all our interests.
>
> A west kept alive on a drip feed of transfer payments would not ultimately benefit the east, either politically or economically. The tensions between a relatively affluent North and a more impoverished South have had a serious

8 House of Commons, *Debates*, 22 Oct. 1993.

impact on both the economy and political systems of at least two of our European neighbours, Italy and Belgium. Given the existing divisions within the island, it does not seem sensible to accentuate our problems by creating new disputes as a result of unbalanced development.

No doubt our neo-classical economists will tell us that the shift to the east is inevitable and therefore to be welcomed. It was an economist who coined the phrase 'the best is the enemy of the good'. But I have always been baffled by the description of economics as the 'dismal science' since so many of its practitioners spend so much time claiming that 'the worst is the friend of the good'.

I do not believe in the inevitability of the decline of the west. Balanced development is in our collective interests. Just as it has been accepted that the European Community has a responsibility to promote convergence between the richer and poorer member states, the respective metropolitan centres have a duty and self-interest in the welfare of all the territory under their jurisdiction.

Bringing about such balanced development requires a new model of centre-periphery relations.

Two different models prevailed in the two jurisdictions until relatively recently. For many years the Republic operated in, to use Professor Garvin's phrase, a 'periphery-dominated centre' mode. The political representatives of the western periphery dominated the legislature and executive, and tried to model an entire society on an illusory image of the west. Unfortunately, this image idealized the factors that forced massive immigration from the west to Britain and the USA. Clearly that model did not ultimately serve the interests of the west. Indeed, the great advances of the west were secured when Sean Lemass broke its political hegemony.

Here, in the North, particularly west of the Bann, and nowhere more blatantly than in Derry, we suffered from being a satellite-centre-dominated periphery. Neglected by the official centre in London, we were stifled by the satellite centre at Stormont. The result was political stultification and economic stagnation.

Neither of these two approaches worked. The problem is that we have not found a new and more effective relationship between the two wests and their respective metropolitan centres. Here in Derry we have tried to elaborate a new approach that calls into question both the notion of centre and periphery, which for want of a better word, I will call polycentric.

The concept of polycentric is useful but double-edged. It is obviously a helpful tool of economic analysis, and serves as a foundation for any coherent strategy of balanced development. Obviously, if decision makers in centres recognize the specific problems caused by geographical remoteness, they are more likely to take our interests into account. Similarly, if ministers and civil servants in Dublin, Belfast and London understand that they, given the global nature of the economy, are also someone else's periphery, they are more likely to respond sympathetically [...]

The most important lesson we have learned in Derry over the last few years is that, from where we stand, we are the centre. We are, in a sense, a periphery-centred periphery. But that is only a foundation for a strategy of peripheral development based on multiple centres – in our case, Belfast, London, Dublin, Brussels and the USA.

I am not pretending that we don't have serious difficulties in our city. But most visitors seem to detect a certain frame of mind that has resulted in Derry being one of the few expanding centres in the west.[9]

Downing Street Declaration

Hume's primary and immediate political focus of attention remained his expectation that both governments would respond to his dialogue with Adams by committing themselves to a new political initiative. However, progress remained slow and prospects seemed to suffer a serious setback when the PIRA detonated a bomb in a fish shop on the Shankill Road in Belfast, which killed ten people and injured fifty-seven others. Compounding the situation, this atrocity was followed by another, a week later, when, in retaliation, loyalist paramilitaries entered the Rising Sun bar in the Co. Derry village of Greysteel, and shot dead seven and injured thirteen. Despite the heightening of tension that followed these horrific events, and Prime Minister Major's apparent rejection of the Hume-Adams proposals, Hume persisted in pressing his case for the two governments to move the process forward and avail of what he firmly believed was a real opportunity to bring the PIRA violence to an end. In his conference address a few weeks after these horrific attacks, Hume appealed directly to the prime minister, saying:

> The key to opening the doors [to talks], the key of peace, that will lead to all of this, now exists. John Major is in possession of that key. It will require no great effort from him to turn that key and open the door to our new future, based on agreement and respect for diversity. It is a key that will threaten no section of our people for it is a key that will open the door to a future that must be agreed by all of them.[10]

As speculation mounted that both governments were preparing a significant initiative in response to the Hume-Adams dialogue, unionist fears once again

9 Address to the conference 'Ireland, west of the Shannon, west of the Bann – what future?', Derry, 16 Oct. 1993. 10 Address to the SDLP's annual conference, 27 Nov. 1993.

mounted about what it might contain, especially as far as Irish unity was concerned. In an interview with John Humphrys of the BBC, Hume addressed this issue, emphasizing that the outcome of any negotiations would have to be an agreement to which all sides would assent. Accused of trying to impose unity on unionists, he replied:

> [H]ave you heard me saying that it's the people of Ireland who are divided and that the answer is agreement among the people of Ireland?
>
> Humphrys: Yes I heard you say that […]
>
> Hume: How could that be imposing Irish unity? […] Do you not understand that an agreement could take any form? Of course it could take the form of Irish unity, but it could take any other form as well. The only form it will take is the form that the people of Ireland, North and South, agree to, and as I have said repeatedly in public, whatever form that agreement takes, whatever form it takes, as long as it's agreement, and I have said repeatedly to the nationalist community that it's people who are divided, not territory. The traditional nationalist mindset here is that this is our land, and my argument against that is that it's people who are here and it's people who are divided. Without people, it's only a jungle and you can't bring people together, only by agreement and whatever form that agreement takes as long as it's an agreement, the quarrel is over and then at last we'll start working together, and as we work together, presumably, the old prejudices will be eroded and away down the road somewhere in a new Ireland, whose model will probably be very different from any of the old traditional ones that we have arguing about for the last fifty years.[11]

The kind of response from both governments for which Hume had been calling came when they jointly issued the Downing Street Declaration a few weeks later, on 15 December. Since he could claim some authorship of the declaration, Hume warmly welcomed it, saying:

> May I express to the prime minister and to Mr Reynolds [the taoiseach] my deep appreciation for the enormous amount of energy that they have put into trying to grasp the hope of peace – a hope which is shared by the masses of people on both islands? Having read the joint declaration, I think that it is one of the most comprehensive declarations that has been made about British-Irish relations in the past seventy years. My appeal to all sections of

11 Interview with John Humphrys, *On the Record*, BBC, 5 Dec. 1993.

our people is to read the entire statement in full and to have no knee-jerk reactions but to study it carefully and in full before responding.

As the house will be aware, it has been the consistent position of my party that the British-Irish quarrel of old, the quarrel of sovereignty, has changed fundamentally in the evolution of the new interdependent and post-nationalist Europe of which we are members, but the legacy of that past is the deeply divided people. I welcome the fact that the declaration identifies the problem as the deeply divided people of Ireland. I also welcome the fact that it recognizes that that division can be healed only by agreement, and by an agreement that earns the allegiance and agreement of all our traditions and respects their diversity. I welcome also the fact that the governments have committed themselves to promoting such agreement and to encouraging such agreement, and whatever form that agreement takes, the government will endorse. Does the prime minister agree that the joint declaration is a challenge to all parties to come to the table in a totally peaceful atmosphere to begin the very difficult process – it will be a difficult process – of reaching agreement? If it takes place in a peaceful atmosphere, we will have much more chance of reaching such an agreement. My appeal to everyone who comes to that table is to come armed only with the strength of their convictions and not with any form of coercion or physical force.

Let us remember at this time that it is people who have rights, not territory, and that humanity transcends nationality. May the house share with me at this moment the hope of all our people that today will be the first major step on a road that will remove forever the gun and the bomb from our small island of people.[12]

The declaration made it clear that all parties with a democratic mandate, and which demonstrated a clear commitment to democratic means for resolving differences, would be free to participate in talks, and that the two governments would endorse whatever agreement would emerge from such talks. The expectation now was that the PIRA would respond positively so as to enable Sinn Féin to participate in such talks by at least declaring a ceasefire. The first half of 1994 was devoted to trying to bring that about.

In early January Hume spelled out the implications of the declaration, as he saw them, in an article in the *Irish News*:

When the British-Irish joint declaration was made in December, I made clear that I regarded it as a major step on the road to peace and I asked for it to be considered in detail by all parties before responding.

12 House of Commons, *Debates*, 15 Dec. 1993.

Given the importance of the declaration and its objectives that was not too much to ask. I also recognized that the most important response would be that of the provisional republican movement and that given the nature of their organization that would take time. I also appealed for an absence of knee-jerk reactions. There has been quite an amount of that, some of it irresponsible and inaccurate. There has also been a lot of insensitive and unhelpful language like 'take it or leave it', decontamination periods, gauntlets etc.

Language of that nature is most unhelpful at a very sensitive and important time particularly when the objective is to seek an end to the terrible tragedies that so many families have suffered. Language from some people who would describe themselves as republicans has not been helpful since their response has been based on regarding the declaration as a settlement of our problems, which it is not. That will only come at the next stage of the process involving both governments and all parties, hopefully in a totally peaceful atmosphere.

What the declaration does, among other things, is address the stated reasons for armed struggle given by the IRA. The stated reasons by the IRA for armed struggle were that the British were in Ireland defending their own interests by force – economic and strategic interests – and that they were preventing the Irish people from exercising the right of self-determination.

I have argued that while these reasons were historically correct they are no longer true in today's new Europe. Indeed, following our published dialogue in 1988 in which Sinn Féin spelled out those reasons, reasons to which I drew the attention of the British government and asked them to make clear that they had no longer any selfish economic or strategic interest in Ireland, the then secretary of state, Peter Brooke, stated that very clearly in a speech in 1990.

The statement is repeated in the joint declaration when the prime minister 'reiterates on behalf of the British government that they have no selfish economic or strategic interest in Northern Ireland. Their primary interest – which in my view is an acceptable and necessary political interest – 'is to see stability and reconciliation established by agreement among all the people who inhabit the island'.

They go further and underline that they would work together with the Irish government to achieve such an agreement, an agreement which would naturally have to address all the relationships that go to the heart of the problem.

There remains the question of self-determination. Mr Adams and I agreed in our first joint statement that while the Irish people as a whole had the right to self-determination, they were divided as to how that right was to be exercised and it was the search for agreement and the means of reaching such agreement on which our dialogue would be concentrating.

It is self-evident that the means of reaching such agreement could not possibly be through force since an agreement by coercion is a clear contradiction in terms and is in fact impossible. It is implicit in all of that of course that agreement should be able to be made freely and without any outside impediment.

I believe that this principle is clearly accepted by the British government when they declare in the joint declaration, 'The British government agree that it is for the people of the island of Ireland alone, by agreement between the two parts respectively, to exercise their right to self-determination on the basis of consent, freely and concurrently given, North and South, to bring about a united Ireland if that is their wish.'

To underline this commitment to self-determination by agreement among our divided people 'they reaffirm as a binding obligation that they will, for their part, introduce legislation to give effect to this [a united Ireland] or equally to any measure of agreement on future relationships in Ireland which the people living in Ireland may themselves freely so determine without external impediment'.

In addition, the British government, while not using the word 'persuade', commit themselves to 'encourage, facilitate and enable the achievement of such agreement over a period through a process of dialogue and co-operation based on full respect for the rights and identities of both traditions in Ireland' [...]

The challenge that now faces all of us is a clear political challenge – how to heal the deep divisions among the people of Ireland, divisions which have political, social and above all economic implications particularly for areas of high unemployment within the North and border counties.[13]

Later that same month, somewhat irritated at the unwillingness of the republican leadership to respond positively to the declaration, and at the failure of unionists to acknowledge that negotiations could not attempt to coerce them into some form of a united Ireland, Hume spelled out what the declaration stated, particularly on the key issue of 'self-determination':

There has been a lot of public discussion, a lot of careless language, and, indeed, a lot of personal views by politicians, British and Irish, in relation to our future or their preferences about that future. However, at this crucial point it is essential that we concentrate on the facts of our situation in Ireland

13 *Irish News*, 5 Jan. 1994.

and the facts of the joint declaration, facts which to myself are very clear, and facts that already made me declare that it is the most comprehensive declaration in seventy years of history of our relationships within this island.

Let us stay with the facts. The facts are that the people of Ireland have the right to self-determine their future. The facts are that the people of Cyprus have the right to self-determine their future. The facts are that the people of the world have the right to self-determine their future. But the fact that gets consistently forgotten as people make emotional declarations about such rights is that it is people who have rights, not territory. Without people this earth is only a jungle. Humanity is what it is all about and how humanity settles its differences. The essence about settling differences is to respect them. There is not a single stable society in the world that is not based on respect for diversity.

The facts are that the people of Ireland are divided on how to exercise that right. So are the people of Cyprus, so are the people of the former Yugoslavia, so are the people of the world. It is the search for agreement and the means of reaching agreement that is the real task facing those who want to solve such problems. It is also surely a fact that such agreement between divided peoples anywhere cannot be solved by any form of coercion or force. Victories, as history has sadly taught us, are not solutions; they simply leave legacies from which subsequent generations also suffer. [...]

There has been the usual talk about vetoes. Again, the facts are that when you have a divided people each section of it has a veto. That is the negative way of looking at it and we have never had any shortage of negative attitudes on this island. Surely the time has come to be positive and to seek and work for agreement, the challenge of which is to persuade one another that neither side wants victory but rather an agreement that respects our different heritages and identities, which is the only basis for stability in any society.

Indeed, once again, in the declaration, the British government commits itself to 'encourage, facilitate and enable the achievement of such an agreement over a period through a process of dialogue and co-operation based on full respect for the rights and identities of both traditions in Ireland'. If we do not want them to impose a solution, what more can they do? Indeed could we reflect on the question, when at any time in the past seventy years have both governments been committed to using all their influence, energy and resources towards such an objective?

The challenge to both traditions is clear. To the unionist tradition, who have a genuinely different heritage to the rest of us in this island and who have every right to protect that heritage, the challenge is to recognize for the first time that their real strength rests in their own numbers and geography and that the problem cannot be solved without them. The people they need to trust in such a process are themselves, to agree a relationship with those with whom they share this island. It is self-evident that they have consistently distrusted British governments. Now they are being asked to trust themselves and to recognize that the objective is an agreement which must earn the allegiance and agreement of all our traditions, including their own.

The challenge to nationalists is equally clear. It is people who have rights, not territory. It is a particular challenge to Sinn Féin [...] to come to the table armed only with those convictions and their powers of persuasion, as everyone else will have to do, given that the British government is now committed not only to encouraging agreement but to implementing and legislating for whatever agreement emerges. Is all of this not totally in keeping with the peace process as defined in my joint statements with Mr Adams, as involving both governments and all parties, the objective of which would be agreement among our divided people, an agreement that would have to have the allegiance of all our traditions as well as their agreement?

We have reached an historic moment in our island's history and I hope that the moral courage will be there on all sides to seize it. It is self-evident to me that no instant package will end our differences forever, but whatever form our agreement takes, once our quarrel is over and all the talents of our diverse people are committed to working together to build our country, North and South, the healing process will have begun and the old prejudices and distrust will be progressively eroded.

Down the road in the future, out of that process will emerge a new Ireland built on respect for our diversity, whose model will be very different from any of our past traditional models. Will Catholic, Protestants and Dissenters finally come together in our small island and as we approach the twenty-first century in our now post-nationalist and interdependent world? Will we at last remove the gun and the bomb from our island?[14]

Later, Hume reviewed the historical background to the declaration, reminding the PIRA of what true republicanism means, and strongly appealing for a ceasefire to allow for comprehensive negotiations:

If this crucial time in our history is not to be another of the 'ifs' of Irish history, it is time for deep and immediate reflection by all sections of our people and in particular by all our political parties. Let none of us forget that the Provisional IRA, and its members are a product of, among other things, the traditional nationalist philosophy with which we all grew up. A philosophy that the essence of patriotism is – à la 1916 – the nobility of dying for

14 *Irish Times*, 31 Jan. 1994.

Ireland and struggling against British occupation of Ireland. All the major parties in the Dáil were born out of that philosophy and their founders were the progenitors of it. Let me quote the unanimous declaration of Dáil Éireann, not 1918 but 1949:

> Solemnly reasserting the indefeasible right of the Irish nation to the unity and integrity of the national territory,
>
> Reaffirming this sovereign right of the people of Ireland to choose its own form of government and, through its democratic institutions, to decide all questions of national policy, free from outside interference,
>
> Repudiating the claim of the British parliament to enact legislation in violation of those rights, and
>
> Pledging the determination to continue the struggle against the unjust and unnatural partition of our country until it is brought to a successful conclusion;
>
> Places on record its indignant protest against the introduction in the British parliament of legislation, purporting to endorse and continue the existing partition of Ireland, and
>
> Calls upon the British government and people to end the present occupation of our six north-eastern counties and thereby enable the unity of Ireland to be restored and the age-long difference between our two nations brought to an end.

If any politician in Dáil Éireann were to make that declaration today he or she would rightly be accused of using Provo language. I reiterate all of that to underline that it is the responsibility of all of us, particularly Southern nationalists, to do everything in our power to remove that last remaining legacy of that attitude and to bring Sinn Féin, the IRA – its members and supporters – aboard the mass movement that is now afoot for the totally peaceful resolution of our conflict, the consistent victims of which have been the Catholic population of Northern Ireland. Let us not forget either that in the 1918 general elections it was the Catholic population of the six North-Eastern counties that were the only people in nationalist Ireland who did not vote Sinn Féin, particularly the people of West Belfast, because they instinctively were aware of the real Irish problem since they lived right on the frontline and have been throughout our history the main victims of the sectarian pogroms of every generation [...]

The challenge to the IRA is clear. There is no justification of any description for the taking of a single human life. Let them lay down their arms and join everyone else in the real task of breaking down those barriers in our hearts and minds and in tackling the real human problems of economic deprivation, which is what politics is really about – the right to a decent existence for all our people in their own land. They cannot be unaware of the mass movement and strength of the Irish at home and abroad that the peace process has created, and that strength will achieve more than any guns or bombs, without any human tragedies [...]

The real challenge to the IRA now is – are you in the genuine republican tradition of Tone which is to unite Catholic, Protestant and Dissenter, which clearly cannot be done by force, or in the territorial tradition of the Defenders,[15] a tradition of no hope?[16]

Gradually, over the following months, the republican movement became persuaded that acceptable conditions for a ceasefire did exist. When Hume and Adams issued another joint statement on the 28 August, its publication seemed to confirm that prospect:

We met today to review the present situation. In April last year we pointed out that everyone has a solemn duty to assist in the search for a lasting peace. Since then we have applied ourselves unremittingly to this task. As a result there has been an unprecedented focus on the development of an effective peace process.

Last Easter we indicated that we were investigating the possibility of developing an overall political strategy to establish justice and peace in Ireland. We are at present addressing this area in particular and we believe that the essential ingredients of such a strategy may now be available.

A just and lasting peace in Ireland will only be achieved if it is based on democratic principles. It is clear that an internal settlement is not a solution. Both governments and all parties have already agreed that all relationships must be settled.

All that has been tried before has failed to satisfactorily resolve the conflict or remove the political conditions which give rise to it. If a lasting settlement is to be found there must be a fundamental and thoroughgoing change, based on the right of the Irish people as a whole to national self-determination.

The exercise of this right is, of course, a matter for agreement between all the people of Ireland and we reiterate that such a new agreement is only viable if it enjoys the allegiance of the different traditions on this island by accommodating diversity and providing for national reconciliation.

We have publicly acknowledged that the task of seeking agreement on a peaceful and democratic accord for all the people of Ireland is our primary

15 The Defenders were a late-eighteenth-century Catholic rural secret society.   16 *Irish Times*, 12 Apr. 1994.

challenge. We are convinced that significant progress has been made in developing the conditions necessary for this to occur.

We underline that the process in which we are engaged offers no threat to any section of the people on this island. Our objective is agreement among our divided people.

In any new situation there is a heavy onus on the British government to respond positively, both in terms of the demilitarization of the situation and in assisting the search for an agreed Ireland by encouraging the process of national reconciliation.

It is our informed opinion that the peace process remains firmly on course. We are, indeed, optimistic that the situation can be moved tangibly forward.[17]

Three days later, the PIRA declared the long-awaited end to its campaign of terror, and after twenty-four years accepted that the future lay with democratic politics. Hume warmly welcomed the announcement, but was highly critical of the British government's response, which raised questions over whether the cessation of violence would be permanent. It was but one of several issues that would delay the inter-party talks Hume had hoped would follow quite soon after the cessation of violence had been declared:

Mr Hume expressed frustration at calls from the British prime minister, John Major, and the Northern secretary, Sir Patrick Mayhew, over the wording of the IRA ceasefire statement. He couldn't understand the 'nit-picking' over whether there was a difference between the word 'complete', which was in the statement and the word 'permanent', which was absent.

When he engaged in discussion with the Sinn Féin leader Mr Gerry Adams they were seeking a total cessation of violence, and 'out they [the IRA] come today with that statement. I am taking it for granted that it is a permanent cessation of violence and I am amazed at the sort of nit-picking that is going on,' said Mr Hume. The two governments and parties in the North with an electoral mandate should now enter into talks [...] He didn't underestimate the difficulty in reaching agreement but hoped that in a peaceful atmosphere political progress could be made.

'Our quarrel is hopelessly out of date. It is terrible that so many families have been victims of that out-of-date quarrel, and I hope that today is the beginning of a whole new era for our country in which we have left aside forever bombs and bullets.'[18]

---

17 Joint statement by John Hume and Gerry Adams, SDLP, 28 Aug. 1994.   18 *Irish Times*, 1 Sept. 1994.

A week later, in a move to consolidate the peace process, John Hume appeared alongside Taoiseach Albert Reynolds and Gerry Adams on the steps of Government Buildings in Dublin. Their joint statement, drafted by Hume, welcomed the opportunities the ceasefire provided, and announced the establishment of the Forum for Peace and Reconciliation, while stressing the need for unionist agreement in resolving their common problems:

> We are at the beginning of a new era in which we are all totally and absolutely committed to democratic and peaceful methods of resolving our political problems. We reiterate that our objective is an equitable and lasting agreement that can command the allegiance of all. We see the forum as a major instrument in that process. We reiterate that we cannot resolve this problem without the participation and agreement of the unionist people. We call on everyone to use all their influence to bring this agreement about.[18]

18 Joint statement by Taoiseach Albert Reynolds, John Hume and Gerry Adams, 6 Sept. 1994.

1994–8

John Hume moved swiftly to acknowledge the international support for the peace process, notably from the US and Europe. His objective was to ensure that this support would strengthen the process. He stressed what he believed was now a unique opportunity for old enmities to be set aside, and for a new era of peace and partnership to be developed. This was especially the case when the main loyalist paramilitaries also declared ceasefires in October.

In the US, Hume attended a session of the senate's foreign relations committee at which senators welcomed the PIRA ceasefire, and discussed how the US might assist economic development in the border regions. In the European parliament, where Hume received a very warm welcome from members of all parties, he acknowledged the support for the peace process that the European council of ministers and its commission had provided, as well as that from his parliamentary colleagues:

> First of all might I begin by expressing my deep appreciation to the council and to the commission for their statements today? Those statements are extremely encouraging, particularly at the present time. One of the things that we have to do at this stage of our process is give hope to our young people in areas of very high unemployment [...]
>
> I also want to express my deep appreciation to President Hänsch for his statement at the last meeting of this parliament. It was a very moving occasion, in particular the minute of silence observed for all those who have lost their lives in this conflict in Northern Ireland, because 3,500 people from all sections of our community who have lost their lives are victims of our history and of our failure to resolve this problem. The figure is the equivalent of 100,000 being killed in Britain. Not only were 30,000 people maimed but it has been necessary to build thirteen walls to separate and protect one section of a Christian people from another in the city of Belfast, which has the highest rate of churchgoing in Western Europe [...]
>
> I thank my colleagues for their support for direct dialogue with the political wing of the IRA, for many people have heavily criticized me for it. I have seen and lived through conflict for twenty-five years. I have known many of the people killed. My own home on many occasions has been attacked because of my opposition to violence. But given that five governments and

20,000 troops did not stop the killing, I felt that if by direct dialogue you could save a single life, it was my duty to embark upon it. I am glad that in the end my dialogue led to the total cessation that the IRA have announced. I would like to pay a strong tribute to both prime ministers, Prime Minister Major and Taoiseach Albert Reynolds, for putting the matter right at the top of their agenda, because it is the greatest human tragedy facing both countries.

Throughout this I have been very much inspired, I have to say, by my experience of Europe. Because what we have here, with the council present and the commission present in this parliament is the greatest achievement of conflict resolution in the history of the world. When we look back fifty years and see 35 million people dead across this Continent for a second time in this century, we must ask who could have stood up and forecast that we would all be here today – the council, the governments, the commission and representatives of the people then at war. Yet, as I often say, the German people are still German, the French are still French, the English are still English. The lesson of that conflict resolution has to be learned in every area of conflict in the world because we have here in this house the message of peace for everywhere. The answer is very simple, as all profundities are simple: difference is not a threat. That is what war and conflict is about, seeing difference as a threat. There are no two human beings in the entire human race who are the same. Difference is an accident of birth and the accident of birth whether it is creed, colour or nationality, should never be the cause of hatred or conflict. Humanity transcends nationality. That is a fundamental principle of conflict resolution.

Let us now apply to our small island the same principles and let us do what Europe did, build institutions which respect our diversity but which allow us to work our common ground together, which is economics; as I often say, let us spill our sweat not our blood and in so doing begin the evolutionary healing process of breaking down barriers of prejudice, distrust and hatred that have divided our people for centuries [...][1]

Forum for Peace and Reconciliation

The opening session of the Forum for Peace and Reconciliation, established to meet the Irish government's commitment in the Downing Street Declaration to set up a 'national all-party convention', was held in Dublin Castle on 28 October. It was modelled on the earlier Forum for a New Ireland, and, apart from the unionist parties, all parties with an elected mandate agreed to attend. Addressing the

1 European Parliament, *Debates*, 29 Sept. 1994.

inaugural meeting of the forum, Chairperson Judge Catherine McGuinness outlined the forum's main purpose, which was:

> to consult on, and examine ways in which lasting peace, stability and recon-
> ciliation can be established by agreement among all the people of Ireland, and
> on the steps required to remove barriers of distrust, on the basis of promoting
> respect for the equal rights and validity of both traditions and identities. In
> accordance with its terms of reference it will also explore ways in which new
> approaches can be developed to serve economic interests common to both
> parts of Ireland.[2]

Addressing the same session, John Hume, interestingly, did not refer directly to the peace process. Instead, he emphasized the need to seize the opportunity to work together and to build a new, peaceful and prosperous Ireland that would attract unionists. He was particularly anxious that the support and goodwill of the Irish diaspora be enlisted in the process of reconstruction and economic development in Northern Ireland:

> We are not here to talk. We are here to work at the central problem that faces
> the people of this country, which is getting agreement among our divided
> people. That is something that never in our history have we had. Its absence
> is the basic source of the instability because the basis of order in any society
> is agreement on how you are governed.
>
> So our major objective is agreement and I am sure that in this forum's
> work, the unionist people will fully realize that when we use the word 'agree-
> ment' we mean what we say. It is agreement we are looking for, not victories,
> nor defeats. Given the geography and numbers of the unionist people, this
> problem cannot be solved without their agreement. And what the forum has
> to do, I think, is to work on a planned basis as to how we break down barriers
> of distrust and prejudice that are the real borders on this island, the border in
> the hearts and minds of the people. That is the real task of this forum, how
> to do that and to work on a steady basis so that we arrive at that agreement.
>
> While we are doing that, we should do something else. We should work
> our common ground together. I mean that we, who are represented in this
> room, representing the people of this island, the Irish people, are the biggest
> wandering people in this world. The time has come to harness that strength,
> because while many originally wandered, they wandered because of famine,
> poverty and emigration. But now they have reached the top in politics and
> economics with the rest of the world.

---

2 Opening remarks by chairperson Judge Catherine McGuinness, Forum for Peace and Reconciliation, 28 Oct. 1994.

So the time has come to harness all of that energy across the world, because since peace broke out in our streets, we have been very aware of that enormous goodwill because of the strength of the Irish abroad. Let us harness that strength and plan, in this forum, how we do it so as to bring economic regeneration to this island. Because if we harness that, we can be very successful and I believe that the unionist people will work with us on that front [...][3]

Position vindicated

At the SDLP's annual conference, where the party's stance throughout the whole period of violence was seen to have been thoroughly vindicated, and where Hume in particular could feel a deep sense of achievement for all his efforts, his conference speech began with some reflections on the ceasefires, then on his own and the SDLP's role in bringing them about. Critically, he emphasized the need for reconciliation and working together to build a better, more equal and fairer society:

No people anywhere in these islands are more conscious of the necessity for peace than the members of this party and our supporters who have been the frontline for peace and civil rights throughout the past twenty-five years. Without your commitment we would not be where we are today. As your leader it was natural that the cynics and opponents directed their considerable flak in my direction and attempted to divide us. Now they know that since its foundation this party has been a team, devoted at every level to the basic and human rights of all our people. Indeed, what I am saying clearly is that as your leader my role in the peace process would not have been possible without your total solidarity, particularly at some very difficult times for members whose homes were attacked, and in particular without the powerful solidarity of my closest colleagues in the parliamentary party and the party executive. Our critics do not seem to have noticed but the central message of the peace process, repeated regularly throughout, was a total cessation of violence followed by agreement among our divided people, agreement that must earn the allegiance and agreement of all our traditions. That has been the central message of this party at all levels since its foundation. Indeed, if our critics care to look, we are the first party in this island to have the word 'consent' in our constitution, because we have always argued that it is the people of this island who are divided and they can only be brought together by agreement. But let us underline [...] the principle of consent applies to both sections of our divided people.

3 Address to the inaugural meeting, Forum for Peace and Reconciliation, 24 Oct. 1994.

On the political front [...] let us realize that although the situation and prejudices that divide us are deep, the atmosphere for dialogue today is a better atmosphere than at any time in the past. The most obvious reason for that is that violence has ended and people will not want us to go back to the trenches of the past. The other and most powerful reason is that we are living in a new world today, a world very different from the 1920s.

In the 1920s independence and sovereignty were central issues not just to our quarrel on this island but across the world. The world of the 1990s is a different world. We are living through the greatest evolution in the history of the world – the technological, telecommunications and transport revolution. It has made the world a smaller place. It has brought people and their problems closer to one another. It is a world in which we no longer live in independent countries. We are interdependent. We cannot live apart, particularly if we wish to have a decent right to existence. That has been reflected in political evolution, as in the evolution of the European Union and the breaking down of barriers between people who have slaughtered one another for centuries but who today work together through common institutions on fundamental matters of economic concern. Indeed, let us not forget that the era of the nation state has not been and is not an eternal era in our history. It is part of the evolutionary process of humanity. Once upon a time on this island and across Europe we had kings, chieftains, clan systems, city states etc. As the world evolved so did the nature of government, not always without controversy, division or war. Indeed, one could argue that the era of the nation state will go down as the worst era in human history. It led to imperialism and two world wars. As we develop the new era now, particularly together with the Irish abroad, let us begin by tackling the deep legacy that that past has left us – our divided people. Let us use all our energies and resources to heal that division. [...]

As we know, in the past twenty-five years we have lost not just lives but jobs. The Troubles have had a serious economic effect particularly on inward investment and tourism. We can never bring back the lives but with the peace process we can win new jobs and we can rebuild communities that have been broken by violence and unemployment.

We have already begun. The United States has announced a substantial increase in its support for the International Fund,[4] and President Clinton will host a major Irish investment conference next April. Jacques Delors, president of the European commission, and our colleagues in the European Socialist Group are finalizing a package of measures for next month's European

---

4 The International Fund for Ireland was established after the Anglo-Irish Agreement of 1985. Funds for development were made available from several parties, including the US and the EU.

summit. Our party has had a major input into the shaping of both these initiatives.[5]

Talks delayed

In December Hume and Adams issued a further joint statement, stressing the urgency of convening all-party talks. British and unionist insistence that the PIRA decommission its arsenal of weapons had become a precondition to Sinn Féin's entry into talks, which was delaying progress. While acknowledging that 'demilitarization' would happen, Hume and Adams would not accept it as a prior requirement. They called on the British government to adopt a more positive approach:

> the search for a real and lasting peace settlement now needed to be addressed energetically by all sides. There should be no stalling. It was essential [...] that the British should adopt a constructive approach by responding positively and enthusiastically to the new situation which had been created. The demilitarization process should be accelerated and inclusive negotiations aimed at securing agreement and an overall settlement should begin without further delay. The British government has a key role to play in this. They can and should be persuaders for agreement between the Irish people. The search for a political settlement based on dialogue and agreement requires courage, flexibility and imagination.[6]

Frameworks Document

While the prospect of inter-party talks involving Sinn Féin remained in doubt, there was political progress of a kind when the two governments published the Frameworks Document. The document set out for discussion possible institutional arrangements for a new agreement. The arrangements again reflected the three-strand approach John Hume had long advocated, and which had been generally accepted at the inter-party discussions of 1991–2. In welcoming the document, Hume made a special plea to unionists to either accept it, or else propose an alternative:

> I say to the unionist people that I understand their fears and tensions, given the twenty-five years which we have been through. We have said before that this problem cannot be resolved without the participation and agreement of

5 Address to the SDLP's annual conference, 18 Nov. 1994.   6 Joint statement by John Hume and Gerry Adams, 1 Dec. 1994.

the unionist people, because of their geography and numbers. We know that they do not trust governments. All they are now being asked to do is trust themselves, and to come to the table [...]

Let us all recognize that all our past attitudes have brought us to where we are, and have built those terrible walls in Belfast. If those walls are ever to come down, all sides must re-examine those past attitudes and come forward with new arrangements and relationships, which respect our differences but which at last harness all our energies to spill our sweat together, and not our blood, so that the next century will be the first century in the island's history in which we have no killings on our streets, and no young people have to go to other lands to earn a living.[7]

Women's rights

Talks about talks continued over the following twelve months, mainly between the British government and Sinn Féin. Hume had opportunities at several engagements to address not just the Northern Ireland peace process, but wider issues as well. Among these issues were women's rights, citizenship and the process of reconciliation. Hume argued that the issue of women's rights in Northern Ireland had been:

> obscured by the conflict of the past twenty-five years and the centuries of division that had preceded it. In the new climate, I hope that other equally fundamental issues, such as the position of women in society, will get the attention they deserve.
>
> Our membership of the European Union is very important in this respect, as in so many others. The struggle for equal opportunities in these islands has been greatly enhanced by our membership of the European Union. Much of the equal-opportunities legislation in these islands has been inspired by the necessity to conform to the European treaties and legislation. It is therefore a setback to the cause of equal opportunities that the British government has opted out of the Social Chapter. Reversing the opt-out should be the prime objective of all those concerned with inequality.
>
> While providing a legislative framework for equality is essential, it is not enough. We must also address the complex range of social and economic factors which create barriers to equality. Indirect discrimination must be targeted as much as the open form. We have to recognize that democracy as much as prosperity is best served by using all the talents at the disposal of society. Discrimination costs in economic, social and political terms.

7 House of Commons, *Debates,* 22 Feb. 1995.

The cause of equal opportunities is both right in principle, and beneficial in practice. In a statement issued on International Women's Day this year, the social-democratic and labour parties of Europe emphasized that economic crisis should not be used as an excuse to halt progress towards equal opportunities, but rather made it all the more necessary. As we pointed out: 'It is precisely when times are hard that policy on women must be an integral component of economic, employment, environmental, family, financial, social and societal policy [...] The achievement of equal opportunities will be a source of enrichment for all citizens.' The Socialist Group in the European parliament has been in the forefront of the campaign of equal opportunities, and intends to continue to press for legislative and political change.

Turning to more specific policy issues, it is clear that the European institutions are facing a heavy workload in pursuit of equality. Equal opportunities is now one of the issues at the top of the European agenda. For a variety of issues – such as the change in the composition of the workforce, transformation in the nature of work from agriculture and manufacturing to the service sector, the need to reform and preserve the European welfare state – the status of women in society has to be addressed. In addition, the Maastricht Treaty, by giving the European parliament the power to approve or reject the appointment of the commission, has allowed the elected representatives of Europe to oblige the commission to put the issue of equality in the centre of its programme. President Santer himself chairs a commission task force, in which all commissioners can take part, whose task it is to oversee equal opportunities policies in the European Union.

The importance attached to the rights of women can also be seen in the commission's white paper on social policy. Three issues in particular have been identified as priorities: finding a European-wide approach to the desegregation of the labour market, reconciling work and family responsibilities and increasing the role of women in decision-making [...]

Given that poverty is increasingly a problem for women, it is regrettable that the fight against poverty at European level has stagnated. Unfortunately, the Poverty Programme has been blocked by the German government, for reasons which have little to do with the merits of the programme. Once again the European parliament is striving to keep the issue on the agenda in the hope of persuading the council of ministers to return to the previous practice of recognizing the need for Europe to combat poverty collectively.

There is also a need to ensure that women play a more equitable role in decision-making. While experience shows that it is no guarantee that the rights of women will be vindicated solely by placing women in positions of responsibility, I believe that obtaining a critical mass of women in positions of responsibility would be helpful. This is not just a question of elementary justice; such a change would help to make our political institutions more effective in pursuing equal opportunities.

Having said that, few of Europe's political institutions and parties have lived up to their ideals. As you have heard, the European institutions have a long way to go to reconcile rhetoric with reality. Neither is the record in Northern Ireland that good. But I would say two things. I hope that the conference today leads to positive action on equal opportunities in public life, and that it encourages us to push for an equal share of power and responsibility. No one will hand you equality on a plate, however well-intentioned. Equality has to be won, not granted.[8]

Citizenship

Hume delivered the Stevenson Lecture at the University of Glasgow in May 1995, for which the theme was citizenship. Among the key points he addressed was the need to further develop the institutions of the European Union to allow a greater voice for its citizens, as well as focusing on the immediate situation in Northern Ireland. The lecture, along with his address on women's rights, reveal the depth and scope of Hume's reflections on contemporary issues:

Citizenship is one of the more complex concepts in political theory. I am not pretending to be a theorist, but I hope I have something significant to say as a practitioner who has spent most of his adult life attempting to establish a genuine democracy and citizenship in my part of the world. It is much easier to recognize the absence of citizenship than to define what it means. That, perhaps, is why so much attention is paid to the idea throughout Western Europe. It is now an issue because it can no longer be taken for granted, even where democracy is deep-rooted and genuine.

If I had to sum up the idea of citizenship in a sentence, I would say – the recognition within a society that what unites its members is more important than that which divides them. The diverse interests and identities within a society find a way of allowing their differences to be expressed and transcended, while ensuring that everyone feels that they are being fairly treated.

Such a concept of citizenship relies on a threefold combination of identity, identification and integration. First, while recognizing the clash of interests within society, there must be some degree of common identity between its citizens. Second, the vast majority of citizens must identify with the political institutions by which they are governed. Third, there must a sense of integra-

8 Address to the conference 'Women in public life', Belfast, 25 Mar. 1995; copy in editor's possession.

tion within the political system so that people feel a part of the process for which collective decisions are taken about collective futures. They must also feel improvements and remedies can be brought about through political action.

In the mainstream of European politics, citizenship has in practice depended on these factors. Being more specific, post-war Western Europe has until recently based itself on four pillars: democratic control over government and policy; the welfare state; the legal equality of all citizens; and a balance between rights and responsibilities. In recent years, this post-war settlement has been called into question by the rise of right-wing economic and political theories that reduce citizenship to consumerism.

This reductionism is one of the greatest threats to citizenship. A citizen is not just a consumer, he or she is also a producer, a taxpayer, a parent, a child, a voter, a political activist, a voluntary worker etc. The list is endless. A citizen has a wide and diverse range of interests and personas, which may well be sometimes in conflict with one another. A citizen has a combination of economic, social, political and moral needs. We cannot, in a democracy, reduce individuals to monomaniac Sunday shoppers. It seems to me that the greatest danger facing our democracies is the effort to force people into the straitjacket of simplistic labels. For example, we should recognize that altruism is as essential to our societies as self-interest.

It is relatively easy to be a citizen in a political system that takes responsibility for offsetting the negative effects of market economics without destroying initiative and enterprise. Where government is dedicated to using reason and policy to improve the lives and opportunities of its citizens, it is reasonable for people to assume that they do and should have a say in what happens to them. Where governments either cannot or refuse to act, the purpose of politics becomes much more obscure [...] But if the purpose of politics becomes obscure, so then the validity and usefulness of citizenship becomes problematical. [...]

From my earlier remarks, it should be clear what has been missing in Northern Ireland. Northern Ireland did not benefit from the enlightened political leadership shown in mainland Europe, nor from the attitude of mutual recognition of difference and diversity.

As for citizenship, none of the criteria I mentioned above – equality, identity, identification and integration – existed. To make matters worse, these factors were absent in a particularly vicious fashion.

I used to think that Northern Ireland was divided into first- and second-class citizens. I was being unduly optimistic. In reality, there were only second- and third-class citizens. While unionists held the upper hand, one only has to look at the general economic failure of Northern Ireland and the widespread poverty in unionist communities that continues to exist to see that unionist domination did not serve the real interests of its supporters. But in a relatively poor society, there are genuine differences in the degree of deprivation experienced by the two traditions. So discrimination and inequality were real and extremely politically dangerous. The failure of the government of Northern Ireland to promote equality, coupled with the subsequent failure of the British government to put a stop to inequality, led directly to the twenty-five years of violence from which we have just emerged. Any realistic political settlement must ensure that we have equality between our traditions.

Neither have we been able to develop any sense of common identity. One of the major elements in this has been the absence of equality, not just in the social and economic fields but also in terms of politics. While both communities have had their own political identities, they have not been given equal respect by the political authorities. The issue of parity of esteem for unionist and nationalist is crucial for the development of citizenship in our society. I am hopeful that we will succeed in establishing the equal legitimacy, mutually recognized, of the two traditions. The Anglo-Irish Agreement of 1985 made a start in this respect, and the commitment of the British government to parity of esteem in the Downing Street Declaration of 1993 is a significant step towards full equality.

There has also been a failure to develop political institutions with which all our people can identify and to which all our citizens can give their allegiance […]

Finally, neither tradition is integrated into either its ideal or the existing political system. No political party in the North plays a part in government. Neither tradition can make the government accountable to it. But we cannot create accountability except by agreement between our divided peoples. Obviously, neither of our traditions will allow the other to dominate it. So clearly we need a comprehensive agreement on new structures which we will operate together, while recognizing our differences.[9]

'Peace and the healing process'

Later that year, in a lecture at the Royal College of Surgeons of Ireland in Dublin on 'Peace and the healing process', Hume cited the many medical analogies that are used in political discourse, which provided another a fascinating insight into his political thinking:

9 'Citizenship', Stevenson Lecture, University of Glasgow, 3 May 1995; copy in editor's possession.

In one of the most famous pieces of political oratory – the Gettysburg Address – Abraham Lincoln spoke at the end of a bloody civil war about binding the wounds of the nation. This is probably the most famous example of medical analogies being used to describe problems being suffered by, or processes being proffered to, the body politic.

It is not uncommon to hear people despair of the cancer of sectarianism or racism. References are made to paralysis, situations haemorrhaging, crippling effects, pain, hurt, trauma, fractures, mental scars and prognoses in many political commentaries, not only in situations where violence is, or has been, raging.

Over the years I have talked of Ireland's need for a 'healing process' and cautioned against notions of 'instant cures'. On numerous occasions I have found myself advising people to diagnose and treat causes of our political condition instead of scratching or picking at symptoms.

Medical or health analogies are particularly understandable in the context of a dysfunctional polity. They probably proliferate especially in circumstances where such political dysfunctionalism manifests itself in violence, creating trauma which is all too real and literal.

The medical profession has to treat the consequences of such violence, and in our situation has done so with distinction, dedication and determined co-operation spanning all levels and branches of the profession and associated professions.

This can partly be explained by the fact that violence itself generates secondary political malignancies and complications. As Martin Luther King said: 'Violence as a way of achieving justice is both impractical and immoral. It is impractical because it is a descending spiral ending in destruction for all. The old law of an eye for an eye leaves everyone blind. It is immoral because it seeks to humiliate the opponent rather than win his understanding; it seeks to annihilate rather than convert. Violence is immoral because it thrives on hatred rather than love. It destroys community and makes brotherhood impossible. It leaves society in monologue rather than in dialogue' […]

Securing relief from the harrowing and debilitating secondary condition or symptoms does not constitute a cure. Nor does it lessen the need to go on to deal with the underlying problem. We need to be resolved rather than reluctant about moving to the other phases or episodes of treatment and care without which we cannot have a healthy outcome. That is why I am concerned about the lack of movement in this welcome absence of violence by the British government, which is supposed to be a sponsor of the process at hand.

I understand fears, misgivings and nervousness about the process ahead. It will be uncomfortable for all of us but we have no alternative course to stability. People want to be cured but we don't like undergoing operations, just like people want to go to heaven but nobody wants to die. It is surprising what some people will tolerate in terms of toothache before submitting to a dentist.

I suppose we have a particular phobia about losing something. In our situation those in all traditions have an innate fear about having to give something up, even if only vestigial. Anyone planning a successful intervention should be sensitive to such fears without being completely constrained by them. Feeding fears will not build the confidence and comfort necessary for us to undergo and undertake the appropriate interventions and exercises.

As you can tell by now I am given to the idea that politics is concerned with healing the wounds of society, just as you heal the wounds of individuals. Given the attitudes of many people towards politics and its practitioners, this might seem an exaggerated or downright presumptuous claim. Nevertheless, I would argue strongly that healing is what politics should be about [...]

There are a number of similarities between medicine [...] and politics which I would like to consider [...] There are also considerable differences [...]

First, we have a common interest in healing. While you heal individuals, we as politicians have to deal with the defects of society. While you tackle disease and injury, we have to deal with problems of poverty, unemployment and, in much of the world, violence. Of course it would be naive to believe that there is no connection between the individual illnesses you treat and the social ills we as politicians have to address.

Second, we have a common awareness of the limitations of our knowledge and powers. Despite the great progress made over the years there are still diseases that cannot be cured, there are still social evils we have yet to overcome. Indeed, the great successes of the past are not irreversible. No advance is permanent. Each step forward has to be fought for again and again. It is not realistic to expect miracle cures. We cannot resolve immediately all the problems we face. But we can play a part in paving the way for eventual solutions [...]

As far as the differences are concerned, the major one is the gap between achievement and aspiration in our respective professions. While the medical profession has a solid record of achievement, politics and politicians often fail to live up to their aspirations.

The outline above of the nature of politics obviously contains a degree of aspirational thinking on my own part rather than being simply a description of politics as it is today. That is not necessarily a criticism since politics is the realm par excellence of aspiration, and without it we would still be living in caves.

The problem occurs when politicians decide that their role is simply to articulate and reflect the divisions in society. In a divided society such as ours in Ireland, every public representative is, to a greater or lesser extent, a reflection of the deep divisions that exist. That is inescapable, but one does not have to resign oneself to such a limited role, or even worse, make it one's raison d'être. There is a challenge to extend ourselves to leadership rather than to content ourselves with spokesmanship alone.

Unlike doctors, we do not have to swear an oath to do no harm. It probably would not solve anything if we did, given that the divisions in our society mean that oaths are contentious in themselves. But I believe that the real purpose of politics, and the justification of political leadership, is to find ways of overcoming such divisions. Our moral duty is to find a way in which the people of this divided island can agree on how to share it and to begin the process of healing.

A further substantial difference between politics and medicine is the relative weight given to diagnosis. A doctor uses the symptoms to diagnose the illness; too many politicians use the symptoms to ignore the underlying political problems. The cycles of violence that have so disfigured our history perpetuated themselves because they were seen as the problem, not as a symptom of a general political failure to create adequate political institutions. In this divided island only political institutions which will accommodate the different traditions on the island can guarantee a peaceful and democratic future. We need institutions which will allow for the expression rather the suppression of difference.

I have spent many years stressing the need for a serious diagnosis of the nature of the problem in Ireland, for which there was often much criticism. But I was, and remain, convinced that without an adequate definition of the problem and some degree of consensus on the diagnosis, it is impossible to treat it. Without some minimum degree of agreement on the nature of the problem, we would be restricted to the political equivalent of using leeches. Indeed, I would argue that the progress made so far towards a peaceful island has been greatly facilitated by the gradual development of a minimal consensus on diagnosis, though quite naturally the prescriptions remain extremely diverse.

I would like to point out one other major difference between politics and surgery. We operate without anaesthesia, even though some political leaders see themselves as amateur anaesthetists. It is not the job of public representatives to provide unjustified reassurance to their supporters. It is our job to tell our supporters that we have serious problems to overcome and that can only be done if we are all prepared to engage in a radical re-examination of our presuppositions and prejudices and inherited hatreds. We should refuse to even offer the prospect of pseudo-anaesthesia. It is our duty to inform and convince our fellow citizens of the need to take an active part in the creation of a new dispensation in our divided Ireland. This is perhaps the equivalent of the important role of health-education and awareness programmes.[10]

Conditions for talks

Throughout 1995 political talks at varying levels took place. Representatives of the British government eventually met with Sinn Féin while the SDLP and the UUP held a series of meetings to exchange information on their respective proposals. While these contacts clarified some issues, the prospect of negotiations taking place remained unclear. Unionists continued to demand that the PIRA decommission before they would participate, and while they maintained that position the British government remained unwilling to convene talks. To circumvent the problem the SDLP proposed that an international commission of three, headed by President Clinton's envoy to the peace process, Senator George Mitchell, review the situation and recommend how decommissioning might proceed. At the party's annual conference in November Hume outlined what the party had in mind:

> We cannot move forward without dialogue. That is now the major priority and given that agreement is totally central to lasting stability in any divided society it is not asking too much of the British government to make it their clear priority.
>
> It would not be sufficient to criticize the British government, if we did not offer a constructive way out of the impasse. My colleague Séamus Mallon and myself, with the agreement of Sinn Féin, put forward the following proposals to the prime minister for consideration by both governments. These proposals set out a parallel process for talks and arms.
>
> The two governments should agree to launch the preparatory phase of all party talks in the peace process which will, not later than 30 November, lead into substantive political negotiations, in round-table format, to reach an agreed political settlement.
>
> The two governments should agree to ask George Mitchell to head up an international body to ascertain and advise the two governments on the commitment to peaceful and democratic methods of all political parties that will be participating in the round-table negotiations and consequently of their commitment to the removal of all weapons from Irish politics.
>
> The international body should also be asked to ascertain and advise on how the question of arms, now thankfully silenced, can be finally and satis-factorily settled.

10 Address at the Royal College of Surgeons in Ireland, 6 Nov. 1995; copy in editor's possession..

George Mitchell should be assisted by two other figures of international standing likely to inspire widespread confidence. The international body should have the remit of reporting on whether it has established that a clear commitment exists on the part of the respective political parties to an agreed political settlement, achieved through democratic negotiation, and to the satisfactory resolution of the question of arms.

The international body should report to the two governments, who should undertake to consider carefully any recommendations it makes and to give them due weight.

These proposals seem to me to be ordinary common sense. Once again they threaten no one. We are at an historic moment in Ireland when the gun can be taken out of our politics forever, when lasting stability can be created for the first time, and when agreement can be reached among our divided people. Such an agreement is the only basis for lasting stability and it should therefore be the top priority of everyone, governments above all [...][11]

Mitchell Report

The proposals were broadly accepted by both governments and the body was established, consisting of George Mitchell, Harri Holkeri, a former prime minister of Finland, and John de Chastelain, a former chief of staff of the Canadian army. Following its consultations it reported quite quickly the following February.[12] Its chief recommendation was that some decommissioning should take place in parallel with negotiations. When the report was debated in the house of commons, Hume urged that rather than add further delay by calling an election prior to convening all-party talks, as urged by unionists, the British government should arrange for those talks to commence immediately. He was particularly annoyed that Prime Minister Major, whose parliamentary majority was slim, seemed to be favouring the unionist demand for elections, solely in order to retain the support of unionist MPs:

> May I agree with the prime minister's comment that we are dealing with the lives of innocent men, women and children in Northern Ireland? Does he agree that it would be utterly irresponsible for any party to play politics with the lives of those people? It would be particularly irresponsible for a government to try to buy votes to keep themselves in power. Does he also agree that the commission recommends no form of election? It made it clear that that proposal was outside its remit, and that it was making no recommendation, but simply reporting what was said to it.

11 Address to the SDLP's annual conference, 18 Nov. 1995.   12 'Report of the International Body on Decommissioning', Belfast, HMSO, 1996.

May I take this opportunity to express my deep appreciation to the commission for the intensity and urgency with which it has perceived its objectives? Although its members come from three different countries, it has spent Christmas and New Year's urgently dealing [with decommissioning]. I invite the prime minister to read paragraph 18, which points out that similar urgency is needed on the political track. Will he accept that advice and now fix a date for all-party talks, rather than waste time as he has for the past seventeen months? [...] May I make it clear that my party fully and unequivocally supports the six principles in the document, which call for total commitment from all parties to the democratic and peaceful process, and to the total renunciation and rejection of violence? Does the prime minister feel that if all parties committed themselves to those six principles, he could fix a date for all-party talks?[13]

Hume hoped that the PIRA would respond positively to the Mitchell Report by renewing its ceasefire, which had been broken by a bomb attack that killed two people at Canary Wharf in London in February. To this end, along with Gerry Adams, Hume met with the leadership of the organization in what turned out to be a vain attempt to persuade it to do so. He was deeply disappointed at the PIRA's return to violence but he was also critical of the British government's slow response to the original ceasefire, which he believed had contributed to that return to violence. In response to the unionist demands for elections before any negotiations Hume urged, instead, that joint referenda be held, North and South, in which people would be asked whether or not they supported a total cessation of violence and all-party talks. Such referenda, he believed, would put huge pressure on the PIRA to renew its ceasefire:

The IRA attack on London has been a bitter blow, not just to the people of London but to the people of Britain and Ireland. The past seventeen months gave us more than a glimpse of how things could and should be. The desire for peace in Ireland and good relations between our divided people and between the people of Britain and Ireland, has been overwhelming. The latest atrocity cannot be allowed to destroy the hopes of our peoples for the future.

This, however, is no time to despair. The ill-conceived gloating of the 'I told you so' sceptics is distasteful. It is a time for careful analysis. Looking at all the various theories, demands, shopping lists of preconditions and proposals on offer, it is in fact possible to distil the essence of a successful peace process.

There are only two absolutely essential criteria, all the others are merely

13 House of Commons, *Debates,* 24 Jan. 1996.

preferences or wish lists. First, the republican movement must accept once and for all that violence is not acceptable. It is not an optional extra in the political toolkit. The Mitchell Report spelled this out and it is unfortunate that the opportunity to drive the point home was wasted through the government's handling of the report.

Second, all those parties who are serious about creating a lasting peace have to accept that all-party talks (involving all those who renounce violence as an instrument of political strategy) are necessary as soon as possible. The issue is now simple and cannot be evaded. Peace means all-party talks.

No one underestimates the difficulties of such talks, even though most parties accept, in principle, that they will be necessary eventually. Many in all parties will find it difficult to sit down to negotiate, especially when they may well be asked to talk to people who have been associated with the advocacy of violence in the past. But it should not be forgotten that the nationalist community has also suffered grievously at the hands of paramilitaries of all persuasions. Our experience of injustice and discrimination in Northern Ireland is also a reality that appears to have been forgotten. But sitting down to talk is inescapable if we are to create a lasting peace.

The crucial question is of course, how do we get to that conference table? The idea of an election has been suggested. Unfortunately, an election has serious drawbacks, not least of which is the fact that it would confuse, rather than clarify matters. Elections in Northern Ireland have always created tensions rather than relieved them. While some may see an election as a door, I suspect it may be a perpetually revolving door. Such an election would also be flawed in so far as it would not seriously address the problem of ensuring that the republican movement commits itself to purely peaceful methods.

But, clearly, there is a rational kernel in the unionist case, as Mr Trimble and his colleagues believe they require some form of popular mandate in order to take part in all-party talks. At the same time, republicans must be shown that the only mandate the people of Ireland are prepared to give them is to take part in exclusively democratic and peaceful politics.

Combining these two complementary requirements, I have suggested that the governments consider the option of a referendum, North and South, in order that the relevant mandates can be created. Our citizens would be asked two questions. First, are you in favour of a total cessation of violence? Second, are you in favour of all-party talks? The referendum would be held as soon as possible.

This is not a panacea; difficult questions would continue to be faced by all parties in the negotiations. Agendas would have to be agreed. But it would provide a much-needed stimulus to the peace process and create the conditions for a lasting peace in which our political institutions would be acceptable to all.

A referendum would prove more advantageous than an election for a number of reasons. Speed is an obvious advantage. It would avoid all the diversions and confusions of an election: the rivalries between and within parties, the parochial considerations and the personalities that often make it difficult to assess the real meaning of an election.

In addition, a referendum would reorder and clarify the choices available to us.

An election would, inevitably, be dominated by the question of preferred constitutional options. But that is not what we need most at the moment. We all know the preferred options. It is more important to begin talks so that we can identify the feasible options.

To call an election now would put a confused horse in front of a divided cart. A referendum would have the virtue of clarity. The major political questions would be clear and the choices would be clear-cut.

Instead of a parade of parties there would be a poll for peace.

Such a referendum would have a powerful impact on the peace process. It would unite rather than divide our people. Unmediated by parties or politicians, our citizens would have a full say in determining the future of the peace process. The massive longing for peace in our islands could be translated into a strong political voice. It is time to let the people speak.[14]

Inter-party talks

Despite Hume's case that elections would prove divisive, the British government decided that they should be held in May, and along with the Irish government scheduled talks to commence on 10 June. Senator Mitchell was invited to chair the talks, again accompanied by his two colleagues from the decommissioning commission. Alongside the talks a forum for political dialogue was established to provide opportunities for wider discussion between the parties. However, Sinn Féin declined to participate since it was excluded from the inter-party negotiations because the PIRA had resumed its campaign with massive bomb attacks in Britain. The SDLP attended early meetings of the forum, but soon withdrew amidst controversy over Orange Order parades and police behaviour towards protestors. The whole process of dialogue and negotiations that Hume had worked for with so much determination did not appear to be getting off to a very positive start. When the talks commenced, they immediately became embroiled in several weeks of wrangling over procedural matters and over the structure of the agenda. These matters were not resolved until October, but by then further delay was being incurred over paramilitary decommissioning.

14 *Independent*, 14 Feb. 1996.

Frustrations at these delays and at the failure of the PIRA to declare a second ceasefire and allow Sinn Féin to enter the talks marked many of the contributions to debates at the SDLP's annual conference in November. In his address Hume expressed that same frustration:

> [A]fter eighteen months they [all-party talks] had not commenced and the IRA ceasefire broke down leading to the loss of many more innocent human lives. Historians will judge the reasons for the delay by the British government in starting the all-party talks but it is my own strong conviction that had they started soon after the ceasefire we would have lasting peace by now.
>
> However, there is no point in developing arguments on that subject. Let history judge it but let all of us with responsibility do all in our power to have the ceasefire restored and have the current talks take place in a totally peaceful atmosphere with all parties, including Sinn Féin, involved.
>
> I believe that Prime Minister John Major wants to see that happen, that he wants to achieve lasting peace in our country and that his government can achieve it by reiterating in the clearest possible terms the nature, objectives and time frame of the talks, together with the confidence-building measures that can improve the atmosphere of the talks themselves.
>
> In spite of any mistrust that they may have, the eighteen-month ceasefire transformed the mood of the people of Ireland, North and South, strengthened massively the will for peace and created massive international goodwill, particularly in Europe and the United States, which can be translated into real economic benefits for all sections of our people.
>
> I ask the IRA to renew their ceasefire and create the circumstances where all the energies of our people are devoted to building a new Ireland based on respect for both our traditions. In doing so, we will be strengthening the international goodwill towards our country. We will also be recognizing the reality that 1996 is neither 1690 or 1916. We are today in a post-nationalist Europe. We are in a post-nation-state Europe [...] we cannot live apart.[15]

In early 1997, the imminence of a general election brought the question of an electoral pact between the SDLP and Sinn Féin to the fore, the objective of those in favour being to maximize the number of nationalist seats that could be won. Hume outlined the only conditions on which such a pact might be possible: a renewed PIRA ceasefire and that any Sinn Féin candidates elected would take their seats at Westminster. Such conditions proved unacceptable to Sinn Féin. Hume then published one of his most trenchant critiques of the whole republican movement and appealed to nationalist voters not to support a party that continued

15 Address to the SDLP's annual conference, 9 Nov. 1997.

to support IRA violence, and which, he alleged, engaged in intimidation, and in electoral fraud:

> To make an electoral pact with Sinn Féin without an IRA ceasefire would be the equivalent of asking our voters to support the killing of innocent human beings by the IRA. The electorate should be aware that in voting for Sinn Féin, that is what they are voting for. Sinn Féin call it 'the armed struggle'.
>
> Within hours of my making the offer to enter into discussions regarding an electoral arrangement with Sinn Féin in the circumstances of a ceasefire, the Sinn Féin leadership pronounced any hope of an electoral arrangement 'dead', and a few days later Sinn Féin announced its panel of candidates. There were no requests for 'clarification', no requests for discussion of the issues and no pleas for time to consult their own members.
>
> Compared with the agonizing delays in which we awaited their response to every development in the peace process, from the Downing Street Declaration onwards, the speed of their response on this issue was breath-taking. It calls into question the good faith of Sinn Féin in their professed wish for a consensus among nationalists, and it stands in marked contrast to the consideration and sensitivity with which I and my colleagues have attempted to facilitate them in moving from a strategy of undemocratic violence to a strategy of democratic politics. Having availed of our good faith as honest brokers, they now intend to cast us aside, using any means, fair or foul.
>
> Already the preparations are under way. My party has recently revealed evidence of their continuing intention to engage in every kind of electoral malpractice, from multiple registration of their own members, to the forging of medical cards to facilitate vote stealing.
>
> Already there have been brutal and cowardly attempts to intimidate leading SDLP members in Derry who man the polling stations to prevent impersonation and abuse [...]
>
> Nationalist voters must consider the consequences of voting for people who do these things, who pretend to be democrats while stealing people's votes, and who pretend to stand for the rights of the Irish people while defying and denying the will of the Irish people for peace, expressed in election after election these past twenty-five years.
>
> Consider the impact on our fellow Irish citizens south of the border, if Northern nationalists were seen to throw in their lot with the movement that murdered Jerry McCabe and so many other innocent people.[16] Consider the

16 Garda Sergeant Jerry McCabe was murdered by members of the PIRA in the course of a post office robbery in Co. Limerick.

impact upon opinion in Washington, where so many powerful people (including the president) have invested so much political and financial capital in the movement for peace in Ireland, only to have it exploded in their faces at Canary Wharf. And then consider the satisfaction of the British and unionists, as nationalists isolate themselves as never before, and cut themselves adrift from the most powerful international alliance ever to concern itself with our problem, an international alliance so painstakingly built, brick by brick, over the years by the SDLP.

For these will be the consequences if the republicans are successful in their bid to win the leadership of Northern nationalism.

For the plain fact is that the so-called republican movement are the people who got it wrong, consistently, over the last quarter of a century, and the SDLP are the people who got it right. And the consequence of them getting it wrong is that over 3,500 people are dead – the vast majority of them non-combatant civilians – and 25 thousand million pounds worth of damage has been done to the economy of Ireland, North and South.

If you stand for human rights then your methods must respect them, particularly the most fundamental human right, the right to life.

The fact that the republican movement over the last quarter-century has again led a substantial section of the nationalist population down the blind ally of violence – which they now agree has reached a predictable dead-end – has had two tragic consequences. Firstly, it distracted attention from, and shifted the focus of political argument from, those fundamental questions about the nature of the Northern Ireland state, which had been raised by the civil rights movement, and which led to the dismantling of the old Northern Ireland state. By changing the focus of the argument through violence, Sinn Féin allowed the British and the unionists off the hook.

The tragic consequences of the republicans' war was that it tainted and weakened the struggle for change in the North. It disgusted our fellow countrymen in the South, and revolted public opinion elsewhere in the world. Again, the British and unionists were allowed off the hook.

This cannot go on. There must be a ceasefire, so that we can begin to put the pieces together again – difficult though that might be. We can begin to rebuild a viable strategy for achieving a democratic settlement. Without a ceasefire we are going to have to look elsewhere for a means of making progress.[17]

The general election results in May marked both a triumph and a loss for the SDLP. The party achieved its highest ever vote in a parliamentary election, over

17 *Irish News*, 20 Feb. 1997.

190,000 votes, but Joe Hendron, the party's candidate in West Belfast, lost his seat, which Sinn Féin regained. The elections also resulted in a change of government in the UK when, under Tony Blair's leadership, the Labour Party won a significant victory. One of Blair's first initiatives was to set down terms for Sinn Féin's participation in the talks. Hume welcomed Blair's plan and hoped it would receive a positive response:

> I place on record my deep appreciation of the priority that the prime minister has given to the problems of Northern Ireland since taking office. By so doing, he has strengthened enormously among people at grassroots level the will and the wish for peace and, therefore, the pressure to bring about peace.
>
> May I especially welcome the rational and reasonable steps that the prime minister has outlined in the aide-memoire to bring Sinn Féin into talks? The central step has to be a total and complete end to all violence, and I am asking that that happens because not only should there never be violence in our situation, but it is the will of the people of Ireland, North and South, that it stop immediately. Let it now stop immediately and let all parties, for the first time in our history, get together in the real task of reaching agreement that will provide lasting stability. If that is to happen in a totally peaceful atmosphere, all the better, but, if it is not, let the rest of us get together and work quickly and strongly with both governments to reach that agreement, to put it to the people and to provide lasting peace and stability.[18]

When the talks reconvened following the elections, pressure mounted for a new ceasefire, to enable Sinn Féin to participate. In mid-July, Hume and Adams met again and issued the following joint statement, which was seen as heralding such a development:

> In our first joint statement in April 1993 we acknowledged that the most pressing issue facing the people of Ireland and Britain today is the question of a lasting peace and how it can be achieved and committed ourselves to addressing this issue. This has been our primary focus. It is our view that inclusive negotiations are the only way of reaching agreement and achieving a just and lasting peace for all the people of this island. We regret that, despite our collective efforts, inclusive and meaningful negotiations were not put in place and that the unprecedented opportunity created by the IRA cessation of August 1994 was wasted. Our principal concern is that this dreadful mistake is not repeated.
>
> At our meeting last night we reviewed progress in removing the obstacles,

---

18 House of Commons, *Debates*, 27 June 1997.

erected by the previous British government, to an inclusive and meaningful negotiations process. These obstacles have been used tactically to prevent progress in the talks process at Stormont. We welcome the moves that have been made to remove these obstacles by the new Irish and British governments.[19]

A just and lasting settlement will only be achieved if it is based on principles of democracy and equality and has the allegiance of both traditions.

Such a solution requires change, political and constitutional. It is for the Irish and British governments, in consultations with all the parties, to co-operate to bring this about in the shortest time possible and to legislate accordingly.

Our primary objective remains the achievement of a just and lasting peace for all the people of this island. We are committed to our continuing dialogue and to co-operation between our parties and others to bring this about. We reiterate that this process offers no threat to any section of the people of this island. Our objective is agreement and reconciliation.

It is our view that the peace process can be restored and that with political will on all sides we can move towards a new political agreement. There is a heavy onus on both governments, and particularly the British government, to respond positively and imaginatively, both in terms of the demilitarization of the situation and particularly in dealing with the issue of prisoners, in urgently addressing the equality agenda and in assisting the search for agreement among the people of this island.[20]

Two days later the PIRA renewed its ceasefire, thereby opening the door to Sinn Féin's entry to the talks in September 1997. While two of the unionist parties, the DUP and UKUP, withdrew on the grounds that the PIRA had not even commenced decommissioning its weapons, the main unionist party, the UUP, decided to remain, allowing substantive negotiations to finally begin.

Hume for president

Before the talks recommenced in the autumn, Hume had to address the growing number of requests that he accept nomination for the presidency of the Republic, the election to which was scheduled for October. He was at the height of his popularity throughout Ireland, and it was generally understood that if he accepted the nomination that he would become the sole candidate, and so be elected unopposed. Within the SDLP, opinions were divided, with some fearing the effects

19 Elections in the South in June had led to a Fianna Fáil government taking office, with Bertie Ahern as taoiseach.   20 Joint statement by John Hume and Gerry Adams, 17 July 1997.

his absence might have on the peace process. He eventually decided not to allow his name to be put forward. In a brief statement, he outlined his reasons for his decision:

'I can think of no greater personal honour than to become president of Ireland as an agreed candidate and I am very grateful to those public figures who have indicated their support for the proposal, and to the very large number of people from all parts of the country and abroad who have written to encourage me.'

Outlining the reasons for turning down the position, Mr Hume said that throughout his adult life and with his SDLP colleagues, he had been devoted to resolving 'the very serious crisis in the North'.

'It is now at a very crucial stage and therefore I feel it is my duty to stay with my colleagues in the SDLP and to continue to devote all our energies towards achieving a new and agreed Ireland based on a lasting settlement and a lasting peace. I have therefore decided to remain in my present position. It was a very difficult decision.'[21]

Substantive talks

In October the talks at last reached substantive issues, and in making the SDLP's opening speech to the first Strand 1 session, John Hume reflected on the length of time it had taken to get to the talks, and urged that all participants commit themselves to achieving an agreement:

It seems incredible that we have taken so long to get to this point of actually talking to each other about our differences. It would have been even more incredible if we were to leave this table prematurely, without resolving those differences. I believe that however long it takes, however difficult the issues, whatever hiccups there may be along the way, we must not leave this table until our differences are resolved.

If we are to succeed in resolving our differences, then we must face those differences honestly and directly. There is little point in either of us saying to the other, 'We cannot change, so you must.' Neither of us can change what we are. What we can and must change, are our attitudes, our intolerance of difference, our repeated pushing of differences to the point of division. We must begin by accepting each other for what we are, accepting that we have an absolute right to be what we are and that we cannot, either of us, change what we are.

21 *Irish News*, 7 Sept. 1997.

That is where our analysis of the problem begins. With our failure to accept our differences and our failure to devise political structures which accommodate those differences. As a first step, therefore [...] we should seek to identify those requirements which will be necessary to the survival of any new arrangements we may wish to make [...]

Strand 1 is about our relationship – the relationship between unionist and nationalist in Northern Ireland. We should be trying to define who the nationalists and unionists are.

In the New Ireland Forum Report, we, along with the other nationalist parties on this island, defined ourselves as those who identify themselves as part of a nation which extends throughout this island, and who seek the unity and independence of that nation. For historical reasons we may in the past have defined ourselves in terms of separation from Britain, and opposition to British domination of Ireland. The more positive vision of Irish nationalism in recent times has been to create a society that transcends all differences and that can accommodate all traditions in a sovereign independent Ireland united by agreement.

In the Forum Report we attempted to define unionists as those who regard themselves as being British, the inheritors of a specific communal loyalty to the British crown. We discerned three major elements in the identity of unionists, their Britishness, their Protestantism and their belief in the economic advantage of being part of the British state. At the same time we discerned an Irish element in the makeup of unionists, an identification with at least some features of Irish life and culture [...]

It is our belief that these two communities, however they are defined, have certain inalienable rights. If our strategy for dealing with this problem were to be reduced to its most essential core, it would be the need to create new arrangements in this island to accommodate together those sets of legitimate rights:

1. the right of nationalists to effective political, symbolic and administrative expression of their identity;
2. the right of unionists to effective political, symbolic and administrative expression of their identity, their ethos and their way of life.[22]

When the talks eventually concluded in April 1998 with the Good Friday/Belfast Agreement, there was widespread rejoicing in the North, and Hume expressed his own and his party's pleasure at the outcome, not least because the

22 Address to the opening session of Strand 1, 15 Oct. 1997.

SDLP's analysis and its general proposals for a way forward lay at the heart of the agreement:

> We in the SDLP concluded many years ago that we could not lay the basis for agreement against a background of violence and disorder. That is why we entered the process to bring peace to our streets. The peace created the space for these talks, which have now concluded with agreement, hope for the future and what must be a determination to maintain our agreement.
>
> It has long been the view of the SDLP that the task which lay before us was to resolve three sets of relationships – between the two traditions in the North; between North and South and between Britain and Ireland.
>
> That analysis was reflected in the agenda for these talks – the three strands. Equally it has been our view, since the foundation of the SDLP, that we needed a new beginning, based on equal partnership in the North; equal partnership between North and South; [and] a new co-operative relationship between Britain and Ireland. These proposals are reflected in the outcomes we have agreed today. This process is not about the victory or defeat of nationalism or unionism. It is about something greater. Today we can take a collective breath and blow away the bondage of fear which has so damaged our people and our country, difficult and demanding though this will be in the coming days and weeks.
>
> For thirty years we have pursued the politics of acceptance and inclusion rather than exclusion and rejection. For thirty years we have wanted to escape the narrow sectarian mindset which choked generosity and openness of spirit. Today we can witness the start of a new mindset based on tolerance, dialogue and accommodation.
>
> There can be a new dawn in politics on this island. We can agree a comprehensive settlement which allows both our traditions to work together. It will be a new agreed Ireland in which the rights and interests of both the nationalist and unionist traditions will be safeguarded and cherished. We must safeguard this agreement we have worked so hard to accomplish.
>
> The reality of living with difference and affirming identity is that we cannot achieve actualization without mutual accommodation. Martin Luther King got to the heart of it when he said, 'I can never be what I ought to be until you are what you ought to be.' Nationalists cannot be what they ought to be until unionists are what they ought to be, and vice versa.
>
> Only once in a generation does an opportunity like this come along, an opportunity to resolve our deep and tragic conflict. No one should diminish the difficulties we face. No one should deny the tough decisions that have been made and tough choices that have to be made. We must draw reassurance that our agreement today reflects the firmest wish of all our people.

Once before we came very close, only to have our hopes dashed. This time we must succeed. Whatever our anxieties, we have to seize this opportunity. And the opportunities which lie before us are vast – to create a new partnership between our divided people, to banish guns and bombs from our streets forever, to secure economic, social and cultural equality and progress, to build a new Ireland for our children.

This is the beginning.

This agreement will now be put to the people of this island, North and South. The people are sovereign and they will now decide. I have every confidence in their judgment and good sense. I commend this agreement to them.[23]

Later, when the agreement was being debated in parliament, he acknowledged the work and contribution of several members towards creating the circumstances for the talks and for their successful conclusion, especially the contributions of Prime Minister Tony Blair and of his predecessor John Major:

May I place on record our deep appreciation for the detailed work that the secretary of state [Mo Mowlam] and her ministerial colleagues have done in arriving at this agreement? I am sure that, in so doing, I speak for the vast majority of the people of both sections of our community.

May I join her in thanking the prime minister for the priority that he gave to the greatest human problem facing the house? The fact that he gave it such priority gave enormous encouragement to the people at grassroots level who have suffered from this problem, and strengthened the peace process enormously. I pay tribute to the prime minister for so doing.

I also pay tribute, and express deep gratitude, to the right hon. member for Huntingdon [Mr Major] and his colleagues, because they worked hard to help to lay the foundations for the process. I express my deep appreciation to him and to other hon. members who are in the chamber. I include in that the right hon. member for the Cities of London and Westminster [Mr Brooke], because, when the history is written – I know a bit about the history of this process – his role and public statements will be seen to have laid a major foundation. I say to him, 'Thank you.' I add to that our thanks to the leader of the Liberal Democrats [Paddy Ashdown], because he has been consistent in his total support for a common-sense approach to this problem.

It is welcome that the agreement will put in place institutions which will give no victory to either side in our community, but which instead will create

23 *Irish News*, 11 Apr. 1998.

circumstances that respect the identities of both sections of our community, in which they could work together in their common interests.

I have no doubt from my experience that, given the massive international goodwill that there has been towards the agreement, reason will take over once we start working together and leave our quarrel behind us. Harnessing that international support and interest will transform our economy, and give hope to our young people, so that the next century will be the first in our island history in which there will be no killings on our streets and no emigration of our young to other lands to earn a living.[24]

In joint referenda held on 22 May, the agreement was endorsed by almost 72 per cent of the electorate in the North and by more than 95 per cent in the South. The challenge then was to have it successfully implemented.

At the SDLP's 1998 annual conference Hume reflected on what the Good Friday Agreement meant in historical terms, and on what it meant for future relationships within the North, between North and South, and between Britain and Ireland:

Of many things we may be uncertain. But of this we can be sure. The Good Friday Agreement will be judged by history to be a seminal document, a document which sets its stamp on the future course of relations in this island, in this society and between these islands.

The agreement was founded on the unfilled potential that we know to be there, the potential to find agreement in the face of paradox and conundrum, to find an agreed constitutional and political accommodation for our people.

Unionists and nationalists have at last taken the future in their hands, have seized control of their history rather than letting history hold them in thrall.

Our party needs to make no apology for our aspiration to the unity of people.

But let us consider our definition of unity.

What greater unity is possible today than the referendum, North and South, which endorsed the Good Friday Agreement? What greater unity is possible than the unity of the joint endeavours of those elected to serve in the assembly and its executive? What greater unity is possible than the unity of our shared endeavours in the North-South Ministerial Council?

At this point in our history, we have achieved a truly valuable unity:

• the unity of purpose across all previous boundaries of party and tradition that suffuses, informs and directs the institutions and principles of the Good Friday Agreement.

24 House of Commons, *Debates*, 20 Apr. 1998.

- the unity of purpose that directs the new politics on behalf of all of the people in this society.
- the unity of purpose undertaken on behalf of all of the people of these islands, North and South, east and west.

Nationalists, republicans and unionists – we have all travelled far in our thinking and attitudes over the years of this peace process. It has been a very positive journey, the success of which may not be obvious to those who have been directly involved in its creation. What was inconceivable is now commonplace and the norm.

Nationalists and republicans have taken their places in a local assembly. Nationalists and unionists are preparing to share power in an executive.

Unionists have accepted that the North-South Ministerial Council is an essential institution without which neither the assembly nor the executive would be possible.

Unionists have accepted the operating principle of sufficient consensus, of parallel consent, the recognition that both traditions must be recognized as equally valid, symbolically and politically. We have all accepted the expression of the totality of relationships represented by the British-Irish Council.

Without reservation, commissions on human rights and equality are to be established and embedded as essential institutions for the good government of Northern Ireland on a day-to-day, case-by-case basis. The European Convention on Human Rights is being incorporated as a matter of law and justice. And so much more. Prisoners, victims, policing, security normalization, criminal justice have become part of a process of profound change and renewal. We have achieved so much.

We have succeeded not because we have challenged others. We have succeeded because we have challenged ourselves [...]

There has been enormous courage from unionists. I believe David Trimble and his party colleagues share the ideals and values of the peace process, ideals and values grounded in the belief that we can find harmony and concord between us as human beings that transcend traditional ideologies – without damage to those ideologies. In the May referendum the unionist community overcame its reservations about aspects of the agreement like prisoners and decommissioning. They joined in the chorus on this island that said yes. They said yes not to a document over which they had sole authorship and control but to a document that was a collective effort by eight parties, three governments and two traditions, forged with help of the remarkable group of independent chairmen led by Senator Mitchell.[25]

25 Address to the SDLP conference, 14 Nov. 1998.

However, despite those high expectations, implementing the agreement did not prove to be as smooth as Hume had hoped, or had expected. Before it would agree to allow an executive be formed, the UUP demanded some evidence, at least, that the PIRA had commenced decommissioning its weapons. Sinn Féin, however, claimed that the agreement had not imposed any such precondition. An immediate impasse arose. Hume agreed with the Sinn Féin position, but believed that there was an expectation that decommissioning would eventually have to happen, and was critical of the unionist approach, which was preventing the implementation of all other aspects of the agreement:

> There is no precondition of decommissioning in the agreement. Nor is there any other precondition under the agreement. The only real precondition for anything under the agreement was the people's verdict by referendum. It is the will of the people that disarmament takes place as provided for in the agreement as part of the full implementation of the agreement in parallel with its other provisions. This party and all other parties are obliged by our own commitments to work constructively with the independent commission [on decommissioning] and use our influence to achieve such disarmament.
>
> We have to ask ourselves whether adopting tactics or rhetoric which create impediments around this issue is the most constructive contribution that can be made to this task. Is it the best use of a party's own influence to adopt negative postures which do little to enhance or encourage the positive influence which we need others to use to good effect? We must all do all we can to make disarmament happen as soon as possible within the timescale for the commission's work, not least by doing all we can to implement all other aspects of the agreement in their own terms as soon as possible.[26]

Nonetheless, it would be another year before an executive would be formed, when the UUP, in November 1999, was led to expect that decommissioning would soon begin. However, since it did not commence, the executive was suspended in early February and, although reinstated in May, was to experience several further short suspensions before eventually being suspended indefinitely in October 2002, when no decommissioning had taken place. Direct rule from London returned, and the agreement was to remain suspended until 2007.

Nobel Prize

While the process of implementing the agreement was encountering its first difficulties, John Hume, along with David Trimble as leader of the UUP, were the joint

26 Ibid.

recipients of the 1998 Nobel Peace Prize. In his address Hume reiterated many of his often-articulated messages about the need for partnership, and he concluded with the following vision for Ireland in the wake of the Good Friday Agreement:

> I want to see Ireland – North and South – the wounds of violence healed, play its rightful role in a Europe that will, for all Irish people, be a shared bond of patriotism and new endeavour.
>
> I want to see Ireland as an example to men and women everywhere of what can be achieved by living for ideals, rather than fighting for them, and by viewing each person as worthy of respect and honour.
>
> I want to see an Ireland of partnership where we wage war on want and poverty, where we reach out to the marginalized and dispossessed, where we build together a future that can be as great as our dreams allow.
>
> The Irish poet Louis MacNeice wrote words of affirmation and hope that seem to me to sum up the challenges now facing all of us – North and South, unionist and nationalist – in Ireland: 'By a high star our course is set,/Our end is life. Put out to sea.'
>
> That is the journey on which we in Ireland are now embarked.
>
> Today, as I have said, the world also commemorates the adoption of the Universal Declaration of Human Rights. To me there is a unique appropriateness, a sort of poetic fulfilment in the coincidence that my fellow [Nobel] laureate and I, representing a community long divided by the forces of a terrible history, should jointly be honoured on this day. I humbly accept this honour on behalf of a people, who after many years of strife, have finally made a commitment to a better future in harmony together. Our commitment is grounded in the very language and the very principles of the Universal Declaration itself. No greater honour could have been done me or the people I speak here for, on no more fitting a day.
>
> I will now end with a quotation of total hope, the words of a former laureate, one of my great heroes of this century, Martin Luther King Jr.
>
> 'We shall overcome.'[27]

Bloody Sunday Inquiry

One other issue which gave Hume considerable satisfaction in 1998 was Prime Minister Blair's announcement in January that a new inquiry into the Bloody Sunday killings would take place. It was an inquiry that Hume and the families of those killed and injured had long campaigned for. Responding to the prime minister's announcement Hume, said:

27 Address at conferring of Nobel Peace Prize, Oslo, 1998.

May I express my very deep appreciation to the prime minister for his statement? He is very right when he underlines the terrible tragedy that that day was. I know something about it, having been the only public representative on those streets on that day. It is therefore right and proper – this is an objective that no reasonable person should oppose or could oppose – that the full truth be established about what happened on that day.

May I also thank the prime minister for his recognition of the enormous dignity of the families of the victims of that day in their pursuit of that objective – the truth? Let us now hope that the steps he is putting in place will finally produce the full truth and be a major part of the healing process in our divided community.[28]

The Saville Inquiry, named after its presiding judge, was to become the longest public inquiry in British legal history, so exhaustive were its deliberations. Its report would not be published until 2012, and when it was, it exonerated all those killed and was a belated vindication of Hume's decision to boycott the earlier Widgery Inquiry and to campaign for a wider, more comprehensive one.

28 House of Commons, *Debates*, 29 Jan. 1998.

1998–2005

From 1998 until his retirement as an MEP in 2004, and as an MP in 2005, John Hume's role gradually became more that of an 'elder statesman' than a frontline participant in Northern Ireland's politics. While he was elected to Northern Ireland's new assembly, day-to-day leadership of the SDLP team there was exercised by his deputy, Séamus Mallon, who became deputy to First Minister David Trimble of the UUP in the new executive. Nonetheless, until 2001, Hume remained leader of the SDLP.

During this period, the Good Friday Agreement was threatened, primarily because of the issue of decommissioning, and also because of uncertainty over whether the DUP, led by Ian Paisley, would fully participate in a power-sharing executive that included Sinn Féin ministers. So, despite the high hopes of a new beginning, deep-rooted political divisions and suspicions continued to manifest themselves. Delays and setbacks characterized the new institutions, almost from their establishment, and raised questions over whether they would ever function as intended.

Hume, however, remained convinced that the agreement provided the best opportunity for the people of Northern Ireland to overcome their divisions and remove their mutual suspicions, and he was optimistic that it would succeed. Still, he was not blind to the challenges this required. In his address to the SDLP's 1999 annual conference, he acknowledged these, saying that more was needed than the fine words of the agreement. In particular, he pointed to controversies over parades associated with the Loyal Orders, several of which had been causing controversy because of objections by residents in nationalist areas to parades passing close to their homes:

> There are fine words in the Good Friday Agreement about tolerance, mutual respect and reconciliation. We must strive to ensure that they become the touchstones by which we live. There are too many places which are disfigured and divided by raw sectarianism. SDLP members have been at the forefront in fighting sectarianism, often at personal risk. [...]
>
> We need to find, through dialogue and mutual respect for the rights of all, ways to resolve the continuing disputes over parades, particularly that at

1 The annual Orange Order July march at Drumcree, Co. Armagh, had become very contentious because of marchers' insistence on passing close to predominantly Catholic areas.

Drumcree,[1] which has had the most severe and enduring consequences for the residents of the Garvaghy Road and which has blighted the life not just of Portadown but of the North as a whole. In general, the example set in Derry by the Apprentice Boys and the residents is one to be commended.[2]

We want to create a society where the civil rights of all sections of our people are respected and where it is recognized that to every right there corresponds a duty to exercise the right responsibly.[3]

Hume believed that the Good Friday Agreement would be fully implemented despite the fact that two months after the executive had been formed both it and the assembly were suspended when no progress was reported on decommissioning PIRA weapons. In an interview with Jennifer Byrne of ABC, Hume denied that he was 'putting a gloss on it':

> I'm saying that we have made a lot of progress. Yes, we have a setback at the moment, but that setback doesn't remove the progress that we've made. We have peace in our streets, which has transformed the atmosphere, but obviously I regret very much the current impasse and we're working at the moment to try to resolve it because it's what the vast majority of the people want, and it's the duty of every democrat here to implement the will of the people.[4]

Asked why he was so optimistic when Gerry Adams was claiming that the agreement was in tatters, he replied:

> We'll I'm not being optimistic, I'm being positive. When you've been through what we've been through in Northern Ireland it's easy to be negative. In fact, I've said to some politicians that if you took the word 'no' out of the English language they would be speechless. It's very easy to be negative – and if you are, you never go anywhere […] if you go on the positive, and build on the positive you make progress. And the positive is the progress that we've made to date […] we now have a setback, a difficulty on the question of decommissioning. It's a difficult issue I think that is a distraction because paramilitary organizations can decommission their guns on Monday and secretly recommission and get more guns on Tuesday. What is more important than decommissioning is that when they say they have stopped that they are telling the truth – that's what's really important.[5]

2 Hume was among those who successfully negotiated agreements that defused tensions around the annual Apprentice Boys marches in Derry. 3 Address to the SDLP's annual conference, 6 Nov. 1999.
4 Interview with Jennifer Byrne, *Foreign Correspondent*, ABC, 14 Mar. 2000. 5 Ibid.

Martin Luther King Award

Following the Nobel Peace Prize, Hume continued to receive recognition at home and abroad for his role in the peace process. Among his many awards, one that he treasured very highly was the Martin Luther King Award. King had been a special hero and inspiration from the outset of his public career, and he had frequently quoted King's endorsements of non-violence and his quest for justice for the downtrodden. He spoke of this inspiration in his acceptance speech in Atlanta:

> I received this award with a profound sense of pride.
>
> Pride because Martin Luther King has been a wellspring of inspiration personally throughout my life.
>
> Pride because it is received on behalf of all the people of Ireland that have longed for peace through the dark decades of upheaval and violence.
>
> Pride because this award is a symbol of the bonds between those who strive for peace and the inalienable dignity of the individual.
>
> Martin Luther King is for me one of the giants of this country.
>
> We have seen many revolutions in the modern age. We have gone from a horse-and-cart age to commonplace trips to space, all in the span of a human lifetime. This century has seen more than its share of war and bloodshed. Since 1900 vast numbers of people across the globe have lost their lives in the vortex of war. We have seen progress, but we have also seen oppressive ideologies advance and retreat, often leaving in their wake ruins of war and deprivation.
>
> Somewhere along the line we needed to be reminded that the supreme value – above all the 'isms' – was the transcending spiritual worth of every human being.
>
> Martin Luther King embodies for me the commitment to the ideals of a true humanism based on loving not just your neighbour but your enemies.
>
> When he spoke, he spoke with passion about the dreams of the individual for freedom, for peace, for prosperity and for justice. His words burned with the heat of indignation at the injustices suffered by his fellow African Americans in what for generations of white people had been the land of opportunity.
>
> I have long admired and travelled in America. I have admired this great country's welcome for the tired and huddled immigrants who came to its shores, its wealth of resources and human talents. America has been good to Ireland over the past generations. It has been a rock of support in the Northern Ireland peace process. I have wondered at America's economic might and the wealth of its resources. Its democratic revolution has been an inspiration to the world and to all democrats fighting for what they believe in.

But who could not understand the anger of the black community at the closed doors of segregation and exclusion? Who could not stand with Dr Martin Luther King Jr in Washington as he demanded that the promissory note of equality be honoured by the government of the time?

He put a challenge to America to fulfil its promise to all its citizens regardless of colour. He put down a challenge to black America to maintain its righteous rage but express it only peacefully, not to satisfy, in his words, the thirst for freedom by 'drinking from the cup of bitterness and hatred'.

We often talk of slavery, discrimination, oppression, lynch law and marginalization, socially and economically. But who among us can really know the meaning, the actuality of the conditions they name? We can never truly know this from the outside. But we can appreciate the sense of injustice.

And we can begin to understand the human imperative for justice, for equality and for dignity. And through the force of Martin Luther King's words, we can feel our hearts quicken to the beat of his righteousness, of his moral outrage, of his desire for true peace.

Here was a man leading his people out of servitude to the land promised for all by the founding fathers of the United States. By moral force alone, he harnessed the energy, challenged those who sought to delay social and economic liberation for African Americans, and made the most powerful society in the world accept its obligations.

Armed alone with words as the stones he would cast, he tackled the Goliath of racism and segregation and he triumphed.

When he spoke under the shadow of the Lincoln Memorial in 1963, he spoke not just for those who had gathered and not just for those whose cause he was part of. He spoke to everyone who would seek justice where there was injustice, who would seek equality where there was inequality, who would seek rights where there were none. He spoke with the power of the prophet who says there is a land we dream of and we will get there not through violence but with 'soul force', with moral force, spilling our sweat and not our blood.

The power of the idea that he embodied – that moral force alone can break the chains of oppression, of rancour, of division – was the driving force of the civil rights movement and has inspired countless peacemakers across generations and in areas of conflict across the globe.

That was his dream.

This is his legacy.

That will be his greatest prize left to us and those who follow.

The bullet that killed Dr Martin Luther King aimed not only to destroy the man but that idea. It was aimed at him but was designed to hit all those who would choose the creative force of peace and non-violence.

But instead of killing moral force as a weapon of change, it sanctified it through his sacrifice. But as the Bible tells us, in the beginning was the Word, not the bullet. For words and the ideals they embody can never be killed. In my work, I have been sustained by the words 'we shall overcome'.

Fate decreed that I would not only be inspired by Dr Martin Luther King, but that I would find myself facing a challenge of civil rights in Northern Ireland that answered to his call to use moral force to make change [...]

But the dream of equality, freedom and the dignity of the individual that Martin Luther King embodied helped shape the Northern Ireland civil rights movement that emerged during the closing years of the 1960s.

Inspired and guided by the moral philosophy of non-violence espoused by Martin Luther King, I felt it my duty to help shape and guide the growing movement for civil rights in Northern Ireland, and later the SDLP, the party I helped found as a vehicle for non-violent constitutional nationalism.

We did not seek ideological confrontation.

We did not seek to inflict suffering. We believed, in the words of Martin Luther King, in the redemptive quality of unearned suffering.

We believed that we would accomplish more through suffering and enduring for our own beliefs.

We believed in inclusivity, not exclusivity.

We believed in peace, in the ability of human beings to find their common humanity.

We believed that true unity among all Irish people, Protestant and Catholic, nationalist and unionist, was a unity of the heart not merely of the soil [...][6]

Final address as SDLP leader

Hume addressed the SDLP's annual conference in November 2001 for the last time as leader. Not unexpectedly, his address began with reflections on the party's contribution to developments in Northern Ireland. He paid tribute to the contribution of the party's deputy leader, Séamus Mallon, who was also stepping down from his role on the same occasion:

Later today, my friend and colleague, Séamus Mallon will address the conference for the last time as deputy leader of this party. Séamus Mallon is a man for whom I – like so many people from so many backgrounds – have the utmost respect. His commitment to peaceful and democratic politics is

6 Address at conferring of the Martin Luther King Award, Atlanta, 18 Jan. 1999; copy in editor's possession.

second to none. His integrity and honesty have helped him serve the people of Newry and Armagh with distinction for many years. His performance during his tenure as deputy first minister in the assembly proved that it is possible to transcend traditional political boundaries while retaining one's own core beliefs and values. He is an inspirational figure for this party and for the people of Ireland and he deserves our sincere thanks and praise today for his immense contribution to Irish politics.

For over twenty years Séamus and myself have shared the helm of the SDLP. We have worked hard together and with many others to fulfil the objectives of our party. I believe that we can say with some confidence, we have done a reasonable job.[7]

He firmly believed that the SDLP approach had been fully vindicated:

These past thirty years have indeed been difficult. But we always knew that what we were doing was right. We knew that a way out from violence and despair could be found. We knew that a political process that included representatives of all sections of the community in Northern Ireland, as well as the Irish and British governments, had the potential to transform our society on the basis of agreement, consensus and partnership. We knew we had the right ideas to effectively address the fundamental problems in our society.

Over many years, others have come to accept that we were right. What a tragedy it is that so much violence and suffering filled the vacuum created by political inertia and inaction. Too many lives were lost and we know those lives cannot be brought back.

The SDLP has never swerved from our total opposition to violence of any kind. In the past year many of our elected representatives or members of their families from all across the North have suffered in the frontline against sectarian violence. I want them to know that this entire party stands with them as they take their courageous stand against sectarianism and bigotry [...]

What we can do now, what we must do, is ensure that no more lives will be lost, that our young people can grow up in a society that is free and democratic and economically prosperous. That is our job for the years ahead. To fulfil the untold promise of the Good Friday Agreement and build the new Ireland.

Indeed, there is a broader imperative at this time of uncertainty for the world. The full implementation of the Good Friday Agreement can provide the world with a blueprint for conflict resolution. Good people around the

7 Address to the SDLP's annual conference, 10 Nov. 2001.

world need to know that conflict can be ended and that peace, hope and justice can prevail. Equally, those who are intent on perpetuating acts of evil upon the world need to know that their deeds cannot and will not break the human spirit [...]

The tragic events of 11 September impacted upon the entire world. The terrorist attacks on New York and Washington were truly catastrophic. On behalf of the SDLP I want to extend our condolences to President Bush and to the American people as they seek to move forward in these most difficult of circumstances [...]

On decommissioning, he stated:

The IRA initiative to put arms beyond use to the satisfaction of the de Chastelain Commission is very welcome. It represents a massive step forward for the republican movement and has given the political process a new dynamic. No one should underestimate the magnitude of the IRA decision.

That said, no one should lose sight of the fact that the SDLP has consistently demanded that decommissioning begin. Frequently, when we made that demand for decommissioning some in the republican movement criticized us for playing into the hands of unionists. Equally, when we said that decommissioning would happen we were criticized by some unionists who believed it would never happen [...][8]

On policing, he claimed:

With conviction and consistency the SDLP has promoted the need for a brand-new beginning for policing in the North on the basis of the Patten recommendations.[9] [...] The best way to establish basic law and order will be through a new police service, one which fully meets the standards set for it in the Good Friday Agreement and as developed in the Patten Report. Such a service will be one which is representative of and supported by both communities, which is properly accountable and which adheres to the highest and most professional standards. The SDLP was not found wanting when it came to meeting our responsibilities. We have worked hard for thirty years to achieve that new beginning. [...]

We realized that the opportunity to create that new beginning for policing in keeping with the Patten recommendations was available. That is why we decided to nominate to the Police Board. We took a courageous step forward

8 Ibid. 9 The commission of inquiry into the future of policing in Northern Ireland was chaired by Chris Patten, a former minister, and a former governor of Hong Kong.

and I believe that step has received widespread support from the whole community. I want to encourage young people from all sections of the community to join the new police service. I can assure any young person who is considering joining the new service that the SDLP will protect their basic human right to opt into policing as an honourable career choice.[10]

The reform of policing proceeded quite rapidly following the publication of the Patten Report. The service was renamed the Police Service of Northern Ireland and membership gradually became more balanced, as a significant number of young men and women from a Catholic-nationalist background were recruited. As a result, police reform was one of the most positive early achievements of the new political era.

Unionist opposition

A section of unionist opinion, led mainly by Ian Paisley and the DUP, remained opposed to the agreement and sought to have it withdrawn. Hume appealed to them to reconsider:

> To those unionists who remain opposed to the agreement I say this. I under-stand that you have real and legitimate concerns surrounding the future course and shape of the political process. But I implore you to participate fully in shaping that future with the rest of us. Central to the Good Friday Agreement is the principle of consent, a fundamental principle of unionism. The SDLP has always endorsed the principle of consent. We will continue to do so. Anti-agreement unionists must understand that if they are successful in bringing the agreement down they will actually undermine one of the core principles of their own ideology. I call today on anti-agreement unionists to work with us all for the good of all.[11]

Concluding his address, Hume thanked all who, throughout bad days and good, had supported him and the SDLP:

> Your work at grassroots level was vital as we sought to design and develop the new Ireland. With renewed energy and vigour your work will continue to be vital in the months and years ahead as the new SDLP leadership begins its work. Often we have sailed against the wind but always we have kept our rudder true. And we always will steer the course of hope and opportunity, of what we believe to be right, no matter how difficult that course may be.

10 Ibid.   11 Ibid.

Leading the community. Shaping the country. The SDLP [...] [k]eep believing. Keep working. Keep hoping. Keep striving. Keep building. The new agreed Ireland of our dreams is within reach. One day we shall overcome.[12]

International co-operation

Following his resignation as party leader, Hume continued to speak at conferences at home and abroad. Speaking at the function in India where he received the Gandhi Peace Prize, he recalled the ties between India and Ireland and then, drawing inspiration from Gandhi, went on to discuss the transformation in hearts and minds that he believed must be the ultimate goal in conflict resolution:

> On hundred years ago to this day, Gandhi-ji was staying in the home of Gopal Gokhale in Calcutta. Gokhale had visited Ireland a few years previously. With his friends he had arranged for a member of the Irish Party, Alfred Webb, to serve as president of the Tenth Indian National Congress. It is recorded by Webb that Gokhale's knowledge of Irish history was superior to that of many members of the Irish Party itself. So it is safe to assume that a century ago, as those two friends in Calcutta discussed the future of India, the word *swaraj* (self-rule) was mentioned, and with it, the name of Ireland.
>
> In our small island, as in this great subcontinent, political change was an untidy business. In Ireland, as in India, there were divisions that led to partition, and a continuing legacy of pain. The Northern Ireland in which I grew up was a divided society. No one from my background could be in any doubt about the characteristics of the problem. The question was what to do about it.
>
> From the late 1960s on, some of us resolved to seek a fundamental change in our circumstances through peaceful, political means. That was and is the purpose of the political party, the Social Democratic and Labour Party, that it was my privilege to lead until a few months ago. In the SDLP we recognize that in situations of conflict all of us carry a burden imposed on us by the past and must help one another cast off that burden. Our differences of religion and politics are accidental: none of us chose to be born. It is our goal to share the future with those who seem at first potential opponents. We reject the logic of the zero-sum game.
>
> It follows therefore that the key to a successful society is to acknowledge and respect differences and to have institutions that enable us to work together [...]

12 Ibid.

[But] [i]n the long run it is not enough for us to respect differences and set up functioning institutions. We must aim higher, at a transformation of hearts and a healing process. In situations of conflict, some of the parties are first in denial – acting out a pretence, for example, that there is no injustice and that differences are a product of the false consciousness of others. The point of breakthrough is when we move from denial to the acceptance of compromise. But the rational acceptance of a need for compromise is a fragile and eventually fruitless state of mind. We must move on from acceptance to affirmation. To take our own case, within Northern Ireland, across the border in Ireland, among all the peoples of Ireland and Britain, we are learning to affirm a quality of earned friendship. It is something we can try to share with others going through a resolution of inherited historical pain [...]

Europe was an important influence on me and my party. But before that, there was Gandhi-ji. When Gandhi died I had just completed my eleven-plus examinations. I was old enough for India and Gandhi to form part of my mental furniture, long before I could imagine any other country beyond Ireland, Britain, and North America. As a young man in the civil rights movement in Northern Ireland, I was a follower of Martin Luther King. Behind King, there again was Gandhi-ji.

For me and my colleagues, in the generation that bore the wounds of two great European wars, it was easy to hear Gandhi's words. As we defined our political strategy of non-violence, respect for difference, and working together in the common interest, we found ourselves giving expression to something resembling the Gandhian conception of *satyagraha* (action to affirm truth) [...]

I have no doubt that at the level of world politics, Gandhi has helped to shape our goals. But even more fundamentally he has helped us to understand the relationship between ends and means. Too often we are tempted to fall back on the utilitarian principle that the end justifies the means. Mahatma Gandhi turned this around. The idea of *ahimsa* (non-violence) and *satyagraha* suggest that it is the quality of the means – including our readiness to suffer for good ends but not to inflict suffering on others – that provides the justification of the ends. Gandhi's choice of means is natural in a world that is growing smaller. Gandhian methods are the counterpart to the purposes of the United Nations: peace and disarmament, human development, human rights, and the strengthening of international law.[13]

---

13 Speech on receiving the Gandhi Peace Prize, 1 Feb. 2002; copy in editor's possession.

Interdependence

Addressing international audiences Hume never ceased to express his conviction that in a world whose peoples were becoming ever-more interdependent, international political co-operation was also increasingly required.

At a conference in France in 2002 on the theme 'diversity and equality and the future of democracy', he highlighted the trends that underlined this requirement, and the challenges they implied:

> Today the impact of global trade in goods and services, of international capital movements, of massive internal and external population shifts, and the pervasive presence of mass communications mean everyone is affected, and has some knowledge of how and why they are affected by these transformations.
>
> The power of technology to break down barriers and end the isolation of a culture is overwhelming. Nothing like this has been seen before, certainly not in terms of the scale and speed of change.
>
> The internationalization of the economy has transformed living conditions throughout the world. Clearly this globalization has not benefited the world equally, but there are large areas, and hundreds of millions of people, who have seen their lives improved.
>
> Our political systems have also been internationalized to an extent never seen before. All European states work together to further their common interests through organizations such as the European Union, the Council of Europe and the Organisation for Security and Co-operation in Europe. Other regional organizations are emerging in Asia and Africa. The UN is quite rightly the focus of attention in its role as the protector of international law and international peace.
>
> Our common humanity and common interests are more obvious and more important than ever before. At the same time, it is impossible to claim that the world is a more peaceful place. With the various conflicts around the world, and the present international crisis, it has to be recognized that our interdependence is also a source of conflict.
>
> Unfortunately, the more we know of each other, the more significant our differences seem to be.
>
> I believe the task of the twenty-first century is to ensure that our common interests prevail over our differences. That can only be achieved if we face up to the reality of difference and diversity. Difference and diversity must be accepted as normal, legitimate and indeed a source of progress, creativity and richness. There is a crying need for institutions and practices that reconcile diversity and unity.

The challenge of the twenty-first century is to ensure that difference enhances humanity rather than destroys it. We know we have the technological means to destroy each other. But do we have the political means to use our technological sophistication to remove poverty, injustice and disease?

I am optimistic that we do. The clash of civilizations is not inevitable. Indeed a civilization of co-existence and co-operation is just as possible if that is what we decide.

I continue to believe that the pen is mightier than the sword, and it should be employed to bring about peaceful relations between the peoples of the world. The choice between civilization and barbarism remains as relevant and available today as it has been for our ancestors for thousands of years [...]

Difference and diversity must be regarded as essential to life, not as a threat. Democratic politics in the twenty-first century must be about the search to promote ways of living together, not dying together. We must resist those who use difference as a method of generating hatred and violence, and as a way of perpetuating injustice.

But to do so is not just a question of moral persuasion. The need to create political institutions at all levels capable of accommodating difference is crucial. This is no simple task. It involves hard thinking and talking, being prepared to take far-reaching and enlightened decisions, and basing institutions on reason rather than prejudice.

Fundamental rights must be guaranteed to all. I would include among these fundamental rights the right for your identity to be respected by political authorities and by your fellow citizens, the right to earn a living, the right to practice religion freely, as well as the right to use your language. The European Convention on Human Rights has a profound influence that I hope will be reinforced by the eventual incorporation of the EU Charter of Fundamental Rights into EU law. Indeed, I believe one of the basic tasks of EU external policy for the forthcoming decades will be the export of these basic values [...][14]

Breaking the impasse

While he remained optimistic that the Good Friday Agreement would eventually be fully implemented, the continued suspension of its institutions from October 2002 – the executive, the assembly and the North-South Ministerial Council – was a source of considerable disappointment. Invited to address Seanad Éireann (the Irish senate) in May 2004, he spelled out what was required to break the impasse.

14 Address to the conference 'Diversity and equality and the future of democracy', Rennes, 19 Sept. 2002; copy in editor's possession.

In his address he once again invoked the example of the European Union, then about to admit several additional member states, in bringing people previously bitter enemies into a powerful union of mutual benefit:

> It is clear we require, above all else, to overcome two problems, the first of which is to see an end to all paramilitary activity on this island, whether that is from loyalist sources or those who call themselves republicans. This must be accompanied by full decommissioning by all paramilitary organizations and groups and by a total normalization of society in the North. Second, unionists must agree to fully and faithfully implement all power-sharing and partnership required by the agreement, including the Northern Ireland executive and the North-South Ministerial Council.
>
> At this time, we should remember that there are democratic imperatives. The Good Friday Agreement was voted for by a huge majority of the people of Ireland. For the first time in history, the people of this island have actually spoken about how they wish to live together by coming out in strength, North and South, to vote for the Good Friday Agreement. Therefore, it is the duty of all true democrats to implement the will of the people by implementing in its entirety all aspects of that agreement.
>
> One of the great traditions of this house is its ability to cast a wide view over matters of public interest and see beyond the minutiae of day-to-day political concerns in matters of national, European and international interest. This confers significant benefit upon democracy on this island and on the greater good. Therefore, it would be opportune now to consider the wider questions and issues which arise out of the current crisis in the peace process and consider the history of the process thus far in order to consider the present situation and future developments [...]
>
> We cannot heal the wounds of centuries in a few years. The violence of recent decades, in particular, has left deep wounds. The hurt inflicted and suffered will not go away because the agreement has been reached. The agreement cannot take away the pain, but it is the start of the healing process. It has the potential to deliver so much for our island, North and South. Through working the agreement, we can build a society where poverty is eliminated, where we provide the very best in schools and hospitals, where our old people feel safe, where we nurture our sense of community, where there is no place for racism or sectarianism and where everyone, young or old, can realize their full potential. The agreement provides us with the opportunity to truly cherish all of our island's children equally. We must do so in a spirit of co-operation with our partners in the European Union and beyond.
>
> As I already mentioned, the European Union has provided the people of Ireland with many benefits and opportunities. For that reason I am very

enthusiastic about the accession of ten new states to the union on 1 May. This will finally see an end to the artificial division of Europe created after the Second World War. This enlargement will not just see the natural reunification of Europe, but it will add to the cultural and social diversity upon which the union is built. We will see the creation of an enlarged market of more than 450 million European citizens, which will be by far the largest single market in the world. This, in turn, will not just allow countries like ours to benefit through the inflow of new peoples with new energies and talents, it will provide opportunities for our own young people to travel and have new experiences. I am certain our small and medium-sized industries and businesses, North and South, will be able to harness the possibilities opened up by these new markets so as to create new jobs.

I would like to commend the ten countries which are about to join the union, particularly those which less than two decades ago were in the grip of imperial Soviet communism. It is my sincere wish and expectation that in joining the European Union, these countries will be able to share fully the benefits of democracy, human rights and the single market for all their citizens. I commend all those involved in negotiations with these countries for their efforts. I do not think it is too early to look beyond May at developments that will occur after that accession. I look forward, in particular, to the accession of Bulgaria and Romania, which I hope will be ready to join the European Union in 2007. Thereafter, we should welcome those other applicant states which meet the standards set down for membership of the union.

It would be remiss of me not to mention the sterling efforts of the Irish presidency, which at this time is contributing so much to the development of the new Europe. Great efforts are being made to finalize arrangements for 1 May, while at the same time the Irish presidency is pursuing applications for further member states. I commend the priority being afforded to the development of a new European constitution by the presidency following the work of the convention under Valéry Giscard d'Estaing. This is necessary given that our institutions were devised initially to cater for a community of just six states, whereas we will soon have twenty-five member states, and more. I am convinced the constitution should be based on the primacy of a Europe of equal member states. It is not in the best interests of the people of Europe to create a two-tier European Union. That would undermine the most fundamental principles of Europe – equality and respect for difference. The principle of co-operation on which the European project is based must be based on a foundation of equality and inclusiveness. I have every confidence that the current difficulties in devising a new constitution will be overcome. Likewise, I believe the democratic imperative of the agreement will eventually see it is implemented.

Working together in our common interests is the best political medicine we can prescribe. As we do so, and as the healing process evolves and new generations emerge, we can look forward to the emergence of a new Ireland in a new Europe. We do not know where the healing process will take us and how quickly it will proceed but we know it is the best possible way to treat the wounds and divisions of centuries past. In looking towards that future, I am still inspired by the words of Martin Luther King Jr, which I first heard when he accepted his Nobel Prize in 1964. These words, which today give us hope to move forward, were as follows: 'I still believe that one day mankind will bow before the altars of God and be crowned triumphant over war and bloodshed, and non-violent redemptive good will proclaim the rule of the land.'[15]

Farewell to European parliament

In May 2004 John Hume bade farewell to the European parliament where he had served continuously since 1979. He had thoroughly enjoyed his years as a member and, as so many of his speeches and articles reflected, he viewed the parliament as a central institution in the network of the European Union's institutions. Collectively, he saw these institutions as guaranteeing peace and security on the Continent and of having promoted reconciliation between bitter enemies. They, therefore, offered an example to Ireland as it emerged from its conflict. His final plea was that a commissioner be appointed with the special task of promoting peace and the values of the European Union:

> Mr President, I very much regret that this will be my last speech to this parliament, having been here for the past twenty-five years. I have to retire owing to health reasons, but I want to express my deepest gratitude to my colleagues in this parliament, and of course to the commission and the council, for the outstanding support that they gave to peace in Northern Ireland. The special programme for peace and reconciliation and the International Fund for Ireland have done outstanding work in giving great hope to our young people.
>
> I also owe a lot to this parliament and to Strasbourg in terms of my own thinking. I always tell the story of the first time I came here in 1979. I went for a walk across the bridge from Strasbourg in France to Kehl in Germany and I stopped and meditated. I thought then that if I had stood there thirty years ago at the end of the Second World War – the worst half-century in the history of the world, in which 50 million human beings were slaughtered –

15 Address to Seanad Éireann, 3 Mar. 2004.

and had said to myself 'don't worry, it's all over, they will all be united very soon', I would have been sent to a psychiatrist. But it happened, and it is something that in my opinion the European Union does not devote enough attention to. The European Union is the best example in the history of the world of conflict resolution. For that reason, the principles at the heart of it should be sent to every area of conflict.

I know what I am talking about in saying that, because the three principles at the heart of the European Union are exactly the same as the three principles at the heart of our special agreement in Northern Ireland. Principle number one is respect for difference. [...]

Principle number two is institutions that respect differences. All member states are represented in the council of ministers, the European commission and the European parliament.

The third and most important principle is what I call the healing process. The countries involved worked together in their common interests – for economic development, for example – spilling their sweat and not their blood. As they did that, they eroded the divisions of centuries and as a result the new Europe has evolved and is still evolving.

Those same three principles are at the heart of our agreement in Northern Ireland. Both identities fully respect principle number one, respect for difference. As regards principle number two, institutions, a proportional assembly and a proportional government, will involve all sections of society. When they are in place, the third principle will come into play: working together in common interests, spilling sweat and not blood. The barriers of the past in Ireland will be eroded and a new Ireland will evolve.

The world is a much smaller place now that we are living through the biggest revolution in the history of the world in terms of technology, telecommunications and transport. We are therefore in a stronger position to shape that world, particularly in this very historic week [in which ten new states joined the EU] – who could have dreamt that the whole of Europe would be together? Given that it is a smaller world and that we are in a stronger position to shape it, the European Union should decide that our first objective in this new century is a world in which there is no longer any war or conflict.

In order to ensure that is the case – and I am making this appeal to the council of ministers – the European Union should put in place a commissioner, backed by a commission department for peace and reconciliation, whose function would be to send to every area of conflict in the world not arms or soldiers, but the philosophy of the European Union. This commissioner's role would be to promote dialogue about that philosophy and to help create a world in which there is no longer any war or any conflict. I believe that is now possible.

Finally, once again, I express my deepest gratitude to you all for the great support that you give to peace on my own streets. Thank you very much indeed and I regret very much that I am leaving this great parliament.[16]

In an interview with local correspondent Patsy McGowan soon after he had announced his retirement, John Hume reflected on his life in politics, and its effects on him and on his family:

As I have often said I couldn't have done what I did in politics without the outstanding work of my wife, Pat. When you are a public representative you have to do a lot of travelling and you are away from home a lot, and people are still looking for you. So my wife has done an outstanding job not only rearing our family but filling the gap for me. As I always say, I'm a parcel and Pat delivers me [...]

The reason I gave up my seat in Europe was that I was told that for health reasons I had to stop and the stress and strain of the last thirty years was affecting my health, so now I have finished my work and I will miss it very much. I want to express my deepest gratitude to the people of Derry for their support over the last thirty years and without it I wouldn't have been able to do what I did, and indeed, to the people across Northern Ireland who gave me their support as leader of the SDLP [...]

I hope that people would remember me and believe that I worked well for them and I did what I said I would do, and I worked hard for them.[17]

In summary, as McGowan wrote in concluding his interview:

John Hume started out as a man on a mission of reconciliation and peace. He never wavered in his methods, and now when his dream is about to be realized, he has had to step down. Let's hope that the people of this country, all of it, don't forget the contribution he made and the price he paid.[18]

---

16 European Parliament, *Debates*, 4 May 2004.   **17** Interview with Patsy McGowan, *Donegal Democrat*, 24 Apr. 2005.   **18** Ibid.

Sources

Records

Editor's private archive
European Parliament, *Debates*, 1979–2004
Forum for Peace and Reconciliation, *Proceedings*, 1994–6
House of Commons, *Debates*, 1983–2005
New Ireland Forum, *Proceedings*, 1983–4
Northern Ireland Assembly, *Debates*, 1973–2001
Northern Ireland Constitutional Convention, *Proceedings*, 1975–6
Northern Ireland House of Commons, *Debates*, 1969–71
Seanad Éireann, *Debates*, 2004

Newspapers and journals

Belfast Telegraph	*Independent*
Boston Globe	*Irish Independent*
Congressional Record	*Irish News*
Crane Bag	*Irish Times*
Derry Journal	*Studies*
Donegal Democrat	*Sunday Independent*
Foreign Affairs	*Sunday Press*
Hartford Courant	*Ulster Newsletter*
Harvard Magazine	

Broadcast interviews

Byrne, Jennifer. Interview with John Hume. *Foreign Correspondent*, ABC, 14 Mar. 2000
Humphrys, John. Interview with John Hume. *On the Record*, BBC, 5 Dec. 1993
Quinn, John. Interview with John Hume. RTÉ Radio 1, 1992

Books

Curran, Frank, *Derry: countdown to disaster* (Dublin, 1986)

Hume, John, *Guilty parties* (Dublin, 1985)

Hume, John, *Personal views: politics, peace and reconciliation in Ireland* (London, 1996)

Mallie, Eamonn & David McKittrick, *The fight for peace: the secret story behind the Irish peace process* (London, 1996)

Index